# LAW OF SEXUAL HARASSMENT AT WORKPLACE

**PRACTICE & PROCEDURE**

Revised and Updated Edition

**Amish Tandon**

PAPER MISSILE
NIYOGI BOOKS

Published by
NIYOGI BOOKS
Block D, Building No. 77,
Okhla Industrial Area, Phase-I,
New Delhi-110 020, INDIA
Tel: 91-11-26816301, 26818960
Email: niyogibooks@gmail.com
Website: www.niyogibooksindia.com



Design: Shashi Bhushan Prasad

ISBN: 978-93-85285-83-7
First Published: 2017
Revised Edition: 2025



Printed at: Niyogi Offset Pvt. Ltd., New Delhi, India

*Amit Bansal*
JUDGE
HIGH COURT OF DELHI

*Resi. : 10, New Moti Bagh*
*New Delhi-110023*
*Ph. : 011-41750104 (Resi.)*
*: 011-23382129 (Off.)*

May 14, 2025

# FOREWORD

Participation of women in the workforce is one of the crucial denominators of gender parity. Historically, scant attention has been paid to the problems plaguing the urban and rural workspaces which have a direct impact on the well-being and employment opportunities of women. Sexual harassment at the workplace is one such pervasive issue that undermines the dignity, safety, and well-being of individuals, while also disrupting organizational harmony and productivity. The recognition of this problem and the evolution of legal frameworks to address the same mark a significant step toward creating equitable and respectful work environments. In India, the enactment of the Sexual Harassment of Women at Workplace (Prevention, Prohibition and Redressal) Act, 2013 has provided a critical foundation for addressing and redressing grievances related to workplace misconduct.

In this book, Mr. Amish Tandon has taken us through the development of Indian law on prevention of sexual harassment at workplace. It is one of the simplest expositions of statutory provisions, procedural requirements, and case law developments, bridging the gap between legal theory and everyday workplace realities. It underscores the importance of proactive policies, fair inquiry processes, and informed decision-making in safeguarding employee rights and reinforcing organizational accountability.

The author has analyzed India's constitutional obligations towards women's safety and autonomy as well as some significant international conventions of which India is a signatory. In the pursuit to provide a holistic view, the author has also briefly analyzed the laws relating to sexual harassment at workplace in other jurisdictions like USA and United Kingdom.

This book serves as a comprehensive resource dealing with procedural and substantive aspects of law on prevention of sexual harassment at workplace. The book will be a useful practical guide for a wider audience. It would be an insightful read for employers, employees, internal committee members, legal practitioners, and HR professionals.

I would sincerely hope that this book will contribute meaningfully to the ongoing efforts to create safe and inclusive workplaces as well as foster awareness and promote culture of zero tolerance towards sexual harassment.

I would like to congratulate Mr. Tandon on this excellent work and wish him the very best in all his future endeavours.

**(Amit Bansal)**

*ustice Mini Pushkarna*

**HIGH COURT OF DELHI**
Sher Shah Road, New Delhi - 110503
Phone (O) : 011-23074205

May 17, 2025

Today, when the world is evolving at a rapid pace, it is imperative that we, as individuals, be at par with the changing scenario in order to contribute meaningfully to a more inclusive and cohesive society. The progress we aspire cannot be attained unless we maintain individual respect and boundaries.

With more women stepping into professional spaces, there has been a troubling increase in incidents of sexual harassment at the workplace. These regressive societal patterns can often inflict lasting damage on the confidence, dignity, and mental well-being of those subjected to such hostile environments. Such instances not only hinder the professional growth and personal safety of individuals, but also erode the ethical milieu and productivity of institutions, ultimately impeding the nation's progress towards equality and inclusivity. In order to strive towards an inclusive, safe, and equitable professional environment, laws against sexual harassment, are an absolute need.

The enactment of the 'Sexual Harassment of Women at Workplace (Prevention, Prohibition and Redressal) Act, 2013', was one big step which gave impetus to the spirit of the Supreme Court's landmark judgment, *Vishaka and Others Versus State of Rajasthan and Others, (1997) 6 SCC 241*. Yet, over a decade since the law came into force, the challenges of implementation, awareness, and genuine institutional accountability, remain pressing. The need of the hour is not just legal compliance, but a cultural transformation, one that acknowledges and addresses the deep-rooted power dynamics and gender biases that silently perpetuate workplace harassment.

This book seeks to empower and educate all the stakeholders in the workforce with the knowledge and sensitivity required to deal with these issues responsibly. This is further substantiated by providing reference to plethora of judicial pronouncements on the issue, which provide valuable guidance in tackling such situations.

The need of the hour is to call for action and remind ourselves that sensitizing our workplaces is not the responsibility of a few, but a collective obligation, by educating employees, strengthening internal redressal mechanisms, and fostering empathetic leadership, in order to create safer professional environment.

I wish the author the very best for this useful publication that brings to fore the dire need for collective effort to curb the menace of sexual harassment and which provides a gainful insight into the practice and procedure on the law of sexual harassment. It is only through such collective commitment, that we can truly move towards building the inclusive, progressive, and equitable society, we aspire for.

Mini Pushkarna
(Mini Pushkarna)

*Jayant Nath*
Judge

**HIGH COURT OF DELHI, SHER SHAH ROAD
NEW DELHI 110 003 TEL. : +91-11-23383175
RESIDENCE : AB-15, TILAK MARG
NEW DELHI-110001 TEL. : +91-11-23071095**

July 04, 2017

With more and more women joining the workforce the need to provide a safe and secure working environment is imperative. An important step to provide legal remedy against 'sexual harassment at workplace' commenced with the Supreme Court's judgment in the case of 'Vishaka vs. State of Rajasthan' in the year 1997. The Hon'ble Supreme Court formulated guidelines and prescribed an in-house procedure for determination of complaints of sexual harassment in workspaces, until the legislature propounded a statute on the subject. This culminated in the legislation titled 'Sexual Harassment of Women at Workplace (Prevention, Prohibition and Redressal) Act, 2013'.

The law on sexual harassment is a new-age piece of legislation which details the mode and manner of inquiring into and deciding instances of sexual harassment at workplaces. With the advent of greater number of women joining the workforce, this law has gained great relevance.

The author has attempted to provide to the readers a brief, simplistic and clear enunciation of the law on sexual harassment at the workplace. I note a provision-by-provision examination of the law replete with relevant case law.

Written in a systematic manner, the book offers a meticulous examination of the statutory provisions of the relevant case law on the subject. The law on the subject is new and developing. This book should be able to fill in some of the gaps and provide a comprehensive database on this critical legal field. This book would be useful for the entire legal fraternity, as also law teachers, students and other people with interest in the area. This book would also be useful for companies and organisation.

I felicitate the author Mr.Amish Tandon for his efforts and the comprehensive manner in which he has crafted this book. I wish him all success.

Jayant Nath

(JAYANT NATH)

*Justice V. Kameswar Rao*

*High Court of Delhi*
*Sher Shah Road*
*New Delhi-110503*
*Tel. : 011-23074322*

July 06, 2017

I have great pleasure in writing this short Foreword to Mr. Amish Tandon's work on *"Law on Sexual Harassment at Work Place, Practice and Procedure"*.

Mr. Tandon is a young Advocate who was junior to my esteemed colleague Justice Jayant Nath before his elevation to the Bench. I am glad that Mr. Tandon has undertaken to write on the aforesaid important topic. Through this book Mr. Tandon has made an attempt to analyse the issue of sexual harassment, which was brought into focus by the Supreme Court in its landmark judgment in ***Vishaka v. State of Rajasthan (1997) 6 SCC 241.***

The work also refers to the Act enacted by the Parliament in the year 2013, its objectives, features apart from referring to different provisions and their interpretation. It gives an insight on the remedies available to a victim both in criminal law and under the Rules of the organization, so also the obligation of the employer making the work place harassment free. The special feature of the work is Draft Sexual Harassment Policy, which may be referred to and utilized by the employers while drafting their internal Rules.

Mr. Tandon's approach to the subject makes the work very relevant and shall be helpful to each and everyone, who wish to know about the issue, the legal provisions including remedies and the judgments on the same. I congratulate him for this excellent work.

(V. Kameswar Rao)

Amish Tandon, Advocate

*Res. Bungalow No. 45, New Moti Bagh, New Delhi-110 021 Ph. 011-26877132*

*Justice Manju Goel (Retd.)*
*Former Judge High Court of Delhi*
*Former Judicial Member, Appellate Tribunal for Electricity*

**Res. Cum Office:**
R-128, Greater Kailash-I
New Delhi - 110048
Mob: +91 9818000330
E-mail: manjugoel_3@yahoo.com

In any study of law related to gender issues it is important to understand the distinction between sex and gender, sex being a biological construct while gender is a social construct. On account of natural physical differences between men and women, traditionally women have been seen in all societies performing a specified role. Beginning with the child birth and continuing with rearing of children, the women are seen as persons who keep the household and bring up the children. Stereotyping the roles for men and women becomes oppressive when men and women are not allowed to step out of the stereotypes and remain or/are forced to continue within the social construct of their respective rules. Thus discrimination has origins in stereotyping.

There are societies where women are freely accepted at a workplace without violating the stereotypes. In societies where the stereotyping requires the women to remain indoors, they are not viewed favourably at a place of work in which many of the workers are men. Apart from stereotyping of women's roles as homemakers there is further stereotyping that women are weak and can be oppressed. When male sexuality is expressed in an unwelcome fashion towards a woman it becomes harassment. Harassment is a generalised and mild term. Unwelcome expression of sexuality can take different forms from simple harassment to molestation and to rape. Sexual harassment is the culmination of misuse of one's sexuality. If allowed to be perpetrated at a place of work it will deter the women from performing to their best of ability and to enjoy the gains of their talent and work.

In order to understand the significance of safe and gender friendly workplace one has to understand the concepts of equality and discrimination. There can be formal equality alongside inequality or discrimination in substance. The comprehensive definition of discrimination against women available in the Convention for Elimination of All forms of Discrimination Against Women helps us to understand the subject of equality between genders. Discrimination is defined therein in Article 1 of the Part I as under:

> *1.3.1 "For the purposes of the present Convention, the term 'discrimination against women' shall mean any distinction, exclusion or restriction made on the basis of sex which has the effect or purpose of impairing or nullifying the recognition, enjoyment or exercise by women, irrespective of their marital status, on a basis of equality of men and women, of human rights and fundamental freedoms in the political, economic, social, cultural, civil or any other field."*

In order to provide equality with men in the matter of exercise of fundamental freedoms in political, economic, social, cultural, civil or any other field it is necessary that women get access to the workplace without any restriction or hindrance of any kind as much as is available to the men. Any apprehension that the workplace is not safe for a woman to work with dignity will cause hindrance and obstacles for the woman to enjoy equality at work and hence would amount to discrimination.

In some degree or the other, sexual harassment at workplace has been noticed in all places leading to a concern for taking remedial steps. There being no statute to address this evil, the Hon'ble Supreme Court in an unusual exercise of its powers gave certain guidelines in dealing with sexual harassment at workplace, in *Vishaka and others v. State of Rajasthan and others* (1997) 6 *SCC 241.* It led to amendments in various service regulations and to the enactment of Sexual Harassment of Women at workplace (Prevention, Prohibition and Redressal) Act, 2013.

A long drawn struggle and a great deal of emotional inputs have gone in making this legislation. For implementation of law, sensitivity on the part of the law enforcing agencies, including judges and lawyers, is an absolute necessity. What must not be forgotten, however, is that objectivity and rationality must go hand in hand with sensitivity and activism.

This book is an honest effort from Mr. Amish Tandon to take us through the development of law in this area. The book includes not only the judicial pronouncements of the various High Courts and the Supreme Court of India, but also comparable legal precedent in other jurisdictions. I do believe that the book will achieve the end for which it has been attempted.

Justice Manju Goel (Retd.)
Former Judge, High Court of Delhi

11.07.2017

# Contents

# List of Cases

**A**

A. Manimekalan v. The Registrar, 2023 Writ LR 201

A.K. Mukherjee v. State 54 (1994) DLT 461

A.K. Singh v. Union of India W.P. (C) No. 4237/2012 (01.12.2015, Delhi High Court)

A.L. Agarwal v. Delhi University CIC/RM/A/2014/000313-SA (09.12.2015, Central Information Commission)

A.V. Venkateswaran v. Ramchand Sobhraj Wadhwani AIR 1961 SC 1506

Aarti Durgaram Gavandi v. Managing Director, Tata Metaliks W.P. No. 8826/2004 (06.10.2008, Bombay High Court)

Abhilasha Dwivedi v. Department of Women and Child Development NCT of Delhi, WP (Crl.) No. 1639/2019 (19.11.2019, Delhi High Court)

Abigail Wilson v. Jim Putman Appeal No. 15-2522 (13.04.2017, Court of Appeals, 4th Circuit)

Abraham Mathai v. State of Kerala 2024: Ker: 91275

Additional District and Sessions Judge v. Registrar General, High Court of Madhya Pradesh (2015) 4 SCC 91

Aditi Bramta v. State of Himachal Pradesh, CWP No. 1628/2020 (09.07.2020, Himachal Pradesh High Court) Ajahar Ali v. State of West Bengal (2013) 10 SCC 31

Ajahar Ali v. State of West Bengal (2013) 10 SCC 31

Ajay Raj Pal v. State Criminal Misc. No. 3100 of 2005 (19.02.2007, Delhi High Court)

Ajay Raj Pal v. State Criminal Misc. No. 3100 of 2005 (19.02.2007, Delhi High Court)

Ajay Tiwari v. University of Delhi 2020 (1) SCT 381 (Delhi)

Ajay Tiwari v. University of Delhi, 2020 (1) SCT 381 (Delhi)

Aleque Padamsee v. Union of India 2007 (6) SCC 171

Allen v. Tyson Foods, Inc.121 F.3d 642

Alphi Chugh v. State of Haryana Crl. Misc. No. M-29141 of 2012 (19.09.2012, Punjab & Haryana High Court)

Aman Kumar v. State of Haryana AIR 2004 SC 1497

Amjith v. State of Kerala 2024: KER:84389

Amrapali Basumatary v. Union of India W.P. (C) No. 3573/2014 (08.12.2015, Delhi High Court)

Amul v. Union of India OA No. 354/2015 (01.10.2015, Central Administrative Tribunal, Ahmedabad)

Amutha v. The Director of Medical and Rural Health W.P (MD) No. 2109/2022 (21.07.2022, Madras High Court, Madurai Bench)

Binoy Jacob v. State of Kerala, Crl MC No. 847/2022 (01.11.2022, Kerala High Court)

Binu Tamta v. High Court of Delhi W.P. (C) No. 162/2013 (17.07.2013, Supreme Court of India)

Biyat Pragya Tripathi v. Government of Odhisha W.P (C) No. 33000/2022 (15.09.2023, Orissa High Court)

Bradley Miller v. Kenworth of Dothan, Inc. 277 F.3d 1269 (11th Circuit, 2002)

Burlington Industries Inc. v. Kimberly B. Ellereth (97-569)123 F.3d 490 (7th Circuit, 1998)

C

C. Govinda Rajulu v. The State of Andhra Pradesh WP No. 36081/2017 (04.08.2023, Andhra Pradesh High Court, Amravati Bench).

C. J. Paul Chandramohan v. The Bishop Heber College, 2023 (1) CLR 621

C.S.H.N. Murthy v. Tezpur University 2015 (3) GLT 346

Capt. M. Paul Anthony v. Bharat Gold Mines Ltd. JT 1999 (2) SC 456

Chairman and M.D. United Commercial Bank v. P.C. Kakkar (2003) 4 SCC 364

Chairman cum Managing Director, Coal India Limited v. Mukul Kumar Chaudhari 2009 (15) SCC 620

Chandan Kumar Soni v. State of Uttarakhand, Criminal Misc Application No. 1028/2015 (24.12.2020, Uttarakhand High Court)

Charles Welsh v. State of Maharashtra Cri. W.P. No. 5006/2015 (01.04.2016, Bombay High Court)

Chennai Water Supply and Sewerage Board v. T.T. Murali (2014) 4 SCC 108

Chhttar Pal v. The Lt. Governor, National Capital Territory Region (16.05.2008, Central Administrative Tribunal, Delhi)

Chikkathimmegowda v. Deputy Commissioner ILR 1991 Kar 3238

Cinema Collective v. State of Kerala 2022 (2) KLJ 254

Clarinda D'Souza v Mccann Erickson India Limited (2003) 4 Bom CR 292

Commissioner of Police v. Sant Ram, W.P (C) No. 5562/2024 (23.04.2024, Delhi High Court)

Constable Ravinder Rana v. Union of India (2008) ILR 2 Del 915

Court on its own Motion v. State of Jharkhand W.P. (PIL) No. 5497 of 2011 (06.01.2014, Jharkhand High Court)

Cuff v. Gypsy Restaurant (1987) BOI 87-004 (06.02.1987, Human Rights Tribunal of Ontario/Board of Inquiry)

D

D.B. Corp Limited v. Shaila Naqvi, CM (M) No. 705/2022 (21.07.2022, Delhi High Court) D.P. Maheswari v. Delhi Administration (1983) 4 SCC 293

D.B. Singh v. State of J&K, CRMC No. 620/2018 (01.0.2019, Jammu and Kashmir High Court)

D.P. Maheswari v. Delhi Administration (1983) 4 SCC 293

D.S. Grewal v. Vimmi Joshi, Civil Appeal No. 7355 of 2008 (17.12.2008, Supreme Court of India)

Damodar Prasad Singh v. Union of India OA No. 211/2012 (29.01.2014, Central Administrative Tribunal, Patna)

David Hansen v. United States Equal Employment Opportunity Commission, Appeal No. 15-8112 (21.12.2016, 10th Circuit)

De Grace v. Rumsfeld 614 F.2d 796 (1980)

Debdulal Maity v. National Insurance Company Limited W.P. No. 728 of 2014 (07.08.2014, Calcutta High Court)

Debjani Sengupta v. Institute of Cost Accountants of India 2024 SCC Online Cal 12001

Debjani Sengupta v. The Institute of Cost Accountants of India, RVW 129/2019 (04.07.2023, Calcutta High Court)

Delhi Cloth & General Mills Co. Ltd. v. CTO Jaipur (1976) 3 SCC 443

Delhi Transport Corporation v. DTC Mazdoor Congress, (1991) Supp (1) SCC 600

Deputy Inspector General of Police v. S. Samuthiram (2013) 1 SCC 598

Dev Dutt v. Union of India 2008 (8) SCC 725

Dharampal Satyapal Limited v. Deputy Commission of Central Excise (2015) 8 SCC 519

Dharmender v. Union of India OA No. 2135/2015 (08.09.2015, Central Administrative Tribunal, Delhi)

Dinkins v. Charoen Pokphand USA, Inc. 133 F. Supp. 2d 1254 (M.D. Ala. 2001)

Doe v. Belleville 119 F.3d 563 (CA7 1997)

Doe v. Dekalb County 145 F.3d 1441 (11th Circuit, 1998)

Dr. B.N. Ray v. Ramjas College W.P. (C) No. 4427/2008 (21.05.2012, Delhi High Court)

Dr. Kasthurba A.K v. National Institute of Technology W.P. (C) No. 25846/2015 (28.09.2015, Kerala High Court)

Dr. Malabika Bhattacharjee v. Internal Complaints Committee, WPA (141/2020 (27.11.2020, Calcutta High Court)

Dr. Parveen v. Director General, Indian Council of Forestry Research & Education, WP No. 99/2019 (19.03.2019, High Court of Uttarakhand)

Dr. Pushkar Saxena v. Government of NCT of Delhi W.P. (C) No. 7592/2001 (16.05.2012, Delhi High Court)

Dr. R.S. Tyagi v. All India Institute of Medical Sciences OA No. 1619/2011 (13.12.2011 Central Administrative Tribunal, New Delhi)

Dr. S. Vinukumar v. The Government of Tamil Nadu W.P (MD) No. 5486/2022 (25.04.2022, Madras High Court, Madurai Bench)

Dr. Satish Kumar S Hosamani v. State of Karnataka W.P. No. 11147/2024 (S-RES) and Others (05.02.2025, Karnataka High Court)

Dr. Sohail Malik v. Union of India, WP (C) No. 8624/2023 (30.06.2023, Delhi High Court)

Dr. Sushmita Banerjee v. Kolkata Port Trust W.P. No. 76/2016 (03.02.2016, Calcutta High Court)

Dr. Tanya Mander v. Rajiv Gandhi National University of Law CWP No. 960/2019 (22.03.2021, Punjab and Haryana High Court)

Dr. Vijaykumaran C.P.V v. Central University of Kerala (2020) 12 SCC 426

**F**

Fauza Rubbani v. Delhi Woman Commission, WP (C) No. 11749/2019 (02.02.2023, Delhi High Court)

Fye v. Oklahoma Corporation 516 F.3d 1217 (10th Circuit, 2008)

**G**

G.M. Telecom v. M. Krishnan AIR 2003 Ker 152

GAIL (India) limited v. Dr. Duraisamy Baskaran, Writ Appeal No. 153/2021 (28.02.2023, Telangana High Court)

Gambhirdan K Gadhvi v. State of Gujarat (2022) 5 SCC 179

Gamini Bala Koteswara Rao v. State of Andhra Pradesh AIR 2010 SC 589

Gaurav Jain v. Hindustan Latex Family Planning Promotion Trust (2015) 220 DLT 60

Gaurav Jain v. Hindustan Latex Family Planning Promotion Trust LPA No. 145/2015 (06.08.2015, Delhi High Court)

Gayatri Balaswamy v. ISG Novasoft Technologies Ltd. (2014) 6 CTC 602

General Officer Commanding v. CBI 2012 (2) R.A.J 527

Girish Rameshchandra Soni v. State of Gujarat, Special Civil Application No. 11804/2017 (15.09.2017, Gujarat High Court).

Global Health Private Limited v. Local Complaints Committee, WP No. 22317/2017 (16.09.2019, Madhya Pradesh High Court, Indore Bench)

Gokak Mills v. State of Karnataka ILR 1995 Karnataka 1489

Gopinath v. State of Kerala, ILR 2014 (4) Kerala 573

Government of NCT of Delhi v. Naresh Kumar Kataria W.P. (C) No. 2454/2012 (17.04.2013, Delhi High Court)

Gurmeet Singh v. CPIO, Appeal No. CIC/VS/A/2014/003051/BJ (04.01.2017, Central Information Commission)

**H**

H.B. Gandhi v. Gopinath and Sons 1992 Supp. (2) SCC 312

H.C. Bakshi v. Union of India (09.05.2008, Central Administrative Tribunal, New Delhi)

Hall v. A.A. Sheiban Pty Ltd (1989) 85 ALR 503

Harris v. Forklift Systems 510 U.S. 17 (1993)

Himanshu Srivastava v. Union of India O.A No. 200/00865/2015 (01.10.2015, Central Administrative Tribunal, Jabalpur)

Hind Rubber Factory v. Union of India W.P. No. 4516/1984 (30.05.1989

Hindustan Petroleum Corporation v. Sarvesh Berry (2005) 10 SCC 471

Hira Khatoon v. Union of India, WP (C) No. 8198/2024 (18.09.2024, Delhi High Court)

Hira Nath Mishra v. The Principal, Rajendra Medical College (1973) II LLJ 111 (SC)

**I**

Inclusion Foundation v. Union of India, 2023 INSC 927

Income Tax Officer v. M.K. Mohammed Kunhi 1968 SCC Online SC 71

Indian Oil Corporation v. Ashok Kumar Arora, (1997) 3 SCC 72

Institute of Hotel Management Catering Technology and Applied Nutrition v. Suddhasil Dey, WPCR 137/2019, (13.03.2020, Bombay High Court)

**J**

J Mani v. Union of India (2021) 170 FLR 23

Janzen v. Platy Enterprises [1989] 1 S.C.R 1252 (Supreme Court of Canada)

Jaya Kodate v. Rashtrasant Tukoji Maharaj Nagpur University W.P. Nos. 3449, 3450 & 3451 of 2013 (13.06.2014, Bombay High Court)

Jennifer Paul v. Elayn Hunt Correctional Centre, Department of Public Safety and Corrections, State of Louisiana Appeal No. 16-30574 (18.11.2016, 5th Circuit)

Jishu Sengupta v. State of West Bengal CRR No. 1204 of 2016 (04.11.2016, Calcutta High Court)

Johney Reberio v. Union of India, WP (C) No. 14547/2022 (14.10.2022, Delhi High Court)

Joseph Oncale v. Sundowner Offshore Services Inc. (96-568) 83 F. 3d 118

**K**

K Hem Lata v. The State of Tamil Nadu 2018 LLR 477

K. Unnikrishnan v. Lakshwadeep Administration OA No. 344/2008 (11.08.2015, Central Administrative Tribunal, Ernakulam)

K.L. Tripathi v. State Bank of India (1984) II LLJ SC

K.V.M. Abdunnafih v. Union of India OA No. 2055/2010 (24.12.2014, Central Administrative Tribunal, Delhi)

Kali Charna Sabat v. Union of India WP No. 10021/2024 (08.11.2024, Madhya Pradesh High Court, Jabalpur Bench)

Kamala v. Madras Port Trust (1966) I LLJ 690 (Mad)

Kasturba A.K v. National Institute of Technology, W.P. (C) No. 25846/2015 (28.09.2016, Kerala High Court)

Kendriya Vidyalaya Sangthan v. J. Hussain (2013) 10 SCC 106

Kerry Ellison v. Nicholas F. Brady 924 F. 2d 872 (9th Circuit, 1991)

Kilmarnock Equitable Co-operative Society Ltd. v. Commissioners of Inland Revenue [1966] 42 TC 675 (C Sess)

Kuldeep Singh v. Commissioner of Police AIR 1999 SC 677

Kuncha Chandrashekhar v. The State of Andhra, WP No. 10333/2021 (11.04.2023, Andhra Pradesh High Court)

Kusum Ignots & Alloys Limited v. Union of India (2004) 6 SCC 254

**L**

L. Nagaraju v. Syndicate Bank 2014 (2) ALD 758

L.S. Sibu v. Air India Limited W.P. (C) No. 4001/2016 (08.04.2016, Kerala High Court)

Lakhwinder P Singh v. IIHMR, WP (C) No. 844/2017 (21.09.2022, Delhi High Court)

Lalit Popli v. Canara Bank, (2003) 3 SCC 583

Laxman B Parmand v. Nuclear Power Corporation of India Ltd, WP No. 9445/2019 (21.04.2022, Bombay High Court)

Laxmi Salt Works v. State of Gujarat 1991 (4) SCC 1

Leena Doley v. State of Assam 2013 (5) GLT 363

Linda Eastwood v. Union of India W.P. (Crl.) No. 1904/2013 (23.02.2015, Delhi High Court)

Lipsett v. University of Puerto Rico 864 F.2d 881 (1ST Circuit, 1998)

Llampallas v. Mini-Circuits Lab., Inc. 163 F.3d 1236 (11th Circuit, 1998)

Long v. Eastfield 88 F.3d 300 (5th Circuit, 1996)

Lynette Jane Aldridge v. Grant Rodney Booth (1988) 80 ALR 1

**M**

M. Kavya v. Chairman, University Grants Commission W.P. No. 11217/ 2014 (04.12.2014, Madras High Court)

M. Rajendran v. M. Daisyrani, (2018) 3 MLJ 84

M. Sabesh Manikandan v. The Director of Collegiate Education, W.P. (MD) No. 7922/2015 (16.10.2020, Madras High Court, Madurai Bench)

M.C.D v. Ram Kishan Rohtagi AIR 1983 SC 67.

M.P Special Police Establishment v. State of Madhya Pradesh, 2004 (8) SCC 788

Mackinnon Mackenzie & Co. Pvt. Ltd. v. Ibrahim Mahmmod Issak AIR 1970 SC 1906

Madam X v. Chancellor, Punjab University, CWP No. 22684/2018 (15.10.2019, Punjab and Haryana High Court)

Madhavrao Jiwaji Rao Scindia v. S.C. Angre AIR 1988 SC 709

Mahender Kumar v. Linda Eastwood (2015) 2 CAL LT 357

Mahendra Singh Rajawat v. Punjab National Bank, 2023 LLR 390

Major U.R. Bhatt v. Union of India AIR 1962 SC 1344

Manoj Kumar Rana v. Sports Authority of India W.P. (C) No. 8481/2015 (16.09.2015, Delhi High Court)

Manomanium Sunderanar University v. P Govinndraju, WA (MD) No. 428/2020 (20.04.2022, Madras High Court, Madurai Bench)

Maruti Suzuki India Limited v. Tourism Development Corporation Limited (2013) IV AD (Delhi) 615

Mary Nell Dinkins v. Charoen Pokphand USA, Inc. 133 F. Supp. 2d 1254 (M.D. Ala. 2001)

Md. Azimur Rahman v. The University of Jamia Milia (2013) 203 DLT 463

Medha Kotwal Lele v. Union of India (2013) 1 SCC 297

Meena Rawat v. Mr. S.K. Chugh, PIO and Manager (HR) Delhi Transco Limited, CIC/SG/A/2011/000462/12128

Meenakshi Pandey v. Central Bank of India, WP No. 29047/2022 (05.04.2023, Madhya Pradesh High Court)

Mobarik Ali v. State of Bombay AIR 1957 SC 857

Ms. Navneet Kaur v. CPIO, Department of Information Technology (22.03.2006, Central Information Commission);

Ms. X v. Union of India, LPA No. 527/2019 (17.12.2020, Delhi High Court)

Ms. Yangchen Dahdul v. State of Sikkim, W.P. (PIL) No. 5/2015 (25.10.2016, Sikkim High Court)

Mukesh Bansal v. State 2009 (2) JCC 898

Mukesh Khampariya v. State of Madhya Pradesh W.P. No. 21852/2018 (05.10.2023, Madhya Pradesh High Court)

Mukesh Khampariya v. The State of Madhya Pradesh citation is different is index

Munendra Kumar v. Government of NCT of Delhi 2024 SCC Online Del 8186

**N**

N. Rajarathinam v. State of Tamil Nadu (1997) I SLJ 10 (SC)

N. Soundaram v. P.K Pounraj (2014) 10 SCC 616

N.K. Singh v. Union of India (1994) 6 SCC 1998

N.K. Suroya, IAS (Retd.) v. Union of India 2003 (3) SLJ 34 (CAT)

Nagaraj G.K v. Additional Labour Commissioner, Appellate Authority 2024 SCC Online Kar 1056

National Council for Cement and Building Materials v. State of Haryana (1996) 3 SCC 206

National Forensic Science University v. Deepak Chetandas Rawtani LPA No. 410/2024 (01.05.2024, Gujarat High Court)

National Spot Exchange Limited v. Anil Kohli (2022) 11 SCC 761

Nirmal Kanti Chakraborti v. Vaneeta Patnaik, FMA No. 873/2024 (23.12.2024, Calcutta High Court)

Nisha Priya Bhatia v. Union of India (2020) 13 SCC 56

Nitesh Parashar v. Institute of Chartered Accountants of India WP (C) No. 88/2023 (05.01.2023, Delhi High Court)

Nitin Saxena v. State Crl. M.C. 2906/2010 (09.09.2010, Delhi High Court)

Noida Entrepreneurs Association v. NOIDA (2007) 10 SCC 385

Nunan v. Action Traffic Services Pty Ltd. [2013] QCAT 565

**O**

of 2003 (19.02.2009 Supreme Court of India)

Ogden v. Potter 397 F.App'x 938 (5th Circuit, 2010)

Om Kumar v. Union of India (2001) 2 SCC 386

Overseas Tankship (UK) Ltd. v. Morts Docks and Engineering Co. Ltd. (1961) UKPC 1

**P**

P. Govindraju v. The Manomanium Sundaranar University, 2020 (1) Writ LR 249 P. Ramaswamy v. State (2013) 14 SCC 577

P. Kannan v. Commissioner of Municipal Administration 2022 SCC Online Mad 1154

P. Murugesan v. Tamil Nadu State Transport Corporation 2024 SCC Online Mad 2233

P. Ramaswamy v. State (2013) 14 SCC 577

Pankaj Kumar v. Union of India W.P. (C) No. 408/2013 (14.02.2017, Tripura High Court)

Parthasarthi v. State of Andhra Pradesh (1974) 3 SCC 459

Patricia Fuller v. City of Oakland No. 92-16081 (14.02.1995, Court of Appeals, 9th Circuit)

Pawan Kumar Niroula v. Union of India, 2022 (2) SLR 320

Pennsylvania State Police v. Suders 542 U.S. 129 (2004)

Poonam Shahani v. Union of India OA No. 1001/2022

Porter v. Houma Terrebonne 810 F.3d 940 (5th Circuit, 2015)

Pradip Mandal v. Metal Scrap Trade Corporation Limited, WPA No. 888/2020 (19.05.2022, Calcutta High Court)

Prama Bhattacharjee v. The State of West Bengal, 2024 Lab IC 785

Prasad Pannian v. Central University of Kerala, (2020) 6 KHC 687

Prasad Parnian v. Central University of Kerala, ILR 2021 (1) Kerala 131

Pravin Marotirao Daroli v. The State of Maharashtra 2024: BHC-AUG:24385-DB

Prof. Bidyug Chakraborty v. Delhi University W.P. (C) No. 8226/2007 (29.05.2009, Delhi High Court)

PS v. State of NCT of Delhi W.P. (Crl) 767/2015 (29.02.2016, Delhi High Court)

Public Services Tribunal Bar Association v. State of U.P (2003) 4 SCC 104

Puja Dubey v. Union of India W.P (C) 7916/2013 (19.07.2016, Delhi High Court)

Punita K. Sodhi v. Union of India (2010) 172 DLT 409

Punjab & Haryana High Court)

Punjab and Sind Bank v. Durgesh Kuwar, AIR 2020 SC 3040

Punjab National Bank v. Niraj Gupta 2024/DHC/5022

Puran Chand v State of Himachal Pradesh, CWP No. 2225/2020 (14.07.2020, Himachal Pradesh High Court)

Puspanjali Padhy v. Central Public Information Officer, Indian Overseas Bank, File No. CIC/SH/A/2015/000235 (30.03.2016, CIC Delhi)

Puthuppan v. K.S. Girija 2008 (3) KLJ 416

**R**

R. Mohankrishnan v. Deputy Inspector of Police, W.P. No. 10707/2024 (11.06.2024, Madras High Court)

R.S. Saini v. Bureau of Indian Standard (2004) 112 DLT 164

Radha Krishan Industries v. State of Himachal Pradesh 2021 SCC Online SC 334

Raj Kumar Dey v. The State Bank of India, WPA No. 20332/2017 (19.05.2022, Calcutta High Court)

Rajinder Kumar Kindra v. Delhi Administration AIR 1984 SC 1805

Raju Pandurang Mahale v. State of Maharashtra AIR 2004 SC 1677

Ramesh Pal v. Union of India (2014) 2 MP LJ 500

Ranjit Thakur v. Union of India AIR 1987 SC 2386

Rashi v. Union of India, WP (C) No. 3396/2019 (04.12.2020, Delhi High Court)

Regional Director E.S.I Corporation v. Francis De Costa AIR 1997 SC 432

Regional Director, Employees State Insurance Corporation v. Derhin Bai (2012) IV LLJ 324 CG

Rehana Kausar v. UT of J & K 2023 LLR 146

Reinhold v. Commonwealth 151 F.3d 172 (4th Circuit, 1998)

Reliance Energy Limited v. Maharashtra State Road Development Corporation (2007) 8 SCC 1

Research Scholar v. Research Guide & Others 2024:MHC:4046

Reshma MG v. Union of India, O.A. No. 180/00722 of 2014 (19.02.2016, Central Administrative Tribunal, Ernakulam)

Rina Mukherjee v. The State of West Bengal (2014) 143 FLR 51

Rishabh Jha v. Union of India Writ No. 30472/2016 (21.12.2016, Allahabad High Court)

Rishiraj v. State, 2009 (1) JCC 265

Robin Anderson v. CRST International Appeal No. 15-55556 (24.03.2017, Court of Appeals, 9th Circuit)

Robinson v. Jacksonville Shipyards U.S.D.C. M.D. No. 86-927-Civ-J-12 (1991)

Rohit Satindra Sharma v. State of Maharashtra 2024 SCC Online Bom 2718

Ruchika Singh Chhabra v. Air France India (AIR Online 2018 Del 809).

Runa Ray v. Soumen Sarkar, MAT 1070/2021 (27.06.2023, Calcutta High Court)

Rupan Deol Bajaj v. Kanwar Pal Singh Gill AIR 1996 SC 309

Rupesh Hari v. Union of India W.P. (C) No. 6549/2016 (29.07.2016, Delhi High Court)

## S

S. Chitra v. Director of Fire Services W.P. (C) 37598 of 2006 (30.09.2009, Madras High Court)

S. Murugan v. The State of Tamil Nadu, 2019 (2) MLJ 613

S. Raju Aiyer v. Jawaharlal Nehru University LPA No. 330 of 2013 (23.08.2013, Delhi High Court)

S. Ravi Selvan v. Central Board of Indirect Taxes WP No. 17798/2022 (09.09.2022, Madras High Court)

S. Ravichandran Iyer v. Justice A.M. Bhattacharjee (1995) 5 SCC 457

S. Srikanth Joshi v. Board of Management of Aladangady Vyavasaya Seva

S.P. Parasher v. Rehabilitation Council of India W.P. (C) No. 12272/2009

S.P.S Sondhi v. Union of India OA No. 060/1319/2018 (01.11.2023, Central Administrative Tribunal, Chandigarh)

S.R. Tewari v. Union of India 2013 (6) SCC 602

Sabir Ahmed v. The Assam University, WP (C) No, 2509/2018 (21.12.2023, Guwahati High Court)

Sahakari Bank 2007 (5) Kant LJ 484

Saikuttan v. Kerala State Electricity Board, 2020 Lab IC 4324; Devender Rai v. Sangeet Natak Akademi, New Delhi, WP (C) 2893/2023 (14.03.2023, Delhi High Court)

Sakiri Vasu v. State of UP 2008 (2) SCC 409

Samridhi Devi v. Union of India (2005) 125 DLT 284

Samuel Tennyson v. The Principal & Secretary, (2019) 2 Writ LR 265

Sandeep Khurana v. Delhi Transco Limited 135 (2006) DLT 346

Sandra M. Clark; Rhonda R. Knoop v. United Parcel Service, Inc.; Eli Brock 400 F. 3d 341 (6th Circuit, 2005).

Sanjay Babu v. State of Tamil Nadu, Criminal Appeal No. 773

Sanjay Kumar Behera v. State NCT of Delhi Crl. M.C. No. 10/2012

Sanjay Sharma v. Union of India W.P. (C) No. 1292/2021 (24.04.2024, Delhi High Court)

Sanjay Singh v. State 2008 (1) JCC 650

Sardar Vallabhbhai National Institute of Technology v. Ranjit Roy L.P.A No. 1349-50/2015 (22.03.2016, Gujarat High Court)

Sarita Das v. Union India 2014 (2) GLT 662

Sarita Singh v. State of U.P, 2020 (165) FLR 66

Sau. Anuradha R. Kshirsagar v. State of Maharashtra (1990) 3 Bom CR 644

Saudi Arabian Airlines v. Shehnaz Mudbhatkal 1999 (1) Bom CR 643

Saurabh Kumar Mallick v. Comptroller & Auditor General of India, (2008) 151 DLT 261 (DB)

Saurashtra Salt Manufacturing Co. v. Bai Valu Raja (1958) II LLJ 249 (SC)

Secretary, Ministry of Defence v. Prabash Chandra Mirdha (2012) 11 SCC 565

Sh. Onkar Singh v. Union of India (01.08.2007, Central Administrative Tribunal, Delhi)

Shah Jayshree Manilal Pushpaben v. State of Maharashtra (2012) 2 Bom CR 770

Shankarlal Namdeo v. State of Madhya Pradesh 2024 SCC Online MP 5512

Shanoff v.Illinois Department of Human Servs. 258 F.3d 696

Sharanjeet Kaur v. IDBI Bank Limited LPA No. 417/2014 (22.05.2024, Delhi High Court)

Shardaben Murlibhai Gurjar v. State of Gujarat (2015) 2 GLR 1620

Shashi Bala v. SBM Sr. Secondary School 218 (2015) DLT 575

Sheela v. E.S.I Corporation (1991) I LLJ 247 P&H

Sheela v. E.S.I Corporation (1991) I LLJ 247 P&H.

Sheo Ratan Upadhya v. Gopal Chandra Nepali AIR 1965 All 274

Shila Debnath v. National Institute of Technology, WP (C) No. 422/2021 (07.12.2021, Tripura High Court)

Shobha Goswami v. State of Uttar Pradesh (2015) 146 FLR 613

Shoyab Bijani v. State of Gujarat 2013 (56) PTC 534 (Guj)

Shri Lalu Varghese v. State Bank of India, Appeal No. CIC/MP/A/ 2014/001168 (31.03.2015, Central Information Commission)

Shri Milind Mamlekar v. Goa University, WP No. 628/2013 (29.01.2021, Bombay High Court, Goa Bench)

Shri V.K. Bhosale v. CPIO, CIC/SH/A/2014/001862 (15.09.2015, Central Information Commission)

Siddharth Jain v. Shaheed Sukhdev College of Business Studies W.P. (Civil) No. 9862/2015 (17.11.2015, Delhi High Court)

Smt. Kalawati v. United Vaish Co-operative Thrift & Credit Society Ltd. I (2002) CPJ 71 (NC)

Somaya Gupta v. Jawarlal Nehru University, 2018 (VIII) AD (Delhi) 259

Soumen Sarkar v. The State of West Bengal, WPA No. 13267/2021 (16.09.2021, Calcutta High Court)

Soumen Sen v. PIO, National Commission for Women File No. CIC/NCFWO/A/2017/191483 (12.05.2017, Central Information Commission)

State Bank of Patiala v. S.K. Sharma 1996 (3) SCC 364

State (NCT of Delhi) v. Rishi Anand 2017 SCC Online Del 10506

State of Goa v. Summit Online Trade Solutions Private Limited, (2023) 7 SCC 791

State of Gujarat v. N.H. Thakor 2005 CriLJ 2957

State of Haryana v. Bhajan Lal 1992 Supp (1) SCC 335.

State of Haryana v. Rattan Singh (1977) 2 SCC 491

State of Punjab v. Gurmit Singh (1996) 2 SCC 384

State of Punjab v. Major Singh 1967 Cri LJ 1

State of U.P v. Siya Ram Civil Appeal No. 5005/2004 (05.08.2004, Supreme Court of India)

State of Uttar Pradesh v. Chandrika AIR 2000 SC 164

State of Uttar Pradesh v. Gobardhan Lal (2004) 11 SCC 402

State of West Bengal v. Committee for Protection of Democratic Rights,

Stewart v. Miss. Transp. Comm'n 586 F.3d 321 (5th Circuit, 2009)

Su Iccha Foundation v. Union of India WP (C) No. 14675/2023 (17.11.2023, Delhi High Court)

Sujit Baran Mandal v. Union of India, 2020 (1) SLJ 231 (CAT)

Sukalyan Haldar v. State of West Bengal, W.P.A. No. 18829/2023 (08.09.2023, Calcutta High Court)

Suman Saurabh v. The Internal Complaints Committee, 2019 LLR 975

Sumana Bhowmick v. Union of India, WPO 177/2019 & WPA 11842/2019 (03.02.2023, Calcutta High Court).

Sumitra Devi v. Executive Engineer, Udar Asthan Irrigation Division (1997) III LLJ 1058 (Pat)

Sunetra v. Central Board for Workers Education OA No. 349/2012 (13.08.2012, Central Administrative Tribunal, Delhi)

Sunil Manu Prasad Jani v. High Court of Gujarat, Special Civil Application No. 14566/2015 (12.10.2015, Gujarat High Court)

Sunita Kumari v. State of Himachal Pradesh, CWP No. 4074/2019 (10.09.2020, Himachal Pradesh High Court)

Suresh Pathrela v. Oriental Bank of Commerce (2006) 10 SCC 572

Suresh v. The State of Tamil Nadu WP (MD) No. 4491/2014 (24.07.2019, Madras High Court)

Sushma Rani Tirkey v. PIO, Council of Scientific & Industrial Research CIC/CSIRD/A/2016/306867 (28.04.2017, Central Information Commission)

Swatanter Kumar v. The Indian Express Limited 207 (2014) DLT 221

Syndicate Bank v. Venkatesh Gururao Kurati 2006:INSC:50

**T**

T. Arivandandam v. T.V. Satyapal AIR 1977 SC 2421

T. Manikadan v. The State Cr. Rev. Petition No. 404/2016 (10.01.2017, Delhi High Court)

T.R. Sahrawat v. Kendriya Vidyalaya Sangathan OA No. 4341/2012 (06.03.2014, Central Administrative Tribunal, Delhi).

T.T. Chakravarthy Yuvaraj v. Principal, Dr. B.R. Ambedkar Medical College AIR 1997 Ker 261

Tanushree Chopra v. Ministry of Women and Child Development W.P. (C) No. 11759/2015 (17.12.2015, Delhi High Court)

The Managing Director, HDFC Standard Life Insurance Company Ltd v. Suresh Babu, 2022 LR 488

The Research Scholar v. Research Guide & Others 2024:MHC:4046.

Titaghur Paper Mills v. State of Orissa AIR 1983 SC 603

Torres v. Pisano 116 F.3d 625 (2nd Circuit, 1997)

Turkeshwar Sahu v. State of Bihar (2006) 8 SCC 560)

**U**

U.S Verma v. National Commission of Women 163 (2009) DLT 557

Union of India v. Central Administrative Tribunal (2005) 4 Mad LJ 104

Union of India v. Dilip Paul, 2023 INSC 975

Union of India v. H.C. Goel AIR 1964 SC 364

Union of India v. Mudrika Singh, Civil Appeal No. 6859/2021 (03.12.2021, Supreme Court of India)

Union of India v. Naman Singh Shekhawat (2008) 4 SCC 1

Union of India v. P. Gunasekaran (2015) 2 SCC 610

Union of India v. Rema Srinivasan Iyengar, 2020 (3) CTC 281

**X**

X v. Internal Committee, RCA DJ No. 2/2022 (06.07.2022, Industrial Tribunal, Rouse Avenue Court, New Delhi)

X v. The District Magistrate, WP (C) No. 8443/2018 (13.08.2018, Delhi High Court)

**Y**

Yamaguchi v. Widnall 109 F.3d. 1475 [1997]

Yasharay Mack v. Otis Elevator Company 326 F.3d 116 (2nd Circuit, 2003)

Yashoda Tiwari v. Western Coal Fields Limited W.P. No. 4509/2014 (02.03.2015, Madhya Pradesh High Court)

# Preface

Sexual harassment is one of the synonyms of 'gender discrimination' or 'gender inequality'. It is one of the antitheses to gender equality. There is no country with perfect gender equality. All countries suffer some loss in achievements when gender inequality is taken into account.

In India, the case of Vishaka v. State of Rajasthan was momentous; it provided a vantage point to recognise and to give the issue of 'sexual harassment' the attention it deserved. This judgement provided to women the armoury to challenge this negative social practice and give a turning point to this subject. Subsequently, the Sexual Harassment of Women at Workplace Act, 2013, was enacted after a decade and a half. This new law shall shape how work cultures are assessed *qua* women.

Generally speaking, the concept of sexual harassment at the workplace can be examined from a variety of vantage points. However, this authorship has primarily focussed on the commercial angle of the issue. This book attempts to holistically analyse the Indian law on sexual harassment at the workplace by resorting to a point-by-point examination of all components thereof.

An attempt has been made to explain the subject in the simplest (possible) language while keeping intact the legal aspect(s) of the subject. As regards judicial precedents, this work attempts to cover all relevant judgements passed by Indian courts from 1997 (when this subject entered the Indian legal domain) until March 2025. It is hoped that exhaustive case-law coverage will come in handy for the stakeholders and interested parties.

From a procedural front, this work has attempted to cover all procedural aspects of internal sexual harassment investigation, which should come in handy for complaints committees which conduct internal investigations/inquiries on complaints of sexual harassment. Moreover, this work contains a draft sexual harassment policy and a conciliation policy which may be utilised by organisations for developing (and updating) their internal policies on the subject.

For ease of understanding, this authorship offers a section-by-section analysis of the Act, along with a reflection of the general scheme of law on sexual harassment. This work is complete with views and thoughts of the author on various issues which still remain unaddressed by courts (due to the infancy of this law). This work hopes to serve the needs of lawyers, law students, organisations, and NGOs as well as all persons interested in gaining insight into this law.

CHAPTER 1

# Introduction

Women constitute nearly one half of the global population. Within the next decade approximately one billion women are likely to enter the global workforce.

Studies indicate that an increase in female workplace participation, or a reduction in the gap between women's and men's work participation, results in faster economic growth, as women bring valuable skill sets and diversity of thought. Therefore, it is a good idea for women to enhance their presence and contribution in workspaces. However, one significant roadblock to an increase in the effective workplace participation of women is the issue of sexual harassment.[1]

## SEXUAL HARASSMENT

In common parlance, the term 'sexual harassment' may be described as discrimination or exploitation based on sex. Any unwelcome or unwarranted conduct of a sexual nature, whether deliberate or not, would normally fall within the ambit of this term.

In the context of employment law, sexual harassment may be described as any unwelcome sexual conduct that has

1 Women's employment prospects can be seriously impaired when women are subjected to gender-specific violence, such as sexual harassment at the workplace.

the purpose or effect of violating the dignity of a person, or of creating an intimidating, hostile, degrading, humiliating or offensive environment for employees. This can include unwelcome physical, verbal or non-verbal conduct.[2] Sexual harassment may be classified as an antithesis of equality and development as it possesses discriminatory undertones and detracts from a productive work environment.

Sexual harassment can occur in all social and economic classes, ethnic groups, jobs and places in society. Recipients of sexually harassing behaviour may experience an array of physical and emotional after-effects, such as anxiety, depression, reclusion, reduced self-esteem, stress disorders, a loss of confidence and morale, etc. If unchecked and uncontained, sexual harassment can hamper the women's ability to earn a living, feel secure, enjoy their working life and participate fully in both their workplace and society at large.

### Sexual Harassment: Concept

Under Indian law, some general attributes or facets of 'sexual harassment' are as follows: (i) the sexual dimension of or the sexual overtones in such conduct; (ii) behaviour or conduct unwelcome by the recipient; (iii) the power imbalance between the perpetrator and the victim; and (iv) the loss or damage occasioned to the victim.[3] Harassment can represent a single, serious incident or persistent abuse.

Indian law recognises freedom from sexual harassment as a human and fundamental right. The harm suffered by a victim of sexual harassment is of such magnitude that legal prohibitions are justified. In India, sexual harassment at work

---

2 *See generally* L. Nagaraju v. Syndicate Bank 2014 (2) ALD 758.

3 Writing unwelcome and unsolicited love letter(s) to women would amount to sexual harassment. D.S. Grewal v. Vimmi Joshi, Civil Appeal No. 7355/2008 (17.12.2008, Supreme Court of India).

in any form is unacceptable behaviour and should neither be permitted nor condoned.

This work address the subject of sexual harassment in the workplace. Efforts have been made to include all possible facets and aspects of this issue. It is pertinent to point out that the primary focus of this work is on Indian law.

Any discussion on a legal topic must commence from its point of emanation and subsequent evolution. In the case of sexual harassment, it is imperative to begin the discourse with the judgement of the Supreme Court of India titled 'Vishaka v. State of Rajasthan'. This judgement laid down the foundation for the law on sexual harassment in the workplace.

## THE VISHAKA CASE

In India, the concept of sexual harassment in the workplace was brought into focus in the year 1997 with the passing of the judgement titled Vishaka v. State of Rajasthan[4] (**Vishaka Case**).

The Vishaka Case was a pathbreaking judgement delivered with the objective of creating an enabling and safe environment at the workplace for the rapidly increasing female workforce.[5] In the Vishaka Case, the Apex Court searched the existing law only to find that there was a total absence of legislative measures to safeguard women against sexual harassment at workplaces. It was deemed absolutely essential to find an effective alternative mechanism to fulfil the urgent social need for suitable methods that would reflect the true concept of gender equality and prevent sexual harassment of working

4 (1997) 6 SCC 241. This judgement had come to be passed in the aftermath of the gang rape of a social worker (in Rajasthan) who had opposed certain discriminatory practices. The focus of the case shifted from a criminal wrong to systemic gender discrimination which needed eradication.

5 The Parliamentary Standing Committee Report (2011) [defined later in the work].

women in all workplaces. It was observed that in the absence of legislative measures, it was imperative to have such guidelines in place, issued through judicial process, to fill the vacuum in existing legislation.[6]

The Supreme Court examined the issue of sexual harassment of working women in the workplace in light of Articles 14, 15, 19 and 21 of the Constitution of India. After examining the relevant constitutional provisions and various international conventions and norms applicable to the field, the court formulated guidelines to provide for the effective enforcement of the basic human right of gender equality and guarantee against sexual harassment and abuse, more particularly against sexual harassment at workplaces, until the enactment of legislation for the purpose (hereinafter referred to as the **Vishaka Guidelines**).

This judgement played a pivotal role in the introduction of a comprehensive definition of the expression 'sexual harassment' to the statute book.

**Vishaka Guidelines**

The aim of the Supreme Court, while formulating the Vishaka Guidelines was: (i) to ensure a fair, secure or comfortable work environment; (ii) to eliminate situations or possibilities where the protector could abuse his trust, and turn predator[7]; and (iii) to provide an assurance to the female members of the Indian workforce that in the event of sexual harassment at the workplace, the employer would take prompt and serious action.[8]

The Vishaka Guidelines are reproduced below for ready reference:

6 *See generally* Puthuppan v. K.S. Girija 2008 (3) KLJ 416.

7 Samridhi Devi v. Union of India (2005) 125 DLT 284.

8 A.K. Singh v. Union of India W.P. (C) No. 4237/2012 (01.12.2015, Delhi High Court). *See also* Leena Doley v. State of Assam 2013 (5) GLT 363.

Having regard to the definition of 'human rights' in *Section 2(d)* of the Protection of Human Rights Act, 1993, taking note of the fact that the present civil and penal laws in India do not adequately provide for specific protection of women from sexual harassment in work places and that enactment of such legislation will take considerable time, it is necessary and expedient for employers in work places as well as other responsible persons or institutions to observe certain guidelines to ensure the prevention of sexual harassment of women:

1. Duty of the Employer or other responsible persons in work places and other institutions:
It shall be the duty of the employer or other responsible persons in work places or other institutions to prevent or deter the commission of acts of sexual harassment and to provide the procedures for the resolution, settlement or prosecution of acts of sexual harassment by taking all steps required.

2. Definition:
For this purpose, sexual harassment includes such unwelcome sexually determined behaviour (whether directly or by implication) as:

- physical contact and advances;
- a demand or request for sexual favours;
- sexually coloured remarks;
- showing pornography;
- any other unwelcome physical verbal or non-verbal conduct of sexual nature.

Where any of these acts is committed in circumstances where under the victim of such conduct has a reasonable apprehension that in relation to the victim's employment or work whether she is drawing salary, or honorarium or voluntary, whether in government, public or private enterprise such conduct can be humiliating and may constitute a health and safety problem. It is discriminatory for instance when the woman has reasonable grounds to believe that her objection would disadvantage her in connection with her employment or work including recruiting or promotion or when it creates a hostile work environment. Adverse consequences might be visited if the victim does not consent to the conduct in question or raises any objection thereto.

3. Preventive Steps:

All employers or persons in charge of work place whether in the public or private sector should take appropriate steps to prevent sexual harassment. Without prejudice to the generality of this obligation they should take the following steps:

- Express prohibition of sexual harassment as defined above at the work place should be notified, published and circulated in appropriate ways.
- The Rules/Regulations of Government and Public Sector bodies relating to conduct and discipline should include rules/regulations prohibiting sexual harassment and provide for appropriate penalties in such rules against the offender.
- As regards private employers, steps should be taken to include the aforesaid prohibitions in the standing orders under the *Industrial Employment (Standing Orders) Act*, 1946.
- Appropriate work conditions should be provided in respect of work, leisure, health and hygiene to further

ensure that there is no hostile environment towards women at work places and no employee woman should have reasonable grounds to believe that she is disadvantaged in connection with her employment.

4. Criminal Proceedings:
Where such conduct amounts to a specific offence under *the Indian Penal Code / Bharatiya Nyaya Sanhita* or under any other law the employer shall initiate appropriate action in accordance with law by making a complaint with the appropriate authority.
In particular, it should ensure that victims or witnesses are not victimized or discriminated against while dealing with complaints of sexual harassment. The victims of sexual harassment should have the option to seek transfer of the perpetrator or their own transfer.

5. Disciplinary Action:
Where such conduct amounts to mis-conduct in employment as defined by the relevant service rules, appropriate disciplinary action should be initiated by the employer in accordance with those rules.

6. Complaint Mechanism:
Whether or not such conduct constitutes an offence under law or a breach of the service rules, an appropriate complaint mechanism should be created in the employer's organization for redress of the complaint made by the victim. Such complaint mechanism should ensure time bound treatment of complaints.

7. Complaints Committee:
The complaint mechanism, referred to in (6) above, should

be adequate to provide, where necessary, a Complaints Committee, a special counsellor or other support service, including the maintenance of confidentiality.

The Complaints Committee should be headed by a woman and not less than half of its member should be women.

Further, to prevent the possibility of any under pressure or influence from senior levels, such Complaints Committee should involve a third party, either NGO or other body who is familiar with the issue of sexual harassment.

The Complaints Committee must make an annual report to the government department concerned of the complaints and action taken by them. The employers and person in charge will also report on the compliance with the aforesaid guidelines including on the reports of the Complaints Committee to the Government department.

8. Workers' Initiative:

Employees should be allowed to raise issues of sexual harassment at workers meeting and in other appropriate forum and it should be affirmatively discussed in Employer-Employee Meetings.

9. Awareness:

Awareness of the rights of female employees in this regard should be created in particular by prominently notifying the guidelines (and appropriate legislation when enacted on the subject) in suitable manner.

10. Where sexual harassment occurs as a result of an act or omission by any third party or outsider, the employer and person in charge will take all steps necessary and reasonable to assist the affected person in terms of support and preventive action.

> 11. The Central/State Governments are requested to consider adopting suitable measures including legislation to ensure that the guidelines laid down by this order are also observed by the employers in Private Sector.
>
> 12. These guidelines will not prejudice any rights available under the *Protection of Human Rights Act*, 1993.

Thus, the Supreme Court created a full-fledged curriculum replete with the mode and manner of inquiry in matters and complaints relating to sexual harassment in the workplace. The Vishaka Guidelines acquired the force of law and took centre stage in every case of workplace sexual harassment for almost a decade and a half.

**Implementation of Vishaka Guidelines**

In Apparel Export Promotion Council v. A.K. Chopra[9], the Supreme Court had an occasion to consider whether the actions of a superior against a subordinate female employee, which were contrary to moral sanctions and did not withstand the test of decency and modesty, would amount to sexual harassment. The court, amongst other observations, held that sexual harassment is a form of sex discrimination, projected through unwelcome sexual advances, requests for sexual favours, and other verbal or physical conduct with sexual overtones, whether directly or by implication, particularly when submission to, or rejection of, such conduct by a female employee was capable of being used to influence her employment or unreasonably interfere with her work performance, and had the effect of creating an intimidating or hostile working environment for her.

9 AIR 1999 SC 625.

**Implementation Related Issues**

The Vishaka Case was delivered on 13 August 1997. While a statutory law was still not in place, instances of sexual harassment at workplaces continued to trouble the judicial conscience. Finally, the Supreme Court, in the case of Medha Kotwal Lele v. Union of India[10], took note of the continued sexual victimisation of women and the lack of effective implementation of the Vishaka Guidelines. The court observed that the Vishaka Guidelines were not being followed in substance and spirit by the state functionaries and all others concerned.

The court ultimately ruled that the implementation of the Vishaka Guidelines must be carried out in both letter and spirit so as to ensure a safe and secure environment for women at workplaces in every aspect, and to enable working women to work with dignity, decency and due respect. It was further clarified that the report of the complaints committee (which makes an inquiry into a complaint of sexual harassment) should not be treated as a mere preliminary investigation or inquiry leading to a disciplinary action, but as a finding/report in an inquiry into the misconduct of the delinquent pursuant to which action would be taken. It was further directed that adequate provisions should be made so that harassment and intimidation of complainants and witnesses are met with severe disciplinary action. Consequently, the court issued a series of directions to the government to formulate internal complaints committees and comply with the law, which are reproduced below:

> 16. In what we have discussed above, we are of the considered view that guidelines in Vishaka should not remain symbolic and the following further directions are necessary until legislative enactment on the subject is in place.

10 (2013) 1 SCC 297.

(i) The States and Union Territories which have not yet carried out adequate and appropriate amendments in their respective Civil Services Conduct Rules (By whatever name these Rules are called) shall do so within two months from today by providing that the report of the Complaints Committee shall be deemed to be an inquiry report in a disciplinary action under such Civil Services Conduct Rules. In other words, the disciplinary authority shall treat the report/findings etc. of the Complaints Committee as the findings in a disciplinary inquiry against the delinquent employee and shall act on such report accordingly. The findings and the report of the Complaints Committee shall not be treated as a mere preliminary investigation or inquiry leading to a disciplinary action but shall be treated as a finding/report in an inquiry into the misconduct of the delinquent.

(ii) The States and Union Territories which have not carried out amendments in the Industrial Employment (Standing Orders) Rules shall now carry out amendments on the same lines, as noted above in clause (i) within two months.

(iii) The States and Union Territories shall form adequate number of Complaints Committees so as to ensure that they function at taluka level, district level and state level. Those States and/or Union Territories which have formed only one Committee for the entire State shall now form adequate number of Complaints Committees within two months from today. Each of such Complaints Committees shall be headed by a woman and as far as possible in such Committees an independent member shall be associated.

(iv) The State functionaries and private and public sector undertakings/organisations/bodies/institutions etc. shall put in place sufficient mechanism to ensure full implementation of the Vishaka guidelines and further provide that if the alleged harasser is found guilty, the complainant - victim is not forced to work with/under such harasser and where appropriate and possible the alleged harasser should be transferred. Further provision should be made that harassment and intimidation of witnesses and the complainants shall be met with severe disciplinary action.

(v) The Bar Council of India shall ensure that all bar associations in the country and persons registered with the State Bar Councils follow the Vishaka guidelines. Similarly, Medical Council of India, Council of Architecture, Institute of Chartered Accountants, Institute of Company Secretaries and other statutory Institutes shall ensure that the organisations, bodies, associations, institutions and persons registered/affiliated with them follow the guidelines laid down by Vishaka. To achieve this, necessary instructions/ circulars shall be issued by all the statutory bodies such as Bar Council of India, Medical Council of India, Council of Architecture, Institute of Company Secretaries within two months from today. On receipt of any complaint of sexual harassment at any of the places referred to above the same shall be dealt with by the statutory bodies in accordance with the Vishaka guidelines and the guidelines in the present order.

## JUDICIAL APPROACH TOWARDS VISHAKA CASE

As mentioned above, prior to the Vishaka Case, there existed no discourse or mechanism to address the issue of sexual harassment of women employees in the workplace. During the time the Vishaka Case occupied the field, the courts observed that all cases of sexual harassment were to be conducted in accordance with the Vishaka Guidelines.[11] In other words, the Vishaka Guidelines had acquired the force of law and it held the

11 *See generally* Arati Durgaram Gavandi v. Managing Director, Tata Metaliks Ltd. (2009) 120 FLR 973 (Bom).

field until the enactment of the Sexual Harassment at Workplace (Prevention, Prohibition and Redressal) Act.[12]

During this period, the court, on various occasions, stressed on the importance of establishing internal complaints committees for redressing issues relating to sexual harassment.[13] One such example is D.S. Grewal v. Vimmi Joshi[14], where the Supreme Court dealt with the issue of sexual harassment of a school principal by a high-ranking official of the school's managing committee. In the said case, amongst other observations, the Supreme Court noted that neither had a mechanism for redressal of the victim's complaints been put in place nor had an appropriate complaints committee been constituted as per the Vishaka Guidelines. The court ultimately reaffirmed the Vishaka Guidelines and directed an inquiry into the matter in accordance therewith.

## RADICAL SHIFT IN REPORTING

Sexual harassment of women in the workplace is now a commonplace issue, experienced by women across all strata of society. As in many other societies, sexual harassment has been long prevalent within the Indian ecosystem. However, in the past, the reporting on such incidents was scarce. It seems that earlier, victims of sexual harassment suffered in silence instead of protesting against such conduct. The reasons for this are

12 The Vishaka Guidelines held the field even in cases where complaints of sexual harassment were pending adjudication as on the date of coming into force of the Act. *See* Bhaskar De Sarkar v. State of West Bengal, W.P. No. 29034/2014 (13.11.2014, Calcutta High Court); Puthuppan v. K.S. Girija 2008 (3) KLJ 416.

13 In 2013, the Gender Sensitisation & Sexual Harassment of Women at the Supreme Court of India (Prevention, Prohibition and Redressal) Regulations, 2013 were enacted to address the offence of sexual harassment taking place in the Supreme Court of India. These regulations were approved and upheld by the Supreme Court in the case of Binu Tamta v. High Court of Delhi W.P. (C) No. 162/2013 (17.07.2013, Supreme Court of India).

14 Civil Appeal No. 7355/2008 (17.12.2008, Supreme Court of India).

numerous: (i) the power imbalance between the perpetrator and the victim; (ii) societal pressure, *viz.* to evade unwarranted glare/ scrutiny of the public; (iii) fear of a retaliation or reprisal from the perpetrator or others the workplace; (iv) protracted, expensive and cumbersome court litigation for redressing the offence of sexual harassment. Resultantly, instances of sexual harassment hardly came to light, allowing this unwanted phenomenon to continue unchallenged, undeterred and unabated.

While the issue of sexual harassment has recently received considerable attention from the relevant quarters, including the judiciary, the legal profession and the media, little has been done to address this evil in its proper perspective. The new enactment on sexual harassment appears to have pumped fresh life into addressing this issue. The next chapter introduces the new law on sexual harassment in India, *viz.* The Sexual Harassment at Workplace (Prevention, Prohibition and Redressal) Act 2013.

CHAPTER 2

# The New Law

Sexual harassment results in violation of various rights of a woman including right to equality, right to life and to live with dignity and the right to practice any profession or to carry on any occupation, trade or business.

Pursuant to the Vishaka Case, the guidelines established therein remained only on paper for a long time. Neither were the guidelines implemented in most workplaces[1] nor was a legislation promulgated in this area. Further, with more and more women joining the workforce (both in organised and unorganised sectors) it started becoming increasingly necessary to ensure an enabling work environment for women through a statute. Ultimately, the Sexual Harassment of Women at Workplace (Prevention, Prohibition and Redressal) Bill, 2012 (hereinafter the "**Bill**") was formulated and brought into circulation. The Bill was passed in the Lok Sabha on 03.09.2012 and in the Rajya Sabha on 26.02.2013. After being passed by both the houses of the Parliament, it received the assent of the President of India on 22.04.2013. It came on the statute book as the Sexual Harassment of Women at Workplace (Prevention, Prohibition and Redressal) Act, 2013 (hereinafter the "**Act**") which came into force on 09.12.2013 thereby superseding the Vishaka Guidelines.

---

1 *See* Medha Kotwal Lele v. Union of India (2013) 1 SCC 297.

## THE OBJECTIVES

The paramount intention of the legislature behind enacting the Act was protection and preservation against sexual harassment at workplace; and redressal of complaints of sexual harassment both in government and private sectors.[2]

The object behind the Act was as follows: (i) To create and maintain a work environment which is conducive for working women in India; (ii) to provide every woman, a safe and secure work environment, free from sexual harassment; (iii) creation of an environment where the woman's integrity, dignity, and privacy is preserved and protected.

### Features of the Act

The Act has been promulgated to provide a safe, secure and enabling environment to every woman, regardless of her age or employment status, free from all forms of sexual harassment, by fixing responsibility on the employers and laying down a statutory redressal mechanism. It is a multifaceted piece of legislation which is applicable to all types of workplaces and provides procedures to effectively tackle the issue of sexual harassment of women and prevent its occurrence. Such procedures include policies which prohibit the act of sexual harassment; and investigation processes for inquiring into a claim of sexual harassment.

Under the Act, sexual harassment is unlawful in every employment situation and employment related relationship. Put differently, sexual harassment is illegal in any and every work related context and includes interactions with clients, contractors and customers. The perpetrators of sexual harassment may include owners, employers, employees, clients,

---

2 The Preamble to the Act states thus '*An Act to provide protection against sexual harassment of women at workplace and for the prevention and redressal of complaints of sexual harassment and for matters connected therewith or incidental thereto.*'

contractors and third parties having business dealings with the work place.

## DEFINITIONS AND INTERPRETATION

The reader would note from an analysis of the definitions of various critical expressions and terms under the Act, the purpose of the legislation is to render maximum possible depth and width to its scope and operation.[3] Please note that the definition of the expression 'sexual harassment' has been dealt with extensively in the immediately succeeding chapter. Other critical definitions are discussed below. At the outset, it is pertinent to point out that the provisions of the Act are attracted only in a workplace scenario and not otherwise. Incidents of sexual harassment occurring in private life can be redressed only by initiating criminal action in accordance with law.[4]

### Workplace

Under the Act, the expression 'workplace' is most important. This expression is required to be widely construed. Its expanse covers private and government establishments. In fact, it even takes within its sweep, the dwelling places/residential homes. Under the Act, the term 'Workplace' includes the following[5]:

i. Any department, organization, undertaking, establishment, enterprise, institution, office, branch or unit which is established, owned, controlled or wholly or substantially financed by funds provided directly or indirectly by the appropriate government or the local authority or a government company or a corporation or a cooperative society.

3 *See generally* Jaya Kodate *infra.*

4 For more *see* chapter titled 'Criminal Remedies'.

5 *See* S. 2 (o) of the Act.

ii. Any private sector organisation or a private venture, undertaking, enterprise, institution, establishment, society, trust, non- governmental organization, unit or service provider carrying on commercial, professional, vocational, educational, entertainmental, industrial, health services or financial activities including production, supply, sale, distribution or service.

iii. Hospital or nursing homes.

iv. Any sports institute, stadium, sports complex or competition or games venue, whether residential or not used for training, sports or other activities relating to it.

v. Any place visited by the employee arising out of or during the course of employment including transportation provided by the employer for undertaking such journey.

vi. A dwelling or a house.[6]

Workplace: Scope and Width

In Saurabh Kumar Mallick v. Comptroller & Auditor General of India[7], the Delhi High Court extensively discussed the concept of workplace. The court opined that the expression 'workplace' cannot be given a narrow or pedantic meaning. It was observed that it was not necessary that a workplace would be only a place where actual office work is performed. Any extension of the place of work where the employer has control of management would also be treated as a workplace. It would typically envisage any situation which is linked to official work or official activity.

In the case in question, an alleged act of sexual harassment had taken place in a hostel/officers mess near the office complex.

6 As a natural consequence of bringing 'domestic workers' within the ambit of the Act, dwelling places have been brought within the definition of the term 'workplace'.

7 (2008) 151 DLT 261 (DB).

The court formulated the following parameters/general guidelines for determining whether the locality of the offence qualifies to be a 'workplace' or not:[8]

a. proximity from the place of work;
b. control of management over such place/residence where the working woman is residing; and
c. such a 'residence' should to be an extension or contiguous part of the working place.

The Act offers an enhanced and highly expanded definition of the term 'workplace'; it goes beyond the traditional 'brick and mortar' definition and includes within its ambit, all places having a linkage with the employment including places visited by the employees arising out of and in connection with the employment and/or having work related consequences.

In Poonam Shahani v. Union of India[9] the question before the court was whether the official residence of the complainant (where the alleged incident of sexual harassment took place) would qualify to be 'workplace' for the purposes of the Act. The court, while relying on the principles explained in Saurabh Kumar Malik supra observed that such questions would need to be determined by the concerned complaints committee through recording of evidence.

<u>Notional Extension of 'Workplace'</u>

As discussed above, the width of the term 'workplace' has been notionally expanded by the Act in recognition of the fact that a woman employee may be subjected to sexual harassment even

8 Please note that, during the said period, the Act had not come into force and the Vishaka Case occupied the field.

9 OA No. 1001/2022 (15.04.2024, Central Administrative Tribunal, Mumbai)

outside the physical boundaries of her workplace; albeit during the course of her employment. This may include harassment by a co-worker outside the precincts of her workplace or by an employee of another workplace visited by her during the course of her employment. The location of the incident of sexual harassment is notionally expanded to include any place 'arising out of or during the course of employment', such as work related trainings, conferences, functions, trips and even transportation provided by the employer.

Arising out of and during the course of employment

Sexual harassment under the Act is prohibited in situations where it occurs away from the workplace but is a culmination or extension of events of the workplace.[10] The legislative intent is clear from the use of the expression 'arising out of and during the course of employment' in the definition of the term 'workplace'.

The expression 'arising out of and during the course of employment' postulates the theory of notional extension of the employer's premises.[11] This theory extends both the 'time' (the work hours of the employee) and 'place' (*viz.* the employment premises) in a reasonable manner.[12] This expression 'arising out of and during the course of employment' has been a subject matter of judicial interpretation in the past, *albeit* in the context of labour and employment statutes such as the Employee Compensation Act, 1923 and the Employees State Insurance Act, 1948. Some important case law which aptly highlight the

10 M. Kavya v. Chairman, University Grants Commission W.P. No. 11217/2014 (04.12.2014, Madras High Court). Note that any act of sexual harassment in private life may not necessarily amount to be sexual harassment at 'workplace' under the provisions of the Act. In such case, the only option available to the aggrieved is to commence criminal action against the perpetrator under the provisions of the Indian Penal Code. *See* Jaya Kodate *supra*.

11 Sheela v. E.S.I Corporation (1991) I LLJ 247 P&H.

12 *See also* Saurashtra Salt Manufacturing Co. v. Bai Valu Raja (1958) II LLJ 249 (SC); Regional Director E.S.I Corporation v. Francis De Costa AIR 1997 SC 432.

expanse of the expression 'arising out of and during the course of employment' are discussed below.

In Kamala v. Madras Port Trust[13] the court held that for an employee to come within the scope of the expression 'arising out of and during the course of employment', she should be able to establish that she was, at the time of the incident, engaged in the employer's business or in furthering that business and was not doing something for her own benefit or accommodation.

In the context of the Employees Compensation Act, 1923 (ESI Act) the Supreme Court, in the case of Mackinnon Mackenzie & Co. Pvt. Ltd. v. Ibrahim Mahmmod Issak[14], analysed the term 'arising out of and during the course of employment' in the following words:

> To come within the Act the injury by accident must arise both out of and in the course of employment. The words 'in the course of the employment' mean 'in the course of the work which the workman is employed to do and which is incidental to it'. The words 'arising out of employment' are understood to mean that 'during the course of the employment, injury has resulted from some risk incidental to the duties of the service, which, unless engaged in the duty owing to the master, it is reasonable to believe the workman would not otherwise have suffered'. In other words, there must be a causal relationship between the accident and the employment. The expression 'arising out of employment' is again not confined to the mere nature of the employment. The expression applies to employment as such to its nature, its conditions, its obligations and its incidents. If by reason of any of those factors the workman is brought within the

13 (1966) I LLJ 690 (Mad).

14 AIR 1970 SC 1906. *See also* Sumitra Devi v. Executive Engineer, Udar Asthan Irrigation Division (1997) III LLJ 1058 (Pat).

> zone of special danger, the injury would be one which arises 'out of employment'. To put it differently, if the accident had occurred on account of a risk which is an incident of the employment, the claim for compensation must succeed, unless, of course, the workman has exposed himself to an added peril by his own imprudent act.

In the case of Regional Director, Employees State Insurance Corporation v. Derhin Bai[15], the Chhattisgarh High Court, in the context of the ESI Act, summed up the position as follows:

> i. The words "in the course of employment" mean in the course of the work which the workman is employed to do and which is incidental to it.
> ii. The words "arising out of employment" are understood to mean "during the course of employment, injury has resulted from some risk incidental to the duties to the service, which, unless engaged in the duty owing to the master, it is reasonable to believe the workman would not otherwise have suffered". In other words, there must be a casual relationship between the accident and the employment.
> iii. Expression "arising out of employment" is again not confined to the mere nature of the employment. The expression applies to (he employment as such to its nature, its conditions, its obligations and its incidents. If by any reason of any of those factors the workman is brought within the zone of special danger, the injury would be one which arises out of employment.
> iv. The onus of proving that the injury by accident arose out of and in the course of employment rests upon the applicant but these essentials may be inferred when the proved facts justify the inference.

15 (2012) IV LLJ 324 CG.

The wide canvass being afforded to the term 'arising out of or during the course of employment' brings to the fore the intention to provide protection and prevention at all possible places where either aggrieved woman works or may be present or may visit in connection with her duty.[16] In the view of the author, the term 'workplace' is intended to include within its ambit all conduct which may have a connection with the work/ employment regardless of the place of occurrence.[17]

Harassment during transport

The term 'workplace' even includes the transportation provided by the employer to the women employee for commuting for work. The legislature recognises the fact that women employees may be sexually harassed during their official journey.[18]

**Employee**

Under the Act, an 'employee' has been defined as a person employed at a workplace for any work on regular, temporary, adhoc or daily basis, either directly or through an agent, including a contractor, with or, without the knowledge of the principal employer, whether for remuneration or not, or working on a voluntary basis or otherwise, whether the terms of employment are express or implied and includes a co-worker, a contract worker, probationer, trainee, apprentice or called by any other such name.[19]

---

16 *See* Jaya Kodate v. Rashtrasant Tukoji Maharaj Nagpur University W.P. Nos. 3449, 3450 & 3451/2013 (13.06.2014, Bombay High Court).

17 In some cases, unwanted, uninvited visits by an offender to the victim's home may also be construed as sexual harassment.

18 Parliamentary Standing Committee on Human Resource Development, 239th Report on The Protection of Women against Sexual Harassment at Workplace Bill, 2010, ¶ 6.26 to 6.28 [hereinafter referred to as the **Parliamentary Standing Committee Report (2011)**].

19 S. 2 (f) of the Act.

The definition of 'employee' is palpably highly expanded and covers all sorts of working women in the workplace. All workplace participants including current and prospective employees also seem to be included in the above definition (such as persons at the stage of interviews, internships, volunteers etc.)[20] All that is to be seen is whether there exists a work related connection, howsoever remote it may be.

### Employer

The Act defines an 'employer' widely in the following words:

i. In relation to any department, organization, undertaking, establishment, enterprise, institution, office, branch or unit of the appropriate government or a local authority, the head of that department, organization, undertaking, establishment, enterprise, institution, office, branch or unit or such other officer as the appropriate Government or the local authority as the case may be, may by an order specify in this behalf.
ii. In any workplace not covered under the above explanation, any person responsible for the management, supervision and control of the workplace is the employer. Management includes the person or board or committee responsible for formulation and administration of policies for such organization.[21]
iii. Thus with regard to the above (i) and (ii), the person discharging contractual obligations with respect to his or her employees is the employer.
iv. In case of a dwelling place or house, a person or a household who employs or benefits from the employment of domestic worker,

20 M. Kavya v. Chairman, University Grants Commission W.P. No. 11217 of 2014 (04.12.2014, Madras High Court).

21 Where, the employer is covered under (i) above, the provisions under (ii) would not apply. The object of (ii) above is to elucidate and enlarge the scope of the term 'employer'; and not narrow down the scope of (i). *See* Gaurav Jain v. Hindustan Latex Family Planning Promotion Trust (2015) 220 DLT 60.

irrespective of the number, time period or type of such worker employed or the nature of the employment or activities performed by the domestic worker is the employer.

The legislative intent behind a wide definition of the term 'employer' is to be able to effectively identify the person responsible for management, supervision and control of every workplace and to fix accountability/responsibility under the Act. The definition is flexible and each case would need to be considered on its own merits.

In Sukalyan Haldar v. State of West Bengal[22] the question before the Calcutta High Court was whether, the secretary of the managing committee of a school (the workplace where the offence of sexual harassment was alleged to have been committed) would qualify the definition of "employer" as contained in Section 2 (g) (ii) of the Act. The Calcutta High Court, while answering in the affirmative, observed that, by mere definition, the secretary of the managing committee would be responsible for the "management of the school". The court also examined other documents which suggested that the said secretary was also exercising control and supervision over the workplace/school.

In Sumana Bhowmick v. Union of India[23] the Calcutta High Court observed that whether or not an accused qualifies to be an "employer" under the provisions of the Act would require a fact-finding exercise in terms of the victim and the accused person's nature of duty, the role of the accused in the management of the company/workplace as well as control over the members of the ICC.

22 W.P.A. No. 18829/2023 (08.09.2023, Calcutta High Court).

23 W.P.O. 177/2019 & W.P.A. 11842/2019 (03.02.2023, Calcutta High Court).

In Women in Cinema Collective v. State of Kerala,[24] the Kerala High Court had the occasion to examine as to whether certain voluntary organizations (of actor artists) which were associated with the film industry would qualify to be 'employers' for the purposes of the Act (as regards its artist/actor members). The organisation had made the following pertinent submissions in this regard: (i) it was only an association of actor/artists in Malayalam feature films; (ii) there was no employer - employee relationship between the association and its members; (iii) the association also did not have any control over film production since its artists members were individually booked directly by the film producers or film production houses, and all remuneration was directly exchanged between the parties; (iv) the only role of the organisation was to assist its members in undertaking any resolution of commercial disputes that cropped up between its members and the film production houses during the film shooting and related activities; (iv) any incident of sexual harassment would require a grievance mechanism not by the association but by the actual employers there in i.e. film producers or film production houses.

The Kerala High Court, while agreeing with the contentions of the voluntary organizations, concluded that insofar as the film industry was concerned, each production unit (where filming and relating activities took place) which would qualify to be a workplace of an individual film and therefore each production unit would have to constitute an ICC to deal with incidents of sexual harassment occurring on the sets at time of filming.

---

24 2022 (2) KLJ 254.

## Aggrieved Woman

Under the Act, the term Aggrieved Woman means:[25]

a. in relation to a workplace, a woman, of any age, whether employed or not, who alleges to have been subjected to any act of sexual harassment[26];
b. in relation to a dwelling place or house, a woman of any age who is employed in such dwelling place or house.

Generally speaking, the term 'aggrieved' refers to one 'having suffered loss or injury'. This term is also defined as feeling resentment at having unfairly treated.[27] Under the Act, only the person who is the target of the harassment[28] or any other person affected by the harassment[29] can initiate action under the Act.

An 'aggrieved women' may be an employee or an outsider. It brings within its ambit all women who not only are employed (whether permanently or temporarily) in the workplace but also non-employees who enter the workplace as clients, customers, apprentices etc.[30] The concept of 'third party harassment' has also been built into the Act.[31]

---

25 S. 2 (a) of the Act

26 The expression 'being subject to' means exposed or open to; prone to or liable to. *See* Hind Rubber Factory v. Union of India W.P. No. 4516/1984 (30.05.1989, Punjab & Haryana High Court); Kilmarnock Equitable Co-operative Society Ltd. v. Commissioners of Inland Revenue [1966] 42 TC 675 (C Sess). Note that when interpretation of an expression arises and such expression is not defined in the Act, the meaning most suitable to the situation will have to be attributed to the expression used. *See generally* Gokak Mills v. State of Karnataka ILR 1995 Karnataka 1489.

27 Leena Doley v. State of Assam 2013 (5) GLT 363.

28 *See* Quid Pro Quo Harassment in the immediately succeeding chapter.

29 Normally, an act of sexual harassment adversely affects the entire workplace. For example, an offender by his general conduct may make various women employees in the workplace uncomfortable. *See* Hostile Work Environment Harassment in the immediately succeeding chapter'.

30 M. Kavya v. Chairman, University Grants Commission W.P. No. 11217/2014 (04.12.2014, Madras High Court); Jaya Kodate *supra.*

31 *See* Parliamentary Standing Committee Report (2011), at ¶ 6.2 & 6.3.

## Seniority/Age of the Victim

Sexual Harassment is not age or status specific. Aspects such as seniority, status or age of the perpetrator and/or the victim are not determinative factors here. The terminology of the expression 'aggrieved woman' under section 2 (a) (i) of the Act is broad enough to cover all women regardless of their age or seniority gap with the perpetrator.[32]

## An Observation

It is critical to note that the Act offers widened definitions to various terms such as 'employer', 'employee', 'workplace' and 'aggrieved person'. The legislature in its wisdom appeared to avoid giving constrained definitions to such terms lest they become roadblocks in the path of a woman seeking a remedy for sexual harassment. The loose or liberal definitions appear to be an attempt to reach women at as many workplaces as possible.[33] The entire Act needs to be viewed as a net cast by the Parliament to cover as many establishments as possible; a net woven by using various concepts as its units giving it spring like qualities.[34] The exhaustive nature of the above terms are elucidated in the following words of the Bombay High Court:[35]

> 33. Mere look at the definition of words "employee" and "employer" reveals that both occupy the fields which are not mutually exclusive. Some posts or designation shall fall under both. A high ranking lady officer occupying managerial or supervisory post in employment of State or Public Body,

32 *See generally* Saurabh Kumar Mallick v. Comptroller & Auditor General of India (2008) 151 DLT 261 (DB).

33 *See* Jaya Kodate v. Rashtrasant Tukoji Maharaj Nagpur University W.P Nos. 3449, 3450 & 3451/2013 (13.06.2014, Bombay High Court).

34 *Ibid.*

35 *Ibid.*

Company or an Institution may become victim of Sexual Harassment. She may exercise administrative powers over several subordinates. So long as she is answerable to somebody else, may be an artificial person, she may in that eventuality, qualify to be an employee. A lady head of the department or principal or chief executive officer may therefore fall under both these definitions Similarly, the "respondent" may also hold these posts and therefore, is covered under both these heads. Normally these concepts are mutually exclusive and will not overlap. But we find that in the 2013 Act these concepts are loosely defined to enable the 2013 Act to reach as many respondents as necessary to advance effectively the object and to curb the mischief. Section 2 itself opens with the qualifying phrase "In this Act, unless the context otherwise requires". Thus question whether respondent is an employee or employer will call for determination in the context of the facts and situation. We find that various concepts have been defined deliberately widely and also wisely. The entire 2013 Act needs to be viewed as a net cast by the Parliament to cover as many establishments as possible; a net woven by using various concepts as its units giving it spring like qualities. Definition of workplace and unorganized sector leave no manner of doubt about the expanse of net foreseen by the Parliament. Concepts like "Employee" and "Employer" in definition clause before us is like a spring which possess property of both expanding and contracting to meet the situation. One spring or concept may be required to be stretched while the other compressed to further the object of such legislation. Parliament appears to have left it to executive to use this legislation giving it adequate elbow-space or manoeuvrability looking to the mischief sought to be prevented and to advance the object firmly. Restricting or curtailing the meaning of any one or more of the concepts and/

> or then expanding the other/s does not cause any damage to the fabric of net but augments its strength or capacity. To us, the "employee" and "employer" appear to be interdependent concepts warranting either narrow or liberal approach in the perspective of the context to preserve the legislative sanctity of definition of "Aggrieved Woman", "Respondent" and to further the object of the 2013 Act. When "Aggrieved Woman" happens to be an employee, concept of "employer" as defined will have to be understood in extremely narrow manner thereby pushing into the fold of "employee" even a high ranking officer or an elected office bearer, whether paid or not but owing some obligation to the superiors or superior body like managing/executive committee or general body.

In Dr. Sohail Malik v. Union of India[36] the Delhi High Court opined that "the rule of purposive construction" is to be adopted while interpreting the provisions of the Act. The Act is in the nature of an ameliorative social welfare legislation, and hence any interpretation which would dilute, or defeat, the purpose of the legislation, which is to ensure a safe working environment for women has, therefore, to be sedulously eschewed.

The Delhi High Court made the following further observations:

> Thus, the avowed objectives of the SHW Act are (i) ensuring that women's right to equality, life and liberty is not violated or compromised, (ii) providing of a secure and friendly work environment, (iii) social and economic empowerment of women, (iv) inclusive growth, (v) creating of an enabling environment for women which is equitous, safe and secure in every aspect, (vi) ensuring women are treated with due respect, decency and dignity at the workplace, (vii) equality in employment, (viii) ensuring women are not subjected

36 W.P. (C) No. 8624/2023 (30.06.2023, Delhi High Court).

to gender-specific violence, (ix) protection and promotion of women's constitutional rights and, at the end of the working day, (x) ensuring that every woman is provided a safe working environment, insulated from any act of sexual harassment, of any form. Each and every one of these objectives is, conspicuously, harasser-neutral. In an era in which – one has to say it, as one sees it every day even in the Court – women are equalling, if not outnumbering, men in professional achievements, there can be no compromise on any of these objectives. Applying Shailesh Dhairyawan and Richa Mishra, therefore, any interpretation, of the provisions of the SHW Act, which downplays, or impedes complete achievement and implementation of, one or more of these objectives, has to be firmly eschewed.

**Unorganised Sector**

The Act is applicable to both organized and unorganized sectors. The term 'unorganised sector' has been defined in the Act as an enterprise owned by individuals or self-employed workers and engaged in the production or sale of goods or providing service of any kind whatsoever, and where the enterprise employs workers, the number of such workers is less than 10 (ten).[37]

**Domestic Worker**

The Act describes a 'domestic worker' as a women who is employed to do the household work in any household for remuneration whether in cash or in kind, either directly or through any agency on a temporary, permanent, part time or full time basis, but does not include any member of the family of the employer.[38]

37 S. 2 (p) of the Act.

38 S. 2 (e) of the Act.

In so far as domestic workers are concerned, the Act recognises residential homes as a 'workplace'. It is pertinent to note that India had, in the past, voted in favour of the International Labour Organisation's Convention for Decent Work for Domestic Workers (No. 189) thereby endorsing home as a workplace.[39]

The domestic sector is a poorly regulated sector in India. Talking of sexual harassment, domestic workers constitute a vulnerable category typically because they comprise of the 'low wage' category having greater financial woes and negligible bargaining power. Induction of 'domestic workers' within the sweep of the Act appears to be a natural consequence of making the Act applicable to the unorganised sectors, including residential homes. However, mere inclusion of the term 'domestic workers' in the Act is not sufficient. Cases of sexual harassment of domestic workers are not easily identified or highlighted. Some level of innovative thinking would be necessary for the purpose of enforcing the provisions of the Act for the benefit of domestic workers. This may be achieved by cooperation and involvement of various agencies such as Police Stations, Resident Welfare Associations, Panchayats, NGO's etc.

## SCOPE OF THE ACT

The Act does not encompass all forms of verbal or physical harassment or abuse occurring in the workplace; it is only directed at 'discrimination because of or based on sex'. Some notable 'exclusions' are same-sex harassment and harassment on account of sexual orientation.

39 *See generally* Parliamentary Standing Committee Report (2011). The said convention defines a 'domestic worker' as one who carries out domestic work in an employment relationship. Workers who carry out domestic work occasionally and not on an occupational basis are excluded from the convention. For more on the said convention. *See also* www.ilo.org.

**Same Sex Harassment**

Same-sex harassment was perhaps not the principal evil the legislature was concerned with when it enacted the Act. Hence, sexual harassment committed by a female perpetrator or that experienced by a male victim does not appear to be specifically encompassed in the Act.

However, recently, there has been a development on this issue In Dr. Malabika Bhattacharjee v. Internal Complaints Committee[40] one of the questions which arose before the court was whether a complaint of sexual harassment could be lodged by a female victim against a female perpetrator. In other words, whether a female could be made an accused of sexual harassment under the Act. The court, while answering in the affirmative, observed that there was nothing in the Act which precluded a same gender complaint being made. The court also went on to observe that the definition of "sexual harassment" cannot be a static concept and must be interpreted against the backdrop of social perspectives. The court finally held that a complaint of sexual harassment against a female perpetrator cannot be turned down at the outset for the reason that the provisions of the Act do not contemplate or envisage "same-sex harassment".

In X v. Internal Committee,[41] a Delhi court examined the objectives of the Act and concluded that these objectives were conspicuously "harasser neutral".

Therefore, in view of this decision, it may be concluded that the accused in a complaint of sexual harassment may either be a male or female. However, male victims continue to be outside the scope of the Act.

---

40 W.P.A. (141/2020 (27.11.2020, Calcutta High Court).

41 RCA DJ No. 2/2022 (06.07.2022, Industrial Tribunal, Rouse Avenue Court, New Delhi).

### Harassment on account of sexual orientation

Harassment on account of sexual orientation has also not found a place in the Act. The following instances may not be actionable under the Act: harassment of a male member of the workplace on the premise that he is not 'masculine enough' or of female member because she is not 'feminine enough'.

However, the author feels that, regardless of the legal position, such forms of harassment must be curbed and addressed for a holistic improvement of the workplace.[42] Ideally, as per the author, workplace harassment which is sexual in content should always be actionable, regardless of the harasser's sex or sexual orientation.[43] In any event, despite the absence of such concepts from the Act, employers are at liberty to qualify them as a workplace misconduct and formulate appropriate internal policies to contain them.

## VULNERABILITY TO SEXUAL HARASSMENT

Sexual harassment occurs across different occupations and industry sectors. While there exists no straitjacket formula to determine which sector/industry suffers the most from this evil, however, in terms of vulnerability, it is important to note the following pertinent points:

a. Women who perform jobs which are perceived to be subservient in nature may experience higher rates of sexual harassment.
b. Women who work in relative isolation along with a fewer number of co-workers may also be more vulnerable to sexual harassment.
c. Traditionally male dominated work environments are at a

42 *See generally* Joseph Oncale v. Sundowner Offshore Services, Inc. (96-568) 83 F. 3d 118.

43 *See generally* Doe v. Belleville 119 F.3d 563 (CA7 1997).

higher risk, often because women entering such environment are perceived to be a threat to the men.

## RETROSPECTIVE OPERATION OF THE ACT

The Act does not have any retrospective operation. In other words, it may not be possible to take cognizance of offences (of sexual harassment) occurring prior to 09.12.2013 under the Act.[44]

In this regard, it is relevant to advert to the following excerpt from the case of Mahender Kumar v. Linda Eastwood:[45]

> 7. It is the case of the petitioner that they cannot be charged for any offence punishable under The Sexual Harassment of Women At Work Place (Prevention, Prohibition and Redressal) Act, 2013, which came into force with effect from 23.4.2013 and the same being a penal statue cannot have retrospective operation. I find the said act was passed in the Parliament and then got the assent of the President on 22nd April, 2013 and was came into force on being notified in the official Gazette of India by the Central Government, on December 9, 2013. Therefore, the cognizance taken on 29th August, 2013 by the learned Court below for such offences is absolutely illegal and without jurisdiction, being hit by sub-article (1) of Article 20 of the Constitution. Furthermore, it is well-settled no penal statutes have any retrospective operation. (sic)

44 It is a cardinal principle of statutory interpretation that every statute should be considered to be *prima facie* prospective unless it is expressly or by necessary implication read to have retrospective operation. *See* Saudi Arabian Airlines v. Shehnaz Mudbhatkal 1999 (1) Bom CR 643.

45 (2015) 2 CAL LT 357.

CHAPTER 3

# Sexual Harassment: Meaning and Scope

Generally speaking, gender discrimination refers to application to any woman of any unwelcome, undesirable or unjustified condition which would not be applied to a man. When this gender discrimination acquires sexual overtones, it takes the shape of sexual harassment.

The expression 'sexual harassment' has no peripheries or straightjacket meanings. Simply put, sexual harassment is a form of sex discrimination which possesses the following attributes: (i) It is related to the aspect of 'sex'; (ii) It consists of sexual overtones or implications; (iii) It is unwelcome (not mutual).

## SEXUAL HARASSMENT AT WORKPLACE

Legally speaking, sexual harassment at workplace may be described as a form of discrimination projected through unwelcome sexual advances, request for sexual favours and other verbal or physical conduct with sexual overtones, whether directly or by implication, particularly when submission to or rejection of such a conduct by the female employee is capable of being used for affecting the employment of the female employee and unreasonably interfering with her work performance; or can have the effect of creating an intimidating or hostile working environment for her.[1] Under Indian law, no woman can be subjected to sexual harassment at any workplace.[2]

In Janzen v. Platy Enterprises Ltd.[3] the Supreme Court of Canada, in light of its Human Rights Code[4], undertook a detailed discussion on the concept of sexual harassment and made the following critical observations:

> In keeping with this general definition of employment discrimination, discrimination on the basis of sex may be defined as practices or attitudes which have the effect of limiting the conditions of employment of, or the employment opportunities available to, employees on the basis of a characteristic related to gender.
>
> Common to all of these descriptions of sexual harassment is the concept of using a position of power to import sexual requirements into the workplace thereby negatively altering the working conditions of employees who are forced to contend with sexual demands.

---

1 Apparel Export Promotion Council v. A.K. Chopra AIR 1999 SC 625.

2 S. 3 of the Act.

3 [1989] 1 S.C.R 1252.

4 Section 19 of the Human Rights Code reads:
19 (1) No person who is responsible for an activity or undertaking to which this Code applies shall (a) harass any person who is participating in the activity or undertaking; or (b) knowingly permit, or fail to take reasonable steps to terminate, harassment of one person who is participating in the activity or undertaking by another person who is participating in the activity or undertaking.
19 (2) In this section "harassment" means (a) a course of abusive or unwelcome conduct or comment undertaken or made on the basis of any characteristic referred to in subsection 9 (2); or (b) a series of objectionable and unwelcome sexual solicitations or advances; or (c) a sexual solicitation or advance made by a person who is in a position to confer any benefit on, or deny any benefit to, the recipient of the solicitation or advance, if the person making the solicitation or advance knows or ought reasonably to know that it is unwelcome; or (d) a reprisal or threat of reprisal for rejecting a sexual solicitation or advance.

The court went on to define 'sexual harassment' in the following words:

> Without seeking to provide an exhaustive definition of the term, I am of the view that sexual harassment in the workplace may be broadly defined as unwelcome conduct of a sexual nature that detrimentally affects the work environment or leads to adverse job-related consequences for the victims of the harassment. It is, as Adjudicator Shime observed in Bell v. Ladas, supra, and as has been widely accepted by other adjudicators and academic commentators, an abuse of power. When sexual harassment occurs in the workplace, it is an abuse of both economic and sexual power. Sexual harassment is a demeaning practice, one that constitutes a profound affront to the dignity of the employees forced to endure it. By requiring an employee to contend with unwelcome sexual actions or explicit sexual demands, sexual harassment in the workplace attacks the dignity and self-respect of the victim both as an employee and as a human being.

Recently, the Tripura High Court[5] described 'sexual harassment' at the workplace as a sexually oriented behaviour aimed at and attributed to a woman at the workplace. In the view of the court, an unusual conduct or behaviour to a woman employee at the workplace which is not generally expected and from which an inference may be drawn that the behaviour was because of the fact that the victim was a woman would amount to sexual harassment.

While there exists no cut and dry formula to ascertain what constitutes sexual harassment, the generally accepted position

5 Pankaj Kumar v. Union of India W.P. (C) No. 408/2013 (14.02.2017, Tripura High Court).

is that such behaviour: (i) is related to or about sex; (ii) is intimidating and coercive; (iii) is unwelcome, unreciprocated and not mutual.

**Manifestations of Sexual Harassment**

Broadly speaking, there exists 3 (three) significant manifestations of sexual harassment in a work environment:

a. Abuse of Authority: A demand by a person in authority for sexual favours in order for the victim to obtain or retain certain job benefits such as increments, promotion, transfer or the job itself.
b. Creating a Hostile Environment: Any unwelcome sexual conduct which interferes with an individual's work performance or creates an intimidating, hostile or offensive work environment. Typically creation of a hostile environment requires a pattern of offensive conduct, however in some cases one isolated severe incident may be sufficient to constitute a violation.
c. Retaliation or Reprisal: Conduct such as refusal to grant sexual favour/give in to sexual demands, to make a complaint of sexual harassment, to act as a witness of the victim etc. may result in retaliation or reprisal, which includes but is not limited to scuttling the victim's future prospects in the organization, tampering with evaluation reports, creating needless gossip about the victim, levying false charges against her etc.

Each of the above manifestations are discussed in detail in this work.

**'UNWELCOME' CONDUCT**

The expression 'unwelcome' in the context of 'sexual harassment' is a very important element or keyword. It essentially refers to the advances, requests or conduct which was not solicited or invited by the employee, which the employee regards as undesirable or offensive.[6] It must be noted that it is not mere unwelcome conduct which is proscribed under the Act; such conduct must be coupled with sexuality or sexual overtones.

Any form of sexual approach or behaviour that is "unwelcome" will come under the definition of "sexual harassment".[7]

**Reciprocated Behaviour**

Generally speaking, the term 'unwelcome' is wholly unconnected with mutual attraction or friendship between people; or for that matter any conduct which is consensual, reciprocated or welcomed by the victim.

However, forced submission to the sexual overtures of the perpetrator does not indicate 'welcomeness'. A victims passivity or consent or participation obtained through pressure, coercion or intimidation or the victims failure to actively object, will neither make the relationship between the parties consensual/ mutual nor make the harassers conduct acceptable.

In Ajay Tiwari v. University of Delhi[8] the Delhi High Court explained the expression "consent" (in the context of sexual harassment), in the following words:

> "Consent" is essentially a physical act. Consent may either be express or implied. Conscious failure to put up a resistance, to an act which is being committed, may indicate consent. At all times, however, the issue of whether the alleged victim of an act, consented, or did not consent, to the doing thereof, would have to be gauged on the basis of the manner in

6 Lynette Jane Aldridge v. Grant Rodney Booth (1988) 80 ALR 1.

7 See generally Prasad Parnian v. Central University of Kerala ILR 2021 (1) Kerala 131.

8 2020 (1) SCT 381 (Delhi).

> which the victim acted, herself or himself. It is precisely for this reason that "consent" itself, is rarely a defence to an act of oppression or assault. "Consent" may become a defence, where it is free. This is for the obvious reason that a victim of an assault, or an act of oppression, may consent to the doing thereof, owing to circumstances beyond the victim's control, which may partake of coercion. Consent, given under coercion, or without volition, is no consent at all.

**Determining unwelcome conduct**

Whether one's behaviour or conduct is welcome or not is a subjective question. To ascertain this, it is important to examine how the conduct in question was perceived or experienced by the recipient rather than the intention behind it.[9] Further, it is irrelevant that the behaviour in question may not have been unwelcome to others or was an accepted feature of the work environment in the past.[10] Additionally, whether or not the perpetrator is aware that his conduct is 'unwelcome' is wholly irrelevant.

In Ajay Tiwari v. University of Delhi[11] the Delhi High Court delved into the expression "unwelcome conduct" in some detail and observed thus:

> The word "welcome" - or, equally, the word "unwelcome" - on the other hand, denotes a state of mind. If a person welcomes an act, that, by itself, denotes free, voluntary and willing consent. An act is "welcome" when there is an active element of conscious and willing acquiescence, by the person,

9 The 'unwelcomeness' of the alleged conduct must be evaluated from the standpoint of the victim and not the perpetrator. For instance, continuation of a relationship/association with the accused despite his indiscretion may indicate that the accused's conduct was not unwelcome.

10 *See generally* Hall v. A.A. Sheiban Pty Ltd (1989) 85 ALR 503.

11 2020 (1) SCT 381 (Delhi).

> to the doing of the act. Contrariwise, an act is "unwelcome", when the person, on whom the act is perpetrated, does not invite the doing thereof, or "welcome" the act. Examination of the question of whether an act, performed by one person or another, is "welcome", or "unwelcome", would necessarily involve an element of psychoanalysis of the purported victim.

### View of the Committee Report

The Verma Committee Report[12] had suggested that the definition of the expression 'unwelcome' should ideally give weight to both objective as well as subjective criteria in order to ensure that women of differing perceptions and comfort levels are given appropriate protection. The relevant excerpt of the report is as follows:

> Therefore, we suggest that after the definition of "sexual harassment", the following explanation may be inserted: "Explanation: In determining whether the behaviour or act complained of is unwelcome, one of the factors to be given due weight shall be the subjective perception of the complainant."

As seen above, the report had suggested the insertion of an *explanation* to the definition of the term 'sexual harassment'. While this suggestion did not make its way into the Act, it nevertheless serves as an indicator on how one can assess and tell behaviour which is sexually harassing.

## SEXUAL HARASSMENT AND INDIAN LAW

The term 'sexual harassment' is worded in a wide manner. The focus is on how the conduct was perceived and

12 Report of the Committee on Amendments to Criminal Law, dated 23.01.2013, by Justice J.S. Verma *et al* (hereinafter the "**Verma Committee Report**").

experienced by the recipient rather than the intention behind it.

The guidelines issued in the Vishaka Case have formed the basis of the definition of the expression 'sexual harassment' in the Act. The Act defines this term in the following words:[13]

> 2 (n) "sexual harassment" includes any one or more of the following unwelcome acts or behaviour (whether directly or by implication) namely:-
>
> i. physical contact and advances; or
> ii. a demand or request for sexual favours; or
> iii. making sexually coloured remarks; or
> iv. showing pornography; or
> v. any other unwelcome physical, verbal or non-verbal conduct of sexual nature;
>
> 3 (2) The following circumstances, among other circumstances, if it occurs or is in relation to or connected with any act or behaviour of sexual harassment may amount to sexual harassment:
>
> i. implied or explicit promise of preferential treatment in her employment: or
> ii. implied or explicit threat of detrimental treatment in her employment; or
> iii. implied or explicit threat about her present or future employment status: or
> iv. interference with her work or creating an intimidating or offensive or hostile work environment for her; or
> v. humiliating treatment likely to affect her health or safety.

---

13 S. 2 (n) & 3 (2) of the Act.

## Definition Analysis

The Primary Elements

As per section 2 (n) of the Act, the term 'sexual harassment' includes any one or more of the following unwelcome acts or behaviour (whether directly or by implication) namely:

a. physical contact and advances; or
b. a demand or request for sexual favours; or
c. making sexually coloured remarks[14]; or
d. showing pornography; or
e. any other unwelcome physical, verbal or non-verbal conduct of sexual nature (the "**Primary Factors**").

As is evident, the definition of the term 'sexual harassment' is inclusive in nature i.e. it is an extensive definition which would include other aspects apart from the five categories mentioned above. The legislature has, in its wisdom, left it open to examine the facts and circumstances of each situation to ascertain whether the conduct in question amounts to sexual harassment.[15]

The above factors are primary in nature and are *per se* sufficient to constitute sexual harassment under the Act. As is evident from the above, sexual harassment includes various forms of offensive behaviour.

The Corresponding Elements

Additionally, as per section 3 (2) of the Act, the following circumstance(s), among other circumstance(s), if present in relation to or connected with any act

14 Comments on age, competence etc. of the women may, in some situations, qualify to be sexually coloured remarks. *See* Mahendra Kumar Singh v. Linda Eastwood CRR No. 3451/2013 (18.06.2014, Calcutta High Court).

15 *See* Pankaj Kumar v. Union of India W.P. (C) No. 408/2013 (14.02.2017, Tripura High Court).

or behaviour of sexual harassment, may amount to sexual harassment:

a. implied or explicit promise of preferential treatment in employment; or
b. implied or express threat of detrimental treatment in employment; or
c. implied or explicit threat of present or future employment status; or
d. interference with her work or creating an intimidating or offensive or hostile work environment for her; or
e. humiliating treatment likely to affect her health or safety (the "**Corresponding Factors**").

While the provisions of Section 2 (n) are general, Section 3 (2) is more specific in nature. The Corresponding Factors are incidental or corresponding to the Primary Factors, meaning thereby, that these, independently, may not constitute 'sexual harassment'. However, the presence of such factors in conjunction with the Primary Factors may constitute the offence of 'sexual harassment' under the Act.

Sections 2 and 3 of the Act cannot be read in isolation of each other. The provisions serve as an acknowledgement of the fact that for the purposes of the Act, "sexual harassment" can be of varied form. Nirmal Kanti Chakraborti v. Vaneeta Patnaik.[16]

In Vaneeta Patnaik v. State of West Bengal,[17] the Calcutta High Court observed that the "circumstances" envisaged under Section 3 (2) of the Act must occur in relation to or in connection with any act or behaviour of "sexual harassment" as described under Section 2 (n) of the Act.

---

16 FMA No. 873/2024 (23.12.2024, Calcutta High Court).

17 W.P. A. No. 10583/2024 (22.05.2024, Calcutta High Court).

An Instance: Acts such as meting out bad or humiliating treatment, misbehaviour such as shouting etc., by themselves, without any sexual overtones, may not constitute 'sexual harassment' under the Act, albeit they may constitute a misconduct under the service rules or the employment policies of the concerned organisation.

While the Corresponding Factors are antithetical to the development of an organisation, without any connection with the Primary Factors, their occurrence or presence is not actionable under the Act.

The objective behind segregating such Corresponding Factors and making them un-punishable independently (under the Act) is perhaps to ensure that 'non-sexual' misconduct occurring in an organisation are not dragged within the ambit of the Act. Organisations are at liberty to draft suitable policies for redressing and resolving acts of 'non sexual' misconduct and misbehaviour.

**Single Incident**

Even a single episode or one-off incident may be sufficient to constitute sexual harassment. The definition of sexual harassment under the Act can include a single action and provides no warrant for necessarily importing a continuous or repeated course of conduct.[18] Hence, even a singular or isolated incident may be sufficient to constitute 'sexual harassment' under the Act.

**Cyber or Virtual Harassment**

Any act committed by the perpetrator *via* the internet (such as through unsolicited emails, stalking, dissemination of obscene material etc.) which qualifies the above definition of the term 'sexual harassment' would be covered within the ambit of the Act.

---

18 Hall v. A. Sheiban Pty. Ltd. (1989) EOC 92-250.

## THE REASONABLE PERSON AND REASONABLE WOMAN STANDARDS

Sexual harassment is essentially a subjective concept. There is no straitjacket formula to discern sexual harassment.[19]

Different individuals may perceive and react to behaviour in different ways. For example, a person may think that his conduct is inoffensive, when in fact the recipient finds it offensive. Similarly, what may be acceptable socially or in private life may be considered inappropriate in a work context. Therefore, it becomes pertinent to correctly earmark the means to identify sexual harassment.

Previously, sexual harassment was discerned on the basis of the 'reasonable person' standard. Succinctly speaking, the test of 'reasonable person' rests on the following question: How would a hypothetical 'reasonable person' perceive the alleged conduct? However, it was soon realized that this standard may not be the right approach for various reasons including the following: (i) Conduct which many men consider unobjectionable may offend many women;[20] (ii) Men and women are vulnerable in different ways and offended by different behaviour.

In Kerry Ellison v. Nicholas F. Brady[21] the court formulated the 'reasonable women' standard for determining whether an act qualifies to be sexual harassment or not. In this regard, the court held that it is the victim's perspective and not stereotyped notions of acceptable behaviour which should be taken into account. The court observed as follows:

---

19 It is pertinent to note that there exists no precise formula to determine how much of the 'behaviour' would result in liability. Typically, both 'qualitative' and 'quantitative' factors would need to be balanced. *See generally* Victoria Zetwick v. County of Yolo Appeal No. 14-17342 (23.02.2017, Court of Appeals, 9th Circuit).

20 *See generally* Lipsett v. University of Puerto Rico 864 F.2d 881 (1st Circuit, 1998).

21 924 F. 2d 872 (9th Circuit, 1991). *See also* Robinson v. Jacksonville Shipyards U.S.D.C. M.D. No. 86-927-Civ-J-12 (1991).

We believe that in evaluating the severity and pervasiveness of sexual harassment, we should focus on the perspective of the victim. Courts "should consider the victim's perspective and not stereotyped notions of acceptable behaviour." If we only examined whether a reasonable person would engage in allegedly harassing conduct, we would run the risk of reinforcing the prevailing level of discrimination. Harassers could continue to harass merely because a particular discriminatory practice was common, and victims of harassment would have no remedy.

We therefore prefer to analyze harassment from the victim's perspective. A complete understanding of the victim's view requires, among other things, an analysis of the different perspectives of men and women. Conduct that many men consider unobjectionable may offend many women. A male supervisor might believe, for example, that it is legitimate for him to tell a female subordinate that she has a 'great figure' or 'nice legs.' The female subordinate, however, may find such comments offensive. Men tend to view some forms of sexual harassment as "harmless social interactions to which only overly-sensitive women would object". The characteristically male view depicts sexual harassment as comparatively harmless amusement.

In order to shield employers from having to accommodate the idiosyncratic concerns of the rare hyper-sensitive employee, we hold that a female plaintiff states a prima facie case of hostile environment sexual harassment when she alleges conduct which a reasonable woman would consider sufficiently severe or pervasive to alter the conditions of employment and create an abusive working environment.

The analogy behind adopting the 'reasonable women' standard is that it is for a women to decide what sort of behaviour she welcomes or tolerates. Further, men and women often perceive sexual conduct very differently and it is an accepted position that women are the principal sufferers of sexual harassment. A 'reasonable women' perspective is considered more apt because a sex blind reasonable person standard may tend to be male biased and may ignore the experiences of women.[22] Hence, arguments (of the harasser) such as the behaviour in question does not offend other women at the workplace or that it was acceptable at the workplace would be inconsequential. The intent of the harasser is not material. Indian courts also seem to adopting this basis.[23]

In Sukalyan Haldar v. State of West Bengal[24] the expression "faltu meye" was construed by the adjudicating authority as "cheap woman", and as a lewd remark; and consequently, the usage of such expression was held to amount to sexual harassment (for being a sexually coloured remark). The matter travelled to the High Court wherein it was contended by the accused that the expression "faltu", in common parlance, meant spare, unnecessary or useless, and consequently, it would not qualify to be a "lewd expression". The High Court, in this regard, observed that whether the subject remark was lewd or not had to be determined totally in the context of which it was made. The expression "faltu meye" could be used in various contexts. The interpretation of the subject expression would depend entirely on the backdrop. Hence, it would be imperative for the adjudicating authority to closely examine the background in which the comment had come to be made or passed by the accused.

22 Kerry Ellison v. Nicholas F. Brady 924 F.2d 872 (9th Circuit, 1991)

23 *See* Jishu Sengupta v. State of West Bengal CRR No. 1204/2016 (04.11.2016, Calcutta High Court).

24 W.P.A. No. 18829/2023 (08.09.2023, Calcutta High Court).

In Vinod Narayan v. The Presiding Officer[25] certain remarks were made by the accused (the supervisor) of the delinquent on the following lines: (i) the accused made a comment with regard to the length and volume of the complainant's hair and started singing a song relating to her hair. (ii) the accused made a comment in respect of another male employee in the presence of female employees. As regards the first incident, the Bombay High Court observed that such comments did not contain any sexual overtones. In fact the complainant herself did not perceive such comments as sexual harassment when they were first made. This became evident from a subsequent whatsapp exchange between the parties where the accused was found professionally motivating the complainant and the complainant thanking the accused of his support and motivation. As regards the second incident, the High Court that such comments did not amount to sexual harassment in as much as these related to another male employee and were not directed at the complainant at all.

In the view of the author, determining each situation on a case to case basis, considering all circumstances involved, taking a view of the matter through the eyes of the victim and that of a reasonable woman should be the preferred outlook while discerning an allegation of sexual harassment.

## MODES OF SEXUAL HARASSMENT

The Act does not prescribe any restricted or limited definition of the expression 'sexual harassment'. Sexual harassment may have various forms. It may be physical, verbal or even non-verbal.[26] Harassment may be direct or indirect, overt or covert. Use of particular language or gestures even without specifically calling these actions as sexual harassment may still qualify its definition

25 2025: BHC: AS-12952.

26 *See* Directive 2006/54/EC dated 05.07.2006 of the European Parliament.

under the Act.[27] Sexual harassment may exist in a range from mild demeanours to severe behaviour. It may include physical conduct ranging from touching to sexual assault; verbal acts such as sexual innuendoes, suggestions, hints or advances, insults, inappropriate sexual inquires etc.; non-verbal forms such as sexual gestures etc. In its subtle forms, sexual harassment may include sexual jokes or comments; inappropriate gestures etc. In its extreme forms sexual harassment may include acts such as voyeurism, assault, advances [both physically as well as online (*via* emails, sms etc.)].

Generally speaking, it may be difficult to enumerate all potentially inappropriate conduct which would fit the definition of the term 'sexual harassment' under the Act. Mentioned below are a brief range of unwanted activities which may constitute sexual harassment. Each of the below acts, whether separate or in combination with other, would be actionable under the provisions of the Act.

a. sexual solicitation, advances and propositions.
b. repeated invitations to go out after prior refusal.
c. direct or indirect threats or bribes for sexual activity.
d. demanding hugs or kisses.
e. making unnecessary physical contact.
f. deliberately blocking ones movements.
g. giving derogatory or sex specific names.
h. leering, ogling or inappropriate staring.
i. sexual jokes and anecdotes, including vulgar humour.
j. making sexual comments about appearance, clothing, body parts etc.[28]

---

27 *See* Md. Azimur Rahman v. The University of Jamia Milia (2013) 203 DLT 463.

28 In N.K. Suroya, IAS (Retd.) v. Union of India 2003 (3) SLJ 34 (CAT) the court indicated that persistent remarks and complements on a woman's dress and looks may amount to be 'sexually coloured' and qualify as 'sexual harassment'.

k. asking personal (and unwanted) questions on one's sexual life etc.
l. display or dissemination of materials with sexually illicit or graphic content. including pornographic photos, calendars, screensavers etc.
m. threats to penalize a person who refuses to comply with sexual advances.
n. procreating a sexualised environment.

### Online Sexual Harassment

Sexual harassment may be physical or virtual (by electronic means). Carrying out any of the above acts through electronic means would be included in the definition of sexual harassment.[29]

## FORMS OF SEXUAL HARASSMENT

There broadly exist 2 (two) types of sexual harassment:

a. Quid Pro Quo
b. Hostile Work Environment

Typically, harassment that does not result in a tangible employment action is traditionally referred to as 'hostile work environment' harassment, and harassment that does result in a tangible employment action is traditionally referred to as 'quid pro quo' harassment.[30] The terms 'quid pro quo' and 'hostile work environment' do not appear in the Act. Both these terms first appeared in academic literature and later found their way into decisions of courts.[31]

### Quid Pro Quo

Simply put, Quid Pro Quo indicates a reciprocal relationship. It means 'something in place of something' or 'this for that'. In the

29 Sending unsolicited, obscene, abusive or threatening emails is one mode of online sexual harassment. Cyber stalking is another mode of sexual harassment.

30 Dinkins v. Charoen Pokphand USA, Inc. 133 F. Supp. 2d 1254 (M.D. Ala. 2001).

31 *See* Burlington Industries Inc. v. Ellereth (97-569)123 F.3d 490 (7th Circuit, 1998).

context of sexual harassment, it refers to sexual advances by a person in a position of power or authority.

In this form of harassment, some form of benefit is made the basis for seeking sexual favours. The concept of Quid Pro Quo is concerned with the unlawful exploitation of a position of power, in the context of unwelcome sexual requests or conduct. Typically, this form of sexual harassment occurs between a superior and his subordinate because the senior is often in a position to take tangible employment actions against the subordinate and/or direct her daily work activities.[32]

A consistent feature of this type of harassment is that it entails job related consequences for the target. Examples: Seeking sexual favours in return of a promotion, salary increment, out of turn favours etc. The negative impact for the women for not being pliant may include assignment of less desirable or worse duties, work schedules, etc. Further, any threat issued to the women for not submitting to the harassers advances would also come under this class of harassment.

Typically, the complainant may need to establish that a tangible employment action resulted from her refusal to submit to the perpetrators sexual demands.[33] However, the

32 For the purpose of this type of harassment, the expression 'superior' would refer to those persons who possess the power to effect a significant change in the employment or work status of the women and would include those responsible for: managing performance, quality, efficiency; training employees; organising work; coordination and control; planning and scheduling etc.

33 A tangible employment action is the 'means by which a superior brings the official power of the enterprise to bear on the subordinates'. A tangible employment action constitutes a significant change in employment status, such as hiring, firing, failing to promote, reassignment with significantly different responsibilities, or a decision causing a significant change in benefits. *See* Yasharay Mack v. Otis Elevator Company 326 F.3d 116 (2nd Circuit, 2003); Dinkins v. Charoen Pokphand USA, Inc. 133 F. Supp. 2d 1254 (M.D. Ala. 2001). A significant change in employment can occur regardless of whether the individual retains the same salary and benefits. For example, actions that significantly increase an employee's work responsibility or block her opportunity for promotion or salary increases are improper. *See* Reinhold v. Commonwealth 151 F.3d 172 (4th Circuit, 1998).

author feels that unwanted sexual advances is a serious offence in itself and hence need not be linked to some sort of disadvantage or detriment to one individual's employment prospects. A victim of harassment need not wait for a tangible employment action to occur to establish a case of a *quid pro quo* sexual harassment.

**Hostile Work Environment**

Sexual harassment need not always be motivated by sexual gratification. It may be based on hostility or an attempt to make the target feel unwelcome in their environment. Hostile work environment is the most common form of harassment. This is a form of harassment which simply creates an offensive work environment. Any conduct (with sexual overtones) which makes or tends to make the woman's work environment hostile, intimidating or offensive. For example, sexual remarks, comments or jokes, display of pornography etc.

Simply stated, a sexually hostile workplace is one in which a women is made to feel uncomfortable or offended on account of behaviour possessing sexual characteristics. When the workplace is permeated with such discriminatory conduct, hostile work environment is said to be created. In such cases, a harasser need not be a direct boss or a supervisor. He may be a co-worker, a colleague in another division of the workplace, or even a person not employed in the victims workplace but a mere visitor or a person notionally connected with the victim's workplace (such as a client, vendor, contractor etc.). Further, aspects such as the status or position of the parties in the organisational hierarchy; work relationship etc. are inconsequential in this category.

Unlike the case of a Quid Pro Quo harassment, it is not necessary that the offending conduct must be directed towards a specific individual. In other words, a woman has the right and the *locus* to complain about a sexually hostile working environment even if the conduct in question was not specifically targeted at her.

While generally repetitive conduct is witnessed in such form of harassment, however, a single isolated incident, in the appropriate facts and circumstances, may also be sufficient.[34]

The following parameters may need evaluation for ascertaining 'hostile work environment': (i) the frequency of the conduct; (ii) the severity of the conduct; (iii) whether the conduct is physically threatening or humiliating, or a mere offensive utterance; and (iv) whether the conduct unreasonably interferes with the employees job performance.[35]

## Quid Pro Quo and Hostile Work Environment: The Indian Law Perspective

In Alphi Chugh v. State of Haryana[36] the court described the concepts of Quid Pro Quo and Hostile Harassment in the following words:

> It would be appropriate to mention about two broad types of sexual harassment: quid pro quo harassment and hostile environment. Quid pro quo, or this for that, involves the victim being promised a benefit in exchange for sexual favours, including requests for dates. Quid pro quo can only be committed by someone who has the power to make employment decisions. When quid pro quo occurs, the victim's submission to or rejection of the conduct is used as a basis for employment decisions. Hostile environment

34 Repeated incidents of verbal harassment that continue despite the employees objections may indicate hostile work environment. Shanoff v. Illinois Department of Human Servs. 258 F.3d 696.

35 Bradley Miller v. Kenworth of Dothan, Inc. 277 F.3d 1269 (11th Circuit, 2002). The harassment need not necessarily be shown to be so extreme that it produces tangible effects on job performance, in order to be actionable.

36 Crl. Misc. No. M-29141 of 2012 (19.09.2012, Punjab & Haryana High Court).

sexual harassment occurs when the conduct of the harasser creates a hostile, offensive or intimidating environment. Factors which may determine a hostile environment include: the verbal and/or physical nature of the conduct, frequency of the conduct, hostility and offensiveness of the conduct, the working relationship to the harasser (trainer or supervisor), perpetuation of the conduct by others, if there is more than one victim. Behaviours that may contribute to a hostile environment include: discussing sexual activities, touching unnecessarily, commenting on physical attributes, displaying sexually suggestive pictures, using demeaning or inappropriate terms, such as "Babe" telling sexual jokes and innuendo, and using indecent gestures. Sexual favouritism may take the form of implicit quid pro quo harassment and/or hostile work environment harassment. Sexual favouritism occurs when one or more individuals are given preferential treatment by a person in a dominant or power role. The people who are not given the preferential treatment can claim sexual favouritism.

The complainants are victims of quid pro quo and hostile environment sexual harassment at the hands of petitioner for unwelcome sexual advances, requests for sexual favours, verbal or physical conduct of a sexual nature. The conduct of the petitioner explicitly or implicitly affected complainant's employment and created an intimidating, hostile or offensive work environment. The complainants were traumatised. Passing in training has essential served as weapon in the hands of petitioner of such a heinous crime against female young trainees.

## Quid Pro Quo versus Hostile Work Environment

A classic point of distinction between Quid Pro Quo Harassment and a Hostile Work Environment Harassment is this: A Quid Pro

Quo harassment is connected with or related to some offer of a tangible employment action against or in favour of the victim. In such a case, the perpetrator relies upon his apparent or actual authority to extort sexual consideration from an employee. Therein lies the quid pro quo. In that case, the perpetrator uses the means furnished to him by the employer to accomplish the prohibited purpose. He acts within the scope of his actual or apparent authority to hire, fire, discipline or promote. On the contrary, considerations such as grant or denial of employment benefit are irrelevant in case of a hostile work environment.[37]

## 'NON-SEXUAL' HARASSMENT

Every behaviour which is unwanted and/or offensive may not necessarily qualify to be sexual harassment. Some types of conduct may be generally unacceptable but not necessarily actionable under the provisions of the Act. Sexual harassment must be distinguished from other forms of harassment.[38]

### Bullying

In common parlance, bullying may be described as any act or conduct which may be distressing to others. It involves unreasonable behaviour directed towards a person or a group of people at a workplace that creates a risk of health and safety. It includes acts like shouting, nagging, taunting, pestering or use of inappropriate language towards others, excessive or unjustified criticism, trivialising or dismissing one work and achievements, personal insults, excluding, marginalising or isolating others, intimidation, spreading misinformation etc.[39] However, there

37 Barbara J. Henson v. City of Dundee 682 F. 2d 897.

38 Note that the Act does not set forth a general civility code. It may be reasonable to separate the significant from the trivial harms, which involves filtering out the ordinary tribulations of the workplace. Abigail Wilson v. Jim Putman Appeal No. 15-2522 (13.04.2017, Court of Appeals, 4th Circuit).

39 *See generally* L. Nagaraju v. Syndicate Bank 2014 (2) ALD 758.

is a fine line between bullying and sexual harassment. Any act of bullying without sexual undertones may not constitute an offence of sexual harassment.

Use of intemperate language against a female employee (without any sexual overtones) may not, by itself, constitute sexual harassment under the Act.[40]

In Abhilasha Dwivedi v. Department of Women and Child Development NCT of Delhi[41] the Delhi High Court observed that merely shouting at the complainant by the accused in anger, by itself, could not be considered as "sexual harassment" within the meaning of Section 2 (n) of the Act.

While an act of bullying may be punishable under the applicable service rules of the organisation, it shall not be actionable under the Act. Although Indian law does not contain any specific legislation dealing with bullying at workplace, employers may consider providing suitable policies to check this activity for they have a general duty of care towards their employees.

In Chhttar Pal v. The Lt. Governor, National Capital Territory Region[42] the question before the court was whether mere use of abusive or un-parliamentary language without sexually coloured remarks would qualify as a misconduct *simplicitor* or as sexual harassment at workplace. Answering in favour of the former, the court observed as follows:

> 10......That apart, the language used by the applicant may be abusive, but would that amount to hurling abuses or would be termed as sexually coloured remarks, is the question. We have given our anxious thoughts to the question referred to above, and are of the view that whereas the abusive language

---

40 *See generally* Union of India v. Rema Srinivasan Iyengar 2020 (3) CTC 281.

41 W.P. (Crl.) No. 1639/2019 (19.11.2019, Delhi High Court).

42 (16.05.2008, Central Administrative Tribunal, Delhi).

used by the applicant would also have a demoralizing effect on working women in general and Ms. Kamini in particular, but the same cannot be said to be sexually coloured remarks, and thus exploitation of a female at workplace.

12. In view of the authoritative pronouncement of the Hon'ble Supreme Court, analyzing the definition of sexual harassment as extracted above, we are in no doubt whatsoever that even though, the applicant might have used choicest abuses, the same shall not even remotely lead to an inference of the applicant making demand or request for sexual favour. The abusive outburst of the applicant may be actuated because of his disliking or even hatred towards complainant, for the reasons known to him, and the same may cause anguish and harassment as well, but the remarks cannot be termed to be sexually coloured. The same could be said to be so if they may have overtones or undertones of sexual advances, or request for sexual favour, but the same is not indeed the tenor of the abusive language indulged in by the applicant. There is also absolutely no evidence led in this case also to show that if the complainant was to reject the overtures of the applicant, she would be harmed in any manner whatsoever in her service graph. The applicant, in our view, cannot be held guilty for sexually harassing a woman at workplace, even though at the same time it has to be held that the behaviour, in which he had indulged himself, would also be misconduct calling for some punishment. Inasmuch as, while fixing the quantum of punishment, the disciplinary and appellate authorities have held the applicant guilty of sexual harassment of woman at workplace as well, the orders passed by them dated 20.7.2004 and 5.11.2004 respectively, need to be set aside. We order accordingly. We, however, remit the matter to the disciplinary authority for re-determining the quantum

of punishment by excluding the charge of sexual harassment of woman at workplace.

**Harassment based on sexual orientation**

There also exists a fine line of distinction between harassment based on sex and that based on sexual orientation. For example, in case a women is harassed because she does not act sufficiently feminine or does not have effeminate mannerisms/ qualities, then such conduct would qualify as harassment based on sexual orientation. The Act does not encompass such form of harassment.

**Discrimination on account of inefficiency at work**

In the Union of India v. Rema Srinivasan Iyenger[43] the Madras High Court observed that any efforts made by a superior employee to push a women employee to execute work as per his discretion and prerogative would normally not be considered sexual harassment. It was observed that every employer has a right to extract work from the employees in the manner deemed fit. A complaint of sexual harassment would normally not be maintainable in relation to any steps taken by an employer/superior employee against a female employee on account of her inefficiency at work or for any other related official reason.

## GENDER SPECIFIC NATURE OF SEXUAL HARASSMENT

Generally speaking, sexual harassment is gender neutral *viz.* both men and women can be the perpetrators or the victims of sexual harassment. Sexual harassment laws in many countries such as the United Kingdom, Ireland, Italy, France, Germany, Portugal, Spain, Netherlands etc. are gender neutral. However, the same cannot be said for Indian law.

43 2020 (3) CTC 281.

The Act is gender specific i.e. it applies only for the benefit of women.[44] The absence of a gender neutral character of the Act appears to indicate a presumption of the legislature that only women can be subjected to (be victims of) sexual harassment; or that only women need protection from sexual harassment.

According to the author, while it may be true that, given the traditional power equation prevalent in the Indian society, women are more likely to face the evil of sexual harassment, however, gender must not be given precedence over human rights. Sexual harassment is a form of discrimination of human rights and all must be equally protected from such discrimination.

To sum up, while Indian law does not provide any provisions for dealing with the issue of sexual harassment committed by men against men; or women against men, however, organisations are free to draft their sexual harassment policies in such manner so as to cover these aspects. It is highly recommended that employers provide for internal policies to envisage situations where men are victims of sexual harassment.

## NEGATIVE EFFECTS OF SEXUAL HARASSMENT

As mentioned above, sexual harassment is a form of sex discrimination. It is unwelcome conduct of a sexual nature that detrimentally affects the work environment or leads to adverse job-related consequences for the victim.[45]

Sexual harassment results in procreation of artificial barriers to employment solely based on gender considerations. In other words, sexual harassment can and often will impact on the employee's job performance, discourage employees from

---

44 In Amrapali Basumatary v. Union of India W.P. (C) No. 3573/2014 (08.12.2015, Delhi High Court), the court appeared to disagree with an argument that the Act was not gender neutral. As per the author, this view of the court may not be correct.

45 Janzen v. Platy Enterprises [1989] 1 S.C.R 1252 (Supreme Court of Canada).

remaining on the job or keep them from advancing in their careers.[46] Sexual harassment leads to an insecure and hostile work environment, which discourages women's participation in work, thereby adversely affecting their social and economic empowerment and the goal of inclusive growth.[47]

Victims of sexual harassment experience multidimensional losses. Consequentially, their movements become guarded and their vulnerability increases multi-fold. The results of sexual harassment can often be long lasting and traumatic. Specifically speaking, the following are some of the adverse effects of sexual harassment:

a. It threatens and dilutes a woman's confidence and self-esteem.
b. It is demoralising, humiliating and source of misery.
c. It can lead to depression and other stress related ailments.
d. Reduced concentration and productivity.
e. Increased absenteeism from work thereby often resulting in loss of income for the victim.
f. Decreased revenue turnover for the organisation.[48]
g. Emotional or mental injury for a woman is a natural result of sexual harassment at workplace. The moment harassment is established, emotional and mental injury is to be presumed.[49]

The subsequent chapters will hold discussions on how to contain and successfully manage the problem of sexual harassment at work places.

46 *See* Harris v. Forklift Systems 510 U.S. 17 (1993).

47 Shardaben Murlibhai Gurjar v. State of Gujarat (2015) 2 GLR 1620.

48 *See generally* L. Nagaraju v. Syndicate Bank 2014 (2) ALD 758.

49 *See* Gayatri Balaswamy v. ISG Novasoft Technologies Ltd. (2014) 6 CTC 602. It is not necessary that the victim should have suffered concrete psychological harm or injury for the harasser's conduct to be considered unlawful under the Act. *See generally* Harris v. Forklift Systems Inc. 114 S.Ct.367 (1993).

CHAPTER 4

# The Complaints Committee

The Act provides for constitution of certain grievance redressal forums for the purpose of inquiring into and adjudicating a claim of sexual harassment. The Act contemplates establishment of 2 (two) classes of forums (discussed below) to deal with the issue of sexual harassment at the workplace ("**Complaints Committee**"). These two forums operate in different spheres and are not intertwined.

Complaints Committees are independent and impartial disciplinary bodies constituted for carrying out investigation of a claim of sexual harassment in an unbiased and objective manner. The functions of the Complaints Committee are fact finding, educational and conciliatory. The constitution of the committee(s) is to serve both as preventive as well as punitive.[1]

No ombudsman or any other person/authority can be a substitute for a complaints committee required under the Act for looking into complaints of sexual harassment.[2]

The employer does not possess the jurisdiction to enter upon an examination of a complaint of sexual harassment and draw

1 *See* Gayatri Balaswamy v. ISG Novasoft Technologies Ltd. (2014) 6 CTC 602.

2 If the law requires a particular act to be done in a particular manner, it shall be done only in that manner and not otherwise. *See* Gayatri Balaswamy v. ISG Novasoft Technologies Ltd. (2014) 6 CTC 602.

a view thereon. A complaint of sexual harassment can only be made to a complaints committee. The employer does not have the jurisdiction to examine the complaint to decide as to whether a prime facie case of sexual harassment is made out or not. Once a complaint of sexual harassment is received by the employer, the only option available with it is to forward the same to the concerned complaints committee for an inquiry under the provisions of the Act. The next steps are to be taken by the complaints committee.

In Poonam Shahani v. Union of India[3] a complaint of sexual harassment made to the employer was, at the very outset, examined by the disciplinary committee of the employer (instead of the ICC) and dismissed with a finding that the complaint did not, prima facie, disclose a case of sexual harassment. The court, while relying on the above-mentioned principles, rejected this approach of the employer and the disciplinary committee.

## INTERNAL COMPLAINTS COMMITTEE

As per Section 4 of the Act, every employer of a workplace is mandated to constitute an Internal Complaints Committee to look into, evaluate and adjudicate every claim of sexual harassment committed in their workplace ("**ICC**").[4] An ICC may be described as an institutional body required to be constituted by every private employer, government or governmental institution that employs 10 (ten) or more individuals.

### Constitution and Scope of ICC

Normally, an ICC is required to be constituted at every office of the workplace. Where the offices or administrative units of the

3 OA No. 1001/2022 (15.04.2024, Central Administrative Tribunal, Mumbai).

4 The power to deal with the complaint of sexual harassment is vested only with the complaints committee. The complaint cannot be decided by the management of the organization in which the employee works. *See* Aarti Durgaram Gavandi v. Managing Director, Tata Metaliks W.P. No. 8826/2004 (06.10.2008, Bombay High Court).

workplace are located at different places or at divisional or sub-divisional levels, an ICC is required to be constituted at all such administrative units or offices.[5]

**One ICC-Many Workplaces**

The above rule (calling for a separate ICC for every office) is not inflexible.[6] A separate ICC may be desirable where the workplaces are geographically separate or inconveniently located.[7] Conversely, in specific situations, a single ICC may cover more than one workplace. In Jaya Kodate v. Rashtrasant Tukoji Maharaj Nagpur University[8], a question which arose for consideration was whether in case of a junior and senior college operating from the same premises, the constitution of a common ICC (for both colleges) would be justified. The court, while replying in the affirmative, observed as follows:

> 36. Whether this noble object of the 2013 Act can be allowed to be defeated by the technicalities like need of a separate ICC for each establishment of the Employer. Surprisingly, here the Aggrieved Women urge for such separate ICCs while the Respondents attempt to point out unity and integrity of otherwise two separate establishments. Standards 11th and 12th constitute a Junior College and student thereof is examined by the Maharashtra Higher Secondary and Secondary Board at the end of 12th class. Service conditions of teaching and non-teaching staff therein are regulated by Maharashtra Employees of Private Schools (conditions of service) Regulations Act, 1977 and 1981 Rules

5 S. 4 (1) of the Act.

6 *See* Jaya Kodate v. Rashtrasant Tukoji Maharaj Nagpur University W.P. Nos. 3449, 3450 & 3451/2013 (13.06.2014, Bombay High Court).

7 *See also* Parliamentary Standing Committee Report (2011) at ¶ 8.13.

8 W.P. Nos. 3449, 3450 & 3451/2013 (13.06.2014, Bombay High Court).

framed there under. Students passing 12th standard may then take admission in Senior College of same management or go to other Colleges or Streams. It is not necessary for management to run both the types of Colleges. Service conditions of teaching and non-teaching staff in Senior Colleges are regulated by Maharashtra Universities Act and Statutes or Rules framed there under as per UGC guide lines. Recruitment process to both theses Colleges is different. Hence, legally Junior and Senior Colleges form two distinct and independent establishments which have no functional integrality. Thus, even if very same management may run both these type of Colleges, they can never be clubbed together. Hence, ideally there need to be two ICCs for both these establishments. However the problem arises when the staff and students of both these establishments use same classrooms, same playground, library or laboratory and other common facilities like office room, waiting hall or common room or rest rooms. The staff of otherwise distinct establishments must thus be frequently coming in contact with each other and this may lead to frictions or problems like one dealt with in the 2013 Act. A situation where Aggrieved Woman is from Junior College and Respondent is from a Senior College or vice-versa, therefore, may also emerge. It is workplace for all of them. When above definition of workplace is scrutinized in this background, it does not contain a bar against providing a single ICC for such a single or common workplace. It may at the most only desire a separate ICC for distinct workplaces when the same are geographically separate or inconveniently located. This obligation is cast upon the employer for the convenience of Aggrieved Woman. Common or one ICC in a contingency like present one is definitely helpful to all and also to smoothly deal with the allegations of Sexual

Harassment at one go avoiding the duplication and other related difficulties.

37. We therefore find the constitution of one/common ICC for a junior college and senior college in this case justified.

**Members of the ICC**

Courts have emphasised on the need for employers to have in place robust internal mechanisms to effectively tackle/counter the problem of sexual harassment.[9] Law requires that the complaints committee(s) should be broad based and have all necessary representation. An ICC is required to consist of the following members to be nominated by the employer:[10]

a. A presiding officer (PO) who shall be a senior level woman at the workplace.
b. In case a senior-level woman employee is not available, then the PO shall be nominated from other offices or administrative unit of the workplace. However, in case such other offices or administrative units also not have a senior-level woman employee, then the PO shall be nominated from the workplace of the same employer or other department or organization.
c. At least 2 (two) members from amongst the employees preferably committed to the cause of women or who have experience in social work or have legal knowledge.
d. The Act contemplates participation of outside persons in the ICC. 1 (one) member is required from amongst non-governmental organizations or associations committed to the cause of women or a person familiar with the issues relating to sexual harassment (External Member). The objective of providing for an External Member is to keep on the complaints committee an independent

9 *See* Vidya Akhave v. Union of India W.P. No. 796/2015 (04.10.2016, Bombay High Court).

10 S. 4 (2) of the Act.

and impartial person who is in a position to command respect and ensure compliance from other members of the committee as well as the management of the concerned organisation/employer.[11]

**Presiding Member of the ICC**

The Presiding Member (PO) should be a senior level woman employee of the employer. In case a senior level woman employee is not available, then the PO should be from other offices or administrative units of the employer. As a last case situation, a PO may be nominated from other workplaces or other organisations. In the view of the author, there is no leverage provided to the employer in so far as the seniority of the PO is concerned. It is not necessary that the PO must be senior to the accused. However, she must be a senior level employee as per the employer's hierarchy.

In Abhilasha Dwivedi v. Department of Women and Child Development NCT of Delhi[12] a challenge was made to the constitution of the entire ICC by the complainant on the pretext that the PO of the committee was a colleague of the accused and that both worked in the same department of the organisation. The Delhi High Court, while rejecting the challenge, observed that it found no reason to doubt the integrity or the independence of the ICC for, *inter alia*, the following reasons:

a. Merely because the PO was a colleague of the accused would, by itself be no ground to doubt her independence.
b. The ICC was, ultimately, an internal committee and was bound to include some members from the same department.
c. The ICC in the said case comprised of 4 members and there was no ground whatsoever to doubt the independence of the other 3 members.

11 Jaya Kodate v. Rashtrasant Tukoji Maharaj Nagpur University W.P. Nos. 3449, 3450 & 3451/2013 (13.06.2014, Bombay High Court).

12 W.P. (Crl) No. 1639/2019 (19.11.2019, Delhi High Court).

d. There was no material on record, even though remotely suggest that the complainant had any reasonable ground to apprehend that the ICC was biased against her.

**External Member of the ICC**

The objective of providing for an External Member is to keep on the complaints committee an independent and impartial person who is in a position to command respect and compliance from other members of the committee as well as the management of the concerned organisation/employer. The presence of an External Member may assist in the following: (i) preventing the possibility of any undue pressure or influence from the senior levels; (ii) improved co-ordination between the members of the committee; and (iii) ensuring objectivity in the deliberations and findings of the committee.

**External Member obviates bias**

In Ms. X v. Union of India[13] the court observed that an ICC has many members, including an outsider, so as to enable a joint application of minds to evaluate the statements made by a complainant and to assess its credibility. It also serves as a safeguard for the accused, as false complaints are very much possible and for which the Act has made clear provisions, including to punish such a complainant for false and malicious complaints and false evidence.

In Punjab and Sind Bank v. Durgesh Kuwar[14] the "external member" of the ICC also happened to be a panel advocate of the employer bank (at the time when the inquiry was being conducted by the ICC). While making reference to Section 4 (2) (c) of the Act, the Supreme Court observed that such panel

13 LPA No. 527/2019 (17.12.2020, Delhi High Court).

14 AIR 2020 SC 3040.

advocate may not qualify to be a "truly independent third-party external member" for the purposes of the legislation. The Supreme Court further observed that this is a significant facet which goes to the root of the constitution of the ICC.

However, in S Ravi Selvan v. Central Board of Indirect Taxes[15] the Madras High Court did not dislodge an external member of the ICC (also a panel advocate of the department) for, *inter alia,* the following reasons: (i) the external member was not an employee but an advocate representing not only the concerned office but also other government departments; (ii) that she was only one amongst a panel of advocates of the concerned government department; (iii) she had been appointed to the ICC as an external member much before a complaint was lodged by the complainant; (iv) no specific allegations of bias had been made against the external member by the accused for the complainant.

**Women representation in the ICC**

It is important to note that at least 50% (fifty percent) of the total members nominated to the ICC are required to be women.[16] This appears to be a confidence building provision for the complainant because, given the nature of the complaints, a complainant may be more comfortable (and feel free to speak out) with more women being at the helm of the investigative process.

**Qualities of Committee Members**

All appointments to the complaints committee must be on the basis of the appointee's integrity and judicious approach. All appointees must possess the requisite knowledge, orientation and sensitivity towards the issue of sexual harassment. Additionally, as far as

15 W.P. No. 17798/2022 (09.09.2022, Madras High Court).

16 S. 4 (2) *proviso* of the Act.

possible, an employer must ensure appointment of person(s) with sound judicial knowledge. Presence of the above qualities in the member(s) of the committee would aid in mitigation of the possibility of biased or injudicious decision-making.

**Tenure of ICC Members**

The PO and every member of the ICC shall hold office for a maximum period of 3 (three) years from the date of their nomination (Term).[17] The Act does not contain any provision either permitting or prohibiting re-appointment of a member after completion of the Term.

**Allowances of ICC Members**

The External Member shall be paid the following allowance by the employer for holding the proceedings of the ICC: (i) Allowance of Rs. 200 (Rupees Two Hundred) per day for holding the proceedings of the ICC; and (ii) Expenses incurred in travelling by train (in three tier air conditioned coach) or air conditioned bus and auto rickshaw or taxi OR the actual amount spend on travel whichever is less.[18]

**Removal of ICC Members**

The PO or other member of the ICC may be removed from office in any of the following situations:

a. if he contravenes the provisions of section 16[19]; or
b. if he has been convicted for an offence or an inquiry into an offence under any applicable law is pending against him; or

---

17 S. 4 (3) of the Act.

18 R. 3 of the Rules. The allowances offered under the Act appear to be quite less and non-commensurate with today's times.

19 S. 16 of the Act prohibits information relating to the sexual harassment from being published, communicated or made known to the public. For more, *see* chapter titled 'Confidentiality'.

c. he has been found guilty in any disciplinary proceedings or a disciplinary proceeding is pending against him[20]; or
d. if he has abused his position as to render his continuance in office prejudicial to public interest.

Any vacancy created on account of the above reasons shall be filled by a fresh nomination by the employer.[21]

**Casual Vacancy**

A vacancy in the ICC prior to conclusion of the Term may be termed as a casual vacancy. Casual vacancies normally arise through death, resignation or disqualification[22] of sitting members. A case of casual vacancy shall be filled by a fresh nomination by the employer.

**Employer Nominates ICC Members**

The Act provides a free hand to the employer to constitute the ICC in the manner it deems fit (as long as the above described mandatory requirements are complied with). In Madam X v. Chancellor, Punjab University[23] a question which arose was whether an employer, while considering names for constituting an ICC, was prohibited from taking inputs from any sources. In the facts of that case, the employer university, while constituting the ICC, had obtained inputs from the senate and syndicate of the university (internal bodies of the university). The High Court observed that the Act does not prohibit/bar an employer

20 In case a complaint of sexual harassment is made against a sitting member of the complaints committee, then he must be replaced. No man can be a judge of his own cause.

21 S. 4 (5) of the Act.

22 If a complaint of sexual harassment is made against a sitting member of the ICC, or if there exists a conflict of interest between such member and the accused or the complainant, then he should be replaced by another.

23 C.W.P. No. 22684/2018 (15.10.2019, Punjab and Haryana High Court).

from obtaining or considering inputs from any sources while considering names for inclusion in and for constitution of the ICC. There was no warrant for implying or reading any such prohibition/bar in the statute.

The formation of a complaints committee is within the exclusive domain of the employer. There is no requirement in law for seeking the views of the accused in the context of formation or constitution of a complaints committee. See The Research Scholar v. Research Guide & Others.[24]

**Constitution of ICC through Service Rules**

Many organisations are governed by service rules. A question which arises for consideration is "what happens in case of a conflict between the service rules and Section 4 of the Act as to the constitution of an ICC". It is important to understand as to which mechanism will prevail in case of a conflict. In Runa Ray v. Soumen Sarkar[25] this issue came up for consideration before the Calcutta High Court. In this matter, the relevant UGC Regulation of 2015 (which were applicable to the concerned organisation/college) contained certain specific provisions as to constitution of the ICC *viz.* presence of two non-teaching employees as nominated members of the committee who were "preferably" committed to the cause of women or who had experience in social work or have legal knowledge. In this case, while the above specific requirement under the UGC Regulations was not complied with by the employer, however, the committee so constituted did conform to the requirements of Section 4 of the Act. On the basis of the above, the submission which was advanced before the High Court was that non-compliance with the above discussed UGC Regulation was not fatal in view of

24 2024:MHC:4046.

25 MAT 1070/2021 (27.06.2023, Calcutta High Court).

the fact that the committee in question was constituted in the manner provided under Section 4 of the Act. The Calcutta High Court was however of the view that the ICC was required to be constituted exactly in terms of the UGC Regulations of 2015 which were specific to the field of university and college education. In addition, the Calcutta High Court also observed that the expression "preferably" used in the UGC Regulations, constitutes a desirable condition for nomination of a candidate but does not debar the organisation from nominating employees who otherwise fulfil the essential criterion of being in the non-teaching category and are otherwise competent to be nominated to the ICC in accordance with the relevant UGC Regulation.

**UGC Regulations versus the Act**

In The Research Scholar v. Research Guide & Others[26] there were some differences between the provisions providing for constitution of a complaints committee under the Act and those under the UGC Regulations. While the provisions relating to nomination of a presiding officer were more or less similar in both statutes, however, the distinguishing feature was that, in the case of the UGC Regulations, the complaints committee was also required to comprise of three students (in case the victim. It was argued by the accused that the constitution of the complaints committee (in accordance with the UGC Regulations) was flawed in as much such constitution was in direct conflict with Section 4 of the Act (which did not provide for nomination of students to the complaints committee). This argument of the accused was rejected by the High Court with the observation that in the event of conflict between the provisions of the UGC Regulations Act and the Act, the UGC Regulations would prevail. Reliance in this regard was placed by the High Court on the decision of the

26 2024:MHC:4046

Supreme Court in Gambhirdan K Gadhvi v. State of Gujarat[27] which had upheld the binding nature of UGC Regulations.[28]

**Challenge to Constitution of the Committee**

The general law is that the complaints committee, if not constituted in accordance with the provisions of the Act, can be challenged by the parties to the inquiry proceedings. Courts have, on various occasions, set aside inquiry proceedings for want of proper constitution of the complaints committee. In fact, in Pawan Kumar Niroula v. Union of India[29] a committee constituted prior to the enactment of the Act (in a proper manner as per the then prevailing legal position) but not being in terms of Section 4 of the Act, was held to have lost statutory force after enactment of the Act.

On the other hand, there have also been instances where, in peculiar facts of the case, high courts have refused to entertain a challenge to the constitution of the complaints committee in view of past participation to the proceedings by the parties concerned.

In Rehana Kausar v. UT of J & K[30] the High Court of Jammu and Kashmir had the occasion to examine such a situation. In the facts of the case, the complainant had participated in an inquiry proceedings conducted by the ICC. At no stage did she express her resentment, protest or demur to her participation before the ICC. It is only after the inquiry report was issued by the committee did the complainant (being dissatisfied with

27 (2022) 5 SCC 179

28 In Gambhirdan K Gadhvi v. State of Gujarat (2022) 5 SCC 179 the subject matter of the dispute was relating to the appointment of a vice chancellor. The Supreme Court observed that appointment of a vice chancellor cannot be made dehors the applicable UGC Regulations even if the relevant state legislation contained diluted eligibility criteria (when compared with the eligibility criteria prescribed under the UGC Regulations).

29 2022 (2) SLR 320.

30 2023 LLR 146.

the same) alleged defective constitution of the committee. The High Court found no infirmity with the inquiry process. It was ultimately concluded as follows:

a. The procedure adopted by the committee while conducting its inquiry was in accordance with law and the principles of natural justice had been adhered to. Therefore at this point, it was impermissible for the complainant to turn around and try to wriggle out of the inquiry report on the premise that it's constitution was defective/not in accordance with law.
b. By participating in the inquiry proceedings without any demur, the complainant had acquiesced in the constitution of the committee and had, at no stage, lodged any protest either regarding the functioning of the committee or regarding its constitution. Consequently, she could not challenge the constitution of the committee once the result went against her.
c. While arriving at its conclusions, the High Court drew an analogy from other judicial precedents (in the context of selection processes) which hold that when a person takes a chance and participates in the selection process, thereafter he cannot, (because the result is unpalatable), turn around to contend that the process was unfair or that the selection committee was improperly constituted.
d. The High Court also distinguished other judgments being relied upon by the complainant (wherein a challenge to the constitution of the committee was made after the issuance of the inquiry report of the committee) by observing that in those cases the complainant had, from the very beginning, lodged a protest with regard to constitution of the committee. However, in the present matter, the complainant far from raising any objection, had in fact vigorously participated in the proceedings until the issuance of the inquiry report.

## Manner of Functioning of the ICC

The status of the ICC is that of an inquiry committee; a fact finding committee for disciplinary action.[31] The ICC is a singular committee and is expected to function like a single body. There should be a collective application of mind and a combined report from the members.

In Jaya Kodate v. Rashtrasant Tukoji Maharaj Nagpur University[32] the Bombay High Court, while stressing on the need of a joint inquiry/deliberation/determination by an ICC, observed as follows:

> Section 13 speaks of a ICC as one entity. When there are total 4 members on ICC, a report or decision by the majority is not ruled out. But when the ICC is a single committee and there is provision for quorum, it is expected to function as a single body. Highlighted part of Section 13 (supra) leaves no manner of doubt that in such a serious matter of public importance, the Parliament expected a collective application of mind and a combined report. When such fact finding body is comprised of more than one member, it is inherent that all hear the controversy together and are benefited by the experience and expertise of each other by sharing/exchanging their views. If every body sits as an individual without any dialogue with the other members and then submits his findings also without deliberations or consultation with the others, very purpose of providing a multi-membered body gets frustrated. Such separate report then becomes a separate report of the several individuals submitting it and may suffer from individual's prejudices or drawbacks. A joint inquiry committee is prescribed to eliminate such elements specific

31 *See* L.S. Sibu v. Air India Limited W.P. (C) No. 4001/2016 (08.04.2016, Kerala High Court).

32 W.P Nos. 3449, 3450 & 3451/2013 (13.06.2014, Bombay High Court).

> to every individual and to bestow advantage of the expertise of every individual in his own field. Persons from different walks of life with varied knowledge and experience as also different approaches come together to form one committee. This artificially created person i.e. one committee (here ICC) therefore must get colour of personality of its every constituent and in the process, bias or prejudices of one are bound to be diluted by the character of the others. Such an artificial body acquires its personality only when the several members forming it sit together, share their view points and gain advantage of the perspective of the other members. This exchange may lead to a combined single inquiry report i.e., a unanimous decision by all. In a given case, one of the learned member may not agree with the view of majority but then, he will be electing to disagree after having advantage of the wisdom of others. His disagreement therefore evidences itself or surfaces in joint deliberations and others also get an opportunity to weigh his view-point. Other members therefore get a chance to know the view of minority and to decide to disagree with it by majority. Thus, reasons for agreement or disagreement are not pre-decided and evolve out of process of joint discussion. When an individual on such multi-membered ICC avoids to speak with others, he robs the artificial person of one facet of its character desired by the Parliament and such ICC is therefore never legally complete or born. Thus, report signed and submitted by majority members of such an ICC without undertaking exercise of joint deliberations is void and unacceptable.

During the prevalence of the Vishaka Guidelines, a school of thought existed that ICCs should be constituted only at the time of filing of a complaint of sexual harassment and should be disbanded upon completion of the inquiry process. However, this issue was put to rest by the Act through induction of provisions requiring a permanent ICC. Having in place a permanent complaints body may have the following benefits:[33]

a. Helps in confidence building of the complainant.
b. Introduces impartiality to the investigative process.
c. Provides easy and timely access to victims and avoids delay due to procedural exigencies.

Recently, in Aurelenio Fernandes v. The State of Goa[34] the Supreme Court observed that constitution of an ICC was a statutory duty of every employer. It directed the government authorities to carry out a survey to identify the number of employers who have constituted an ICC under the Act, and to ensure full compliance by the employers in this regard. Various other directions were also passed by the Supreme Court, including but not limited to, directions to the district officer to upload all details of complaints committees constituted under the Act, directions to every Indian state to consider instituting a she-box for the purposes of registering complaints of sexual harassment etc.

## LOCAL COMPLAINTS COMMITTEE

The Act contemplates establishment of a Local Complaints Committee (hereinafter the "**LCC**") at the district level(s) to address complaints of sexual harassment pertaining to the following categories:

i. Cases where the perpetrator of the harassment is the employer himself[35];

---

33 Parliamentary Standing Committee Report (2011), at ¶ 8.2.

34 Misc Application No. 22553/2023 (03.12.2024, Supreme Court of India)

35 It is a settled principle of law that no person can be a judge in his own cause. It is thus imperative that a neutral (and third party) body investigates a complaint of sexual harassment made against the top management of an organisation.

ii. Organizations having less than 10 (ten) employees[36]; and

iii. Women workers in the unorganized sector, including domestic workers.

### ICC First : LCC Second

In Rashi v. Union of India[37] the Delhi High Court observed that the basic scheme of the Act is for appointment of an ICC and only if no alternative is available, should the victim/complainant be asked to approach the LCC. It appears that the view of the Delhi High Court (especially in the context of cases where the perpetrator is a high-ranking official) is that, at the first instance, efforts to constitute an independent ICC should be attempted by the organisation. The LCC should be approached only if the same is not possible in the facts of the case.

In Fauza Rubbani v. Delhi Woman Commission[38] an ICC was not constituted by the concerned organisation. In such a situation, the Delhi High Court observed in the absence of the ICC (which was supposed to be constituted by the employer in accordance with the provisions of the Act) the complainant may approach the concerned LCC with her complaint. Additionally, the court also imposed a penalty of Rs. 50,000/- on the employer (in accordance with Section 26 of the Act) for its failure to constitute an ICC.

### Notification of District Officer

The appropriate government may notify any of the following officers as district officer (for each district) under the Act: (i) District Magistrate; (ii) Additional District Magistrate; (iii) Collector; or (iv) Deputy Collector (hereinafter referred to as District Officer).[39]

36 S. 6 (1) of the Act.

37 W.P. (C) No. 3396/2019 (04.12.2020, Delhi High Court).

38 W.P. (C) No. 11749/2019 (02.02.2023, Delhi High Court).

39 S. 5 of the Act. The expression "may" in S. 5 of the Act is to be read as "shall". *See* Initiatives For Inclusion Foundation v. Union of India, 2023 INSC 927.

In Initiatives For Inclusion Foundation v. Union of India[40] the Supreme Court observed that the notification of a district officer is mandatory. The Supreme Court observed as follows:

> The District Officer is the most important functionary in the system and is tasked with keeping the redressal and monitoring framework both intact and smoothly running. The District Officer performs multiple roles, including the following: (i) The District Officer is responsible for payment of allowances to the chairman and members of the LCC, which it receives from the agency set up by the state government (See S. 8 of the Act & R 5 of the Rules); (ii) The district officer also perform the duty in terms of enforcement i.e. taking steps for recovery of money as areas of land revenue, if the respondent fails to pay any sum so directed by the ICC/LCC (See S. 13 (3) proviso of the Act).

### Jurisdiction of an LCC

Every District Officer shall constitute an LCC to receive and adjudicate complaints of sexual harassment from establishments where either the ICC has not been constituted due to having less than 10 (ten) workers (including the unorganised sector) or where the complaint is against the employer himself.[41]

The District Officer shall designate 1 (one) nodal officer in every block, taluka and tehsil in rural or tribal area and ward or municipality in the urban area, to receive complaints and forward the same to the concerned LCC within a period of 7 (seven) days.[42] The jurisdiction of the LCC shall extend to the areas of the district where it is constituted.[43]

40 2023 INSC 927.

41 S. 6 (1) of the Act.

42 S. 6 (2) of the Act.

43 S. 6 (3) of the Act.

## Scope of Powers of LCC

The LCC does not exercise any supervisory or appellate jurisdiction over the ICC. In Sukalyan Haldar v. State of West Bengal,[44] the LCC, while adjudicating a claim of sexual harassment, amongst other things, adjudicated upon the constitution of the ICC and directed a reconstitution of the ICC in compliance with the provisions of the Act. These observations of the LCC were brought into question before the Calcutta High Court. It was argued that the statute did not provide the LCC with the power or authority to pass such directions. The Calcutta High Court, after examining the provisions of the Act, observed that nothing in the said Act conferred jurisdiction on the LCC to adjudicate upon the propriety or legality of the constitution of the ICC and/or pass directions on the concerned institution/workplace to take steps regarding constitution of the ICC. At best, the LCC could have approached the appropriate authorities for imposition of penalty against the concerned institution/workplace in accordance with the provisions of Section 26 of the Act.

## Composition of an LCC

The LCC shall consist of the following members to be nominated by the District Officer:[45]

a. A chairperson to be nominated from amongst the eminent women in the field of social work and committed to the cause of women;
b. 1 (one) member to be nominated from amongst the women working in the block, taluka or tehsil or ward or municipality in the district;
c. 2 (two) members, of whom at least one shall be a woman, to be nominated from amongst such non-governmental organizations or associations committed to the cause of women or a person familiar with the issues relating to sexual harassment (External Members).

44 W.P.A. No. 18829/2023 (08.09.2023, Calcutta High Court).

45 S. 7 of the Act.

d. The concerned officer dealing with social welfare or women and child development in the district shall be a member *ex officio*.[46]

At least one of the above nominees shall, preferably, have a background in law or legal knowledge. Further, at least one of the nominees shall be a woman belonging to the Scheduled Castes or the Scheduled Tribes or the other Backward Classes or minority community notified by the Central Government from time to time.[47]

**Person committed to the cause of women**

The Act does not define the expression 'person committed to the cause of women'. The Parliamentary Standing Committee Report, 2011 described a 'person committed to the cause of women' as one who has done outstanding work for women and is sensitive to the concerns of women.[48]

**Person familiar with the issues relating to sexual harassment**

A person familiar with the issues relating to sexual harassment is one who has expertise on issues relating to sexual harassment and may include any of the following: (i) a social worker with at least 5 (five) years experience in the field of social work which leads to creation of societal conditions favourable towards empowerment of women and in particular in addressing workplace sexual harassment; or (ii) a person who is familiar with labour, service, civil or criminal law.[49]

---

46 by virtue of one's position or status.

47 S. 7 (1) *proviso* of the Act.

48 *See* Report, at ¶ 3.16. This is a truly broad based description and following the same would lend great latitude to the appointing authority in identifying the correct person for the job.

49 R. 4 of the Rules.

In sum, in the view of the author, the following people may be most qualified to be appointed as External Members of a complaints committee.

i. Social workers or members of NGO's who work in the area of women empowerment.
ii. Lawyers/other persons having sufficient experience in the areas of labour, service, civil or criminal law.

**Tenure**

The Chairperson and every member of the LCC shall hold office for a maximum period of 3 (three) years from the date of their nomination (Term).[50] The Act does not contain any provision either permitting or prohibiting a re-appointment of a member after completion of the Term.

**Allowance**

The Chairperson shall be paid the following allowance(s) by the District Officer for holding the proceedings of the LCC: Rs. 250 (Rupees Two Hundred and Fifty) per day.

The External Members shall be paid the following allowance by the District Officer for holding the proceedings of the LCC: (i) Allowance of Rs. 250 (Rupees Two Hundred and Fifty) per day; and (ii) Expenses incurred in travelling by train (in three tier air condition) or air conditioned bus or auto rickshaw or taxi OR the actual amount spend on travel whichever is less.[51]

**Grants & Audit**

The Central Government may make monetary grants to the State Government towards utilisation for payment of the above allowances. The State Government may set up an agency and

50 S. 7 (2) of the Act.

51 R. 5 of the Rules.

transfer the grants to the said agency. The agency shall further pay to the District Officer such sums as may be required for making the above payments. The accounts of the agency shall be maintained and audited in such manner as may be prescribed in consultation with the Accountant General of the State.[52]

### Removal of ICC Members

The Chairperson or a Member of the LCC may be removed from office in any of the following situations:

a. if he contravenes the provisions of section 16; or
b. if he has been convicted for an offence or an inquiry into an offence under any applicable law is pending against him; or
c. he has been found guilty in any disciplinary proceedings or a disciplinary proceeding is pending against him; or
d. if he has abused his position as to render his continuance in office prejudicial to public interest.

Any vacancy created on account of the above shall be filled by a fresh nomination by the District Officer.[53]

### Casual Vacancy of ICC Members

A vacancy in the LCC prior to conclusion of the Term may be termed as a casual vacancy. Casual vacancies normally arise on account of factors such as death, resignation or disqualification of the sitting members. A case of casual vacancy shall be filled by a fresh nomination by the District Officer.

52 S. 8 of the Act. In this regard, please note that the Women and Child Development Department of the Government of Madhya Pradesh has promulgated The Madhya Pradesh Sexual Harassment of Women at Workplace (Prevention, Prohibition and Redressal) Setting up of Agency, Accounts and Audit Rules, 2014 *vide* Notification No. 1379-1866-13-L-2 dated 20.08.2014 for *inter alia* implementing the provisions of Section 8 of the Act. These Rules designate the State Women Resource Centre as the agency for the purposes of the Act.

53 S. 7 (3) of the Act.

### Duties and Powers of the District Officer

The District Officer shall have the following primary functions:[54]

a. To monitor the timely submission of reports furnished by the LCC.
b. To take all necessary measures for engaging non-governmental organizations for creation of awareness on sexual harassment and the rights of women.

### Submission of Annual Reports by the Committees

Every ICC and LCC is required to prepare an annual report and submit the same to the concerned employer and the District Officer.[55] Such annual report shall contain the following particulars:[56]

a. Number of complaints of sexual harassment received in the year.
b. Number of complaints disposed off during the year.
c. Number of cases pending for more than 90 (ninety) days.
d. Number of workshops or awareness programs carried out against sexual harassment.
e. Nature of action taken by the employer or District Officer.

The District Officer is required to forward a brief report on the above received annual reports to the State Government.[57] Strict and scrupulous compliance with such mechanism (of annual reports) would aid the government in developing and maintaining an organised (and centralised) database on the subject which would, in turn, improve data

54 S. 20 of the Act.

55 S. 21 (1) of the Act.

56 R. 14 of the Rules & S. 22 of the Act. *See generally* Office Memorandum F. No. 11013/2/2014-Estt.A-III, dated 02.02.2015, Department of Personnel & Training, Ministry of Personnel, Public Grievances and Pensions, Government of India.

57 S. 21 (2) of the Act.

accessibility, management and sharing on the issue of sexual harassment.

## DUTIES OF COMPLAINTS COMMITTEES

As discussed earlier, the concept of a complaints committee has been promulgated by the Act to look into and investigate cases of sexual harassment. In fact, it is pertinent that such committees are viewed as courts in their own right. Every committee has a duty of care and the degree of responsibility when it comes to determining cases of sexual harassment. Some critical responsibilities of a committee while evaluating a sexual harassment claim are as follows:

a. Every committee, when approached with a complaint of sexual harassment, should fully inform every complainant of her rights. Every complaint must be addressed responsibly and in an impartial manner. This is imperative so as to instil in the victim, a sense of confidence over the investigative body. The committee has to maintain a balance even between the interest of the complainant and the avoidance of injustice to the accused. Therefore, even the accused must be intimated of his rights so that he may be able to present his defence in the matter.
b. The investigation should be complete, objective and thorough. Each party, including the witnesses and others with information on the matter, should be examined. An unbiased determination should be made and the results communicated to the concerned parties in accordance with law.
c. If sexual harassment is proved, then prompt and efficacious corrective action must follow. Such corrective action should be devised (as per law) in such way that it (as far as practicable) remedies the complainant's loss and also prevents further harassment from taking place in the organisation both *qua* the complainant as well as other potential victims.

## Obligations of the Complaints Committee

In Linda Eastwood v. Union of India[58] the following pivotal obligations of the complaints committee were highlighted by the Delhi High Court:

a. The procedure for adjudication should be fair and unbiased.[59]
b. It must be insured that there is no undue pressure or influence on the complaints committee from the senior levels of the organisation.[60]
c. The accused must not take any active part in the decision of formation/constitution of the complaints committee.
d. The credentials of the members of the committee should be absolutely without blemish. No member of the committee should have any personal interest in the matter being inquired into.
e. The committee must ensure that no injustice is done.

Separately, in the author's view, all members of the complaints committee ought to also do the following:

a. Monitor the working environment to ensure that acceptable standards of conduct are being maintained by all.

---

58 W.P. (Crl.) No. 1904/2013 (23.02.2015, Delhi High Court).

59 Any specific incidents of bias should ordinarily be reported to the employer who may then take appropriate action. Kasturba A.K v. National Institute of Technology, W.P. (C) No. 25846/2015 (28.09.2016, Kerala High Court). Any failure on this account may result in the inquiry getting vitiated or stayed. If allegations of bias are established against one member of the complaints committee, then on this basis, that committee may not be permitted to conduct the inquiry. *See* Office Memorandum F. No. 11013/2/2014-Estt (A-III), dated 16.07.2015, Department of Personnel & Training, Ministry of Personnel, Public Grievances and Pensions, Government of India.

60 Mere acquaintance of a member of the Complaints Committee with the accused or the complainant should normally not be the reason to raise a plea of bias, unless the relations are such which could affect the outcome of the proceedings. Normally, at preliminary stages of the proceedings, it may be difficult to ascertain whether the relationship is capable of influencing the decision making process of the committee. It is only after completion of the probe that such aspects can be determined. *See* Kasturba A.K v. National Institute of Technology, W.P. (C) No. 25846/2015 (28.09.2016, Kerala High Court).

b. Meet periodically, even if there exists no live case, to review preparedness; and to ensure functionality.[61]
c. Model appropriate behaviour themselves.
d. Promote the sexual harassment policies of their organisation to the hilt.

Ideally, all members of the complaints committee must possess a demonstrated understanding of and ability to deal with sexual harassment issues. While the complaints committee is the master of its procedure, it must carry out its duties in consonance with the principles of natural justice.[62]

**Conduct of Proceedings by Complaints Committee**

In Rashi v. Union of India[63] the Delhi High Court summarised the following broad principles regarding constitution/conduct of proceedings in the ICC:

a. Members of an ICC must be impartial, unbiased, independent minded and fair.
b. Members of an ICC must not have any conflict of interest with any of the parties in the matter.
c. Neutrality and objectivity must be maintained in the conduct of the proceedings. There should be no cause for bias for or against any of the parties.
d. Members of an ICC must possess blemish-free credentials.
e. The external members should be truly external and should not be, in any way, connected with either the organization or with any party.

61 *See generally* Office Memorandum F. No. 11013/2/2014-Estt.A-III, dated 02.02.2015, Department of Personnel & Training, Ministry of Personnel, Public Grievances and Pensions, Government of India.

62 *See also* Chapter titled 'Procedure'. Note that the committee is not bound by the rigid limitations regarding the admissibility of evidence and the degree of proof applicable before criminal courts.

63 W.P. (C) No. 3396/2019 (04.12.2020, Delhi High Court).

f. In cases where persons who have been at the helm of the affairs are themselves the accused in a complaint, the ICC cannot be one of their choice or comprise of persons who have worked under them.
g. There should be no undue pressure or influence on the ICC from the senior levels.
h. The ICC should follow a clear and precise procedure to deal with sexual harassment complaints.
i. The principles of natural justice should be followed scrupulously.
j. The proceedings should lend confidence and assurance to the complainant and make her comfortable.
k. The inquiry proceedings should inspire confidence of the court.

**Bias**

Existence of bias disqualifies a committee member from his/her post. In simple terms, bias is the result of any member of the ICC having any pecuniary or personal interest in the matter. In order to succeed on an argument of bias, the alleging party must be able to establish "real likelihood" or a "real existence" of bias. Mere apprehension of bias would not be sufficient.

In M.P Special Police Establishment v. State of Madhya Pradesh[64] the Supreme Court, *inter alia,* observed that actual bias would lead to automatic disqualification where the decision-maker is shown to have an interest in the outcome of the case.

In Parthasarthi v. State of Andhra Pradesh[65] the Supreme Court explained the test of bias in the following words:

> The tests of "real likelihood" and "reasonable suspicion" are really inconsistent with each other. We think that the reviewing authority must make a determination on the basis

64 2004 (8) SCC 788.

65 (1974) 3 SCC 459.

> of the whole evidence before it, whether a reasonable man would in the circumstances infer that there is real likelihood of bias. The Court must look at the impression which other people have. This follows from the principle that justice must not only be done but seen to be done. If right minded persons would think that there is real likelihood of bias on the part of an inquiring officer, he must not conduct the inquiry.

**Bias Requires Strong Evidence**

In S Ravi Selvan v. Central Board of Indirect Taxes[66] the Madras High Court observed that an allegation that some members of the ICC belong to the same department as one of the parties to the complaint may not, by itself, be sufficient to prove bias. Allegation of bias must be supported with conclusive and undisputed evidence. This judgement also indicates that normally courts refrain from taking judicial notice of allegations of bias especially when the investigation in the matter is ongoing before the ICC (unless of course such allegation is duly supported with incontrovertible evidence).

In Somaya Gupta v. Jawarlal Nehru University,[67] the Delhi High Court observed that where the constitution of an ICC is not specific to a case; but is constituted to enquire into all cases of sexual harassment, then in such case it will be difficult to hold that the constitution of such ICC is vitiated by any bias (specific conclusive evidence of bias excepting).[68]

66 W.P. No. 17798/2022 (09.09.2022, Madras High Court).

67 2018 (VIII) AD (Delhi) 259.

68 In Soumen Sarkar v. The State of West Bengal, W.P.A. No. 13267/2021 (16.09.2021, Calcutta High Court), the High Court reconstituted the ICC to dispel any allegation of bias as also to dispel the reservations expressed by the accused about certain members thereof. In the view of the author, the approach of the court, in ordering a re-constitution of the ICC, despite its preliminary view that the ICC appeared to be properly constituted in terms of law, may not be correct.. This observation of the Single Bench of the Calcutta High Court was reversed in appeal by the Division Bench of the Calcutta High Court in Runa Ray v. Soumen Sarkar, MAT 1070/2021 (27.06.2023, Calcutta High Court).

**Disqualification of one Member**

In the above judgement of *Somaya Gupta,* the Delhi High Court also observed that just because the Presiding Officer/Chairperson of the ICC was disqualified to act in the matter (since she was a witness to the alleged incident of sexual harassment), it would not automatically entail that the entire ICC must be reconstituted. This was more so because there existed no allegation against any other member of the ICC. In such cases, it would be sufficient for the disqualified member to be substituted by another member (with the rest of the ICC remaining intact).

**DELAY IN ADJUDICATION**

One major obstacle en-route of effective decision making by the committee is delay. Some reasons for delay in internal inquiries are as follows:

a. Unfamiliarity of the complaints committee with the applicable investigative procedure.
b. Lack of firmness in dealing with dilatory tactics deployed (or attempted to be deployed) by the accused during the course of the proceedings.
c. Pre-occupation of the complaints committee members with their regular duties and responsibilities.

Some ways of avoiding such delay:

a. The employer must promptly nominate all members of the complaints committee (with the desired qualifications and capabilities) in compliance with the provisions of the Act.
b. When a claim of sexual harassment is made or an inquiry is underway, the members of the committee should be relieved of their normal duties (to such extent as may be necessary or possible) in order to enable them to devote complete and careful

attention to the completion of the inquiry and submission of the final report.

c. The members of the complaints committee must familiarize themselves with the relevant rules and procedure.
d. Periodic trainings of the members would also be helpful.
e. All time lines for adjudication (provided in the Act) must be scrupulously followed.
f. All dilatory attempts made by the parties to the complaint must be dealt with in a firm manner.

## SENIORITY OF THE MEMBERS OF THE COMPLAINTS COMMITTEE

There is some divergence of views of different high courts as to the requirement of a senior level employees to at as the presiding officer of a complaints committee. In Shobha Goswami v. State of Uttar Pradesh[69] a question which arose for determination was whether the presiding member of an ICC needs to be senior to the accused. The court observed that there was nothing in the Act which required the presiding member to be senior to the accused. It was sufficient that the presiding member was of a senior level in the organisation.[70] Hence, lack of seniority of any member of the ICC (*vis-a-vis* the accused) would not vitiate the inquiry.[71]

A similar view (as above) was taken in the case of P Govindraju v. The Manomanium Sundaranar University[72] wherein, *inter alia*, it was observed that the composition and constitution of an ICC is not dependent upon the rank of the delinquent. Hence,

---

69 2015 (146) FLR 613.

70 *See also* H.C. Bakshi v. Union of India (09.05.2008, Central Administrative Tribunal, New Delhi).

71 *See generally* Office Memorandum F. No. 11013/2/2014-Estt.A-III, dated 09.09.2016, Department of Personnel & Training, Ministry of Personnel, Public Grievances and Pensions, Government of India.

72 2020 (1) Writ LR 249.

in other words, the members of the ICC need not necessarily be senior to the delinquent. It would be sufficient compliance for the purposes of Section 4 of the Act that the presiding member of the ICC is a senior level employee at the workplace.

A different view, however, was taken on this issue by the Madras High Court in Dr. S. Vinukumar v. The Government of Tamil Nadu.[73] In this matter, the presiding officer of the ICC was at a level/position equivalent to that of the accused. The High Court, while opining that a higher level officer should be appointed as the presiding officer, made the following observations:

a. The expression "senior level employee" used in Section 4 of the Act should be interpreted constructively with reference to the purpose and object sought to be achieved under the Act.
b. The word "senior level" indicates not a mere senior officer but an officer who should be working in a higher cadre than that of the delinquent.
c. Even appointment of an equivalent level officer should be eschewed to prevent prejudice to either party. In all circumstances, the senior level officer must be working in the higher rank than that of the delinquent official for the purposes of conducting an inquiry by the ICC.

In A. Manimekalan v. The Registrar[74] the presiding officer of the ICC was a junior level employee of the concerned organization (despite the fact that there were many other women at senior positions employed in the organization). The Madras High Court observed that the constitution of the ICC was violative of Section 4 of the Act.

---

73 W.P (MD) No. 5486/2022 (25.04.2022, Madras High Court, Madurai Bench).

74 2023 Writ LR 201.

In M. Rajendran v. M. Daisyrani[75] certain allegations of sexual harassment were made against the Dean of a College. It was found that the ICC had been constituted by the dean himself and most members of the committee were subordinate to him. Under these peculiar circumstances, the Madras High Court ordered a fresh constitution of an independent committee which was impartial and fair.

In Rashi v. Union of India[76] a complaint of sexual harassment was made against a high-ranking official of a government department. In that context, the Delhi High Court observed that where the accused is a high-ranking or a highly placed official of an organisation, then in such case, it may be desirable to ensure that at least a majority of the members of the ICC are not from the same department (in order to obviate any allegation of unfairness or bias).

In Binani Chattopadhyay v. Union of India[77] a somewhat different view was taken by the Calcutta High Court, in the peculiar circumstances of that matter. In that case, the presiding officer of the ICC was a junior level employee. However, the organisation concerned in that matter was, at the relevant time, undergoing a process of winding up its activities and was operating with skeleton staff. The High Court, keeping in mind this peculiar fact, did not fault the appointment of a "not so senior officer" as the presiding officer of the ICC.

## SENIORITY BY EXPERIENCE

The word "seniority" used in Section 4 of the Act includes the concept of "seniority by experience". In Research Scholar

---

75 (2018) 3 MLJ 84.

76 W.P. (C) No. 3396/2019 (04.12.2020, Delhi High Court).

77 2023 LLR 480.

v. Research Guide & Others[78] an argument was raised by the accused that the constitution of the complaints committee was flawed in as much as both the presiding officer and the accused were heads of departments of their respective divisions of the educational institution and were therefore of the same status. It was argued that Section 4 of the Act provided that the presiding officer of the complaints committee must necessarily be senior to the accused. On the other hand, it was argued by the institution that the presiding officer of the complaints committee was "senior to the accused" in the sense that she was "senior by experience" since she was appointed as a department head earlier than the accused and consequently had spent more time in the capacity of "department head". Also, the institution pointed out that in the overall combined seniority of the faculty members of the institution, the presiding officer of the complaints committee ranked higher in seniority than the accused. The High Court rejected the argument of the accused in this regard and upheld the submission of the institution that in the facts and circumstances of the case, the presiding officer, by virtue of experience and overall seniority, passed muster under Section 4 of the Act.

## INVESTIGATIVE PROCESS OF THE COMPLAINTS COMMITTEE

Sexual harassment is a sensitive issue. It requires tactful handling of the parties involved. The complaints committee must undertake its tasks with the correct approach and sensitivity. What is required is an orderly and systematic investigation to take the inquiry to its logical end. The following investigative processes may, among other things, be adopted by a complaints committee while adjudicating a claim of sexual harassment.

78 2024:MHC:4046

a. Commence with verifying all facts of the case.
b. Unearth all evidence in the matter.
c. Examine and analyze every view point and representation made by the parties.
d. Take into account the submissions/representations of the witness and other persons in the know of things.
e. Take into account every piece of evidence. More specifically, this may include emails, employment records, SMS, call records, CCTV footage etc.
f. Maintain all documentation pertaining to the case, including the complaint, replies, witness statements etc.
g. Ensure confidentiality of the processes as well as of the documents.

It is important to note that, the recommendations of a complaints committee can be set aside in case of, *inter alia*, its improper constitution[79] or its flawed approach in adjudicating the matter.[80]

In fact courts propagate proper compliance with the laid down procedures for conducting inquiry proceedings by the ICC. In Shila Debnath v. National Institute of Technology[81] the complainant was not granted an opportunity of hearing by the ICC before making its report. The High Court observed that when a particular procedure is provided in a statute, it is the duty of the ICC to comply with the same. Infraction of a laid down procedure renders the inquiry proceedings of the ICC as unsustainable. Ultimately the High Court set aside the inquiry report and ordered a fresh inquiry into the matter.

---

79 Normally a finding that the inquiry proceedings were vitiated on account of the complaint committee's improper constitution would result in the court remitting the matter back to the employer to take suitable steps for constituting another committee in accordance with law and causing the matter to be decided afresh. *See* U.S Verma v. National Commission of Women 163 (2009) DLT 557.

80 *See* Punita K. Sodhi v. Union of India (2010) 172 DLT 409.

81 W.P. (C) No. 422/2021 (07.12.2021, Tripura High Court).

Similarly, in the cases of Suresh v. The State of Tamil Nadu[82] and K Hem Lata v. The State of Tamil Nadu,[83] the Madras High Court directed a reconstitution of the ICC and dictated fresh timelines for completion of the inquiry by the newly constituted complaints committee.

82 W.P. (MD) No. 4491/2014 (24.07.2019, Madras High Court).

83 2018 LLR 477.

CHAPTER 5

# Procedure

This chapter details the procedures for inquiring into and adjudicating a complaint of sexual harassment. At the outset, it is important to note that the course of action enumerated in the Act is broad based and leaves sufficient scope for the complaints committee(s) to carve out their own procedure. However, at the same time, it sets out the boundaries and stipulates certain parameters which have to be mandatorily complied with by the committees during the course of the inquiry.[1] Under the Act, the investigative and adjudicatory procedure must revolve around the following pivots: principles of natural justice and fair opportunity to the parties.

## THE PROCEDURE FOR ENQUIRY

Before embarking on a detailed discussion, it is first important to highlight the following points:

---

1 It is mandatory to hold an inquiry when a claim of sexual harassment is made. *See* Dr. R.S. Tyagi v. All India Institute of Medical Sciences OA No. 1619/2011 (13.12.2011 Central Administrative Tribunal, New Delhi). *See generally* Sandeep Khurana v. Delhi Transco Limited 135 (2006) DLT 346 wherein, in the context of the Central Civil Services (CCA) Rules, 1964, the court stated that the procedure for conducting an inquiry under Rule 14 of the said rules, as far as possible, must be adhered to.

a. The Act is in addition to and not in derogation to any other applicable law.[2] In other words, it is meant to supplement and not supplant.

b. The investigative procedure prescribed under the Act for redress of a complaint of sexual harassment is to be resorted to where no other statute (covering the aspect of sexual harassment) is applicable to or no statutory service rules exist in the concerned organisation.[3]

## Making a Complaint

Any aggrieved woman may make, in writing, a complaint of sexual harassment at workplace to the ICC or the LCC, as the case may be, within a period of 3 (three) months from the date of the incident, and in case of a series of incidents, within a period of 3 (three) months from the date of the last incident.[4]

The above described time period of 3 (three) months may be extended by another period of 3 (three) months, with reasons to be recorded in writing, in case the complaints committee is satisfied that the circumstances were such which prevented the woman from filing a complaint on time.[5] Complaints which are time barred run the risk of being turned down by the complaints committee.[6]

2 S. 28 of the Act.

3 However, it goes without saying that, even in cases where another statute/ service rules are applicable, any lacunae or vacuum therein may be filled by drawing on or taking the benefit of the provisions of the Act. In case of any inconsistency between the other statute/service rules and the Act, the other statute/service rules shall prevail. *See generally* Debjani Sengupta v. The Institute of Cost Accountants of India, RVW 129/2019 (04.07.2023, Calcutta High Court).

4 S. 9 (1) of the Act.

5 S. 9 (1) Proviso of the Act. The said proviso makes it obligatory for the ICC to record its reasons. *See* Nirmal Kanti Chakraborti v. Vaneeta Patnaik. FMA No. 873/2024 (23.12.2024, Calcutta High Court)

6 *See generally* Debdulal Maity v. National Insurance Company Limited, W.P. No. 728 / 2014 (07.08.2014, Calcutta High Court).

Any unwelcome act or behaviour if repeated at short intervals by the same person would come within the purview of the expression "series of incidents". See Nirmal Kanti Chakraborti v. Vaneeta Patnaik.[7]

**Limitation for filing a complaint**

Typically, every offence of sexual harassment should be reported immediately, however, the legislative viewpoint seems to be that reporting the incident 'as soon as reasonably possible' will also suffice. Consequently, law prescribes an upper cap of 6 (six) months for filing a complaint. However, it is imperative that the reporting must be made within the time boundaries set by law.[8] Even courts have generally opined that there should be a limitation period for filing complaints of sexual harassment.[9]

The object of putting a time limit is to ensure timely approach by the complainant and to eradicate the possibility of resurrection of any stale claims (Nirmal Kanti Chakraborti v. Vaneeta Patnaik).

The court, while examining a plea of limitation, must read the pleadings in its entirety and in the event it is found that it cannot be decided as an issue of law as it largely depends upon the facts so pleaded in the evidence in this regard to be produced, then in such case, the court should postpone the determination to the stage of final decision (Nirmal Kanti Chakraborti v. Vaneeta Patnaik).

Where, in the context of limitation, the statute provides for an outer cap, then in such case, the court can exercise its discretion within the circumference of this outer limit and cannot transgress

7 FMA No. 873/2024 (23.12.2024, Calcutta High Court).

8 It is pertinent to note that no such limitation period was prescribed under the Vishaka Guidelines.

9 *See* Swatanter Kumar v. The Indian Express Limited 207 (2014) DLT 221; Rishabh Jha v. Union of India, Writ No. 30472/2016 (21.12.2016, Allahabad High Court).

such limit even in a deserving case. See generally National Spot Exchange Limited v. Anil Kohli.[10] This judgement (although in the context of the Indian insolvency regime) is relied upon in the context of limitation under the Act in Nirmal Kanti Chakraborti v. Vaneeta Patnaik.

**The Criticism to Limitation**

While there exist various advantages of filing a complaint of sexual harassment expeditiously (the incident is fresh in the mind of the complainant, as also the witnesses; evidence does not get damaged, destroyed or escapes memory etc.) however, restricting the time period for making a complaint is also viewed as being counterproductive to the redressal. This is because the delay in making complaints may often be because the victim is, at the relevant point in time, in a vulnerable position or afraid to speak out because of various factors such as fear of reprisal, the social stigma/reprobation, lack of sufficient evidence etc. A power or status imbalance between the harasser[11] and the victim is another common reason for delay in making a complaint of sexual harassment.

In the context of criminal law, courts have observed that in sexual offences, delay in lodging an FIR may be due to a variety of reasons, including the reluctance of the victim or her family members to go to the police and complain about the incident which concerns the reputation of the victim and the honour of her family.[12]

As per the author, the outer limit of 6 (six) months prescribed for filing a complaint of sexual harassment appears to be

10 (2022) 11 SCC 761.

11 Please note that, the words accused, harasser, delinquent, perpetrator and respondent have been used synonymously or interchangeably in this chapter (and this work). Similarly, the terms aggrieved, complainant and victim have been used synonymously.

12 State of Punjab v. Gurmit Singh (1996) 2 SCC 384.

reasonable to ensure that there is no denial of justice on account of short timelines and is the adjudicatory process diluted. Simultaneously limitation will also ensure that a claim of sexual harassment is not made an endless process. It may be noted that, under the applicable criminal law, the limitation for making a complaint of sexual harassment with the police authorities is larger.[13]

**Judicial Precedents on Limitation**

Judicial precedent indicates that courts tend to adopt a liberal approach when it comes to matters of limitation for filing complaints of sexual harassment at the workplace.

In X v. the District Magistrate[14] a complaint of sexual harassment was filed by a complainant with the concerned LCC after a lapse of the limitation period prescribed under Section 9 (1) of the Act. The LCC dismissed the complaint on grounds of limitation. The matter travelled to the Delhi High Court. The Single Bench of the Delhi High Court, after examining the provisions of Section 9 of the Act, upheld the decision of the LCC to dismiss the complaint on grounds of limitation. An appeal was preferred against the said order of the Single Bench before the Division Bench of the Delhi High Court. The Division Bench however adopted a more liberal view and without getting into the merits of the matter, relegated the parties back to the LCC and permitted the complainant to file the communications/documents (which were being referred to before the High Court) before the LCC to re-consider the issue of limitation on the basis of the documents/communication.

However, a somewhat different view was taken by the Madhya Pradesh High Court in Mukesh Khampariya v. State

---

13 *See* Chapter titled 'Criminal Remedies'.

14 W.P. (C) No. 8443/2018 (13.08.2018, Delhi High Court).

of Madhya Pradesh[15] where the High Court, after examining Section 9 (1) of the Act leaned towards strict compliance with the limitation period prescribed therein.

In Vaneeta Patnaik v. State of West Bengal[16] the Calcutta High Court observed that the question of limitation is a mixed question of law and fact, and therefore, this issue should not be decided by the complaints committee at the threshold stage itself without evidence. The High Court observed that the complaints committee, at the threshold stage, should accept the allegations made in the complaint at its face value,[17] including those on the aspect of limitation.

In R Mohankrishnan v. Deputy Inspector of Police[18] the Madras High Court observed that, in so far as grave offences of sexual harassment are concerned, the same would be considered a "continuing wrong" or a "continuing misconduct" and hence computation of limitation for such offences ought to be made accordingly. The Madras High Court further observed that while computing limitation in sexual harassment cases, strict interpretation and hyper technicalities should be avoided.

In 2023, the Rajya Sabha introduced a Bill to amend the Act. One of the notable amendments proposed to the Act is the enhancement of the limitation period to 1 (one) year. The Bill has not yet become law. The Statement of Objects and Reasons of the Bill are self-explanatory and are reproduced below:

> Section 9 stipulates a limitation period of three months for filing complaints, further extendable by three months,

15 W.P. No. 21852/2018 (05.10.2023, Madhya Pradesh High Court).

16 W.P. A. No. 10583/2024 (22.05.2024, Calcutta High Court).

17 In this regard, reliance was also placed by the Calcutta High Court on the principles of the civil procedure code, 1908, more specifically Order 7 Rule 11 (d) thereof. *See generally,* Urvashiben v. Krishnakant Manuprasad Trivedi, (2019) 13 SCC 372.

18 W.P. No. 10707/2024 (11.06.2024, Madras High Court).

provided that the Internal Committee or Local Committee (as the case may be) is satisfied that the circumstances were such which prevented the woman from filing a complaint within the said period. This limitation period is inapposite since in cases involving sexual harassment, women may be so traumatized as to render filing of the complaint impossible until such time they have recouped their strength. Placing a maximum limit of six months on such complaints does great injustice to the aggrieved woman.

This Bill intends to remedy these problems by amending the Sexual Harassment of Women at Workplace (Prevention, Prohibition and Redressal) Act, 2013. It provides that the basic limitation period for filing complaints shall be fixed at one year, which shall be further extendable, without any upper limit, by the Internal Committee or Local Committee (as the case may be), upon satisfaction that the circumstances prevented the woman from filing the complaint within the limitation period

### Manner of making a complaint

The Act requires every complaint to be in writing. Where the complaint cannot be made in writing, a member of the ICC or the LCC, as the case may be, shall render all necessary assistance to the aggrieved woman for making the complaint in writing.[19] Where the woman is unable to make a complaint in writing on account of reasons such as physical or mental incapacity, death etc. then the following persons shall be entitled to make a complaint on her behalf:[20]

19 S. 9 (2) of the Act. Note that there is no provision under the Act which entitles the complaints committee to take *suo moto* action/cognizance in the matter. *But see* Office Memorandum F. No. 11013/2/2014-Estt (A-III), dated 16.07.2015, Department of Personnel & Training, Ministry of Personnel, Public Grievances and Pensions, Government of India.

20 R. 6 of the Rules.

a. Where the aggrieved woman is unable to make a complaint on account of her physical incapacity, a complaint may be filed by any of the following: (i) a relative or friend; (ii) her co-worker; (iii) an officer of the National Commission for Woman or State Woman's Commission; or (iv) any person who has knowledge of the incident, with the written consent of the aggrieved.
b. Where the aggrieved woman is unable to make a complaint on account of her mental incapacity, a complaint may be filed by any of the following: (i) a relative or friend; (ii) a special educator[21]; (iii) a qualified psychiatrist or psychologist; (iv) the guardian or authority under whose care she is receiving treatment or care; or (v) any person who has knowledge of the incident, jointly with her relative or friend or a special educator or qualified psychiatrist or psychologist, or guardian or authority under whose care she is receiving treatment or care.
c. Where the aggrieved woman, for any other reason, is unable to make a complaint, then the same may be filed by any person who has knowledge of the incident, with her written consent.
d. Where the aggrieved woman is dead, a complaint may be filed by any person who has knowledge of the incident, with the written consent of her legal heir.

No Complaint without complainant

There exists no provision under the Act which permits the making of an anonymous complaint or a third party complaint (*viz.* a complaint by a third person in the know of the incident(s) without the knowledge or consent of the complainant).[22]

This position was upheld in the case of P Govindraju v. The

21 A 'special educator' is a person trained in communication with people with special needs in a way that addresses their individual differences and needs. *See* R. 2 (f) of the Rules.

22 There exists no provision in the Act which authorises the aggrieved person to make an anonymous complaint or a complaint on a no name basis. *See generally* Parliamentary Standing Committee Report (2011), at ¶ 4.1.

Manonium Sundaranar University[23]. In this case, an inquiry under the provisions of the Act was initiated on the basis of an anonymous note and a CD received by the vice chancellor of the employer university alleging sexual harassment. The Madras High Court observed that this amounted to a violation of Section 9 (1) of the Act in as much as the inquiry was not initiated on the basis of a complaint received by the aggrieved woman but was initiated pursuant to receipt of an anonymous note.

In Sujit Baran Mandal v. Union of India[24] the ICC had entered upon an inquiry pursuant to a complaint being preferred by a colleague of the complainant. In fact, no complaint was ever lodged by the complainant herself. It was observed by court that the provisions of the Act do not provide for third-party complaints. It was further held that the action of the ICC in taking cognizance of a third party complaint was beyond its jurisdiction.

In Abraham Mathai v. State of Kerala[25] the Kerala High Court emphasised on the mandatory requirement of a written compliant for commencement of inquiry by the ICC. The High Court also indicated that the ICC does not have authority to commence a *suo moto* inquiry (*sans* a complaint from the complainant).

In Prasad Pannian v. Central University of Kerala[26] it was observed by the Kerala High Court that, in order to trigger an inquiry under the Act, the requirement for a complaint by the complainant (whether oral or written) was mandatory.

<u>Filing of Additional Complaints</u>

In Union of India v. Dilip Paul[27] a question which arose before the Supreme Court was whether a complainant could prefer

23 2020 (1) Writ LR 249.

24 2020 (1) SLJ 231 (CAT).

25 2024: Ker: 91275

26 2020 (6) KHC 687

27 2023 INSC 975.

an additional or subsequent complaint against the same accused with the complaints committee. In the said matter, a complainant filed an additional complaint against the same accused during the pendency of the first complaint. However, this second complaint was filed at an early stage itself and in fact even before the complaints committee held its first hearing in the matter. This filing of a "subsequent or additional complaint" was objected to by the accused. The Supreme Court rejected this objection of the accused on the following premise: (i) The provisions of the Act did not inhibit filing of an additional complaint with the complaints committee. (ii) The additional complaint has been preferred promptly by the complainant even before the first hearing of the committee. The Supreme Court further observed that the issue whether an additional complaint should be entertained by the complaints committee must be ascertained keeping in mind the stage of its filing (i.e. whether it was filed at an earliest point of time or whether it was filed at a later stage in order to prejudice the accused).

**Jurisdiction of complaints committee**

In the case of a complaint of sexual harassment, the general rule is that the complaints committee of the organization to which the victim and the harasser belong, shall be entitled to make an inquiry into the said complaint. Normally, there exists no difficulty in cases where both the parties belong to the same workplace or organisation.

However, there may be times where the complainant and the harasser do not belong to the same workplace. In cases where the parties belong to different workplaces, the work place where the incident of sexual harassment took place, would have jurisdiction over the matter.[28] However, there may be practical difficulties where the harasser does not belong to the workplace

28 *See* Parliamentary Standing Committee Report (2011), at ¶ 6.16.

where the incident of sexual harassment took place, primarily because the complaints committee or the victim's organisation may not have any control over the harasser. In such cases, in the view of the author, the following steps may be adopted:

i. The complaints committees and the organisations of the complainant and the harasser may work *in tandem* for a seamless inquiry process and effective implementation of the recommendations of the committee (which makes the adjudication).
ii. Further, a criminal complaint (as envisaged under Section 19 (h) of the Act) may also be filed against the harasser.

Below is a tabulation of the committees which would have jurisdiction in different situations.

| S. No. | Place of occurrence of Harassment | Committee having jurisdiction | Comments |
|---|---|---|---|
| 1. | Harassment by another co-employee (whether senior, subordinate or contemporary) at the workplace of the victim regardless of the working location of the accused | ICC of the workplace of the victim | Additionally, a criminal complaint (as contemplated under S. 19 (g) of the Act) may also be made |
| 2. | Harassment by a co-employee at a place visited by the victim during the course of her employment | ICC of the workplace of the victim | - Do - |
| 3. | Harassment by an outsider at the workplace of the victim | ICC of the workplace of the victim | - Do - |
| 4. | Harassment by an outsider at his workplace when the victim is present at his workplace in connection with her employment | ICC of the workplace of the accused | - Do - |
| 5. | Harassment by an Employer | The LCC which has jurisdiction over the workplace of the Employer. | - Do - |

- In case the workplace having jurisdiction employs less than 10 (ten) people then the complaint shall be adjudicated by the relevant LCC.[29]
- As mentioned above, in all cases of sexual harassment, apart from initiation of a departmental inquiry with the concerned complaints committee, the victim possesses a concurrent remedy of invoking criminal action.[30]

In Dr. Sohail Malik v. Union of India[31] a submission was made by the accused before the Delhi High Court that the Act does not extend to situations where the complainant and the accused belong to different organizations or to different employers. It was further argued that the Act does not contemplate any remedy or redress if the harassment is perpetrated by a person belonging to a different department/organisation and is hence not subject to the disciplinary control of the organisation where the complainant is working. The Delhi High Court rejected these arguments and observed that there is nothing in the Act, which limits its scope only to cases where the women employee is sexually harassed by another employee working in her own office. The court observed that the Act applied even where the accused worked elsewhere. The Delhi High Court made the following further observations in this regard:

a. The provisions of the Act do not insulate, from action thereunder, men who sexually harass women in offices other than those in which they are themselves working.
b. There is nothing in the Act which would restrict its application only to cases where the accused and the complainant are part of the same department/organization.

29 For more, *see* chapter titled 'Complaints Committee'.

30 For more, *see* chapter titled 'Criminal Remedies'.

31 W.P. (C) No. 8624/2023 (30.06.2023, Delhi High Court).

c. The expression "in accordance with service rules applicable to the Respondent" in Section 11 (1) of the Act itself indicates that the statute has kept in mind the possibility where the accused may be covered by service rules which are not those which apply to the complainant or to the department that the complainant is working.
d. A similar view can also be made in accordance with Section 13 (3) (i) of the Act, which requires the ICC, on its finding that the complaint of sexual harassment has been proved, to recommend, to the employer or the district officer "to take action for sexual harassment as a misconduct in accordance with the service rules applicable to the Respondent". This provision caters to a situation in which the Respondent is governed by independent service rules.
e. The definition of the expression "employer" used in Section 2 (g) of the Act is wide and general in nature, and does not, in any manner, limit its scope only to the organisation of the employee who complains of sexual harassment.
f. The rule of purposive construction/interpretation is to be adopted while interpreting the provisions of the Act.
g. Under Section 13 (1) of the Act, the employer (of the ICC which has inquired into the matter and made the report thereon) can forward the findings of the ICC to the employer who has disciplinary control over the accused, to take action on the basis thereof.

## Conciliation

The complaints committee may, before initiating an inquiry and at the written request of the aggrieved woman, take steps to settle the matter between her and the accused through conciliation.[32]

### Conciliation: The Concept

Conciliation is a voluntary and confidential process which, if initiated by the complainant, involves attempts at arriving at an amicable resolution between the parties and bringing a

32 S. 10 (1) of the Act.

closure to the matter. The goal of conciliation is not fact-finding. Its principal object is to discuss the allegations and arrive at an agreement that is satisfactory to all parties. Two points are important here. One, conciliation can be resorted to only at the behest of the complainant. Two, monetary settlement cannot be made a basis of the conciliation.[33]

### Objective of Conciliation

Conciliation is typically an informal procedure which focuses on resolution and sustenance of a working relationship rather than substantiation of a complaint. Conciliation may be apt where the allegations are of a less serious nature or where the complainant is not interested in an inquiry (against the harasser) as such and simply wants the offending behaviour to cease.

In some situations (for instance, where the misconduct is mild or where the perpetrator is apologetic for his behaviour) the victim may simply want a 'closure' instead of a 'punishment' for the perpetrator. This may be achieved through the informal procedure of conciliation, which can bring about a swift and early settlement between the parties.

However, in the view of the author, such procedures are not recommended where the allegations of misconduct are serious in nature.

### Conciliation Procedure

Conciliation can be invoked only if requested for by the complainant. In P Govindraju v. The Manomanium Sundaranar University[34] it was observed by the Madras High Court that an accused cannot demand initiation of conciliation proceedings,

---

33 S. 10 (1) *proviso* of the Act. Such move to proscribe monetary settlement from the conciliation process appears to have been made to prevent trivialisation of the offence of sexual harassment and misuse of the conciliation mechanism.

34 2020 (1) Writ LR 249.

as a matter of right. Conciliation could be ordered only when a request was made in this regard from the complainant.

In Kali Charna Sabat v. Union of India[35], the Madhya Pradesh High Court, while examining Section 10 of the Act, appears to suggest that Section 10 imposes an obligation on the complaints committee to first try to settle the matter by way of conciliation, and to proceed with the inquiry only if the conciliation fails. In the view of the author, a complaint committee's obligation to conciliate the matter should arise only if a request is received in this regard from the complainant and not in any other circumstances.

Where a settlement is arrived at between the parties, the ICC or the LCC, as the case may be, shall record the settlement and provide the same to the employer or the district officer to take necessary action.[36] Copies of the settlement, as recorded, shall also be supplied to the aggrieved woman and the accused. Once a settlement has been arrived at, no further inquiry shall be conducted in the matter[37], except where the accused breaches any term or condition of the settlement.[38]

If the process of conciliation does not yield any satisfactory result or outcome, or if the misconduct continues unabated, then in such case, the formal adjudicatory procedure as envisaged under the Act must be resorted to.

As per the author, conciliation should ideally be resorted to only where the offence is minor in nature. However, (unlike various other foreign jurisdictions) the Act does not carve out a distinction between major and minor offences. Therefore, the instrumentality of conciliation must be resorted to with abundant caution.

35 W.P. No. 10021/2024 (08.11.2024, Madhya Pradesh High Court, Jabalpur Bench)

36 S. 10 (2) of the Act.

37 S. 10 (3) of the Act.

38 S. 11 (1) of the Act.

## Benefits of Conciliation

Some benefits of conciliation are as follows:

a. It is a voluntary and confidential process.
b. It avoids lengthy and unnecessary litigation.
c. It may also help parties in identifying ways to repair a working relationship.
d. It presents an opportunity to the parties to resolve the case informally and amicably. It often helps in removing any animosity surrounding the matter.
e. An investigation in the matter can still be made if the accused breaches any term or condition of the settlement arrived at.

## Time Limit for invoking Conciliation

No time limits are prescribed under the Act for invoking the conciliation process. Hence, conciliation can be resorted to by the complainant at any time prior to the conclusion of the inquiry by the complaints committee.

## The Criticism of Conciliation

The instrumentality of conciliation has been a subject matter of much criticism in the past. The Verma Committee Report was not in favour of introducing conciliation related provisions in the Act. The relevant excerpt of the Verma Committee Report in this regard is as follows:

> We note that Section 10(1) of the Sexual Harassment Bill, 2012 stipulates that on receipt of complaint of sexual harassment, conciliation must be attempted between the complainant and respondent. This is in violation of the mandate prescribed by the Supreme Court in Vishakha, which was a direction to the State 'to ensure a safe workplace/educational institution for women'. In this

> context, we think that the attempts to get justice cannot be muscled by attempts at conciliation.
>
> There are certain areas, such as contractual matters where there could be conciliation, but in matters of harassment and humiliation of women an attempt to compromise the same is indeed yet another way in which the dignity of women is undermined. We are in agreement with the objections raised by many women's organisations that the said provision actually shows very little regard for the dignity of women. We think that Section 10(1) of the Bill, in so far as it proposes conciliation as a first step, must be deleted.

In view of the author, another point of criticism could be the potential of this mechanism being used as a tool or device for unscrupulous organizations or parties who, in a bid to protect their image and reputation may attempt to cajole an unassuming victim to settle the matter.

An Observation

According to the author, while conciliation may be an acceptable procedure in case of minor offences, it should certainly not be made applicable to situations where the offence is a major one. This is because in case of a successful conciliation, the accused would normally be let off by tendering a simple apology or other mild punishment. Adopting a similar recourse in case of intense offences may not prove to be a deterrent for the offender. This surely would be antithetical to the purpose and objective in the Act. This mechanism, if inappropriately applied, may be prove to be detrimental to the interests of the victim(s).

Monetary Compensation: No Basis for Settlement

The Act provides that monetary compensation cannot be made a basis of a settlement between the parties. The element of monetary settlement appears to have been deliberately left out of the conciliatory process for the following reasons:[39]

a. It may result in creation of a situation where punishments would be bargained with money.
b. Money may not be adequate redressal for loss of dignity suffered by a victim of sexual harassment.
c. A 'monetary settlement' would trivialise a grave act of sexual harassment.

Proposal for Removal of Conciliation

In 2023, the Rajya Sabha introduced a Bill to amend the Act. One of the notable amendments proposed to the Act is the removal of the concept of conciliation. The Bill is not yet law. The Statement and Objects of the Bill in this regard are self-explanatory and are reproduced below for ready reference.

> Section 10 provides the aggrieved woman with the option of settling the complaint through conciliation. This provision is highly problematic since it fails to take into account the possibility of influencing, coercing, pressuring or intimidating the complainant to arrive at a settlement. While there are certain areas (such as contractual matters) where conciliation may be fruitful, an attempt to reach a compromise in matters of sexual harassment of women greatly undermines the dignity of women.

## The Inquiry Process

General Rule: Upon receipt of a complaint of sexual harassment by the harasser's organisation, the complaints committee shall proceed to make an inquiry into the complaint in accordance with the service rules applicable to the harasser, and where no such rules exist, in the manner prescribed.

39 *See* Parliamentary Standing Committee Report (2011), at ¶ 13.5 & 13.6.

Domestic Workers: In case of a domestic worker, the LCC shall, if a *prima facie* case exists, forward to the police, within a period of 7 (seven) days, for initiation of criminal action.[40]

Breach of Settlement: Where the aggrieved woman informs the complaints committee that any term or condition of the settlement arrived at in conciliation has not been complied with by the harasser, the complaints committee shall proceed to make an inquiry into the complaint or, as the case may be, forward the complaint to the police.[41]

## Pre-examination of complaint

In Debdulal Maity v. National Insurance Company Limited[42] the Calcutta High Court considered the question as to whether the complaints committee, upon receipt of a complaint of sexual harassment, is duty bound to mechanically proceed with an inquiry without looking into the contents of the complaint and applying its mind or whether, at this stage, the complaints committee is required to apply its mind on the contents of the complaint as well. The court, held as follows:

a. The scheme of the Act does not preclude a complaints committee in receipt of the complaint to apply its mind to arrive at a *prima facie* finding as to whether the offence complained of constitutes 'sexual harassment' under the Act or whether an incident of 'sexual harassment' has occurred in the workplace and thereafter decide the best course available *viz.* whether to conciliate (subject to a written request of the complainant) or proceed with an inquiry under the Act.[43]

---

40 S. 11 (1) of the Act. *See also* Chapter titled 'Criminal Remedies'.

41 S. 11 (1) *First Proviso* of the Act.

42 W.P. No. 728/2014 (07.08.2014, Calcutta High Court).

43 An analogy may be drawn with the provisions of Order 7 Rule 11 of the Civil Procedure Code, 1908 which entitles the court to dismiss the suit at the very outset for failing to disclose a valid cause of action. *See* T. Arivandandam v. T.V. Satyapal AIR 1977 SC 2421; Clarinda D'Souza v Mccann Erickson India Limited (2003) 4 Bom CR 292.

b. For a complaints committee to conciliate, it has to apply its mind as to the nature of the complaint and the gravity of the offence.

In Institute of Hotel Management Catering Technology and Applied Nutrition v. Suddhasil Dey,[44] the Bombay High Court observed that if a complaint of sexual harassment is, *prima facie*, found to have substance and is worthy of being inquired into, then in such case the committee shall call upon the accused and explain to him what the allegations against him are; and thereafter proceed with the inquiry process. It therefore appears that there exists an inherent requirement for the ICC to arrive at a *prima facie* assessment as to the substance of the complaint made before it by the victim.

From the above it appears to the author that despite a written request of the complainant (for conciliation), in case the complaints committee is of the view that the offence (complained of) is grave and/or needs to be inquired into, then in such case, it may proceed with an inquiry regardless.

<u>Lodging of Complaint: Mandatory for ICC Action</u>

A written complaint is a mandatory pre-requisite for conduct of an inquiry by the ICC. While an oral complaint can be made to any member of the ICC (if the complainant is not in a position to give a complaint in writing), however, the need for a complaint for conducting an inquiry is mandatory.[45] The Act does not permit any *suo moto* action or inquiry by the ICC.[46]

44 WPCR 137/2019 (13.03.2020, Bombay High Court).

45 *See* Prasad Pannian v. Central University of Kerala (2020) 6 KHC 687 & Abraham Mathai v. State of Kerala 2024: Ker: 91275

46 *See* Girish Rameshchandra Soni v. State of Gujarat, Special Civil Application No. 11804/2017 (15.09.2017, Gujarat High Court).

## The Inquiry Mechanism

Inquiry proceedings can be initiated by the ICC only after receipt of the complaint from the complainant (and not earlier). In Manomanium Sunderanar University v. P Govinndraju[47] the Madras High Court observed that an inquiry commenced by the ICC even prior to receipt of the complaint from the complainant should be regarded as unsustainable and bad in law.

The Sexual Harassment Rules of 2013 (Rules) prescribe the manner in which an inquiry for a complaint of sexual harassment should be carried out.[48] Summarised below is such procedure.

a. The complainant shall submit to the complaints committee 6 (six) copies of the complaint along with supporting documents and the names and addresses of the witnesses (collectively "**Complaint**").
b. On receipt of the complaint, the complaints committee shall send 1 (one) copy of the same to the Respondent within a period of 7 (seven) working days.[49]

47 WA (MD) No. 428/2020 (20.04.2022, Madras High Court, Madurai Bench).

48 Such procedure shall apply only when: (i) no service rules exist with respect to the concerned workplace; or (ii) service rules exist for the workplace but are silent or incomprehensive. The general law is that service rules, wherever applicable, shall hold the field. Sardar Vallabhbhai National Institute of Technology v. Ranjit Roy L.P.A No. 1349-50/2015 (22.03.2016, Gujarat High Court). Any gaps in the service rules can be filled up by drawing upon the provisions of the Act and the Rules. In case of conflict the service rules shall prevail.

49 Notice to the opposite party is the first and an important step in the adjudicatory process. Any proceedings taken without notice would violate the principles of natural justice. It is a *sine qua non* of a fair hearing. The components of a fair hearing are as follows: (i) Provision of all material which the complainant wishes to produce or rely on during the adjudication process; (ii) An opportunity to the opposite party to rebut the allegations and such material. Separately, note that failure to furnish copies of documents such as the complaint and statements recorded during investigation amounts to a violation of Article 311 (2) of the Constitution of India. *See also* The Managing Director, HDFC Standard Life Insurance Company Ltd v. Suresh Babu, 2022 LR 488, wherein, *inter alia,* it was observed that non-furnishing a copy of the complaint to the accused; and non-furnishing a copy of the findings of the ICC to the accused, would vitiate the inquiry process under the Act.
*But see* Bhagwan Chand Saxena v. Export Inspection Council of India W.P. (C) No. 11353/2005 (19.09.2013, Delhi High Court) which appears to suggest that documents which are not relied upon by the committee need not be supplied to the delinquent.

c. The Respondent shall file his reply to the complaint along with his list of documents, names and addresses of witnesses, within a maximum period of 10 (ten) working days from the date of receipt of the complaint.

d. The complaints committee shall make an inquiry in accordance with the principles of natural justice.[50]

e. The parties are not allowed to bring in any legal practitioner to represent them in their case at any stage of the proceedings before the complaints committee.[51]

f. Quorum: In conducting the inquiry, a minimum of 3 (three) members of the complaints committee, including the Presiding Officer or the Chairperson, as the case may be, shall be present.

g. The inquiry shall be completed within a period of 90 (ninety) days.[52]

As is evident from the above, with certain safeguards, the complaints committee is basically the master of its procedure. While ensuring that the principles of natural justice are upheld

50 The principles of natural justice are not inflexible and may differ in different circumstances. *See generally* Hira Nath Mishra v. The Principal, Rajendra Medical College (1973) II LLJ 111 (SC); Dev Dutt v. Union of India 2008 (8) SCC 725.

51 Generally, every litigant has a right to counsel. Right to counsel is the rule and the prohibition of counsel is an exception, which exception must arise from statute or other exceptional circumstances. *Inter alia,* the following statues contain similar proscriptions: (i) The Industrial Disputes Act 1947; (ii) The Banking Ombudsman Scheme 2006. Under the provisions of the Industrial Disputes Act 1947, a legal practitioner is restrained from representing any party in the labour court without the consent of the other party and the permission of the court. Under the Banking Ombudsman Scheme 2006, no party has a right of legal representation before the Banking Ombudsman. There exist certain advantages of not having legal representation: (i) it saves costs for the parties thereby making the process an inexpensive one; (ii) it creates parity in the sense that the poor litigants are protected from the richer ones; and (iii) it reduces technicalities from the adjudicatory process. Additionally, a cross examination by a legal mind may have the result of muzzling the complainant which may preclude her for deposing freely before the committee. However, notwithstanding the above, under the Act, there appears to be no embargo in law for the employer to nominate an officer of the organisation to provide advice and assistance to the parties.

52 S. 11 (4) of the Act. This provision seems to be directory, since no penalty appears to have been envisaged in the Act for its violation. However, prolonging such investigations would only result in rendering protection to the delinquent.

and maintained, the inquiry can be conducted with little formality and technicalities; and with maximum expedition.

However, at the same time, it is imperative for the ICC to comply with the basic procedures of inquiry set out herein above. Any failure of the ICC in this regard may result in setting aside of the inquiry report; an ordering of a fresh inquiry.[53]

A settlement cannot be thrust upon the complainant. It would be illegal for the ICC to drop proceedings on the basis of a settlement which has not been approved by the complainant. (Sarbajaya Banerjee v. The State of West Bengal).[54]

After the ICC concludes its inquiry and submits its findings, then in such case, the disciplinary authority need not commence a fresh inquiry. It can proceed further on the basis of the ICC report (G. Kishor Kumar v. The Director of Medical and Rural Health Services).[55]

### Discrete inquiry by ICC

In A. Manimekalan v. The Registrar[56] upon receipt of a complaint of sexual harassment, a discrete inquiry was carried out by the ICC without following the procedures for inquiry/ investigation provided under the provisions of the Act and the Rules (including Sections 11, 12, 13 of the Act & Rule 7 of the Rules). The Madras High Court observed that the holding of such discrete inquiry by the ICC was impermissible in nature. It was further observed by the High Court that failure on the part of the ICC to adhere to the prescribed procedures under the Act was violative of principles of natural justice. Consequently, the Madras High Court set aside the report of the ICC.

---

53 *See generally* Aditi Bramta v. State of Himachal Pradesh, C.W.P. No. 1628/2020 (09.07.2020, Himachal Pradesh High Court).

54 WPA No. 13588/2024 (13.02.2025, Calcutta High Court).

55 2024: MHC: 3629

56 2023 Writ LR 201.

Validity of ICC Report based only on pleadings of parties

In Kali Charna Sabat v. Union of India[57] the ICC prepared its report only on the basis of the complaint of the complainant and the reply filed by the accused. The High Court set aside this ICC report for the reason that it failed to comply with the principles of natural justice. The High Court observed that an inquiry conducted by the ICC should be a full-fledged inquiry complying with principles of natural justice. It was observed that in the absence of an opportunity to the parties to appear before the committee, to lead evidence and to cross examine, the inquiry process would remain incomplete and result in an improper ICC report.

ICC not to prevent cross examination

Typically, in an inquiry, an ICC cannot deprive the delinquent from cross examining the witnesses or shield the witnesses from cross examination except where there exist proper reasons for doing so. The general rule is that when prejudicial statements are made, then they cannot be used against any person without giving him an opportunity to act and contradict. The ICC is required to verify the capability of the complainant and the witnesses to depose before it fearlessly and without any intimidation. If the ICC, for any good reason, is of the opinion that the complainant may not be able to withstand the cross examination, then in such case, the ICC may adopt any other measure (interrogatories etc.) to ensure that the rights of representation of the accused are not compromised in any manner.[58]

However, if the accused declines to avail the opportunity of cross-examination, then in such case, he may not be later be permitted to challenge the ICC report by arguing that principles

57 W.P. No. 10021/2024 (08.11.2024, Madhya Pradesh High Court, Jabalpur Bench)

58 *See generally* Vijay Gajanan Mane v. Union of India, MANU/CA/1194/2024

of natural justice are violated in as much as an opportunity of cross-examination has been denied to him.[59]

In Dharampal Satyapal Limited v. Deputy Commission of Central Excise[60] the Supreme Court observed that applicability of principles of natural justice is not dependent on any statutory provision. These principles must be mandatorily applied irrespective of the fact as to whether there is any statutory provision or not.

In Commissioner of Police v. Sant Ram[61] the Delhi High Court observed that principles of natural justice must be complied with under any and all circumstances. In this matter, the complaints committee completed an inquiry process in haste and declared the accused is guilty without conducting the statutorily prescribed departmental inquiry. The complaints committee proceeded on the assumption that since the accused is police personnel, the complainant needed to be protected and further the witnesses would not come forward to depose against him in a regular inquiry. The Delhi High Court observed that even though the charges against the accused are very serious and the interests of the complainant deserved to be protected, it would not automatically imply that principles of natural justice as also the provisions of the Act could be given a complete go by based on such presumptions. The Delhi High Court set aside the inquiry.

Inquiry as per Service Rules

Section 13 of the Act & Rule 7 and 9 of the SH Rules provide that where certain service rules are applicable to the employer in question, then in such case the inquiry procedures must be carried out in the manner prescribed under such service rules.

59 *See generally* Vijay Gajanan Mane v. Union of India, MANU/CA/1194/2024

60 (2015) 8 SCC 519.

61 W.P (C) No. 5562/2024 (23.04.2024, Delhi High Court).

Typically, when the ICC returns a finding of guilt against the accused, then in such case, the disciplinary authority of the employer is required to conduct disciplinary proceedings before imposing any penalty on the accused. However, the mode and modality of conduct of such disciplinary proceedings are entirely based on the concerned service rules of the employer organisation.

In Debjani Sengupta v. The Institute of Cost Accountants of India and Others[62] the Calcutta High Court had the occasion to examine the interplay between the procedures of inquiry by an ICC of an organisation into a complaint of sexual harassment, on the one hand, and the service rules (applicable to the organisation), on the other hand, for the purposes of disciplinary action (in the context of imposition of a major penalty). The Calcutta High Court, after analysing the provisions of the Act, the Rules and the relevant service rules, made the following pertinent observations:

a. Where service rules exist, the report of the ICC is to be considered a fact-finding report or a preliminary report with regard to allegations of sexual harassment; and the employer is then bound to proceed under the service rules before imposing any major penalty on the accused.
b. On the basis of the recommendations made by the ICC, the employer is mandated to initiate disciplinary proceedings in accordance with the service rules. Only in cases where no service rules exist, is the ICC empowered to recommend punishment, but in all cases where service rules exist, the disciplinary authority is required to proceed by initiating disciplinary proceedings before imposing any major penalty.
c. Once the charge of sexual harassment is proved by the ICC, the basis for proceeding against the accused employee for committing

62 W.P. No. 4806 (W)/2019 (03.05.2019, Calcutta High Court).

the misconduct of sexual harassment already exists. In other words, with the findings of the ICC, the ground for inquiring into the truth of any imputation of misconduct or misbehaviour would already be in existence.

In Debjani Sengupta v. The Institute of Cost Accountants of India[63] in further litigation between the parties the High Court further clarified that the employer, on the recommendation of the ICC, was mandated to initiate disciplinary proceedings in terms of the service rules of the employee and only in cases where there were no service rules, the ICC was empowered to recommend punishment. Reliance was also placed by the High Court on Section 28 of the Act to indicate that the Act did not override the service rules. It was held that once a charge of sexual harassment was proved before the ICC, the basis of proceeding against the accused for committing the misconduct of sexual harassment had been established. The findings of the ICC would be the charges and the foundation of misconduct, mandating the employer to proceed in accordance with the service rules.

In Nisha Priya Bhatia v. Union of India[64] the Supreme Court of India emphasised that an inquiry into a complaint of sexual harassment under the Act and a disciplinary inquiry under the service rules are two separate inquiries conducted under two separate dispensations, and are not to be considered as one cohesive process. The Supreme Court went on to observe that in matters of departmental enquiries, prosecution, penalties, proceedings, action on inquiry report, appeals *et cetera* in connection with the conduct of the employee, the relevant service rules operate as a self-contained code for departmental action.

Succinctly speaking, the Supreme Court laid down the law as follows: (i) the inquiry under the Act constitutes a separate

63 RVW 128/2019 (04.07.2023, Calcutta High Court).

64 Civil Appeal No. 2365/2020 (24.04.2020, Supreme Court of India).

inquiry of a fact-finding nature; (ii) post conduct of such fact-finding inquiry by the concerned committee, the matter goes before the department for a departmental inquiry under the relevant departmental rules; (iii) accordingly thereafter action should follow.

The relevant excerpt of the aforesaid judgement of the Supreme Court is reproduced below:

> "95. Be that as it may, in our opinion, the Petitioner seems to have confused two separate inquiries conducted under two separate dispensations as one cohesive process. The legal machinery to deal with the complaints of sexual harassment at workplace is well delineated by the enactment of The Sexual Harassment of Women at Workplace Act, 2013 (hereinafter "2013 Act") and the Rules framed there under. There can be no departure whatsoever from the procedure prescribed under the 2013 Act and Sexual Harassment of Women at Workplace (Prevention, Prohibition and Redressal) Rules, 2013 (for short, "the 2013 Rules"), either in matters of complaint or of inquiry there under. The sanctity of such procedure stands undisputed. The inquiry under the 2013 Act is a separate inquiry of a fact-finding nature. Post the conduct of a fact-finding inquiry under the 2013 Act, the matter goes before the department for a departmental inquiry under the relevant departmental Rules [CCS (CCA) Rules in the present case] and accordingly, action follows. The said departmental inquiry is in the nature of an in-house mechanism wherein the participants are restricted and concerns of locus are strict and precise. The ambit of such inquiry is strictly confined between the delinquent employee and the concerned department having due regard to confidentiality of the procedure. The two inquiries cannot be mixed up with each other and similar procedural

> standards cannot be prescribed for both. In matters of departmental inquiries, prosecution, penalties, proceedings, action on inquiry report, appeals etc. in connection with the conduct of the government servants, the CCS (CCA) Rules operate as a self-contained code for any departmental action and unless an existing Rule is challenged before this Court on permissible grounds, we think, it is unnecessary for this Court to dilate any further."

It is however relevant to point out that the judgement of Nisha Priya Bhatia (above) related to pre- 2013 Act era (when the Vishaka guidelines were in effect). However, the Bombay High Court in Laxman B Parmand v. Nuclear Power Corporation of India Ltd[65] after examining the judgement of Nisha Priya Bhatia, applied its principles in the context of the Act as well.

Therefore, in the view of the author, on a harmonious application of the above judgment with the Act, once the ICC/LCC arrives at a finding of guilt in a complaint of sexual harassment, then in such case, the departmental inquiry in accordance with service rules would be required to be made. However such departmental inquiry would be limited to proceedings in connection with the penalty to be levied.

Service Rules are Mandatory

In Manomanium Sunderanar University v. P Govinndraju[66] the Madras High Court held that in cases where there existed service rules for an organization, the same were also required to be complied with. Mere inquiry by the ICC (under the provisions of the Act) may not suffice the purpose. The departmental inquiry as per the service rules should also be conducted.

65 W.P. No. 9445/2019 (21.04.2022, Bombay High Court).

66 W.A. (MD) No. 428/2020 (20.04.2022, Madras High Court, Madurai Bench).

In Pradip Mandal v. Metal Scrap Trade Corporation Limited[67] a question which arose before the Calcutta High Court was whether in case of a complaint of sexual harassment, the disciplinary authority of the employer organisation had to initiate a fresh inquiry or could it take disciplinary action by treating the ICCs report to be the report of the inquiring authority. The court, amongst other things, observed that a complaint of sexual harassment was inquired into by the ICC (as per the Act) whereas the disciplinary action is taken under the service rules. In the facts of that matter, the High Court observed that disciplinary action would have to start by treating the ICC report as the inquiry report under the relevant service rules and thereafter proceed in accordance with the said service rules before inflicting punishment upon the delinquent.

### Authority of Employer to order fresh inquiry

In Mukesh Khampariya v. State of Madhya Pradesh[68] after conclusion of the inquiry by the ICC, the police headquarters (which was the employer therein) ordered another inquiry into the matter. This order of fresh inquiry was brought into question before the Madhya Pradesh High Court. The Madhya Pradesh High Court examined the provisions of the Act and observed that there existed no enabling provision under the Act to conduct any further inquiry at the direction of the police headquarters. It was observed that in the absence of showing any source of power to the employer to pass such orders/directions, the order of the police headquarters was bad in law.

### Legal Representation

While the courts have upheld the bar on legal representation and held that lawyers should not be permitted to defend any charges

67 W.P.A. No. 888/2020 (19.05.2022, Calcutta High Court).

68 W.P. No. 21852/2018 (05.10.2023, Madhya Pradesh High Court).

during the course of inquiry by a complaint committee, however, in certain instances courts have permitted the parties to obtain the services of a defence assistant (such as a retired employee), especially in matters relating to examination of witnesses.[69]

In Johney Reberio v. Union of India[70] the accused sought to be represented in the inquiry proceedings of the ICC by a person of legal background. The Delhi High Court, while examining Rule 7 (6) of the Rules, observed that its intent was to disallow a legal practitioner from representing the parties at any stage of the proceedings before the ICC. In fact, the High Court observed that the expression "legal practitioner" should not be given a restricted meaning. In other words this expression should not only include "advocates" registered under the provisions of the Advocates Act, 1961 but even law graduates. The High Court concluded that the parties, in ICC proceedings, cannot be represented either through advocates or even by a next friend.

Fair Trail

The procedure prescribed in the Act should ordinarily be followed in letter and spirit. The departmental inquiry should be fair and in compliance with the principles of natural justice. Incumbents of the complaints committee must have no nexus with the parties concerned. The investigative and determinative process should be shorn of favouritism, prejudice or bias.[71]

The parties (as well as the witnesses) should be allowed to make statements freely and without fear. The Committee's endeavour should not be to needlessly exculpate or condemn the

69 *See generally,* M. Sabesh Manikandan v. The Director of Collegiate Education, W.P. (MD) No. 7922/2015 (16.10.2020, Madras High Court, Madurai Bench)..

70 W.P. (C) No. 14547/2022 (14.10.2022, Delhi High Court).

71 Ordinarily, incidents of bias must be reported to the employer who may take appropriate action thereon. Mere acquaintance of any member of the complaints committee with the accused may not be sufficient to raise a plea of bias. *See* Dr. Kasthurba A.K v. National Institute of Technology W.P. (C) No. 25846/2015 (28.09.2015, Kerala High Court).

perpetrator. No assumptions about innocence or guilt should be made prior to conclusion of the investigative process.[72] Not only should the perpetrator have a fair opportunity to repudiate the allegations levelled against him but also the complainant should be satisfied that the investigation was fair.

Right to access official records

During the course of the inquiry, parties may seek official records of the organization in order to substantiate or defend their case (such as employment records, appraisal or performance reports, attendance records, camera footage etc.). In this regard, it may be noted that the right of the parties to access official records is not unlimited and it is open to the employer to deny such access if in its view it contains other sensitive information or that it is not desirable in the public interest to allow such access. The grant of official records should be the rule and their denial, an exception. Denial of official records should be spare.[73]

Standard of Proof

A moot question which arises for consideration is 'what is the standard of proof with which a claim of sexual harassment must be weighed by the complaints committee during the course of inquiry'. The answer is as follows: In departmental inquires, a complainant must show that, on a 'balance of probabilities', there appears to have been a contravention of the provisions of the Act. Put differently, this means that a complainant must gather sufficient evidence to show that the alleged conduct 'more likely than not' took place, and that the conduct qualified to be sexual harassment within the meaning of the Act. This burden of

72 *See generally* Additional District and Sessions Judge v. Registrar General, High Court of Madhya Pradesh (2015) 4 SCC 91.

73 *See generally* Archana Sharma v. Geological Survey of India, CIC/YA/A/2016/000059 (01.07.2016, Central Information Commission).

proof for establishing harassment in departmental proceedings is not as strong or stringent as the 'beyond a reasonable doubt' standard required for establishing guilt in criminal matters.

## Right of Representation and Supply of Records

The parties shall, during the course of inquiry, be given an opportunity of being heard and a complete copy of the complaint shall be made available to them so as to enable them to make a representation before the complaints committee.[74] However, mere supply of the complaint without supplying copies of all annexures/attachments may not serve the purpose.[75]

The purpose behind giving to an accused a right of representation is to enable him to satisfy the complaints committee that he is innocent of the allegations made against him. The accused should get a fair opportunity to challenge, explain and controvert the allegations made against him in the complaint.

## Ex Parte Decision

The complaints committee shall have the right to terminate the inquiry proceedings or to give an *ex-parte* decision[76] if the complainant or the accused fail, without sufficient cause, to present themselves for 3 (three) consecutive hearings. However, such an order may not be passed by the complaints committee without giving a prior written notice of 15 (fifteen) days to the party concerned.[77] The legislature clearly intends that wilful abstention of the parties from the committee proceedings needs to be viewed seriously and consequences (such as ex-

---

74 S. 11 (1) *Second Proviso* of the Act.

75 *See* Prof. Bidyug Chakraborty v. Delhi University W.P. (C) No. 8226/2007 (29.05.2009, Delhi High Court).

76 The term 'ex-parte' order generally refers to orders granted on the request of and for the benefit of one party only in the absence of the other party.

77 R. 7 (5) of the Rules.

parte orders) should follow.[78] In fact, once a charged officer is correctly proceeded *ex-parte*, thereafter, he may not be able to subsequently challenge the proceedings on the grounds of unfairness or incompleteness.[79]

Powers of Civil Court

During the course of the inquiry, a complaints committee may require information/documents of diverse nature for the purpose of better discharge of its functions. Under the Act, for the purpose of making an inquiry, the complaints committee has been vested with the same powers as are vested in a civil court under the Code of Civil Procedure, 1908 (CPC) in respect of the following matters:[80]

a. summoning and enforcing the attendance of any person and examining him on oath[81];
b. requiring the discovery and production of documents;
c. any other matters which may be prescribed.

Hence, the complaints committee possess trappings of a civil court for the purpose of inquiring into a complaint of sexual harassment.

It may be noted that the Verma Committee Report was not in favour of vesting the complaints committee with powers of a civil court. The Report stated as follows:

---

78 *See generally* Bhagwan Chand Saxena v. Export Inspection Council of India W.P. (C) No. 11353/2005 (19.09.2013, Delhi High Court).

79 *See* Major U.R. Bhatt v. Union of India AIR 1962 SC 1344.

80 S. 11 (3) of the Act. *See also* Reshma MG v. Union of India, O.A. No. 180/00722 of 2014 (19.02.2016, Central Administrative Tribunal, Ernakulam).

81 Under Indian law, a civil court can enforce its summons under Order XVI of the Civil Procedure Code, 1908 by use of sanctions such as issuing warrants of arrest, ordering furnishing of security for attendance etc.

As far as Section 11(ii) is concerned, which has enabled the internal complaints committee to be given powers of a civil court for summoning discovery and production of documents is concerned, this amounts to colourable legislation because powers of courts cannot be simply conferred upon domestic committees, particularly when the composition of the internal committee does not have any legal background.

## General Principles regarding Inquiry

In Syndicate Bank v. Venkatesh Gururao Kurati[82] the Supreme Court made the following observations as regards procedure of an inquiry including aspects relating to supply of documents to the delinquent, cross examination of the parties etc.:

> ....In our view, non-supply of documents on which the enquiry officer does not rely during the course of enquiry does not create any prejudice to the delinquent. It is only those documents, which are relied upon by the enquiry officer to arrive at his conclusion, the non-supply of which would cause prejudice, being violative of principles of natural justice. Even then, the non-supply of those documents prejudice the case of the delinquent officer must be established by the delinquent officer. It is well-settled law that the doctrine of principles of natural justice are not embodied rules. It cannot be put in a straitjacket formula. It depends upon the facts and circumstances of each case. To sustain the allegation of violation of principles of natural justice, one must establish that prejudice has been caused to him for non-observance of principles of natural justice.'
>
> From the above decisions, the following principles would emerge:

82 2006:INSC:50

> (i) The enquiries must be conducted bona fide and care must be taken to see that the enquiries do not become empty formalities.
> (ii) If an officer is a witness to any of the incidents which is the subject-matter of the enquiry or if the enquiry was initiated on a report of an officer, then in all fairness he should not be the enquiry officer. If the said position becomes known after the appointment of the enquiry officer, during the enquiry, steps should be taken to see that the task of holding an enquiry is assigned to some other officer.
> (iii) In an enquiry, the employer/department should take steps first to lead evidence against the workman/delinquent charged and give an opportunity to him to cross-examine the witnesses of the employer. Only thereafter, the workman/delinquent be asked whether he wants to lead any evidence and asked to give any explanation about the evidence led against him.
> (iv) On receipt of the enquiry report, before proceeding further, it is incumbent on the part of the disciplinary/punishing authority to supply a copy of the enquiry report and all connected materials relied on by the enquiry officer to enable him to offer his views, if any."

In Research Scholar v. Research Guide & Others[83] the Madras High Court emphasized that an inquiry should be conducted by a complaints committee in the manner it deems appropriate (as long as principles of natural justice are complied with). Sufficient latitude should be given to the complaints committee. The courts should not step into the shoes of the complaints committee or dictate the way an inquiry should be conducted. The relevant excerpts of the judgement are reproduced below.

---

83 2024:MHC:4046

> 129....We appreciate the Committee for having taken efforts to protect her dignity. The Research Guide/Professor was aware of the nature of the complaint. He was asked to give his explanation. It is not his grievance that his version was not even received by the Committee. They gave him fair opportunity. They enquired into the issue in the manner which the Committee felt appropriate. The Court cannot step into the shoes of the Committee and dictate the manner in which the inquiry should be conducted. Leverage should be given to protect the privacy of the individual and understand the emotional stress of a trial process. The Court must also understand that if the Research Guide/Professor had deliberately evaded effective participation then, he cannot turn around and complain about the procedure adopted. Opportunities can only be afforded. The onus was always on the Research Guide/Professor to take up the opportunity and participate in the enquiry.

## Rules of Evidence in Departmental Inquiry

It is a settled legal position that in a domestic inquiry there is no requirement of strict evidence (as per the Indian Evidence law).[84] In other words, technical rules of evidence have no application in departmental proceedings. Hence, in a case of sexual harassment, the inquiry committee can adopt its own procedure in conformity with the principles of natural justice.[85] The Supreme Court, in the case of State of Haryana v. Rattan Singh[86] upheld the above position in the following words:

84 Union of India v. Central Administrative Tribunal (2005) 4 Mad LJ 104.

85 Gaurav Jain v. Hindustan Latex Family Planning Promotion Trust LPA No. 145/2015 (06.08.2015, Delhi High Court).

86 (1977) 2 SCC 491. *See also* Chennai Water Supply and Sewerage Board v. T.T. Murali (2014) 4 SCC 108.

> 4. It is well settled that in a domestic inquiry the strict and sophisticated rules of evidence under the Indian Evidence Act may not apply. All materials which are logically probative for a prudent mind are permissible. There is no allergy to hearsay evidence provided it has reasonable nexus and credibility. It is true that departmental authorities and Administrative Tribunals must be careful in evaluating such material and should not glibly swallow what is strictly speaking not relevant under the Indian Evidence Act. For this proposition it is not necessary to cite decisions nor text books, although we have been taken through case-law and other authorities by counsel on both sides. The essence of a judicial approach is objectivity, exclusion of extraneous materials or considerations and observance of rules of natural justice. Of course, fairplay is the basis and if perversity or arbitrariness, bias or surrender of independence of judgment vitiate the conclusions reached, such finding, even though of a domestic tribunal, cannot be held good.

In Union of India v. Dilip Paul[87] the Supreme Court while delving into this aspect, observed as follows:

a. In a domestic inquiry, strict and sophisticated rules of evidence may not apply. The connotation "evidence" cannot be understood in a narrow technical sense as to include only that evidence adduced in a regular court of law when a person is examined as a witness by administering the oath.
b. There should not be any allergy to "hearsay evidence" provided it has reasonable nexus and credibility.
c. The simple point is, whether there was some evidence or was no evidence.

87 2023 INSC 975.

d. It is open to the adjudicating authority to accept, rely and evaluate any evidence having probative value and come to its own conclusion, keeping in mind judicial approach and objectivity, exclusion of extraneous material and observance of rules of natural justice.

The 'reasonable person' and 'reasonable woman' standards

Earlier, in judging whether the harasser's conduct was sufficient to justify legal action for sexual harassment, courts applied the 'reasonable person' standard, *viz.* considering whether a hypothetical reasonable person would have found the alleged harassing conduct offensive. However, subsequently, this concept evolved and courts adverted to the 'reasonable woman' standard by noting that while determining sexual harassment, the focus ought to be on the perspective of the victim and not that of a 'reasonable person'.[88] In other words, in determining an allegation of sexual harassment, due regard must be had to how the victim perceives the conduct/behaviour of the harasser and the effect it has on her.

Whether the perception of the harassed individual was conveyed to the accused may not be very material in most situations.[89] In other words, it would not be open to the accused to defend himself by projecting that in his understanding, the alleged action against the victim was unoffending.[90] However, each case must be decided on its own merits.

---

88 *See* Kerry Ellison v. Nicholas F. Brady 924 F.2d 872 (9th Circuit, 1991).

89 The intention of the harasser may not matter. A lack of intent may not be a defence to an allegation of sexual harassment under the Act.

90 *See* Additional District and Sessions Judge v. Registrar General, High Court of Madhya Pradesh (2015) 4 SCC 91. *See also* S. Ravichandran Iyer v. Justice A.M. Bhattacharjee (1995) 5 SCC 457 which devised an 'In-House Procedure' for holding inquiries against judges.

## Circumstantial or Indirect Evidence

There may not always exist direct evidence in a case of sexual harassment. Circumstantial evidence gains significance in cases of sexual harassment since such incidents normally take place behind closed doors or in isolation. In appropriate cases, circumstantial evidence may, in itself, be sufficient to arrive at a conclusion that sexual harassment had taken place.[91]

Some markers of circumstantial evidence are as follows:

a. Employment records which reveal aberrations (such as denial of promotion or increments despite a good professional record; unexplained requests for transfer; sudden increase in leaves etc.)
b. Personal records maintained by the victim.
c. Verbal and physical harassment may be proved by obtaining the testimony of an objective third party. Complaints from other members of the workforce about any offending conduct by the perpetrator may also come in handy.
d. In case the victim suffers emotional distress (as a consequence of the harassment) then her counsellor may also be able to serve as a professional witness.[92]

## Victim Testimony

As stated above, direct proof of sexual harassment may be hard to come by as the nature of the behaviour is such that it usually occurs inconspicuously. Often, the sole witness of an incident of sexual harassment is the complainant herself and circumstantial evidence may not always be sufficient to indisputably corroborate her case. Consequently, issues of credibility (of the complainant) may arise in sexual harassment claims. However, it is a settled position that a conviction

---

91 N.K. Suroya, IAS (Retd.) v. Union of India 2003 (3) SLJ 34 (CAT).

92 *See generally* L. Nagaraju v. Syndicate Bank 2014 (2) ALD 758.

can be made on the sole (and uncorroborated) testimony of the complainant, provided that the version given by the complainant infuses confidence in the mind of the adjudicatory authority.[93] It may be noted that, so long as there exists a preponderance of probability, a harasser can be indicted even on the basis of the complainant's testimony.[94]

Aberrations in the Complaint

In C. J. Paul Chandramohan v. The Bishop Heber College[95] the accused had assailed an inquiry report of the ICC on the premise that there were certain defects in the complaint; and also for the reason that the complaint (which ought to have been submitted to the ICC) was in fact submitted before the principal of the employer college. The Madras High Court while rejecting the challenge made by the accused, observed as follows:

a. Certain mistakes in the complaint i.e. non-mentioning of date or addressing the complaint to the wrong authority would not vitiate the complaint itself.
b. It is suffice if the allegations are substantiated for the purposes of initiation of action under the provisions of the Act. In other words, the seriousness of the allegations in the complaint are to be looked into, not the date and the addressee of the complaint. Even if such complaints are addressed to a wrong authority, such authority is duty-bound to place such complaints before the correct authority for necessary action.
c. The genuineness of the complaint and the seriousness of the

93 *See* Reshma MG v. Union of India O.A. No. 180/00722 of 2014 (19.02.2016, Central Administrative Tribunal, Ernakulam); Pankaj Kumar v. Union of India W.P. (C) No. 408/2013 (14.02.2017, Tripura High Court).

94 N.K. Suroya, IAS (Retd.) v. Union of India 2003 (3) SLJ 34 (CAT). *See also* N. Rajarathinam v. State of Tamil Nadu (1997) I SLJ 10 (SC).

95 2023 (1) CLR 621.

allegations raised alone are to be considered by the competent authority and if such allegations are sufficient enough to conduct an inquiry, then the process must be initiated in accordance with the provisions of the Act.

Continuation of proceedings despite the departure of the accused from the organization

In Binani Chattopadhyay v. Union of India[96] one of the issues which came up for consideration before the Calcutta High Court was whether an ICC could continue its inquiry proceedings against an employee/accused even if such person had left the employment of the employer during the pendency of such proceedings. While observing in the affirmative, the Calcutta High Court observed that continuation in service of the accused cannot be taken as a condition precedent for continuation of an inquiry and making a recommendation under the provisions of section 13 (3) of the Act.

Proving a claim of Harassment

Most harassment cases are an uphill battle given the nature of workplace harassment: It often occurs out of sight and is not always physical. Typically, harassment victims will need impartial witnesses, proof of its occurrence and proof that the harassment has affected them, in some capacity. In order to succeed in a harassment claim, the complainant may require hard proof such as personal and official records, emails, video, witness statements, which to an unbiased observer would clearly show harassment.

Cross Examination

An important component of 'fair trail' is the right of cross examination of the parties and their witnesses. Cross-examination is a very important tool for testing the truthfulness and credibility of the parties. An accused should be given an

96 2023 LLR 480.

opportunity to cross-examine the complainant and the witnesses who have deposed against him.[97]

In Vinod Bharti v. Union of India[98] it was observed that failure to give an opportunity of cross examination amounts to violation of principles of natural justice and vitiates the inquiry process.

In Avinash Mishra v Union of India[99] the court observed that the procedure adopted in an inquiry must be fair, and all material (rendered by the parties) should be considered in a fair, reasonable and dispassionate manner. Barring rare instances where the security of the witness or the victim would be in peril[100] cross-examination should not be denied.

In Dr. Pushkar Saxena v. Govt of NCT of Delhi[101] the court balanced the two interests; i.e. of the sensitivity and sensibility of the witnesses with the public interest in affording the accused with fair opportunity. Consequently, the following options were given to the accused: (i) cross-examination of the witnesses through the services of a female assistant; (ii) submitting a questionnaire to the witness in the presence of the committee and in the absence of the charged official (interrogatories).

It appears from the above, under special circumstances, in the case of an inquiry into allegations of sexual harassment, cross examination need not necessarily be in the presence of the delinquent since sometimes his very presence may result in putting pressure upon the witnesses and may discourage them from coming out with the truth.[102]

97 Dr. Pushkar Saxena v. Government of NCT of Delhi W.P. (C) No. 7592/2001 (16.05.2012, Delhi High Court).

98 OA No. 2998/2021 (02.03.2024, Central Administrative Tribunal, Delhi Bench).

99 2014 (215) DLT 714 (DB).

100 *See* Union of India v. Tulsiram Patel AIR 1985 SC 1416.

101 W.P. (C) 7592/2001 (16.05.2012, Delhi High Court).

102 *See* Dr. B.N. Ray v. Ramjas College W.P. (C) No. 4427/2008 (21.05.2012, Delhi High Court).

However, another viewpoint is that cross-examination is vital to the proceedings before the ICC; and should normally be made in the presence of the parties concerned. The right of cross-examination is recognized as a basic right of fair hearing; and a failure to extend an opportunity of cross-examination in course of an inquiry/trial would defeat Article 21 of the Constitution. In fact, in some cases, courts have nullified proceedings of inquiry under the Act for, amongst other things, the reason that the accused was not extended an opportunity of cross-examination of the complainant by the ICC on the pretext of protecting the victim and the witnesses.[103]

In P. Murugesan v. Tamil Nadu State Transport Corporation[104] denial of an opportunity to the accused to cross examine the complainant and the witnesses resulted in the inquiry process been vitiated.

Power of Complaints Committee to put independent questions to parties

In Samuel Tennyson v. The Principal & Secretary, Madras Cristian College (Autonomous) Tambaram East[105] the approach of the ICC in putting independent questions to the participants of the investigation (during the cross examination exercise) was assailed. The Madras High Court upheld this approach on the ground that the ICC also donned the role of an inquiry committee and any other approach would have the effect of reducing the complaints committee to a mere recording machine. While arriving at this conclusion, reliance was placed by the Madras

103 *See* Union of India v. Shibram Sarkar, (2019) 6 WBLR (Cal) 167 & Institute of Hotel Management, Catering Technology and Applied Nutrition v. Suddhasil Dey, WPCT No. 137/2019 (13.03.2020, Calcutta High Court).

104 2024/MHC/2231

105 Writ Appeal No. 2962/2019 (30.04.2024, Madras High Court).

High Court on the decision of the Supreme Court in Union of India v. Dilip Paul.[106]

In Union of India v. Dilip Paul[107] the Supreme Court affirmed the view that complaints committee is empowered to also put questions to the witnesses during the inquiry. The Supreme Court made the following observations:

a. There appears to be neither any statutory bar nor any logic to restrict the power of the complaints committee to put questions to the witnesses. The complaints committee, being an inquiry authority, must be allowed to put questions if a proper, fair and thorough inquiry is to take place.
b. The Supreme Court further referred to Section 165 of the Indian Evidence Act, 1872 to observe that the complaints committee cannot be denied the privilege of discovering or obtaining proper proof of relevant facts.
c. The only exception to the above position carved out by the Supreme Court was where allegations of personal bias was made against the committee members.

Haste in Conduct of Inquiry Proceedings

In Aureliano Fernandes v. State of Goa[108] the Supreme Court disapproved the conduct of the complaints committee in conducting the proceedings in haste. In the matter the inquiry proceedings were vitiated for, amongst other things, the following reasons: (i) the "tearing hurry" in which the proceedings were conducted and and concluded by the complaints committee (within less than one month); (ii) the

106 2023 INSC 975. *See also* Vilas V Pawar v. Union of India OA No. 770/2023 (05.10.2023, Central Administrative Tribunal, Mumbai Bench) which reaffirms the principle that it is the ICC which is the inquiring authority.

107 2023 INSC 975.

108 Civil Appeal No. 2482/2014 (12.05.2023, Supreme Court of India).

unilateral advancing of dates of hearings by the committee; (iii) the "almost back-to-back" hearings which were conducted by the committee without cause or reason (which limited the time for the parties to prepare and participate in the matter in an effective manner).

Fair Opportunity

It is important that a fair opportunity is given to the accused to defend the allegations made against him. There exists no precise rule for defining fair opportunity. In L.S. Sibu v. Air India Limited[109] the Kerala High Court elaborated on this principle in the following words:

> 17. The fundamental principles relating to the principles of natural justice is that when a prejudicial statements are made, the same shall not be used against any person without giving him an opportunity to correct and contradict. In sexual harassment complaint, sometimes the complainant may not have courage to depose all that has happened to her at the work place. There may be an atmosphere restraining free expression of victim's grievance before the Committee. The privacy and secrecy of such victims' also required to be protected. It is to be noted that verbal cross examination is not the sole criteria to controvert or contradict any statement given by the aggrieved before any authority. Primarily, in a sexual harassment complaint, the committee has to verify and analyse the capability of the aggrieved to depose before them fearlessly without any intimidation. If the Committee is of the view that the aggrieved is feeble and cannot withstand any cross examination, the Committee can adopt such other measures to ensure that the witnesses statement is contradicted or corrected by the delinquent in other manner.

109 W.P. (C) No. 4001/2016 (08.04.2016, Kerala High Court).

> The fair opportunity, therefore, has to be understood in the context of atmosphere of free expression of grievance. If the Committee is of the view that the witness or complainant can freely depose without any fear, certainly, the delinquent can be permitted to have verbal cross examination of such witnesses. In cases, where the Committee is of the view that the complainant is not in a position to express freely, the Committee can adopt such other method permitting the delinquent to contradict and correct either by providing statement to the delinquent and soliciting his objections to such statement.
>
> 18. What is reminded here by this Court to the Committee is that a fair opportunity should be given to the delinquent in such manner the Committee think fit to consider. There is no easy and precise rule defining fair opportunity.

In Delhi Transport Corporation v. DTC Mazdoor Congress[110] the Supreme Court of India highlighted the importance of a reasonable opportunity to the employee to put forth his case in a domestic inquiry and the requirement of an employer to comply with the principles of natural justice and fair play, in the following words:

> "202. ......It is now well settled that the 'audi alteram partem' rule which in essence, enforces the equality clause in Article 14 of the Constitution is applicable not only to quasi-judicial orders but to administrative orders affecting prejudicially the party-in-question unless the application of the rule has been expressly excluded by the Act or Regulation or Rule which is not the case here. Rules of natural justice do not supplant but supplement the Rules and Regulations. Moreover, the Rule

110 (1991) Supp (1) SCC 600.

> of Law which permeates our Constitution demands that it has to be observed both substantially and procedurally……. Rule of law posits that the power is to be exercised in a manner which is just, fair and reasonable and not in an unreasonable, capricious or arbitrary manner leaving room for discrimination……"

In Aureliano Fernandes v. State of Goa[111] the Supreme Court, while reiterating the right of an employee to be granted a reasonable opportunity of being heard in a departmental inquiry went on to cite various other judgments which go on to observe that even in a case where a statue to silent (with no positive words in the statute regarding grant of an opportunity of hearing), even in such case, the principles of natural justice must be observed by the relevant authority.

Exception to Verbal Cross Examination

Ordinarily, an accused must be given an opportunity to cross examine the complainant, unless there exist reasonable grounds for taking away such right of cross examination (such as the complainant being a student or a disabled person etc).[112]

If the version or statement of the person (who has testified) is in dispute, then right to cross-examination must invariably form a part of fair play. However, there may be no requirement of

111 Civil Appeal No. 2482/2014 (12.05.2023, Supreme Court of India).

112 Cross-examination of the witness by the complaints committee cannot be a substitute for the right of cross-examination by the delinquent. *See* H.C. Bakshi v. Union of India (09.05.2008, Central Administrative Tribunal, Delhi). Normally, cross examination of a witness should be conducted in the presence of the delinquent, but this may be avoided in case there exists a possibility of the presence of the delinquent putting pressure on the witness. *See* K.L. Tripathi v. State Bank of India (1984) II LLJ SC; Balvir Singh v. Union of India W.P. (C) No. 8321/2015 (31.08.2015, Delhi High Court). *But see* Union of India v. Shibram Sarkar (2019) 6 WBLR (Cal) 167 & Institute of Hotel Management, Catering Technology and Applied Nutrition v. Suddhasil Dey WPCT No. 137/2019 (13.03.2020, Calcutta High Court).

cross-examination when there is no dispute between the parties with respect to the facts of the matter.[113]

In the cases of Union of India v. Shibram Sarkar[114] and Institute of Hotel Management, Catering Technology and Applied Nutrition v. Suddhasil Dey[115] the Calcutta High Court observed that normally, the right of cross-examination to the accused should not be denied. However, in case where the right of the accused to cross-examination is denied (for any good or valid reason) or in case where the victim seeks protection (from the accused during cross examination) then in such case, the version of the complainant/victim should have the following elements: (i) the versions of the complainant (regarding the incident of sexual harassment) should not be self-contradictory; (ii) where witnesses are involved, the version of the complainant should be duly corroborated by the said witnesses. The courts should take the version of the complainant to be believable only the above-described elements are met or satisfied.

## Cross Examination by Interrogatories

In certain occasions it may be felt by courts that the complainant and the accused must not be confronted with each other. In such situations courts may devise alternate means of examination. In Bidyug Chakraborty v. Delhi University[116] the court ordered withholding of the identity of the witnesses and permitted a cross examination by means of a questionnaire to be conducted through a Local Commissioner.[117] Similarly, in Dr. B. N Ray

113 K.L. Tripathi v. State Bank of India (1984) II LLJ SC.

114 (2019) 6 WBLR (Cal) 167.

115 WPCT No. 137/2019 (13.03.2020, Calcutta High Court).

116 W.P. (C) No. 8226/2007 (29.05.2009, Delhi High Court).

117 *See also* T.R. Sahrawat v. Kendriya Vidyalaya Sangathan OA No. 4341/2012 (06.03.2014, Central Administrative Tribunal, Delhi).

v. Ramjas College[118] the court stated that whilst the principles of natural justice should be followed in the procedures of the University's ICC, it is not imperative that the complainant(s) in a case of sexual harassment need be cross examined in the presence of the accused. In case of complaints made by girl students against any member of the staff, in order to preserve anonymity of the complainant(s), their names and other particulars (which may expose their identity) may be withheld but the core contents of the complaint must be supplied to the accused.[119]

In Vimalkant Bhanuprasad Shrimali v. IDMC Limited[120] the Gujarat High Court observed that submission of written questionnaire for the purposes of cross-examination of the witness (instead of verbal cross examination) may be considered a valid exercise in the context when the aggrieved woman and the delinquent are under the same employment. In this matter, at the stage of cross-examination, the accused was given a questionnaire to fill in by the ICC for setting up questions which he would want the complainant to respond to in the cross-examination. However, the accused refused to submit any written questions and later challenged the inquiry process for being violative of principles of natural justice "on account of being denied an opportunity of verbal cross examination". The High Court, after examining the provisions of the Act, observed that the necessity to submit written questions for the purposes of cross-examination of the complainant/witness, instead of a verbal cross examination, may be considered a valid exercise in the context when the complainant and the delinquent are under the same employment. The reasoning

118 W.P. (C) No. 4427/2008 (21.05.2012, Delhi High Court).

119 Government of NCT of Delhi v. Naresh Kumar Kataria W.P. (C) No. 2454/2012 (17.04.2013, Delhi High Court).

120 SCA No. 16219/2020 (19.04.2022, Gujarat High Court).

given by the High Court was that if the complainant/witnesses in favour of the complainant are confronted in person with the delinquent, then it is possible that it would put them under stress and in an awkward position. Consequently they may not be able to depose freely and without fear. The High Court consequently rejected the challenge made by the accused on this ground.

In The Managing Director, HDFC Standard Life Insurance Company Ltd v. Suresh Babu[121] a question which arose for consideration before the High Court was whether failure to give an opportunity to the accused for verbal cross examination of the complainant would vitiate the inquiry made under the Act. The following observations may be culled out from a review of this decision:

a. Verbal cross-examination is not the sole criteria to controvert the disposition of the complainant/witnesses in inquiries into complaints under the Act.
b. Specifically in the context of sexual harassment cases, the ICC, depending on the circumstances, can adopt such other methods by permitting the delinquent to contradict and/or correct through written objections of the delinquent on the complaint.
c. What is ultimately important is that the accused should be aware of the evidence that has been given and the statement that is affecting him.
d. Hence, denial of cross-examination will not, under all circumstances, vitiate the inquiry on the ground of violation of principles of natural justice.

To sum up, in the case of sexual harassment, while conducting an inquiry, no straitjacket formula can be applied and what has

121 2022 LR 488.

to be kept in mind is that the inquiry must be conducted in good faith and after giving a fair opportunity to both sides.[122]

Complaints Committee: Regulator of Cross Examination

The general rule is that a cross examination should be conducted with minimum interference. However, the court should not sit as a silent spectator while the parties (and the witnesses) are being cross-examined. It must effectively control the recording of the evidence. While every latitude should be given to the defence to test the veracity of the victim's claims and the credibility of her version through cross-examination, the court must also ensure that cross-examination is not made a means of causing harassment or humiliation to the victim.[123]

Generally speaking, the following should be done by the complaints committee during the course of the cross examination process:

i. Cross examination should be curtailed to issues which are relevant.
ii. Collateral matters may be gone into for the limited purposes of testing the credibility of the witness and not beyond.
iii. Repetitive and unduly procrastinated cross examinations must be avoided. Where possible, strict time lines (and sessions) may be fixed for conducting the cross examination.
iv. Irrelevant, offensive, indecent, insulting or humiliating questions should not be posed to the victim or the witnesses.
v. The committee may explore the possibility of imposing costs on the party which does not conduct the cross examination with expedition and in compliance with law.

122 Balvir Singh v. Union of India W.P. (C) No. 8321/2015 (31.08.2015, Delhi High Court).

123 State of Punjab v. Gurmit Singh (1996) 2 SCC 384.

## Past Conduct or History of the Delinquent

Normally, past conduct or history of the perpetrator may not become a pivotal issue while inquiring into a complaint of sexual harassment. Past conduct, at best, qualifies to be a collateral issue which may be gone into for the limited purpose of ascertaining whether the perpetrator is 'habitual' of similar misconduct. A negative finding on this issue may hamper the credibility of the perpetrator. However, it is important that the complainant raises such issues in her complaint for the same to be considered by the complaints committee during the investigative process. In Chhttar Pal v. The Lt. Governor, National Capital Territory Region[124] a question which arose was whether previous conduct of a perpetrator could be taken into consideration for returning a finding of guilt on the charge of sexual exploitation when the same was not mentioned in the complaint filed by the complainant. Replying in the negative, the court observed as follows:

> 9.....We have given our anxious thoughts to the question as mentioned above, and are of the view that unless previous conduct of the applicant was subject matter of charge emanating from the statement of imputation of misconduct or misbehaviour, the evidence led on that behalf cannot be looked into. The applicant was not called upon to show cause with regard to his previous behaviour, and it would be against principles of natural justice and against settled law to return a finding of guilt on the basis of evidence which was not subject matter of charge in the statement of imputation of misconduct or misbehaviour.

However, a somewhat different view is taken by the Gujarat High Court in Vimalkant Bhanuprasad Shrimali v. IDMC Limited.[125]

124 2008 SCC online CAT 1311 (16.05.2008, Central Administrative Tribunal, Delhi).

125 Special Civil Application No. 16219/2020 (19.04.2022, Gujarat High Court).

In this matter, during the inquiry process by the ICC, amongst other things, it was found that the accused had faced allegations of sexual harassment even in his past employment. This "past conduct" was taken as the valid consideration by the ICC while making a recommendation of "termination of employment of the accused". This approach of the ICC was approved by the High Court. It therefore appears that where an offence of sexual harassment is proved, past record of the accused may be taken to be a relevant consideration, at least while taking a decision on the severity of the penalty/punishment.

**Interim Relief**

During the pendency of an inquiry, on a written request of the aggrieved woman, the ICC or the LCC, as the case may be, may recommend the following interim actions to the employer:[126]

a. Transfer of the aggrieved woman or the accused to any other place.
b. Grant of leave to the aggrieved woman for a period of 3 (three) months. Such relief shall be in addition to what she would otherwise be entitled to and would not be debited against her leave account.[127]
c. Restrain the accused from reporting on the work performance of the aggrieved woman or writing a confidential report, and assign the same to another officer of the organisation.[128]
d. In case of an educational institution, restrain the accused from supervising any academy activity of the aggrieved.

---

126 S. 12 of the Act & R. 8 of the Rules.

127 *See generally* Office Memorandum F. No. 13026/2/2016-Estt.A-III, dated 15.03.2017, Department of Personnel & Training, Ministry of Personnel, Public Grievances and Pensions, Government of India.

128 It is important to remove any charge from the accused which gives one party excessive powers over the complainants job conditions.

Although not mentioned in the Act, wherever possible, the complainant may also be afforded a 'work from home' option until the completion of the inquiry.

Once the recommendations are made, the employer shall implement the same and send a report of such implementation to the complaints committee.[129] Whenever recommended by the complaints committee, interim reliefs ought to be granted by the employer to the complainant.[130]

Objective of Interim Relief

The humiliation faced by a victim of sexual harassment can remain with her. It is revisited and compounded when the victim and the perpetrator have to continue to work in the same setting. The imbalance in the power equation between the perpetrator and the victim could further exacerbate the problem.[131] It is for precisely this reason that the concept of interim reliefs/protective orders has been promulgated by the Act *viz.* to separate the victim and the perpetrator for mitigation of post-harassment after-effects on the victim and for an unbiased/uninfluenced adjudication of the complaint by the complaints committee.[132]

The objective of interim relief is to make the complainant comfortable during the inquiry process. The underlying theme is prevention or mitigation of the possibility of a reprisal or future harassment. Therefore, removing or disassociating the

129 S. 12 (3) of the Act.

130 Special attention to 'interim reliefs' should be given to institutions such as schools and universities. *See* M. Kavya v. Chairman, University Grants Commission W.P. No. 11217/2014 (04.12.2014, Madras High Court).

131 Punita K. Sodhi v. Union of India (2010) 172 DLT 409.

132 *See generally* Manoj Kumar Rana v. Sports Authority of India W.P. (C) No. 8481/2015 (16.09.2015, Delhi High Court). This judgment indicates the importance of separating the perpetrator and the victim especially during the course of the inquiry.

victim from the source of the problem may serve as a useful tool in preventing retaliations from the accused.[133]

Courts have upheld and approved "transfers" being made during the pendency of the inquiry by the ICC. Courts have recognised the fact that during an adjudication of a complaint by the ICC, there exist every possibility of animosity between the complainant and the accused. Further, any attempt by the accused to influence the witnesses also cannot be ruled out. Hence, a transfer being made during pendency of inquiry by the ICC is in consonance with Section 12 of the Act and a permissible course in law.[134]

The mechanism of transfer envisaged under Section 12 of the Act is an exception to the general law on transfer based on administrative exigencies or in public interest. The transfer under Section 12 of the Act is like a statutory transfer which gets triggered only when the pre-requisites of this provision are met (i.e. the pendency of an inquiry by the complaints committee and a written request from the complainant seeking the transfer)[135].

In Amutha v. The Director of Medical and Rural Health[136] a transfer order was passed by the employer transferring the complainant (during the pendency of her complaint of sexual harassment). In fact, in that matter, even the complaint of sexual harassment was pending adjudication for several years. The High Court viewed such transfer as punitive and set aside the transfer order. Additionally, the High Court directed expeditious

133 The Vishaka Guidelines incorporated the salutary rule that the perpetrator and the complainant should not remain in the same place (or work together) while the inquiry is underway. This rule has found its way in the Act as S. 12.

134 *See generally* Saikuttan v. Kerala State Electricity Board, 2020 Lab IC 4324; Devender Rai v. Sangeet Natak Akademi, New Delhi, W.P. (C) 2893/2023 (14.03.2023, Delhi High Court); Mahendra Singh Rajawat v. Punjab National Bank, 2023 LLR 390.

135 *See generally* Dr. Parveen v. Director General, Indian Council of Forestry Research & Education W.P. No. 99/2019 (19.03.2019, High Court of Uttarakhand)

136 W.P (MD) No. 2109/2022 (21.07.2022, Madras High Court, Madurai Bench).

disposal of the complaint of sexual harassment by the concerned complaints committee.

There is no provision in the Act which provides for any protective interim relief to the witnesses. However, interim reliefs similar to what are available to the aggrieved may also be provided to the witnesses in appropriate circumstances. The victims and the witnesses must be protected from all sorts of pressure and hostility prior to, during and subsequent to the inquiry.

Transfer on Administrative Grounds during inquiry

In Himanshu Srivastava v. Union of India[137] a question which arose for consideration was whether a complainant of sexual harassment could be transferred (on administrative grounds) during the course of inquiry even when she had not requested for a transfer under the Act. The court observed that the Act provides a facility to a complainant to make a request for transfer of herself or the accused. However, this does not preclude her *bona fide* transfer on administrative grounds if the circumstances of the case so require.

Transfer as Final Punishment

While transfer is permissible as an interim measure/relief, the same cannot be imposed as a final punishment on the parties. In Meenakshi Pandey v. Central Bank of India[138] the Madhya Pradesh High Court, after examining the provisions of the Act, observed that the range of punishment prescribed under the Act does not include transfer of the parties. In other words, there is no power to transfer by way of punishment. Further, this judgement also appears to suggest that transfer (even as an interim measure)

137 O.A No. 200/00865/2015 (01.10.2015, Central Administrative Tribunal, Jabalpur).

138 W.P. No. 29047/2022 (05.04.2023, Madhya Pradesh High Court).

should be reasonable and justifiable e.g. should not be made to a far off places etc.

General Principles relating to Transfer

In Dr. Parveen v. Director General, Indian Council of Forestry Research & Education,[139] after examining various judicial precedents, the following principles relating to the aspect of transfer (in the context of government employees) were highlighted:

a. Unless there is a term to the contrary in the contract of service, a transfer order is a normal incidence of service.
b. In a transferable post, an order of transfer is a normal consequence and personal difficulty is a matter for consideration of the department, and not for the court.
c. Courts or tribunals are not appellate forums to decide on the transfer of employees made on administrative grounds.
d. Orders of transfer should normally not be interfered with by a court of law in the exercise of its discretionary jurisdiction. Typically, courts or tribunal should not substitute their own decisions in matters of transfer, or that of the competent authorities.
e. Unless the order of transfer is shown to be an outcome of a mala fide exercise of power or as violative of any statutory provision or is passed by an authority not competent to do so, it cannot be lightly interfered with by a court of law as a matter of course.
f. Transfers are normally not to be interfered by courts or tribunals, except in rare cases where they have been made in a vindictive manner.
g. Where an employee is transferred, he must comply with the order, but if there is any general difficulty in proceeding on transfer, it is open to him to make a representation to the competent authority

139 W.P. No. 99/2019 (19.03.2019, High Court of Uttarakhand),

for stay, modification or cancellation of the transfer order. If the said transfer order is not stayed, modified or cancelled, then in such case, the concerned employee must carry out the order of transfer. In the absence of any stay of the transfer order, the employee has no justification to avoid or evade the transfer, merely on the ground of having made a representation, or on the ground of his difficulty in moving from one place to another. If he fails to proceed on transfer, then in such case, he will expose himself to disciplinary action under the relevant rules.

h. Transfer of an employee, on administrative grounds, or in public interest, should not be interfered with unless there are strong and compelling grounds rendering the transfer order improper or unjustifiable.

In Shankarlal Namdeo v. State of Madhya Pradesh[140] during the course of pendency of an inquiry under the Act, the accused was transferred to a location which was at a significant distance from his original location, outside city limits. This transfer was made only on account of pendency of the above said inquiry. In fact, the inquiry proceedings were at a standstill at the behest of the complainant herself. The High Court made the following observations in the matter:

a. For a transfer to qualify as a statutory transfer (in terms of Section 12 of the Act) it should be made on the recommendation of the ICC.
b. The transfer of the accused merely on account of pendency of the proceeding under the Act was unjustified in the absence of a recommendation for such transfer by the ICC, coupled with the fact that the said proceedings had been brought to an indefinite standstill by the complainant herself. The court observed that such

140 2024 SCC Online MP 5512

a transfer amounts to victimisation and harassment of the accused.

c. Looking into the allegations being made in the matter by both the parties, the competent authority was always at liberty to make suitable arrangements to maintain a cordial atmosphere at the workplace. In this backdrop, the court granted liberty to the concerned authority to transfer the accused to a nearby location and that too, only during the pendency of the inquiry under the Act.

## Completion of Investigation

Section 13 of the Act deals with the procedure subsequent to submission of the inquiry report. On completion of an inquiry, the ICC or the LCC, as the case may be, shall provide a report of its findings to the employer or the district officer, as the case may be, within a period of 10 (ten) days from the date of its completion.[141] Further, a copy of such report shall also be made available to the concerned parties.[142]

Where the ICC or the LCC, as the case may be, arrives at a conclusion that the allegation(s) against the accused have not been proved, it shall recommend that no action be taken in the matter.[143]

Where the ICC or the LCC, as the case may be, arrives at a conclusion that the allegation(s) against the accused have been proved, it may recommend the following action(s):[144]

a. to take action for sexual harassment as a misconduct in accordance

141 Ss. 13 and 11 of the Act clearly indicate that the inquiry conducted by the complaints committee is not a preliminary inquiry but a full fledged fact finding inquiry. L.S. Sibu v. Air India Limited W.P. (C) No. 4001/2016 (08.04.2016, Kerala High Court).

142 S. 13 (1) of the Act. Law warrants a strict compliance with the provisions of Ss. 11 and 13 of the Act. *See generally* Puspanjali Padhy v. Central Public Information Officer, Indian Overseas Bank, File No. CIC/SH/A/2015/000235 (30.03.2016, CIC Delhi).

143 S. 13 (2) of the Act.

144 S. 13 (3) of the Act.

with the provisions of the service rules applicable to the accused; or where no such service rules exist, in such manner as prescribed under the Act.[145]

b. award of monetary compensation in the manner prescribed.

The employer or the district officer, as the case may be, shall act upon the recommendations[146] within a period of 60 (sixty) days of its receipt.[147]

Simply stated, the complaints committee, subsequent to the conclusion of the inquiry, is empowered to do the following: (i) dismiss the complaint in case the allegations are unsubstantiated; or (ii) make recommendations (as mentioned above) in case the allegations are substantiated.[148] The recommendations made by the complaints committee may depend on various factors, including the following: severity or frequency of the harassment, the level of repentance, if any of the harasser, the past conduct

145 The findings of the complaints committee must include a definitive conclusion and a clear finding that the facts alleged in the complaint have been proved (or not proved) against the accused. *See* Ashok Kumar Singh v. University of Delhi W.P. (C) No. 7371/2016 (16.02.2017, Delhi High Court).

146 The expression 'recommendations' here are not mere suggestions but the order of the committee which decides on the guilt of the accused and the consequent punishment of the accused. These 'recommendations' are subject to the appellate provisions envisaged under S. 18 (1) of the Act. *See* Ashok Kumar Singh *ibid.*

147 S. 13 (4) of the Act.

148 Once a procedure is followed and only the operative portion of the report falls foul of S. 13 (4) of the Act, then in such case, the complaints committee, while issuing a fresh report, may rely on and adopt the reasoning, discussions and conclusions afforded in the previous report. *See* Ashok Kumar Singh *supra.* *See also* C.S.H.N. Murthy v. Tezpur University 2015 (3) GLT 346. *See also* The Managing Director, HDFC Standard Life Insurance Company Ltd v. Suresh Babu, 2022 LR 488, wherein, *inter alia,* the court suggested that a *de novo* inquiry may not be conducted in cases where there is a significant time gap between the inquiry process and the date of the proceedings between the court. In other words, for instance, if the High Court (whether in writ or appellate proceedings originating from inquiry proceedings under the Act) finds infirmities in the inquiry process, but also simultaneously observes that a long time has passed since the conduct of the inquiry, then in such case, the court may not order a fresh inquiry into the matter but may resort to other remedies.

of the harasser etc. Normally, the action proposed against the harasser should be one which assures generally the workforce, and more specifically the victim that sexualised behaviour is unacceptable. The recommendations should be commensurate to the offence committed.

### Time Limit for completion of inquiry: Whether mandatory or directory

A question which arises is whether the 90 (ninety) day time limit given to the complaints committee to complete the inquiry process is mandatory or directory in nature. In Pankaj Kumar v. Union of India[149], this question arose before the Tripura High Court. The High Court, while holding this time period to be directory, made the following observations:

a. Section 11 (4) of the Act nowhere provides the consequence for failure to complete the inquiry within 90 (ninety) days.
b. Ordinarily, as per the principles of statutory interpretation, when a provision (which provides a time period) is not coupled with any penal or adverse consequences for failure to complete the task for which the time period is assigned, then in such case, such provision is to be considered as directory in nature.
c. Consequently, inquiry proceedings before a complaints committee are not invalidated merely on account of the breach of the time limit of 90 (ninety) days specified in Section 11 (4) of the Act. Further, inquiry proceedings are not required to be terminated upon breach of this 90 (ninety) day time line.
d. Any other view (than the one taken above) would give to an offender an opportunity to escape on account of procedural technicalities. This would act as an encouragement for offenders and as discouragement for victims.

149 W.P. (C) No. 408/2013 (14.02.2017, Tripura High Court).

A similar view was taken by the Delhi High Court in Nitesh Parashar v. Institute of Chartered Accountants of India[150] wherein the High Court observed that a complaint of sexual harassment and the inquiry proceedings emanating therefrom cannot be quashed merely for the reason that the ICC failed to complete the inquiry within the time lines prescribed under Section 11 (4) of the Act. It was further observed that complaints of sexual harassment deserved to be treated with a certain of seriousness and responsibility; and ought to be taken to their logical conclusion.

In S.P.S Sondhi v. Union of India[151] the court, while relying on the above discussed case law on the subject, refused to invalidate an inquiry merely for breach of the timelines prescribed under Section 11 (4) of the Act. It was also noted that the accused in that matter had not been able to establish any prejudice to him on account of crossing of the timeline of 90 (ninety) days.

**Limitation**

In the view of the author, the aspect of limitation under the Act should be viewed in a liberal manner by courts except where the delay is excessive and inexplicable. In some situations however, the aspect of limitation may (along with other factors) be taken into account, especially where the accused alleges that the complaint of sexual harassment made against him is an afterthought or a counter blast by the complainant (for example, a revenge tactic or an arm twisting tactic; or an effort to neutralise the accused or the employer into taking action against the complainant in connection with work or performance related reasons). For instance, in Mukesh Khampariya v. The State of Madhya

150 W.P. (C) No. 88/2023 (05.01.2023, Delhi High Court).

151 OA No. 060/1319/2018 (01.11.2023, Central Administrative Tribunal, Chandigarh).

Pradesh[152] a complaint of sexual harassment was lodged by the complainant against the accused (her supervisor) as a counter measure to certain steps taken by the accused against her in connection with her dereliction of duty at work. Amongst other things, the Madhya Pradesh High Court took cognizance of the five month delay by the complainant in lodging the complaint of sexual harassment.

**Two ICC Inquiries on the same complaint**

In Mukesh Khampariya v. The State of Madhya Pradesh[153] a complaint of sexual harassment was rejected by the ICC for want of sufficient evidence. The findings of the ICC were upheld in the departmental appeal as well. However, strangely, the concerned employer directed conduct of a fresh inquiry against the accused on the same complaint. In this context, the Madhya Pradesh High Court, while rejecting such conduct of the employer, observed that there exists no provision in the Act allowing for conduct of another inquiry on the same complaint.

**Mere Suspicion versus Actual Proof**

In Mukesh Khampariya v. The State of Madhya Pradesh[154] the accused was held guilty by the ICC solely on account of the fact that the complainant was filing repeated complaints against the accused. This approach of the ICC was rejected by the Madhya Pradesh High Court. The High Court further observed that suspicion however strong cannot take the place of proof.

<u>Proceedings before the Disciplinary Authority</u>

Service rules of various organisations (PSUs etc.) provide that, after conclusion of the inquiry by the ICC, if a major penalty

152 2024 (1) MPLJ 351.

153 2024 (1) MPLJ 351.

154 2024 (1) MPLJ 351

is required to be imposed on the delinquent, then in such case, prior to imposing any penalty, disciplinary proceeding needs to be conducted by a designated disciplinary authority (which authority, amongst other things, grants to the delinquent and opportunity of hearing/providing explanations prior to imposition of any penalty). The Supreme Court in the case of Dr. Vijaykumaran C.P.V v. Central University of Kerala[155] has observed that once the ICC arrives at a conclusion of guilt of the accused in its inquiry, then in such case, the complaint must be taken to its logical end by initiating departmental or regular inquiry as per the relevant service rules of the organization. In such cases, a regular inquiry or departmental action (as specified in the service rules) is a mandatory requirement. This position has also been upheld in Sabir Ahmed v. The Assam University.[156]

Scope of Powers of ICC

The scope of authority of an ICC (pursuant to an inquiry), was discussed in some detail by the Delhi High Court in the case of Bibha Pandey v. Punjab National Bank.[157] In the said matter, the ICC, after making an inquiry into a complaint of sexual harassment, observed that the allegations of sexual harassment were not substantiated (for the case was one of a consensual relationship between the parties). However, the ICC went further and made various remarks/comments on the conduct of the parties to the complaint and recommended that the employer "takes suitable action" against them. Objecting to such conduct of the ICC, the Delhi High Court made the following observations:

155 (2020) 12 SCC 426.

156 W.P. (C) No, 2509/2018 (21.12.2023, Guwahati High Court).

157 W.P. (C) No. 3249/2017 (16.12.2020, Delhi High Court).

a. If allegations of sexual harassment are not proved before the ICC, then in such case, the ICC can only recommend to the employer to not take any action in the matter.
b. If, on the other hand, a case of sexual harassment is made out, then the recommendation of the ICC can only be for taking appropriate action for misconduct, in accordance with the provisions of the service rules as contained within Section 13 (2) and 13 (4) of the Act.
c. The part of the ICC's report wherein comments were made about the conduct of the parties and further suggestions were made to take suitable action against them, were held by the court to be beyond the jurisdiction of the ICC and its statutory mandate recognized by Section 13 (2) of the Act.
d. The court further went on to observe that "moral policing" was not the job of the management or the ICC. Any consensual relationship amongst adults should be of no concern of the management or the ICC, so long as the said relationship does not affect the working and the discipline of the organization, and is not contrary to the rules/code of conduct binding the said employees. The ICCs jurisdiction is restricted to the allegations of sexual harassment and whether a complaint is made out or not, to that effect.
e. Therefore, the Delhi High Court was of the view that the ICC's authority to inquire into complaints of sexual harassment is derived from and is to be strictly regulated by the provisions of the Act.

<u>Demeanour of witness in the inquiry process</u>

In the case of Union of India v. Shibram Sarkar[158] & Institute of Hotel Management, Catering Technology and Applied Nutrition v. Suddhasil Dey[159] a question which came up for consideration before the Calcutta High Court was whether the demeanour of a

158 (2019) 6 WBLR (Cal) 167.

159 W.P.C.T. No. 137/2019 (13.03.2020, Calcutta High Court).

witness could be taken note of/recorded by the ICC during the inquiry process. In the said matter, a witness to the proceeding was exhibiting certain body language and expression (during the course of her examination) that appeared to indicate to the ICC that she was under some pressure and was perhaps not disclosing the truth out of fear. The ICC took written note of such conduct of the witness. The accused objected such procedure of the ICC. The Calcutta High Court observed the although a departmental inquiry is not conducted with the rigidity of a criminal trial, there is no legal embargo to note the demeanour of a witness while her statement is being recorded in the course of a departmental inquiry. After all, every departmental inquiry ought to be conducted fairly and without any element of bias. If indeed the body language, expressions, pauses in conversation and look in the eyes of the witness was so very vital for the ICC to arrive at a conclusion that the concerned witness was not disclosing the truth out of fear, then it was the duty of the ICC to record the same while recording the statement of the said witness.

Witness Testimony: Relevance

The views of the witnesses often hold significant importance in the inquiry. Also, in appropriate cases, the exoneration of the accused by the ICC (pursuant to an inquiry) is also taken to be one of primary grounds for setting aside criminal proceedings instituted against the accused for the same set of allegations. For instance, in Pravin Marotirao Daroli v. The State of Maharashtra[160] the Bombay High Court, while hearing a petition for quashing of an FIR (instituted by the complainant citing outraging of her modesty) gave weightage to the views of certain other lady officers who were present at the time of the incident (witnesses). As per the complainant, the conduct of the accused in moving his hands on a paperweight in a peculiar fashion while talking

160 2024:BHC-AUG:24385-DB

had resulted in outrage of her modesty. On the other hand, the witnesses had stated that, for the conduct of the accused, they did not feel that their modesty was outraged by the conduct of the accused. The complainant had lodged a criminal complaint as well as a complaint with the ICC under the Act, for the same set of allegations. The ICC, pursuant to an inquiry, had arrived at a conclusion that no act of sexual harassment was committed by the accused. Thereafter, the Bombay High Court, while considering the petition of the accused for quashing of FIR, considered this exoneration by the ICC as a ground for quashing of the FIR.

Procedure: Disciplinary Proceedings: Suspension

Ideally, in the case of a suspension of an employee, any inquiry proceedings (or disciplinary proceedings) must be concluded within a reasonable time. While there is no quarrel with the proposition that an employer has a right to suspend an employee (to prevent him from further perpetuating misconduct or tinkering with the evidence) however, at the same time, prolonged suspension can become punitive for the accused.

In the view of the author, there would be no automatic lapse of suspension just because the inquiry of the ICC is not completed within the timelines prescribed under the Act. Hence, merely delay in completion of an inquiry (in which the accused is placed under suspension) would neither result in an automatic lapse of the suspension nor would it erode the power of the competent authority to extend the suspension (for justified reasons).[161]

161 *See generally* Munendra Kumar v. Government of NCT of Delhi 2024 SCC Online Del 8186; Vikash Kumar v. Union of India (2023) 6 HCC (Del) 78; P. Kannan v. Commissioner of Municipal Administration 2022 SCC Online Mad 1154; State (NCT of Delhi) v. Rishi Anand 2017 SCC Online Del 10506. These decisions are rendered in the context of service law and disciplinary proceedings. These decisions lay down the proposition that delay in filing of chargesheet by the disciplinary authority would not result in automatic lapse of suspension of the accused nor would it extinguish the power of the competent authority to pass further orders of suspension.

Multiple Inquiries

The normal rule is that there can be only one inquiry on a complaint of sexual harassment. A further inquiry in the matter can be held in some specific circumstances only. Normally, *de novo* inquiries cannot be ordered or conducted without sufficient cause.[162]

In Suman Saurabh v. The Internal Complaints Committee[163] a second inquiry was sought to be initiated by the employer against the accused (on the same charges and the same complaint) despite the fact that the first inquiry had been completed and was a subject matter of challenge before the appropriate appellate forum. The court while setting aside the initiation of the second inquiry, drew on the principle of "double jeopardy" (as envisaged under Article 20 (2) of the Constitution of India) which provides that no person shall be prosecuted and punished for the same offence more than once.

In Vineeth Shamil v. Air India Charters Ltd[164] the ICC of one (subsidiary) organization enquired into a complaint of sexual harassment of the complainant and found the accused as not guilty. Subsequent to the above, the complainant approached the National Commission for Women (NCW) which directed the parent/holding organization to take action on the complaint of the complainant. Accordingly the parent/holding organization initiated a fresh inquiry into the same matter through its own ICC. This action of the parent/holding organization (of initiating a fresh inquiry into the matter) was challenged before the Kerala High Court. The Kerala High Court, while disagreeing with such approach, observed that the holding organization (a separate legal entity) could not have directed a fresh inquiry by its own ICC. There was no provision

162 *See* C.S.H.N. Murthy v. Tezpur University 2015 (3) GLT 346.

163 2019 LLR 975.

164 W.P. (C) No. 4457/2016 (04.09.2019, Kerala High Court).

of law which permitted such course of action. The court further observed that an inquiry had already been conducted by the employer of the parties (i.e. the subsidiary organization) and since the findings of this inquiry had not been challenged on any legally sustainable ground, the action taken by the parent/ holding organisation to conduct another inquiry into the matter through its own ICC was without jurisdiction.

The Report

The significance of an inquiry report in a departmental proceeding cannot be over-emphasized. In Pankaj Kumar v. Union of India[165] the court observed that the report submitted by the complaint committee should be treated as a fact finding/ report in an inquiry into misconduct of the delinquent. In other words, no further inquiry into the facts of the case is required. Inquiry report is to be treated as the final fact-finding report upon which necessary action is taken by the employer.

Reasons in support of the ICC Report

It is a well-settled principle of law and natural justice that the report of the complaints committee should be duly supported by reasons. The conclusions of the committee made out in the report (whether or not a case of sexual harassment is made out) should have adequate reasons and explanations.

In Union of India v. Shibram Sarkar[166] & Institute of Hotel Management, Catering Technology and Applied Nutrition v. Suddhasil Dey[167] the Calcutta High Court, by emphasising on the importance of reasons in a report by a complaints committee, went on to observe that it is not the law that whenever a victim of

165 W.P. No. 408/2013 (17.02.2014, Tripura High Court).

166 (2019) 6 WBLR (Cal) 167.

167 WPCT No. 137/2019 (13.03.2020, Calcutta High Court).

sexual harassment at workplace asserts her case then in such case, a presumption should be drawn that the harassment had indeed taken place and it is for the accused to disprove the charge. The rebuttal of the accused (and the evidence in support thereof) must be considered by the committee. If the evidence of the accused does not appeal to the committee to be creditworthy, and in such case, adequate reasons must be assigned for the same in the report.

In Mukesh Khampariya v. State of Madhya Pradesh[168] the Madhya Pradesh High Court observed that the findings of the committee is required to be based on evidence. The findings cannot be based on surmises, conjectures or suspicions. Suspicion, however strong it may be, cannot be substituted for proof.

Findings of the ICC to be clear and decisive

It is obligatory on the part of the ICC to ensure that its findings are clear decisive and well-reasoned. Vague findings and recommendations are to be rejected. In Vinod Narayan v. The Presiding Officer[169] the Bombay High Court rejected the report of the ICC on the ground that the findings recorded therein were vague in nature. The High Court observed thus:

> 10. Perusal of the findings recorded by the ICC would indicate that the same are vague in nature. The Committee has not discussed each article of charge in relation to the evidence appearing on the record. The ICC has merely made vague recommendations by recording a general finding that 'all serious allegations were confirmed by multiple witnesses that were interviewed by the committee'. Beyond this finding, there is no discussion in the report of the ICC about the evidence appearing on record in respect of each article of charge.

168 W.P. No. 21852/2018 (05.10.2023, Madhya Pradesh High Court).

169 2025: BHC: AS-12952

> 11. In my view, therefore the report of the ICC is clearly vague as the same is drawn without discussing the evidence on record. Most importantly, the ICC has not considered the issue whether the allegations levelled against the Petitioner in first two incidents really constitute sexual harassment to the complainant. The allegation involved in third incident had nothing to do with Petitioner's actions. Still said incident was unnecessarily incorporated in the report of the ICC...

## Action under Service Rules

Section 13 (4) of the Act stipulates that if the ICC concludes that a case of sexual harassment is made out, then action is required to be taken against the accused in accordance with the applicable service rules. The Act does not contemplate any action against the accused without an inquiry by the complaints committee.

In Sarita Singh v. State of U.P[170] a complaint of sexual harassment was filed by the complainant against the accused. However, instead of initiating an inquiry by the ICC, direct proceedings were launched by the employer against the complainant under the applicable service rules for the initiation of false and malicious proceedings against the accused and consequently punishment was also inflicted upon the complainant for the same. The High Court deprecated this practice and observed it to be a violation of Sections 13 (3) & 13 (4) of the Act. The court went on to observe that once a complaint of sexual harassment was made, it was the paramount responsibility of the competent authority to proceed and to take cognizance of the same under the provisions of the Act and an inquiry under the applicable service rules could be made basis the report of the concerned complaints committee.

---

170 2020 (165) FLR 66.

In National Forensic Science University v. Deepak Chetandas Rawtani[171] it was observed by the Gujarat High Court that it was mandatory for employers to follow their service rules (for inquiry process and awarding punishment etc.) even if the ICC had pronounced on the guilt of the delinquent and had made recommendations of punishment against the delinquent. In this matter, the relevant service rules required the employer to issue a show cause notice to the delinquent along with an opportunity of hearing before punishment. However, the employer had, on the basis of the observations and recommendations of the ICC (which declared the delinquent to be guilty of sexual harassment) proceeded to straightaway terminate the employee without issuance of a show cause notice and an opportunity of hearing. A single bench of the Gujarat High Court rejected this conduct of the employer and set aside the termination order. The Division Bench of the Gujarat High Court affirmed the judgement of the Single Bench.

In a disciplinary proceeding, the recommendations of the ICC are to be considered as an inquiry report. Generally, in any disciplinary proceeding, after submission of the inquiry report, the disciplinary authority considers the same and if it concludes that further action is required to be taken on the basis of the said report, then in such case, it is required to give an opportunity to the delinquent to respond to this report, consider the response of the delinquent and arrive at a finding of punishment.[172]

## Disciplinary Proceedings after superannuation of the Delinquent

Unless the service rules (applicable to the delinquent) specify otherwise, no disciplinary proceedings can be initiated against

171 LPA No. 410/2024 (01.05.2024, Gujarat High Court).

172 Debjani Sengupta v. Institute of Cost Accountants of India 2024 SCC Online Cal 12001

the delinquent post his superannuation. In Debjani Sengupta v. Institute of Cost Accountants of India[173] the ICC proceedings against the delinquent resulted in an inquiry report holding him guilty of sexual harassment. The said inquiry report was challenged before the High Court which allowed the challenge and set aside the report along with directions to the ICC to carry out a fresh inquiry. While continuation of such fresh inquiry, the delinquent superannuated. Thereafter, the fresh inquiry report also held the delinquent guilty of sexual harassment. The matter once against travelled to the High Court. The question before the High Court at this stage was whether disciplinary proceedings could be initiated against the delinquent after his superannuation. The High Court answered in the negative and observed that no disciplinary proceedings could be initiated against the delinquent under such circumstances.

Employers Role after ICC Report

The report of the complaints committee is an important element in the adjudicatory process.[174] One view of courts is that the employer is duty bound to comply with the recommendations made by the complaints committee. The employer merely has a facilitation role in the scheme of adjudication; it is only required to effectuate the findings and recommendations of the committee, subject to applicable service rules.[175]

In Raj Kumar Dey v. The State Bank of India[176] it was observed that the recommendations of the ICC are binding on the employer. It is not open to the employer to ignore the recommendations of the ICC.

173 2024 SCC Online Cal 12001

174 L.S. Sibu v. Air India Limited W.P. (C) No. 4001/2016 (08.04.2016, Kerala High Court).

175 L.S. Sibu v. Air India Limited W.P(C) No. 4001/2016 (08.04.2016, Kerala High Court).

176 W.P.A. No. 20332/2017 (19.05.2022, Calcutta High Court).

Another view of courts is that there exists an option with the employer/disciplinary authority to either accept or reject the recommendations of the ICC. In Institute of Hotel Management, Catering Technology and Applied Nutrition v. Suddhasil Dey[177] the Calcutta High Court was of the view that the language employed in Section 13 (4) of the Act does not make it imperative for the disciplinary authority to act on the recommendations of the ICC by accepting it. The expression "act upon the recommendation" used in the said provision would mean either accept or reject the recommendation, for reasons to be recorded in writing. If the recommendations were binding, it would cease to be a recommendation and partake the character of a command which was not the legislative intent. It is entirely for the disciplinary authority to decide the next course of action upon giving the recommendations (of the ICC) due consideration.

Typically, the employer must ensure that every complaint of sexual harassment reaching the complaints committee is dealt with in compliance with law and the recommendations of the committee are acted upon expeditiously.[178]

**The Punishment**

Once a case of sexual harassment is proved, punishment follows. Once an offence is proved, the requirement of taking action is not merely subjective to the incident, or to the facts of a case; it is to comply with and sub-serve a wider societal purpose.[179]

In the context of sexual harassment, the punishment in a sense is not merely one imposed by the employer simply because it feels that such behaviour mandates discipline, but is

177 WPCT No. 137/2019 (13.03.2020, Calcutta High Court).

178 *See* Parliamentary Standing Committee Report (2011), at ¶ 16.6.

179 *See* A.K. Singh v. Union of India W.P. (C) No. 4237/2012 (01.12.2015, Delhi High Court)

also one which assures the female members of the work force that such behaviour is illegal and intolerable in the workplace.[180] The nature of the penalty imposed on the delinquent, *inter alia,* serves the following purposes: (i) A signal to the female employees in the establishment that the employer is intolerant of such misbehaviour;[181] (ii) While assuring a safe workplace, it signals the willingness of the employer to address such issues with seriousness and promptitude.[182]

**The Principle of Proportionality**

At the stage of punishment, the principle of proportionality gains relevance. The principle of proportionality may be pithily articulated as follows: 'the punishment must be commensurate to the offence'.[183] The principle of proportionality warrants that the action of the disciplinary authority must be commensurate to the proved misconduct by the delinquent.[184] The sentence must suit the offence and the offender.[185]

There is no gainsaying the importance of displaying sensitivity while considering appropriate penalty for proved misconduct of sexual harassment. In other words, a hammer

---

180 *Ibid.*

181 *See generally* Arvind v. Union of India W.P. (C) No. 5863/2014 (21.09.2015, Delhi High Court).

182 *See* A.K. Singh v. Union of India W.P. (C) No. 4237/2012 (01.12.2015, Delhi High Court).

183 Proportionality must normally take into account the 'adequacy' and 'public interest' elements.

184 Arvind v. Union of India W.P. (C) No. 5863/2014 (21.09.2015, Delhi High Court). *See also* Jyoti Prakash v. Inquiry Authority 2024 SCC Online Ori 2108.

185 *See* Ranjit Thakur v. Union of India AIR 1987 SC 2386. The principle of proportionality applies both to choice as well as quantum of punishment; and is a well defined concept of judicial review. *See* T.T. Chakravarthy Yuvaraj v. Principal, Dr. B.R. Ambedkar Medical College AIR 1997 Ker 261; Rishabh Jha v. Union of India, Writ No. 30472/2016 (21.12.2016, Allahabad High Court).

cannot be used to swat a fly.[186] Conversely, a punishment of reprimand *simplicitor* for grave offence would amount to failure justice.

One is expected to take into consideration measures, magnitude and degree of misconduct and all other relevant circumstances and exclude irrelevant matters before imposing punishment.[187] Therefore, the punishment must be commensurate with the gravity of the offence and the likely effect it would have on the perpetrator.[188]

## The Proportionality Parameters

Some factors which make up the elements of a proportionate punishment for proven indiscipline or misconduct are as follows:[189]

a. the nature and severity of the misconduct.
b. the frequency of the misconduct.
c. the extent which the harassment has affected the victim.
d. the propensity of the delinquent.
e. the nature of the penalty proposed or imposed in other comparable cases.
f. in some situation, the further career prospects of the complainant and (sometimes) of the delinquent.
g. in certain situations, perhaps exceptionally so, familial circumstances of the complainant or the delinquent may be relevant.

186 Arvind v. Union of India W.P. (C) No. 5863/2014 (21.09.2015, Delhi High Court).

187 *See* Chairman cum Managing Director, Coal India Limited v. Mukul Kumar Chaudhari 2009 (15) SCC 620.

188 *See generally* Apparel Export Promotion Council v. A. K. Chopra AIR 1999 SC 625.

189 Arvind v. Union of India W.P. (C) No. 5863/2014 (21.09.2015, Delhi High Court).

h. the age of the delinquent may be a relevant factor in some circumstances; yet it may be irrelevant in others.[190]

Upon conclusion of the inquiry, once the complaints committee recommends and the employer implements the penalty, courts would be slow in interfering with such order (in the context of punishment), unless it arrives at a conclusion that the penalty imposed on the delinquent is shockingly disproportionate to the misconduct committed by him.[191] Barring this, only in rare and exceptional cases (such as long delay in adjudication etc) would the courts venture to substitute their own view as to the quantum of punishment.[192]

Imposition of Punishment: What should be Disregarded

Conversely, there are various factors which may be disregarded while making a determination of punishment. No weightage should be given to aspects such as rank/position of the offender, his performance or value to the organisation etc. Further, in line with settled principles, the character of the women should not ideally be taken into account. In other words, the moral character of the victim should not be taken into consideration.[193]

190 It becomes a relevant factor when the delinquent is a student. *See* Rishabh Jha *supra*. While punishing a student offender, the focus should, *inter alia*, be on reformation and rehabilitation. For critical parameters (to be kept in mind) while imposing punishment on students for offences, *see* Siddharth Jain v. Shaheed Sukhdev College of Business Studies W.P. (Civil) No. 9862/2015 (17.11.2015, Delhi High Court); T.T. Chakravarthy *supra*.

191 Om Kumar v. Union of India (2001) 2 SCC 386. *See also* C. Govinda Rajulu v. The State of Andhra Pradesh W.P. No. 36081/2017 (04.08.2023, Andhra Pradesh High Court, Amravati Bench).

192 *See generally* Vidya Akhave v. Union of India W.P. No. 796/2015 (04.10.2016, Bombay High Court).

193 Parliamentary Standing Committee Report (2011), at ¶ 7.8. *See also* S. 53A of the Indian Evidence Act 1872 (Now S. 48 of the Bharatiya Sakshya Adhiniyam, 2023), which *inter alia* provides that, in case of sexual offences, where the question of consent is an issue, the character of the victim or of such person's previous sexual experience with any person shall not be relevant on the issue of such consent or the quality of consent.

Any regard to any such (irrelevant) factor(s) could vitiate the adjudicatory process.

To sum up, the punishment for sexual harassment must be sufficient to: (i) convince employees that the management takes complaints of sexual harassment very seriously; and (ii) deter offensive behaviour in others. All penalties/punishments must be apt for the offence and should have a consistent and 'across the board' application.

**Monetary Damages**

The Act provides for damages in case of proved sexual harassment. An award of monetary compensation to the aggrieved woman is made where the complaints committee arrives at a finding of guilt of the accused. The provision for monetary compensation is regardless of the service rules applicable to the inquiry.[194] Put differently, the victim shall be entitled to monetary compensation once her case is sustained by the complaints committee irrespective of whether the service rules applicable to her, envisages the concept of monetary compensation or not.

In Debjani Sengupta v. Institute of Cost Accountants of India[195] the Calcutta High Court clarified this position by observing that monetary penalty can be recommended by the ICC notwithstanding anything in the service rules applicable to the delinquent.[196]

<u>Determination of Compensation</u>

The Act empowers the complaints committee to recommend payment of compensation to the victim by the accused if the

194 S. 13 (3) of the Act.

195 2024 SCC Online Cal 12001

196 Debjani Sengupta v. Institute of Cost Accountants of India 2024 SCC Online Cal 12001

accused is declared guilty.[197] For the purpose of determining compensation, the following factors shall be taken into account:[198]

a. the mental trauma, pain, suffering and emotional distress caused to the aggrieved.[199]
b. the loss in the career opportunity on account of sexual harassment.[200]
c. medical expenses incurred by the aggrieved for physical or psychiatric treatment.
d. the income and financial status of the delinquent.
e. feasibility of such payment being made in lump sum or in instalments.

In determining compensation, the following additional factors may also be taken into account:

a. The nature, magnitude and gravity of the harassment.
b. The duration of the harassment.
c. The frequency of the harassment.
d. The age of the victim.
e. The vulnerability of the victim.
f. The psychological impact of the harassment upon the victim.[201]

<u>The Proportionality Theory in Monetary Compensation</u>

The doctrine of proportionality applies to the aspect of monetary compensation as well. In recommending compensation, the

197 S. 11 (2) of the Act.

198 S. 15 of the Act.

199 Emotional or mental injury for a woman is an automatic and natural result of sexual harassment at workplace. Gayatri Balaswamy v. ISG Novasoft Technologies Ltd. (2014) 6 CTC 602.

200 The fact that the victim instituted proceedings (for sexual harassment) after termination of her service or her resignation would be insignificant in so far as such proceedings are concerned. Gayatri Balaswamy v. ISG Novasoft Technologies Ltd. (2014) 6 CTC 602.

201 Cuff v. Gypsy Restaurant (1987) BOI 87-004 (06.02.1987, Human Rights Tribunal of Ontario/Board of Inquiry).

complaints committee should not display such severity that the respondent suffers hardship disproportionate to the misconduct.

Courts would not normally interfere with punishment imposed in a proven case of sexual harassment, unless the punishment is disproportionate to offence or shocks the conscience of the court.[202]

Under common law, for harassment to be found as warranting a high damage award, courts would normally examine the following elements: (i) whether the offence occurred more than once; (ii) whether the harasser was informed that the conduct was not welcome, or the harasser should have known that it was unwelcome; (iii) whether the offensive conduct has a physical or mental impact on the victim stemming from the interaction.

Quantum of Charges

The Act is not concerned with the quantity or percentage of charges which are established against the delinquent. As long as the commission of an offence of sexual harassment is shown to have taken place, appropriate punishment must follow. In The Research Scholar v. Research Guide & Others[203] the Madras High Court observed thus:

> 137. The learned Single Judge, in the course of the order, had stated that only 50% of the charges had been proved. We are not able to understand that observation. Even if there is a slight indication or even if there is intention to commit sexual or mental or emotional harassment and the said allegation is made out, the perpetrator, must be punished. Harassment is a deeply sensitive issue and touches the heart and soul of the person who suffers in silence….

202 Kendriya Vidyalaya Sangthan v. J. Hussain (2013) 10 SCC 106.

203 2024:MHC:4046

Recovery of Compensation from the offender

The Act prescribes the mode of recovery of compensation from the offender. At the first instance, the compensation shall be deducted by the employer from the salary of the offender. However, in case such amounts cannot be deducted from his salary (due to him being absent from duty or cessation of his employment), then the employer may direct the offender to pay the amounts directly to the aggrieved woman. In case the offender fails to pay such amounts then the monies may be recovered from the offender as arrears of land revenue.[204]

**Action against the Guilty**

Where the complaints committee arrives at a conclusion that the accused has committed sexual harassment, it may recommend the following action(s) against him:[205]

a. In cases where service rules exist, action in accordance with such service rules.
b. In cases where no service rules exist, any suitable action, including the following: a written apology, warning, reprimand or censure[206], withholding of promotion, withholding of pay rise or increments, terminating the accused from service, requiring the accused to

204 S. 13 (3) (ii) of the Act. *See also* The Revenue Recovery Act, 1890.

205 S. 14 of the Act & R. 9 of the Rules.

206 In common parlance, the terms 'censure' and 'warning' are often used interchangeably. However, there exists some distinction between these two terms. An order of 'censure' is a formal act intended to convey that the person concerned has been guilty of some blameworthy act or omission for which it has been found necessary to award him a formal punishment. On the other hand, there may be times when it is found necessary to criticise the conduct of the accused, but taking all circumstance into consideration, it may be felt that, while the matter is not serious enough to justify the imposition of the formal punishment of 'censure', it calls for some informal action such as the communication of a written warning, admonition or reprimand. This would qualify to be a 'warning'. *See generally* MHA OM No. 39/21/56-Ests. (A) dated 13.12.1956.

undergo a counselling session or requiring the accused to carry out community service.[207]

ICC recommends and the Employer Implements

It appears that the findings of the complaints committee are recommendatory in nature and the ultimate power of execution lies in the hands of the employer.[208] Put differently, complaints committee can only recommend to the employer and the employer alone shall take further action in the matter.[209]

Notwithstanding the punishments provided above (or those recommended by the complaints committee), an employer can impose only such punishment which is provided for under the relevant service rules. In other words, in case of any inconsistency in the punishments provided under the service rules of the employer and those recommended by the complaints committee, the service rules shall take precedence.

Forfeiture of Gratuity

In GAIL (India) limited v. Dr. Duraisamy Baskaran[210] a question which arose before the Telangana High Court was whether it was permissible in law to forfeit the gratuity of an offender as a consequence of the ICC returning a finding of guilt against him. In this regard, the Telangana High Court examined Section 4 (6) (b) (ii) of the Gratuity Act 1972 which provides that gratuity payable to an employee may be wholly or partly forfeited if, *inter alia*, the services of such employee have been terminated

207 *See generally* Nitin Saxena v. State Crl. M.C. 2906/2010 (09.09.2010, Delhi High Court).

208 It is a settled law in labour/service jurisprudence, that the authority having the power to appoint shall alone have the power to punish or dismiss the errant employee. *See generally* Union of India v. V.S. Jaitha W.P. (C) No. 9695/2008 (01.08.2016, Kerala High Court).

209 B.M. Sanjeeva v. Union of India W.P. No. 26794/2010 (03.07.2014, Madras High Court).

210 Writ Appeal No. 153/2021 (28.02.2023, Telangana High Court).

for any act (committed during the course of his employment) which constitutes an offence involving moral turpitude.

The High Court examined various Supreme Court decisions in the context of gratuity (and it's forfeiture) and culled out the following principles regarding the same:

a. Gratuity is a property of the employee, is a welfare measure to improve the service conditions of employees; and consequently is an obligation of the employer being one of the minimum conditions of service of an employee.
b. The Gratuity Act 1972 is a close knit scheme and a complete code containing detailed provisions concerning a scheme for gratuity, including but not limited to the principles for quantification thereof as well as the conditions in which it may be denied to an employee.
c. The expression "offence" appearing in Section 4 (6) (b) (ii) of the Gratuity Act 1972 means "any act or omission made punishable by any law for the time being in force". Hence, it is not the "conduct of a person involving moral turpitude" that triggers forfeiture of gratuity but the "conduct or act constituting an offence involving moral turpitude" which triggers such forfeiture. Therefore, from a collective reading of the above, under Section 4 (6) (b) (ii) of the Gratuity Act 1972, forfeiture of gratuity would be permissible only if the termination of an employee is for: (i) any misconduct which constitutes an offence involving moral turpitude, and; (ii) convicted for the same by a court of competent jurisdiction.

Consequently, the Telangana High Court concluded that gratuity could not be forfeited merely based on the findings of an ICC (in the absence of any material on record to show: (i) lodging of any complaint by the victim against the accused for an offence involving moral turpitude; and (ii) in the absence of any conviction of the accused by a court of competent jurisdiction).

A similar issue came up for consideration before the Delhi High Court in Punjab National Bank v. Niraj Gupta[211]. In this matter, a complaint of sexual harassment was lodged against the accused with the ICC. The ICC, after an inquiry, returned a finding of guilt against the accused. Thereafter, disciplinary proceedings were initiated against the accused by the employer organisation on the basis of the report of the ICC. The disciplinary proceedings resulted in a punishment of dismissal from service. However, no court proceedings were initiated against the accused in this context. In the meanwhile, a show cause notice was issued to the accused by the employer organisation stating that his acts amounted to "offence involving moral turpitude in terms of the provisions of the Gratuity Act" thereby warranting a forfieture of gratuity.

The question before the High Court was whether a complaint of sexual harassment, if upheld by the ICC, would *per se,* be considered an "offence of moral turpitude" and be liable for forfeiture of gratuity in terms of the provisions of the Payment of Gratuity Act. The Delhi High Court examined the relevant provisions of the Payment of Gratuity Act, more specifically Section 4 (6) of this Act (pertaining to the principles regarding forfeiture of gratuity) and drew the below mentioned conclusions.

As regards the principles for forfeiture of gratuity, the Delhi High Court identified the following situations in which a forfeiture of gratuity is permissible in law:

a. where the dismissal from service is on account of an act, wilful omission or negligence committed by the employee and the same causes any damage or any loss, destruction of property of the employer. Quantification of the damage or loss caused to the employer would be required in this situation.

211 2024/DHC/5022

b. where the dismissal from service is on account of riotous or disorderly conduct or any other act of violence committed on the part of the employee.
c. where the dismissal from service is on account of any act/ misconduct committed by the employee during the course of employment and the same constitutes an offence involving moral turpitude.

Further, as regards the issue regarding "moral turpitude", the Delhi High Court, while relying on various judicial precedents, observed as follows:

a. The essential pre-requisites for forfeiture of gratuity are that the concerned act should constitute an offence involving moral turpitude resulting in a conviction under law at the time in force.
b. The act/conduct is not for the employer to decide rather it must be strictly decided as per the realm of criminal law and by a court of competent jurisdiction.
c. Forfeiture of gratuity of an employee by the employer would require initiation of criminal proceedings which have been culminated in conviction of an offence involving moral turpitude.

The Delhi High Court ultimately concluded that forfeiture of gratuity of the accused employee by the employer would be impermissible in the event it is only based on the findings of the ICC (and any other consequent disciplinary action emanating therefrom), in the absence of a conviction by a court of competent jurisdiction for such offence.

**Stigmatic Termination**

In service law, a termination order issued to an employee which contains certain reasons for his termination but is not preceded by a full-scale inquiry is generally regarded as stigmatic in nature and is often considered questionable in law.

A question arises as to whether a termination order made pursuant to finding of guilt of the accused in a complaint of sexual harassment (after a full-scale inquiry) would amount to be a stigmatic order of termination. It is a settled possession of law that no punitive or stigmatic orders of termination should be passed without conduct of a proper inquiry into the alleged misconduct of the employee which culminates into a clear finding of guilt.[212]

The general position of law in this regard is that a termination which is preceded by a proper inquiry which ultimately arrives at a finding of guilt of the accused, typically, while being punitive in nature, would not be regarded as a stigmatic order.

In legal parlance, punitive termination is one which is preceded by: (i) a full-scale formal inquiry; (ii) is in the context of allegations involving moral turpitude or misconduct; (iii) which culminates into a finding of guilt. If all the above factors are present, then the termination is regarded as punitive, irrespective of the form and manner of the termination order.

Parallel Proceedings before ICC and LCC

In Kuncha Chandrashekhar v. The State of Andhra[213] a peculiar situation arose where "almost parallel proceedings" were conducted by the ICC and the LCC into the same complaint. In the facts of the case, during the pendency of proceedings before the ICC, the LCC was also constituted. The accused participated in both these proceedings. While the ICC observed that no case was made out against the accused, however the

212 *See generally* Vijaykumaran CPV v. Central University of Kerala, 2020 (12) SCC 426.

213 W.P. No. 10333/2021 (11.04.2023, Andhra Pradesh High Court).

LCC drew a different conclusion and found the accused guilty of sexual harassment. The accused challenge the proceedings of the LCC. The High Court observed that the accused having participated in the inquiry proceedings of the LCC, could now not raise any objection regarding such LCC.

**Action Against False or Malicious Complaint or False Evidence**

A generally accepted position is that any self-respecting lady would normally not raise unfounded or unjustified allegations of sexual harassment.[214]

While the general rule is that the outcome of a complaint which remains un-established or unsubstantiated should not disadvantage the complainant in any way; it is equally important to punish unscrupulous accusers and (sham) witnesses if they knowingly made false allegations or depositions.

Action against the Complainant

The legislative perception appears to be that law against sexual harassment may be misused by certain troublesome and vindictive women and hence certain safeguards and deterrents have been incorporated to prevent such misuse.

Where the complaints committee arrives at a conclusion that the allegations against the Respondent are malicious or the complainant has made the complaint knowing the same to be false[215], or the complainant has produced a forged or misleading document, then in such case, it may, subject to applicable

214 Rina Mukherjee v. The State of West Bengal (2014) 143 FLR 51.

215 The word 'knowingly' means '*mens rea* in the full sense'. Evidence would need to be lead to establish the required guilty knowledge. *See generally* A.K. Mukherjee v. State, 54 (1994) DLT 461; Sheo Ratan Upadhya v. Gopal Chandra Nepali, AIR 1965 All 274; Vissa Television Network Ltd. v. Gemini Television Private Ltd. (2005) 125 CompCas 815 (AP). Normally cogent evidence would be required to come to a finding that the complainant 'knowingly' made false allegations/accusations.

service rules, recommend any action against the complainant, including the following: written apology, warning, reprimand or censure, withholding of promotion, withholding of pay rise or increments, terminating the complainant from service, requiring the complainant to undergo counselling session(s) or requiring the complainant to carry out community service.[216]

This provision appears to have been incorporated in the Act to serve as a deterrent and to ensure that the inquiry mechanism under the Act is not illegally deployed by anyone to further their own selfish ends or as a revenge strategy or to get even on other issues.[217]

The Safety valve

Law provides two safety valves or protectionist measures to the complainant in such situations:

a. Mere inability to substantiate a complaint or provide adequate proof need not attract any action against the complainant.[218] Such a safeguard would ensure that the complainant is not disadvantaged in case a grievance (raised by her in good faith) is found to be unsubstantiated. However, each case must be closely examined in its facts and circumstances before arriving at a conclusion in this regard.
b. The malicious intent on the part of the complainant needs to be established pursuant to an inquiry before any action is recommended against the complainant.[219] Therefore, no

216 R. 10 of the Rules.

217 *See generally* Shah Jayshree Manilal Pushpaben v. State of Maharashtra (2012) 2 Bom CR 770. In the said case, a student caught by her professor using unfair means in an examination made a complaint of sexual harassment against him as a counterblast.

218 S. 14 *First Proviso* of the Act.

219 S. 14 *Second Proviso* of the Act.

complainant shall be proceeded against simply on account of an unsubstantial claim of sexual harassment. No precipitative action should be taken before the malicious intent is proved. All action must be taken only after a thorough investigation since such actions tend to affect the character and credibility of the complainant.[220]

## The Criticism by Verma Committee

The Verma Committee Report was not in favour of any provision for penalising a complainant of sexual harassment. Its observations in this regard are as follows:

> We notice from the provisions of the Bill that Section 14 appears to penalise a woman for filing a false complaint. We think that such a provision is a completely abusive provision and is intended to nullify the objective of the law. We think that these 'red-rag' provisions ought not to be permitted to be introduced and they show very little thought.

## Action against Witnesses

Where the complaints committee arrives at a conclusion that, during the inquiry, any witness had given false evidence or produced any forged or misleading document, then in such case it may recommend action against such witness, including the following: written apology, warning, reprimand or censure, withholding of promotion, withholding of pay rise or increments, termination from service, requiring such person to

220 In Dr. Sushmita Banerjee v. Kolkata Port Trust W.P. No. 76/2016 (03.02.2016, Calcutta High Court), disciplinary action was sought to be taken against a witness of a sexual harassment case with alacrity, despite the fact that the main proceedings were in a state of arrest. The court expressed alarm at such conduct of the complaints committee and stopped the proposed disciplinary action against such witness.

undergo a counselling session or requiring such person to carry out community service.[221]

Employer penalty for non compliance

Failure of the employer to take action against the unscrupulous complainants or witnesses invites penalty of up to Rs. 50,000/-.[222]

## CORRECTIVE MEASURE BY EMPLOYER

The Act provides for little when it comes to curing / minimising/ rectifying the after effects of sexual harassment. However, as per the author, an employer ought to assist victims of sexual harassment in overcoming their inflictions and successfully moving on with their lives.

Although an act of sexual harassment may be not be capable of complete remedy, the following steps (as far as practicable) may be taken by an employer in this regard:

a. Restoration of leaves, if any, taken by the victim as a result of the harassment.
b. Providing extra leaves to the victim, if deemed necessary.
c. Reinstatement of the victim with all consequential benefits, wherever possible.
d. Removal of any adverse employment decision taken with respect to the victim or witnesses (which arose on account of or in connection with the harassment).
e. Monetary compensation.
f. Monitoring the victim and witnesses to ensure that they are not subjected to any reprisal.
g. Not post the victim or the witnesses under any person where

221 S. 14 (2) of the Act.

222 S. 26 of the Act.

there may be reasonable ground to believe that they may be subjected to harassment.[223]

h. In case of any complaint of retaliation or harassment, deal with the issue efficaciously and expeditiously.

i. Other rehabilitative steps, such as counselling of the victim etc.

## VICTIMISATION/RETALIATORY ACTION

The Act makes it illegal to retaliate against an person for opposing practices made unlawful by the statute. Victimisation, in the context of sexual harassment, means subjecting the complainant or the witness to some detriment for initiating or participating in a claim of sexual harassment.[224]

It is unlawful to retaliate against an individual: (i) who oppose conduct(s) that discriminate based on sex; or (ii) files a sexual harassment claim; or (iii) participates in any way in an investigation or proceeding pertaining to sexual harassment (the "**Protected Activity**").[225] The Supreme Court, in the Vishaka Case, obligated the employer to ensure that victims or witnesses are not victimized or discriminated against. A similar sentiment has been echoed by courts on numerous other occasions.[226]

Any action impacting an individual's employment due to reasons such a genuine business downturn or a legitimate business/administrative decision may not amount to victimisation.

---

223 *See generally* Office Memorandum F. No. 11013/7/2016-Estt (A-III), dated 22.12.2016, Department of Personnel & Training, Ministry of Personnel, Public Grievances and Pensions, Government of India.

224 Every woman has a right to claim and enforce her rights under the Act; and every person has the right to participate in any proceedings under the Act in connection with reprisal or threats of reprisal. Law provides protection from reprisal irrespective of whether a claim of sexual harassment is sustained or not.

225 The Supreme Court in D.S. Grewal v. Vimmi Joshi (2009) 2 SCC 210 took note of the phenomenon of retaliatory action.

226 *See* Sh. Onkar Singh v. Union of India (01.08.2007, Central Administrative Tribunal, Delhi) where the court observed that the complainant of sexual harassment and others who come forward to assist and support such complainant in sexual harassment proceedings must not be penalized.

Typically, to establish a case of retaliation, the complainant must be able to show the following:[227] (i) that she engaged in the Protected Activity;[228] (ii) she suffered an adverse employment action; and (iii) there exists a causal link between the Protected Activity and the adverse action.[229] In other words, it must be shown that 'retaliation' played a 'motivating part' in the adverse employment decision.[230] Once the above is established, the burden shifts on the opposite side to demonstrate a 'legitimate non-retaliatory purpose'.[231] Put differently, the opposite side would need to show that it would have taken the same action absent the retaliatory motive.[232]

227 Jennifer Paul v. Elayn Hunt Correctional Centre, Department of Public Safety and Corrections, State of Louisiana Appeal No. 16-30574 (18.11.2016, 5th Circuit); Long v. Eastfield 88 F.3d 300 (5th Circuit, 1996).

228 Normally, the 'adverse employment action' must be 'materially adverse' that is 'harmful to the point that it could dissuade a reasonable person from making or supporting a charge of sexual harassment'. *See* Porter v. Houma Terrebonne 810 F.3d 940 (5th Circuit, 2015). Such a requirement of 'materiality' is intended to separate significant from trivial harms. *See* Aryain v. Wal Mart Stores 534 F.3d 473 (5th Circuit, 2008). Accordingly, this standard may not encompass the 'petty slights, minor annoyances or simple lack of good manners' that employees encounter in the workplace. To determine whether an action is materially adverse, one needs to look to indica such as whether the action affected the 'job title, grade, hours, salary or benefits, or caused 'a diminution in prestige or change in standing'. *See* Stewart v. Miss. Transp. Comm'n 586 F.3d 321 (5th Circuit, 2009).

229 Close timing between the Protected Activity and the adverse action may be an indicator of 'causal connection'. Even otherwise, absent temporal proximity, a causal connection may be shown by aspects such as employment record (of the victim) not supporting the employment action, employers departure from standard policies and procedures etc. *See* Jennifer Paul, *supra.*

230 Fye v. Oklahoma Corporation 516 F.3d 1217 (10th Circuit, 2008).

231 The following may not qualify to be adverse employment action: (i) Late payment of claims, pay etc. *See* Jennifer Paul, *supra;* (ii) Single denial of leave when if affects leave on a specific date and time, but not the employee's amount of or right to take leave in general. *See* Ogden v. Potter 397 F.App'x 938 (5th Circuit, 2010); (iii) Delay in promotion when the claimant ultimately received promotion with retroactive pay and seniority. *See* Anthony v. Donohoe 460 F.App'x 399 (5th Circuit, 2012); (iv) Any reassignment which generally requires additional tasks but is not accompanied by any other change in the employment status. *See* Watts v. Kroger Co. 170 F.3d 505 (5th Circuit, 1999).

232 David Hansen v. United States Equal Employment Opportunity Commission, Appeal No. 15-8112 (21.12.2016, 10th Circuit).

In view of the author, the aspect of retaliation, by itself, constitutes a significant form of sexual harassment. Any form of retaliatory action, such as reprisals (firing from employment, denial of promotion etc.) subjecting one to hostility, scrutiny, social exclusion, negative behaviour, any form of 'bullying', and 'constructive discharge' of the complainant (*viz.* the complainant quitting her job when she can no longer tolerate a hostile work environment) ought to be construed as a notional extension to the offence of 'sexual harassment'; and any person involved in such retaliatory action should be proceeded with under the Act and as per applicable law.

The Act does not appear to contain any specific provision expressly prohibiting a retaliation against a complainant or witnesses for filing a case of sexual harassment or participating in a claim of sexual harassment or for generally speaking out against sexual harassment.[233] Be that as it may, it appears from a reading of Section 19 of the Act that the employer is under an implicit obligation to prevent victimization of the complainant of sexual harassment.

In view of the author, a sexual harassment policy formulated by an employer may contain specific provisions for protecting complainants and witnesses, both during the pendency of a complaint and thereafter.[234]

### Types of Victimisation

Victimization may take various forms. It is now pertinent to refer to some common forms of victimization.

233 *See generally* Parliamentary Standing Committee Report (2011), at ¶ 4.1 & 7.4. The Report had proposed insertion of a 'no retaliatory clause' to protect people who raise *bona fide* issues in connection with sexual harassment, including witnesses. Further, the Bill also contained a provision which elaborately dealt with the issue of victimisation. However, this provision did not make its way into the Act.

234 *See generally* M. Kavya v. Chairman, University Grants Commission W.P. No. 11217/2014 (04.12.2014, Madras High Court).

## Suspension Orders

Suspension orders are a common form of retaliation. Normally, courts may intervene, even at an interim stage, in situations where unjustified adverse action is taken (or sought to be taken) against the complainant or a witness. However, if allegations against the complainant/witnesses are grave or serious in nature (for example financial irregularities, misappropriation etc.) then in such case the court may not be inclined to interfere.[235] In any event, every such case as to be determined on the basis of its facts and circumstances.

## Transfer Orders

Courts have ruled in a cantena of judgments that ordinarily, transfer orders must not be interfered with.[236] In State of U.P v. Siya Ram[237] the Supreme Court held that transfer is not only an incidence of service but also a condition of service.[238] It should not be interfered with if it is an outcome of a *bona fide* exercise or the outcome of an administrative exigency or in public interest.[239] However, the burden should be on the employer to show that the transfer was necessitated by any public interest or on administrative ground.[240] A purely lateral transfer, that is, a transfer that does not involve a demotion in form or

235 *See generally* Shobha Goswami v. State of Uttar Pradesh (2015) 146 FLR 613.

236 Public Services Tribunal Bar Association v. State of U.P (2003) 4 SCC 104. Often, in appropriate circumstances, a transfer may, by itself, be considered to be akin to punishment imposed upon the delinquent. *See* Rupesh Hari v. Union of India W.P. (C) No. 6549/2016 (29.07.2016, Delhi High Court).

237 Civil Appeal No. 5005/2004 (05.08.2004, Supreme Court of India).

238 *See also* Yashoda Tiwari v. Western Coal Fields Limited W.P. No. 4509/2014 (02.03.2015, Madhya Pradesh High Court).

239 However, the transfer should not adversely affect the transferee's official status or infract his career prospects such as seniority, pay scale or secured emoluments. *See* State of Uttar Pradesh v. Gobardhan Lal (2004) 11 SCC 402; N.K. Singh v. Union of India (1994) 6 SCC 1998.

240 Sh. Onkar Singh v. Union of India *supra*.

substance, would not rise to the level of a materially adverse employment action.[241]

In Sunita Kumari v. State of Himachal Pradesh[242] it was observed that courts would not normally annul a transfer order solely on the ground that it may cause personal inconvenience to the employee concerned, as these matters fall within the exclusive domain of the employer.

If the transfer of an employee is being made either in pursuance of or in anticipation of closure of the office where the concerned employee is located, then in such case, the transfer would be considered as routine and not punitive.[243]

In Puran Chand v. State of Himachal Pradesh[244] the court summarized the following principles of law relating to transfer:

a. Transfer is a condition of service.
b. Transfer does not adversely affect the status or emoluments or seniority of the employee.
c. The employee has no vested right to get a posting at a particular place or choose to serve at a particular place for a particular time.
d. It is within the exclusive domain of the employer to determine as to what place and for how long the service of a particular employee is required.
e. A transfer order should be passed in public interest or administrative exigency, and not arbitrarily or for extraneous consideration or for victimisation of the employee or under political pressure.
f. There is very little scope for judicial review by courts/tribunals against a transfer order. Judicial review is restricted only to cases

241 *See* Doe v. Dekalb County 145 F.3d 1441 (11th Circuit, 1998). However, multiple transfers to lesser positions, especially when other employees are not treated similarly, may constitute an adverse employment action. *See* Llampallas v. Mini-Circuits Lab., Inc. 163 F.3d 1236 (11th Circuit, 1998).

242 C.W.P. No. 4074/2019 (10.09.2020, Himachal Pradesh High Court).

243 W.P. No. 18561/2023 (11.10.2023, Andhra Pradesh High Court).

244 C.W.P. No. 2225/2020 (14.07.2020, Himachal Pradesh High Court).

where the transfer order is found to be in contravention of the statutory rules or where *mala fides* are established.

g. In case of *mala fides,* the employee must make specific averments and prove the same by adducing impeccable evidence.
h. The person against whom allegations of *mala fide* is made should be impleaded as a party.
i. Transfer policy or guidelines issued by the state or employers do not have any statutory force.
j. The court does not interfere with a transfer order only on the ground that it will cause personal inconvenience to the employee or his/her family members.

In Sunetra v. Central Board for Workers Education[245] a transfer order had been issued without any real administrative exigency and only for the purpose of preventing a person from appearing before an inquiry committee as a witness in a case of sexual harassment. The court, while disapproving of the transfer order, explained the law on transfer in the following words:

> 13. It is well settled that the power to transfer has to be exercised bona fide and for administrative exigency. Mala fide will take within its sweep arbitrary or colourable excise of power and any other element which goes to establish non-existence of a real administrative (sic). The Hon'ble Supreme Court in the case of State of Punjab v. Gurdial Singh, AIR 1980 SC 319, has explained the import of true mala fide in relation to exercise of power. In the context of transfer, mala fide is not limited to the personal malice of the authority making the transfer. Malafide has two components, i.e., malice in law and malice in fact. Relevant extract of the said judgment herein below:

245 OA No. 349/2012 (13.08.2012, Central Administrative Tribunal, Delhi).

The question then, is what is mala fides in the jurisprudence of power? Legal malice is gibberish unless juristic clarity keeps it separate from the popular concept of personal vice. Pithily put, bad faith which invalidates the exercise of power sometimes called colourable exercise or fraud on power and often times overlaps motives, passions and satisfactions--is the attainment of ends beyond the sanctioned purposes of power by simulation or pretension of gaining a legitimate goal. If the use of the power is for the fulfilment of a legitimate object the actuation or catalysation by malice is not regicidal. The action is bad where the true object is to reach an end different from the one for which the power is entrusted, goaded by extraneous considerations, good or bad, but irrelevant to the entrustment. When the custodian of power is influenced in its exercise by consideration outside those for promotion of which the power is vested the Court calls it a colourable exercise and is undeceived by illusion. In a broad, blurred sense, Benjamin Disraeli was not off the mark even in law when he stated: "I repeat... that all power is a trust that we are accountable for its exercise--that from the people, and for the people, all springs and all must exist." Fraud on power voids the order if it is not exercised bona fide for the end designed. Fraud in this context is not equal to moral turpitude and embraces all cases in which the action impugned is to affect some object which is beyond the purpose and intent of the power, whether this be malice laden or even benign. If the purpose is corrupt the resultant act is bad. If considerations, foreign to the scope of the power or extraneous to the statute, enter the verdict or impels the action mala fides or fraud on power vitiates the acquisition or other official act.

14. The Hon'ble Supreme Court has said that the order of transfer may be silent but the operative reasons are kept in

> hidden. In such circumstances, it is the duty of the Court to find out whether the transfer order was issue in bona fide exercise of power. The Court-has to find out from the material placed before the Court whether the transfer was bona fide one or not. In the case of C. Ramanathan v. Acting Zonal Manager, Food Corporation of India 1980 (1) SLR 309 (Mad.), it has been held that in exercising its jurisdiction, if necessary, it is open to the Court to crack the shell of innocuousness which might wrap the order of transfer and by piercing the veil to find the operative reason behind the order of transfer.

Similarly, in State of UP v. Goobardhan Lal[246] the Supreme Court held as follows:

> 8. A challenge to an order of transfer should normally be eschewed and should not be countenanced by the Courts or Tribunals as though they are Appellate Authorities over such orders, which could assess the niceties of the administrative needs and requirements of the situation concerned. This is for the reason that Courts or Tribunals cannot substitute their own decisions in the matter of transfer for that of competent authorities of the State and even allegations of mala fides when made must be such as to inspire confidence in the Court or are based on concrete materials and ought not to be entertained on the mere making of it or on consideration borne out of conjectures or surmises and except for strong and convincing reasons, no interference could ordinarily be made with an order of transfer.

246 Civil Appeal No. 404/2004 (23.03.2004, Supreme Court of India).

Further, in Dharmender v. Union of India[247] the court stated thus:

> 28. It is thus well settled that in the matter of transfer, the Executive retains the absolute right to transfer a person in public interest and unless there are clear cut malafides established or if it is established that the decision is in violation of a statutory rule it should not be interfered with. Therefore, interference in the cases is warranted only if the transfer orders are issued by an incompetent authority or the transfer orders are established to be based on malafides. Normally, Courts or Tribunals cannot act as appellate forums to decide on transfers on administrative grounds. Further, a government servant cannot disobey a transfer order by not reporting at the place of posting. It is his duty to first report for work where he is transferred and make a representation, if aggrieved with the transfer order.

Thus, from the above, it is palpable that transfers which are motivated by malice or *mala fides*; which result in violation of the service rules or any statutory provision[248] or which are against public interest are impermissible. The modality of transfer should not be converted into a device to procrastinate or scuttle an inquiry of sexual harassment.

Transfers which are punitive or stigmatic may be set aside by courts. For a court to ascertain as to whether an order of transfer is stigmatic or punitive, it would examine the consequences flowing from such order; and as to whether it adversely affects any service conditions i.e. status, service prospects, finances etc.[249]

247 OA No. 2135/2015 (08.09.2015, Central Administrative Tribunal, Delhi).

248 *See* Union of India v. S.L. Abbas (1993) 4 SCC 357.

249 *See generally* Gopinath v. State of Kerala ILR 2014 (4) Kerala 573.

Compulsory Retirement

Another mode of victimisation is compulsorily retiring the victim. The case of Sarita Das v. Union India[250] is a textbook case of this form of victimisation. Here, the victim had filed a case of sexual harassment against the accused. The complaints committee arrived at a finding that the accused was guilty of sexual harassment. The accused was punished with compulsory retirement. Subsequently, the victim herself was charge sheeted and discharged from service for being a part of an alleged conspiracy against the accused. The court held that this was a clear case of victimization of the complainant.

Discharge of the Victim from Employment

In Rina Mukherjee v. The State of West Bengal[251] in the context of an industrial dispute, the services of a complainant (of sexual harassment) were terminated by citing unsatisfactory work performance.[252] The court, while observing that the employer could not adduce substantial proof of unsatisfactory performance, observed that the termination of the women was not *bona fide*. The court held as follows:

> The Industrial Tribunal is a fact finding authority. The Industrial Tribunal has held that the termination of the probationer was not bona fide and in colourable exercise of power. In absence of any evidence to show that the performance of the probationer was unsatisfactory inasmuch as the management has failed to establish the validity, loyality, existence and contents of the letter dated 25th September, 2002 which terms the basis of the formation

250 2014 (2) GLT 662.

251 (2014) 143 FLR 51.

252 *See also* Saudi Arabian Airlines v. Shehnaz Mudbhatkal (1999) 1 Mah LJ 489.

> of opinion, the findings arrived at by Tribunal cannot be said to be perverse. Moreover the management employee did not constitute a committee in terms of the judgment of the Hon'ble Supreme Court in Vishaka (supra). The Tribunal is of the view that the employee suffers termination in view of her protest against sexual and professional harassment. The tribunal can always go into the question to find out if such order is actuated by motives of victimization or other ulterior motives. The Tribunal can always examine the grounds on which the management terminated the service as also other facts only for the purpose of seeing whether it was actuated by ulterior motive in terminating the service and in not confirming her. The Tribunal found such termination punitive and/or stigmatic. Such findings are arrived at on careful consideration of the materials on record and appreciation of evidence. The Employer could not adduce any evidence to show that the performance of the employee was unsatisfactory raising a grave and serious doubt about the bona fide of the discharge order and makes one to feel that she was victimized. In Utkal Machinary Ltd. Vs. Prasah (1966) 1 LLJ 398 the Hon'ble Supreme Court set aside the order of discharge of the probationer during the period of probation since the employer could not produce evidence of unsatisfactory performance of the employee at the factory. Such order of discharge was held to be punitive.

## Constructive Discharge

Constructive discharge occurs when an employer, rather than directly discharging the employee, intentionally creates an intolerable work atmosphere that forces the employee to quit involuntarily. To succeed in a claim of constructive discharge, a victim must show 'deliberate action on the part of the employer' to create working conditions so intolerable that a reasonable person would feel compelled to resign.[253] This may include humiliating demotion, extreme cut in pay, repositioning of victim to unbearable working conditions etc.[254]

<u>Postponement of Increment</u>

This is another form of victimisation. In S. Chitra v. Director of Fire Services[255] the accused made counter-allegations against a victim of sexual harassment. While the sexual harassment complaint of the victim were ignored, the charges made against her by the accused were considered and consequently, by an order, a punishment of postponement of increment for a period of three years was imposed on her. The court observed, *'(i)t is a classic case where the complainant has become the accused and the accused has become the complainant.'* The court directed quashing of this order.

<u>Reprimands and Poor Performance Evaluations</u>

Reprimands and poor performance evaluations, *per se,* may not qualify to be a retaliation (since these occur generally and with some frequency in the workplace and are less likely to involve adverse employment actions like transfers, discharges, declination of promotion etc. Although, in combination (with other forms of retaliations) they may also signify retaliation.[256]

<u>Sexual Harassment by a 'responsible person'</u>

The Karnataka High Court, in the case of S. Srikanth Joshi v. Board of Management of Aladangady Vyavasaya Seva Sahakari

---

253 Whidbee v. Garzarelli Food Specialties Inc. 223 F.3d 62 (2nd Circuit, 2000).

254 *See generally* Pennsylvania State Police v. Suders 542 U.S. 129 (2004).

255 W.P. (C) 37598/2006 (30.09.2009, Madras High Court).

256 *See* Abigail Wilson v. Jim Putman Appeal No. 15-2522 (13.04.2017, Court of Appeals, 4th Circuit).

Bank[257] took up cudgels against the harasser who was a 'chief executive' of the workplace (a bank) and had himself committed in sexual harassment. The court regretted that the 'protector' had turned into a 'predator' and observed that such conduct was unbecoming of an officer who was himself in a fiduciary capacity of a 'responsible person' at the workplace.

## VICTIM ADVISORY

A victim of sexual harassment may explore the below mentioned suggestions for effective prosecution and enforcement.

a. Act: First and foremost, you must act in case you are harassed in a manner which you perceive to be sexual in nature. You must not ignore the sexual behaviour or sit tight over it lest such behaviour escalates towards you or towards any other member of the female workforce. Assertive action on the part of the harassed individual and unequivocal rejection of the inappropriate behaviour is a vital step towards remedying the problem.
b. Check Company Policies: Look up the sexual harassment policy of your organisation, and evaluate for yourself whether the alleged conduct constitutes 'sexual harassment'. You may consult colleagues, friends or lawyers in this regard. Please note that it is imperative that you follow the terms of the sexual harassment policy which your organisation may have in place.
c. Keep a Detailed Record of the Happenings: Note the date, time and place of each incident, what was said and done, and the witnesses of such actions. Preferably, you should be specific and lucid in your recordal. Maintaining a detailed record of the harassment would be useful in case of an inquiry or legal proceedings. If possible, you may request the witnesses to take written notes of what they witnessed. This may aid you (and the

257 2007 (5) Kant LJ 484.

witnesses) at the time of an inquiry. Additionally, if possible, try and make circumspect inquires within your organisation to earmark any other victims (of the offender) and document the results of your inquiries. This may also come in handy during the inquiry process.

d. Warning to the Perpetrator: One important legal requirement for sexual harassment to occur is that the perpetrator's conduct should be 'unwelcome'. Therefore, it may be a good idea to inform the perpetrator that his behaviour is offensive. Often a person may unwittingly commit an act of sexual harassment. Sometimes employees are oblivious to how their conduct is being perceived by others; or sometimes they may simply make mistakes which can be easily purged. It is because of this reason that, wherever possible, it is advisable that a complainant may explore the possibility of giving a prior warning to the perpetrator before pressing charges against him. This may often prove helpful in dissipating situations where the conduct of the offender is unintended or non-deliberate. If such person realises that his behaviour is offending then he may immediately cease such behaviour and in future, be mindful of how his words or expressions may be interpreted by others before he speaks or acts.[258] However this option is completely fact driven. This option need not be exercised in situations where the sexual harassment is clearly deliberate or sufficiently severe or pervasive in nature.

e. Speak to your Employer: If necessary, speak to your employer or superiors about the issue. Gathering support from your colleagues may help you gain confidence. However, do not let them trivialise or dismiss the issue for it may have the result of undermining of your potential complaint against the offender.

f. File a Complaint: File an internal complaint with your organisation's complaints committee, in accordance with the sexual harassment

258 A complaint of sexual harassment will not necessarily be dismissed on the premise that the victim did not directly indicate to the harasser that his conduct was unwelcome. *See* Lynette Jane Aldridge v. Grant Rodney Booth (1988) 80 ALR 1.

policy.[259] It is important that the complaint is specific, definite and clear; and every charge is easily comprehended by the complaints committee as well as the perpetrator.[260] If necessary, a criminal complaint against the perpetrator may also be filed.[261] You must fully co-operate with the investigation. Nothing should be suppressed. Failure to do so may have a negative impact on the investigation process.

g. Be Clear about the Time Lines: Presently, the time lines for pressing charges of sexual harassment before the complaints committee are 3 (three) months from the date of the incident [extendable by another period of 3 (three) months]. Make sure that you strictly adhere to these time lines. It is recommended that any offensive behaviour is reported at the earliest; although failing to report immediately does not affect the merits of the matter.

h. Keep doing your job: Keep doing your job and keep a record of your work. Preferably, keep a track of all job evaluations, reviews, memos, reporting structure etc. These may come in handy in case of any retaliatory action is initiated (or sought to be initiated) against you for filing a claim of sexual harassment. Specifically speaking, keep any eye out for any change in your work patterns or the attitude of your superiors/contemporaries subsequent to filing of the complaint.

---

259 It is settled law that, to sustain a disciplinary proceeding, the charges framed against the accused must be clear, specific and unambiguous. Further, the charges should not be changed during the course of the proceedings. Sarita Das v. Union of India (2014) 2 GLT 662.

260 *See* C.S.H.N. Murthy v. Tezpur University (2015) 3 GLT 346. This would ensure that the perpetrator is unable to challenge any order passed against him by the complaints committee by citing bareness or inadequacies in the complaint.

261 *See* Chapter titled 'Criminal Remedies' for more on criminal actions.

CHAPTER 6

# Confidentiality

Complaints relating to sexual harassment contain sensitive information which must be carefully preserved and protected. The Act upholds this principle and obligates maintenance of adequate confidentiality.

As per the Act, none of the below mentioned information/ documents shall be published, communicated or made known to the public, press and media in any manner:[1]

a. the contents of the complaint.
b. the identity and addresses of the aggrieved woman, respondent and witnesses.
c. information relating to conciliation and inquiry proceedings.
d. recommendations of the complaints committee.
e. any action taken by the employer or the district officer under the provisions of the Act.

## EXCLUSION OF THE RIGHT TO INFORMATION ACT

The Act further clarifies that all material pertaining to sexual harassment shall not be subject to the provisions of the Right to Information Act, 2005. In other words, information relating

1 S. 16 of the Act. Note that S. 16, in the first instance, favours the theory of denial of publicity to the sexual harassment proceedings.

to workplace harassment shall not be made public under any circumstances.[2] This provision safeguards against public disclosure of the identities of the parties to a complaint of sexual harassment. This would also help to prevent victimization of the complainant.[3] Such a provision shall encourage the victim to avail the recourse available under the Act without fear or stigma.

However, the aforesaid rule contains a limited exception: The Act provides that information regarding justice secured to any victim of sexual harassment may be disseminated without disclosing the name, address, identity or any other particulars calculated to lead to the identification of the aggrieved and the witnesses.[4] This limited disclosure does not militate against the interests of the complaint and further may have the following benefits: (i) aid in deterring potential violators from indulging in acts of sexual harassment; and (ii) provide a marker to the employees at the workplace that their organisation takes the issue of sexual harassment very seriously.

## BREACH OF CONFIDENCE

The doctrine of "breach of confidence" is based on the principle of equity and probity; and has largely been developed in India through judicial precedent. The jurisprudence relating to the concept of confidence stems from the 'right to privacy'. The cornerstone of this concept is that a person who receives information from another in confidence must not use it or publish it. Disclosure or use by others of a person's secret or

---

2 S. 16 merely eclipses the 'right to know' of the public, press and media but not of the complainant. *See* Archana Sharma v. Geological Survey of India, CIC/YA/A/2016/000059 (01.07.2016, Central Information Commission).

3 *See* Archana Sharma *ibid.*

4 S. 16 *Proviso* of the Act.

confidential information without proper consent is considered illegal and is actionable in Indian courts.

**Objective of Confidentiality in sexual harassment matters**

Confidentiality is an important part of the sexual harassment law. Confidentiality must be ensured inasmuch as the subject matter of a sexual harassment incident is bound to have 'sensitive' features.[5] All details regarding an inquiry must be kept out of public domain. Compliance with this provision is imperative and must be scrupulously followed.[6] Any leak could tarnish the reputation of the concerned parties as well as of the organization. Therefore, all confidential information requires cautious handling by the concerned persons.

Upholding the confidentiality provision under the Act is, apart from being a statutory obligation, also a moral obligation of the employer. Ensuring the confidentiality of the inquiry would also assist in maintaining the institutional/ organizational credibility.[7]

**Confidentiality in Appellate Forum**

At the request of the victim(s), courts generally consider rendering confidentiality to the parties in case the circumstances so require (such as withholding the names of the parties in the cause title, in-camera proceedings etc.)

In the context of sexual harassment, various High Courts have issued appropriate practice directions for ensuring the

---

5 S. 16 has been enacted as a safeguard measure to check further aggravation of traumatic and stigmatic experience of the victim on account of unwarranted disclosure of her identity. *See* Archana Sharma *supra.*

6 *See generally* Shri Lalu Varghese v. State Bank of India, Appeal No. CIC/ MP/A/ 2014/001168 (31.03.2015, Central Information Commission).

7 S. 16 of the Act would be violated in case of dissemination of the prohibited information to any third party. *See* Shri V.K. Bhosale v. CPIO, CIC/ SH/A/2014/001862 (15.09.2015, Central Information Commission).

confidentiality of the parties who are embroiled in litigation before courts. Towards this end, directions are issued to redact the names and other identifying markers of the concerned parties from the pleadings/case title/memo of the petition which is served to the court and the counsels. The names and other identifying markers of the parties are directed to be retained by the court registry in a sealed envelope.

**Application of the confidentiality provision to the parties**

Section 16 only prohibits undue publicity or publication of the contents of the complaint made under the Act to third parties.[8] This provision does not militate against disclosure of documents and other information to the parties involved. The prohibition under section 16 is against undue publicity among the public, press or media, which by no stretch of imagination can be extended to the parties.[9] The complainant shall be entitled to all records relating to the sexual harassment complaint lodged by her.[10]

8 Shri V.K. Bhosale v. CPIO, CIC/SH/A/2014/001862 (15.09.2015, Central Information Commission).

9 A.L. Agarwal v. Delhi University CIC/RM/A/2014/000313-SA (09.12.2015, Central Information Commission); Ather Parvez v. CPIO, New Delhi Municipal Council File No. CIC/YA/A/2016/001444 (01.05.2017, Central Information Commission).

10 *See* Ms. Navneet Kaur v. CPIO, Department of Information Technology (22.03.2006, Central Information Commission); Gurmeet Singh v. CPIO, Appeal No. CIC/VS/A/2014/003051/BJ (04.01.2017, Central Information Commission). The right of a complainant to secure a copy of the findings of the committee (whether preliminary or final) overrides S. 8 (1) (h) of the RTI Act (which exempts disclosure of such information which would impede the process of investigation or apprehension of prosecution of offenders. *See* Sushma Rani Tirkey v. PIO, Council of Scientific & Industrial Research CIC/CSIRD/A/2016/306867 (28.04.2017, Central Information Commission); Soumen Sen v. PIO, National Commission for Women File No. CIC/NCFWO/A/2017/191483 (12.05.2017, Central Information Commission) *See also* Meena Rawat v. Mr. S.K. Chugh, PIO and Manager (HR) Delhi Transco Limited, CIC/SG/A/2011/000462/12128 where information sought by a woman in connection with a sexual harassment proceeding initiated on the basis of her complaint was directed to be provided to her by the Central Information Commission.

## Management of Confidential Information

Employers must develop appropriate guidelines for dealing with information described as confidential under the Act. Ideally, all information relating to sexual harassment should be protected by practical security safeguards, and should be accessible only by responsible persons.

It may be noted that, achieving confidentiality in such matters is a herculean task. Further, law neither appears to provide sufficient guidance on how to go about this issue nor does it seem to provide appropriate deterrents for its violation. The employer should ideally draw up appropriate policies and mechanisms for achieving and enforcing confidentiality.

## Penalty for breach of Confidentiality

All participants to an inquiry of sexual harassment should be advised to maintain confidentiality. If any person entrusted with the duty to handle the complaint, inquiry or any recommendations or actions to be taken under the Act, contravenes the above-described confidentiality provisions, then he shall be liable for penalty in the following manner:

a. Penalty in accordance with the provisions of the service rules applicable to the violator.
b. Penalty of Rs. 5,000/- in case no service rules are applicable to the violator (to be recovered by the employer).[11]

In view of the author, the penalty of Rs. 5,000/- contemplated in the Act for breach of 'confidentiality' is miniscule and disproportionate to the gravity of the offence.

11 R. 12 of the Rules.

## RAISING THE ISSUE OF SEXUAL HARASSMENT IN PUBLIC DOMAIN

Section 16 of the Act obligates the employers (and its personnel) to uphold confidentiality. One question that arises is whether a victim of sexual harassment is also required to uphold the principles of confidentiality specified in Section 16 of the Act. In Leena Doley v. State of Assam[12] in the context of the Vishaka Guidelines, it was observed that the victim was at liberty to raise the matter of sexual harassment in employee meetings. As a consequence of the above, the matter may get publicized. Such publication was not held to be illegal. Accordingly, a victim of sexual harassment may not be restrained from publicizing her incident of sexual harassment.

12 2013 (5) GLT 363.

CHAPTER 7

# The Appellate Mechanism

As explained in the preceding chapters, post conclusion of an inquiry, the complaints committee makes a report and sends it to the organisation along with its recommendations. The organisation then acts on such recommendations. Often a party to the inquiry is not satisfied with the results and seeks to assail the report of the complaints committee before a superior forum. This is done by filing an appeal before the appropriate forum or a writ petition before the jurisdictional High Court.

In simple terms, an appeal is a 're-appreciation' or 'reconsideration' of a decision (rendered by the original forum) by a higher forum. In an appeal, the correctness of the original forum's decision is tested and scrutinised. In the context of sexual harassment, a decision rendered by the complaints committee (and its consequent implementation by the employer) can be challenged by way of an appeal (in the manner prescribed in the Act).

## THE HIGHER FORA

It is critical to identify the forum which would exercise appellate jurisdiction over a determination made by a complaints committee in a sexual harassments claim. In this regard, the Act provides as follows:

a. If any service rules are applicable to the concerned organisation, then the appeal shall be made in accordance with such service rules.[1] It is crucial to clarify that where service rules exist, an appeal needs to be preferred only in accordance with the provisions of such service rules and in no other manner.[2]

b. If no service rules are applicable to the concerned organisation, then the appeal shall be made before the Appellate Authority prescribed under the provisions of the Industrial Employment (Standing Orders) Act, 1946 ("**Standing Orders Act**").[3]

   Generally speaking, the Standing Orders Act applies only to organisations which qualify to be 'industrial establishments' and which employ more than 150 (one hundred and fifty) 'workmen'.[4] However, the Act has, through deeming fiction, vested in this Appellate Authority with the mandate of hearing and determining appeals under the provisions of the Act irrespective of whether the organisation or qualifies to be an industrial establishment or not; or whether the establishment employs 150 (one hundred and fifty) workmen or nor.[5]

---

1 S. 18 (1) of the Act. *See generally* Amul v. Union of India OA No. 354/2015 (01.10.2015, Central Administrative Tribunal, Ahmedabad) for the interpretation of the terms 'court' and 'tribunal' used in S. 18 (1) of the Act. For more on service rules, *see* chapter titled 'Service Rules and other Legislation'.

2 In Ramesh Pal v. Union of India (2014) 2 MP LJ 500 a central government employee governed by the provisions of the Central Civil Services (Conduct) Rules 1964 was a party in a case of sexual harassment. He challenged the findings of the committee before the High Court by means of a writ petition. He was directed by the High Court to withdraw the writ and to challenge the findings of the complaints committee before the appropriate forum (*viz.* the Central Administrative Tribunal) in accordance with the service rules applicable to him.

3 *See generally* Reshma MG v. Union of India, O.A. No. 180/00722 of 2014 (19.02.2016, Central Administrative Tribunal, Ernakulam); Sunil Manu Prasad Jani v. High Court of Gujarat, Special Civil Application No. 14566/2015 (12.10.2015, Gujarat High Court).

4 Please note that certain states such as Maharashtra, Karnataka and Delhi have enhanced the scope of the Standing Orders Act and made it applicable to industrial establishments employing 50 (fifty) or more workmen. For more, *see* chapter titled 'Service Rules and other Legislation'.

5 *See generally* Tanushree Chopra v. Ministry of Women and Child Development W.P. (C) No. 11759/2015 (17.12.2015, Delhi High Court).

c. In other cases (not covered by any of the above), or in case of orders with no provision for appeal there against, an appropriate remedy may be to prefer a writ petition (judicial review) before the appropriate jurisdictional High Court.[6] A writ petition is also entertainable where pure questions of law are involved, where is absence of any factual dispute or controversy in the matter etc.

## APPEAL

Under the Act, the following situations are appealable:[7]

a. Where the complaints committee, pursuant to an inquiry, arrives at a conclusion that the allegations against the accused have not been proved and consequently recommends to the employer or the district officer (as the case may be) that no action is required to be taken in the matter.[8]
b. Where the complaints committee, pursuant to an inquiry, arrives at a conclusion that the allegations against the accused have been proved and consequently recommends to the employer or the district officer (as the case may be) that action be taken against such accused in the following manner: (i) action for sexual harassment as a misconduct in accordance with the applicable service rules or in the manner prescribed (in case no service rules are applicable);[9] (ii) deduction of appropriate sums from the salary/wages of the accused, and remittance of the same to the aggrieved.[10]
c. Where the complaints committee arrives at a conclusion that a false or malicious complaint has been

6 *See* Articles 226 & 227 of the Constitution of India. *See also* Office Memorandum F. No. 11012/5/2016-Estt.A-III, dated 02.08.2016, Department of Personnel & Training, Ministry of Personnel, Public Grievances and Pensions, Government of India.

7 S. 18 (1) of the Act.

8 S. 13 (2) of the Act.

9 S. 13 (3) (i) of the Act.

10 S. 13 (3) (ii) of the Act.

knowingly[11] filed by the complainant; or the complainant has submitted forged or misleading documents; and recommends action against the complainant in the manner prescribed.[12]

d. Where the complaints committee arrives at a conclusion that any witness to the proceedings has given false evidence or submitted forged or misleading documents, and recommends action against the said witness in the manner prescribed.[13]
e. Where a penalty (in the prescribed manner) is imposed upon a person who, entrusted with the duty to handle or deal with the complaint of sexual harassment, its inquiry or any recommendations or actions to be taken under the Act in connection thereof, breaches his duty.[14]
f. Where the employer or the district officer, as the case may be, fails to comply with any of the recommendation(s) made by the complaints committee under the Act within a period of 60 (sixty) days from the receipt of the recommendations.[15]

## Powers of the Appellate Authority

The appellate authority has a wide scope of examination of the matter. In Union of India v. Shibram[16] it was observed by the Calcutta High Court that in an appeal, the appellate authority has the power and jurisdiction to re-appreciate evidence and arrive at its own conclusion. Contrast this with the powers of the

11 The word 'knowingly' means 'mens rea in the full sense'. Evidence would need to be lead to establish the required guilty knowledge. *See generally* A.K. Mukherjee v. State 54 (1994) DLT 461; Sheo Ratan Upadhya v. Gopal Chandra Nepali AIR 1965 All 274; Vissa Television Network Ltd. v. Gemini Television Private Ltd. (2005) 125 CompCas 815 (AP). Normally cogent evidence would be required arrive at to a finding that the complainant 'knowingly' filed a false or malicious complaint against the 'harasser'.

12 S. 14 (1) of the Act.

13 S. 14 (2) of the Act.

14 S. 17 of the Act.

15 S. 13 (4) of the Act.

16 2019 SCC OnLine Cal 9105.

high court where the court only examines the decision making process and not the decision (unless the findings are based on no evidence, are perverse or are legally untenable).

At this stage, it is important to point out that any challenge to an order passed by the appellate authority would have to be made before the jurisdictional High Court under writ jurisdiction. In writ jurisdiction, the High Court would be guided by the principles of "judicial review" which are discussed in this chapter in an elaborate manner.

Interim Measures by Appellate Authority

In Nagaraj G.K v. Additional Labour Commissioner, Appellate Authority[17], at the stage of appeal against the order of the ICC, an application for interim relief was rejected, *in limini,* by the concerned appellate authority, on the premise that the Act did not contain any express provisions for grant of interim measures at the appellate stage. This order was assailed before the Karnataka High Court in writ proceedings. The High Court, after examining Section 18 of the Act and Rule 11 of the Rules, concluded that, under the Act, at the stage of appellate proceedings, the appellate authority had the power to grant interim measures (stay etc.). The High Court, while arriving at this conclusion, observed that while it was true that the Act did not contain any express provisions dealing with interim measures in appeal, however, at the same time, the Act did not expressly prohibit the same. It was concluded that the appellate authority had an implied power to grant interim measures.[18]

---

17 2024 SCC Online Kar 1056

18 Reliance was placed on Chikkathimmegowda v. Deputy Commissioner ILR 1991 Kar 3238 and Income Tax Officer v. M.K. Mohammed Kunhi 1968 SCC Online SC 71. Further reliance was also placed on the principle that "every court must be deemed possess, by necessary intendment, all such powers as are necessary to make its orders effective".

**Limitation**

Under the Act the limitation period[19] for filing an appeal is 90 (ninety) days from: (i) the date of receipt of the recommendations [under points (a) to (d) above][20]; (ii) the imposition of penalty [under point (e) above]; and (iii) the expiry of the 60 (sixty) day period[21] granted to the employer or the district officer (as the case may be) to comply with the recommendations of the complaints committee [under point (f) above].[22]

A question arises as to whether the above mentioned limitation period of 90 days is fixed or whether it is extendable by providing sufficient cause and explanation.

The issue of limitation and condonation of delay was recently discussed by the Delhi High Court in the case of DB Corp Limited v. Shaila Naqvi[23] In the said matter, an appeal was filed beyond the period of 90 days prescribed under Section 18 of the Act. The Appellate Authority (i.e. the Central Government Industrial Tribunal) had condoned the delay in filing this appeal. The matter travelled to the Delhi High Court which considered the question as to whether the provisions of Section 5 of the Limitation Act 1963 would apply to appeals under Section 18 of the Act. In other words, the question was whether delay in filing appeal under Section 18 of the Act could be condoned by the appellate authority if sufficient cause was shown by the appellant. The Delhi High Court answered in the affirmative and observed that the provisions of the Limitation Act 1963 would be applicable in case of appeals under Section

19 In its legal sense, the word 'limitation' refers to the time within which an action may be brought before the appropriate forum.

20 *See* Dr. Sushmita Banerjee v. Kolkata Port Trust W.P. No. 76/2016 (03.02.2016, Calcutta High Court).

21 S. 13 (4) of the Act.

22 S. 18 (2) of the Act.

23 CM (M) No. 705/2022 (21.07.2022, Delhi High Court).

18 of the Act and consequently observed that any delay in filing appeal, if properly explained by the appellant, should not stand in the way of the matter being decided on merits by the appellate authority. Additionally, the Delhi High Court also observed that the expression "shall" used in Section 18 (2) of the Act was directory and not mandatory in nature.

**Appeal in absence of recommendations by the Complaints Committee**

In Lakhwinder P Singh v. IIHMR[24] the Delhi High Court had the occasion to consider the situations/eventualities in which an appeal could be preferred before an appellate authority under Section 18 of the Act. In the said matter, post an inquiry, the ICC, while holding the accused to be guilty of sexual harassment, did not make any recommendations against him in the report. In other words, while the ICC's report did not exonerate the accused from the allegations of sexual harassment, however, at the same time, the ICC also did not suggest any action to be taken against the accused in this regard (as mentioned in Section 13 (3) of the Act). In any case, the employer terminated the accused from service taking into account his overall conduct and deteriorating performance at work. Interestingly, the employer did not base the termination on the report of the ICC. The accused challenged his termination through an appeal before the appellate authority (i.e. Presiding Officer, Industrial Tribunal, New Delhi). However, the appellate authority dismissed the appeal for being non-maintainable in absence of any recommendations being made by the ICC in the report (under Section 13 (3) of the Act).

The Delhi High Court, upon a conjoint reading of Sections 13 and 18 of the Act, observed that an appeal could be preferred only in the following cases: (i) allegations against the accused not being proved; (ii) allegations against the accused being

24 W.P. (C) No. 844/2017 (21.09.2022, Delhi High Court).

proved and recommendation being made to take action for sexual harassment as misconduct in accordance with law. The Delhi High Court also observed that the ICC did not make any recommendation against the accused and that the termination of the accused was not an outcome of any recommendations by the ICC. Consequently, the Delhi High Court upheld the decision of the appellate authority.

## SCOPE OF JUDICIAL INTERVENTION IN DEPARTMENTAL PROCEEDINGS

Under service law jurisprudence all proceedings initiated in connection with a claim of sexual harassment (whether in private or public sector) are generally classified as 'departmental proceedings'. Post the recommendations/decision of the disciplinary authority/complaints committee, courts have jurisdiction to entertain a challenge thereof as available either under appeal or judicial review.[25] It may be noted that the scope of judicial intervention or judicial review in departmental proceedings is very limited. Discussed below are a series of judgements which elaborate on this aspect.

In the case of Union of India v. Upendra Singh[26] the Supreme Court emphasized that the court cannot take over the function of a disciplinary authority. The truth or otherwise of the charges is a matter for the disciplinary authority to go into and the court has no jurisdiction to go into the truth of the charges or the correctness of the findings recorded by the disciplinary authority. A similar view was adopted by the Delhi High Court in the case of S. Raju Aiyer v. Jawaharlal Nehru University[27] wherein the court observed that, under the appellate or writ stage, it is not required

25 *See generally* R.S. Saini v. Bureau of Indian Standard (2004) 112 DLT 164.

26 (1994) 3 SCC 357.

27 LPA No. 330/2013 (23.08.2013, Delhi High Court).

to re-appreciate the evidence on the basis of which the findings have been returned in a domestic disciplinary proceeding.[28] Further, courts have observed that interference is warranted only if there exists a serious error of law or the findings recorded suffer from error apparent on the face of record.[29]

In Aureliano Fernandes v. State of Goa[30] the Supreme Court, in a case of sexual harassment, while discussing the scope of interference by a High Court in judicial review, observed that the High Court was required to examine the decision-making process and not just the final outcome. In exercise of powers of judicial review, the High Court does not sit as an appellate authority over the factual findings recorded in the departmental proceedings, as long as these findings are reasonably supported by evidence and have been arrived at through proceedings that cannot be faulted on account of procedural illegalities or irregularities.

The Supreme Court further observed that the purpose of judicial review is not only to ensure that the individual concerned receives fair treatment, but also to ensure that the authority, after according fair treatment, reaches a conclusion which is correct in the eyes of law.

In K.V.M. Abdunnafih v. Union of India[31] the court observed as follows:

> 8... It is well settled legal proposition that the principles of natural justice need to be complied with and the employee has to be treated fairly in departmental proceedings which

---

28 *See also* Union of India v. H.C. Goel AIR 1964 SC 364 wherein the Supreme Court observed that it cannot consider the question about the sufficiency or adequacy of evidence in support of the order under challenge.

29 *See* Rina Mukherjee v. State of West Bengal (2014) 143 FLR 51.

30 Civil Appeal No. 2482/2014 (12.05.2023, Supreme Court of India).

31 OA No. 2055/2010 (24.12.2014, Central Administrative Tribunal, Delhi).

> may culminate into imposition of a punishment. However, it is appropriate that the scope of judicial intervention in departmental proceedings be defined at the very outset. The role of judicial intervention in departmental proceedings is indeed limited and circumscribed by pronouncements of Hon'ble Supreme Court and Hon'ble High Courts from time to time. During departmental proceedings, the inquiry officer is face to face with the charged officer and also has the benefit of examination of the documents on which reliance has been placed in the inquiry. He is also a privy to examination of witnesses and their cross-examination as well as proving of the documents adduced as evidence. This benefit is not there either in the appellate court or in tribunal/ high courts, which have to rely upon the evidence recorded during the course of departmental proceedings. It is well settled law that the scope of judicial review is limited and is permissible to the extent of finding whether the process in reaching the decision has been observed correctly, and not the decision as such. However, we cannot reappraise the evidence on record and are to confine ourselves to the main issues concerned with the exercise of jurisdiction, namely, whether departmental proceedings are vitiated on account of mala fide or infringement of any statutory provisions relating to conduct of departmental inquiry or proceedings being barred by some gross procedural laches.

In the case of H.B. Gandhi v. Gopinath and Sons[32] the Supreme Court stated that judicial review is not directed against the decision but is confined to the decision-making process.[33] It cannot extend to the examination of the correctness or the reasonableness of a

32 1992 Supp. (2) SCC 312.

33 *See also* Reliance Energy Limited v. Maharashtra State Road Development Corporation (2007) 8 SCC 1.

decision as a matter of fact. The purpose of judicial review is to ensure that individuals would receive a fair treatment but not test the correctness of the decision taken by the competent authority. In other words, the court sits in judgment not in respect of the correctness of the decision but of the decision-making process and hence, the court may not go into reappraisal of the evidence.

In S.R. Tewari v. Union of India[34] the court held that the findings of the disciplinary authority can be set aside where they are perverse i.e. they have been arrived at by ignoring and excluding relevant material or taking irrelevant inadmissible material into account.[35] The relevant excerpt is as follows:

> 22. The role of the court in the matter of departmental proceedings is very limited and the court cannot substitute its own views or findings by replacing the findings arrived at by the authority on detailed appreciation of the evidence on record. In the matter of imposition of sentence, the scope for interference by the court is very limited and restricted to exceptional cases. The punishment imposed by the disciplinary authority or the appellate authority unless shocking to the conscience of the court, cannot be subjected to judicial review. The court has to record reasons as to why the punishment is disproportionate. Failure to give reasons amounts to denial of justice. The mere statement that it is disproportionate would not suffice.
>
> 24. The findings of fact recorded by a court can be held to be perverse if the findings have been arrived at by ignoring or excluding relevant material or by taking into consideration irrelevant/inadmissible material. The finding may also be

34 2013 (6) SCC 602.

35 *See also* Rajinder Kumar Kindra v. Delhi Administration AIR 1984 SC 1805; Kuldeep Singh v. Commissioner of Police AIR 1999 SC 677; Gamini Bala Koteswara Rao v. State of Andhra Pradesh AIR 2010 SC 589; Babu v. State of Kerala (2010) 9 SCC 189.

> said to be perverse if it is against the weight of evidence, or if the finding so outrageously defies logic as to suffer from the vice of irrationality. If a decision is arrived at on the basis of no evidence or thoroughly unreliable evidence and no reasonable person would act upon it, the order would be perverse. But if there is some evidence on record which is acceptable and which could be relied upon, the conclusions would not be treated as perverse and the findings would not be interfered with.

Procedural infirmities or infractions in the inquiry process would normally be interfered with by courts only if it can be shown that the accused suffered prejudice on account of the same. In Ajay Tiwari v. University of Delhi[36] the Delhi High Court observed that in service jurisprudence, any procedural lapse, even if they exist, would vitiate disciplinary proceedings only if, as a result thereof, the charged officer is subjected to prejudice. In this matter the accused, in the disciplinary proceedings, had admitted all relevant facts on the basis of which a decision had been made against him. In this factual background, the Delhi High Court observed that in the face of such consistent admissions by the accused, any procedural infractions which may have taken place in the disciplinary proceedings would not be sufficient for the court to interfere in the adjudicatory process, in as much as the accused failed to show any prejudice occasion to him on account of such procedural lapse.

**Judicial Intervention in case of Sexual Harassment**

In Gaurav Jain v. Hindustan Latex Family Planning Promotion Trust[37] the Delhi High Court, in the context of sexual harassment, observed that interference against orders by departmental

36 2020 (1) SCT 381 (Delhi).

37 (2015) 220 DLT 60.

authorities/complaints committees would be warranted under the following specific circumstances *viz.*

a. If the order is against the principles of natural justice.
b. If the order is in violation of the rules of the organisation.
c. If the order is in violation of applicable law.
d. If the findings/conclusions of the committee are perverse and which no reasonable man could have arrived at.
e. If the punishment is shockingly disproportionate to the offence.

**Principles governing challenge to disciplinary proceedings**

In Union of India v. Dilip Paul[38] the Supreme Court discussed various principles to be considered while sitting in appeal over findings of a disciplinary committee:

a. An order passed by a disciplinary committee need not be set aside merely because it violates any rules/regulations governing such disciplinary proceedings. The court should examine whether the provisions violated are of substantive nature or procedural in character.
b. Generally speaking, violation of any and every procedural provision should not automatically vitiate the disciplinary inquiry or the order passed. Except cases falling under "no notice" or "no opportunity" or "no hearing" categories, a case of violation of procedural provision should be examined from the point of view of prejudice i.e. whether the violation has prejudiced the delinquent in any manner. If prejudice is found, then in such case appropriate orders should be passed by the court to remedy the situation. If no prejudice is established, then in such case, the disciplinary inquiry/order may not be interfered with.
c. In case of a violation of a procedural provision (which is not of mandatory nature), courts should examine the case from

38 2023 INSC 975.

the standpoint of substantial compliance and prejudice to the delinquent.

d. In case of violation of a procedural provision (which is of mandatory nature) then in such case, the examination of the court should entail aspects such as: (i) whether or not the said provision has been waived by the delinquent; (ii) prejudice to the delinquent; (iii) element of public interest.

e. Where the inquiry is not governed by any rules/regulations, even then the principles of natural justice should be complied with. Even here, the principles of substantial compliance and prejudice to the delinquent will apply.

f. There may be situations where the interest of the state or public interest may call for curtailing the rule of *audi alteram partem.*

**Substantive and Procedural violations in inquiry proceedings**

It is significant to note that violations during an inquiry may broadly be either substantive or procedural in nature. These have to be dealt with differently. The manner of discerning the violations committed during an inquiry process and its consequences was discussed by the Supreme Court in State Bank of Patiala v. S.K. Sharma[39] the relevant excerpts of which are reproduced below.

> "33. We may summarise the principles emerging from the above discussion. (These are by no means intended to be exhaustive and evolved keeping in view the context of disciplinary enquiries and orders of punishment imposed by an employer upon the employee):
>
> (1) An order passed imposing a punishment on an employee consequent upon a disciplinary/departmental enquiry in violation of the rules/regulations/statutory provisions governing such enquiries should not be set aside

39 1996 (3) SCC 364

automatically. The Court or the Tribunal should enquire whether (a) the provision violated is of a substantive nature or (b) whether it is procedural in character.

(2) A substantive provision has normally to be complied with as explained hereinbefore and the theory of substantial compliance or the test of prejudice would not be applicable in such a case.

(3) In the case of violation of a procedural provision, the position is this: procedural provisions are generally meant for affording a reasonable and adequate opportunity to the delinquent officer/employee. They are, generally speaking, conceived in his interest. Violation of any and every procedural provision cannot be said to automatically vitiate the enquiry held or order passed. Except cases falling under -- "no notice", "no opportunity" and "no hearing" categories, the complaint of violation of procedural provision should be examined from the point of view of prejudice, viz., whether such violation has prejudiced the delinquent officer/employee in defending himself properly and effectively. If it is found that he has been so prejudiced, appropriate orders have to be made to repair and remedy the prejudice including setting aside the enquiry and/or the order of punishment. If no prejudice is established to have resulted therefrom, it is obvious, no interference is called for. In this connection, it may be remembered that there may be certain procedural provisions which are of a fundamental character, whose violation is by itself proof of prejudice. The Court may not insist on proof of prejudice in such cases.

As explained in the body of the judgment, take a case where there is a provision expressly providing that after the evidence of the employer/government is over, the employee shall be given an opportunity to lead defence in his evidence, and in a given case, the enquiry officer does not give that opportunity in spite of the delinquent officer/ employee asking for it. The prejudice is self-evident. No proof of prejudice as such need be called for in such a case. To repeat, the test is one of prejudice, i.e., whether the person has received a fair hearing considering all things. Now, this very aspect can also be looked at from the point of view of directory and mandatory provisions, if one is so inclined. The principle stated under (4) hereinbelow is only another way of looking at the same aspect as is dealt with herein and not a different or distinct principle.

(4)(a) In the case of a procedural provision which is not of a mandatory character, the complaint of violation has to be examined from the standpoint of substantial compliance. Be that as it may, the order passed in violation of such a provision can be set aside only where such violation has occasioned prejudice to the delinquent employee.

(b) In the case of violation of a procedural provision, which is of a mandatory character, it has to be ascertained whether the provision is conceived in the interest of the person proceeded against or in public interest. If it is found to be the former, then it must be seen whether the delinquent officer has waived the said requirement, either expressly or by his conduct. If he is found to have waived it, then the order of punishment cannot be set aside on the ground of the said violation. If, on the other hand, it is found that the delinquent officer/employee has not waived it or that the provision could not be waived by him, then the Court or Tribunal should make appropriate directions (include the setting aside of the order of punishment), keeping in mind the approach adopted by the Constitution Bench in B. Karunakar.[40] The ultimate test is always the same, viz., test of prejudice or the test of fair hearing, as it may be called.

40 (1993) 4 SCC 727.

(5) Where the enquiry is not governed by any rules/ regulations/statutory provisions and the only obligation is to observe the principles of natural justice -- or, for that matter, wherever such principles are held to be implied by the very nature and impact of the order/action -- the Court or the Tribunal should make a distinction between a total violation of natural justice (rule of audi alteram partem) and violation of a facet of the said rule, as explained in the body of the judgment. In other words, a distinction must be made between "no opportunity" and no adequate opportunity, i.e., between "no notice"/"no hearing" and "no fair hearing". (a) In the case of former, the order passed would undoubtedly be invalid (one may call it 'void' or a nullity if one chooses to). In such cases, normally, liberty will be reserved for the Authority to take proceedings afresh according to law, i.e., in accordance with the said rule (audi alteram partem). (b) But in the latter case, the effect of violation (of a facet of the rule of audi alteram partem) has to be examined from the standpoint of prejudice; in other words, what the Court or Tribunal has to see is whether in the totality of the circumstances, the delinquent officer/ employee did or did not have a fair hearing and the orders to be made shall depend upon the answer to the said query. [It is made clear that this principle (No. 5) does not apply in the case of rule against bias, the test in which behalf are laid down elsewhere.]

(6) While applying the rule of audi alteram partem (the primary principle of natural justice) the Court/Tribunal/ Authority must always bear in mind the ultimate and overriding objective underlying the said rule, viz., to ensure a fair hearing and to ensure that there is no failure of justice. It is this objective which should guide them in applying the rule to varying situations that arise before them.

> (7) There may be situations where the interests of State or public interest may call for a curtailing of the rule of audi alteram partem. In such situations, the Court may have to balance public/State interest with the requirement of natural justice and arrive at an appropriate decision."
>
> 135. It has to be examined whether the alleged violation of principles of natural justice was of substantive nature or of procedure. It had been held that if it was only relating to procedure then it cannot be said to automatically vitiate the enquiry held.

**Interpretation of Service Rules and Sexual Harassment**

Judicial Precedent suggests a liberal interpretation of service rules in the context of case-relating to sexual harassment. The Supreme Court, in the case of Union of India v. Mudrika Singh[41] cautioned courts from invalidating inquiries into sexual harassment on the basis of hyper technical interpretations of service rules. The Supreme Court observed as follows:

> Before we conclude our analysis, we would also like to highlight a rising trend of invalidation of proceedings inquiring into sexual misconduct, on hyper-technical interpretations of the applicable service rules. For instance, the Sexual Harassment of Women at Workplace (Prevention, Prohibition, and Redressal) Act 2013 penalizes several misconducts of a sexual nature and imposes a mandate on all public and private organizations to create adequate mechanisms for redressal. However, the existence of transformative legislation may not come to the aid of persons aggrieved of sexual harassment if the appellate mechanisms turn the process into a punishment. It is important that courts

41 Civil Appeal No. 6859/2021 (03.12.2021, Supreme Court of India).

> uphold the spirit of the right against sexual harassment, which is vested in all persons as a part of their right to life and right to dignity under Article 21 of the Constitution. It is also important to be mindful of the power dynamics that are mired in sexual harassment at the workplace. There are several considerations and deterrents that a subordinate aggrieved of sexual harassment has to face when they consider reporting sexual misconduct of their superior. In the present case, the complainant was a constable complaining against the respondent who was the head constable - his superior. Without commenting on the merits of the case, it is evident that the discrepancy regarding the date of occurrence was of a minor nature since the event occurred soon after midnight and on the next day. Deeming such a trivial aspect to be of monumental relevance, while invalidating the entirety of the disciplinary proceedings against the respondent and reinstating him to his position renders the complainant's remedy at nought. The history of legal proceedings such as these is a major factor that contributes to the deterrence that civil and criminal mechanisms pose to persons aggrieved of sexual harassment.

The above sentiment was echoed by the Supreme Court in Union of India v. Dilip Paul[42] wherein courts were encouraged to steer clear of hyper technical interpretations in cases of sexual harassment; and focus on an interpretation that metes out procedural and substantive justice to all parties.

### Challenge to disciplinary proceedings at the preliminary stage(s)

Often, inquiry/disciplinary proceedings are challenged by the accused at preliminary or interim stages. Courts loath at

42 2023 INSC 975.

entertaining such challenge. Courts have deprecated the practice of challenge to disciplinary proceedings being made at interim/ preliminary stage, and which often results in delay of the original proceedings as well as multiplicity of proceedings.[43] A similar sentiment has been expressed by courts in the context of sexual harassment cases.[44] However, in exceptional cases courts may intercept proceedings where the complaint not disclosing an offence of 'sexual harassment' at all etc.[45]

In Damodar Prasad Singh v. Union of India[46] the court observed that the charge sheet involving allegations of sexual harassment and indecent behaviour cannot be scrapped at the pre-inquiry stage, when disciplinary proceedings are in progress.[47]

In Samuel Tennyson v. The Principal & Secretary[48] the Madras High Court elaborated the law on this aspect and observed that typically, no challenge should be entertained by courts (especially in writ jurisdiction) against show cause notices or the charge-sheet. The reasoning given was that a mere charge-sheet or show cause notice, by itself, does not give rise to any cause of action, because it does not amount to an adverse

43 *See* D.P. Maheswari v. Delhi Administration (1983) 4 SCC 293; National Council for Cement and Building Materials v. State of Haryana (1996) 3 SCC 206; Avtar Singh v. Delhi Sikh Gurudwara Committee (2006) 8 SCC 487; Maruti Suzuki India Limited v. Tourism Development Corporation Limited (2013) IV AD (Delhi) 615.

44 Tanushree Chopra v. Ministry of Women and Child Development W.P. (C) No. 11759/2015 (17.12.2015, Delhi High Court).

45 *See* Union of India v. V.S. Jaitha W.P. (C) No. 9695/2008 (01.08.2016, Kerala High Court).

46 OA No. 211/2012 (29.01.2014, Central Administrative Tribunal, Patna).

47 *See* Secretary, Ministry of Defence v. Prabash Chandra Mirdha (2012) 11 SCC 565 wherein the court held that a charge sheet *per se* cannot be a subject matter of challenge as it does not adversely affect the rights of the delinquent. Further, the court observed that neither the disciplinary proceedings nor the charge sheet can be quashed at a preliminary stage. *See also* S.P. Parasher v. Rehabilitation Council of India W.P. (C) No. 12272/2009 (23.09.2011, Delhi High Court).

48 (2019) 2 Writ LR 265.

order which affects the rights of any party (unless the same has been issued by a person having no jurisdiction to do so). It is quite possible that after considering the reply to the show cause notice or after holding an inquiry, the authority concerned may drop the proceedings and/or hold that the charges are not established. It is only when a final order imposing some punishment or otherwise adversely affecting the party is passed, that the said party can be said to have any grievance.

In S Ravi Selvan v. Central Board of Indirect Taxes[49] a challenge was made before the Madras High Court to on going inquiry proceedings before the ICC. In the said matter the accused was yet to participate in the inquiry proceedings; he had only sent a reply submitting his explanation to the complaint. In other words, no tangible progress had been made in the inquiry against the accused when the petition challenging the same was presented by him before the High Court. In such a situation, the High Court took a view that such proceedings were premature in nature. The High Court further went on to observe that there were adequate safeguards provided to the accused (under Section 14 of the Act) in the event the complaint was found to be false and malicious. In sum, the courts are not inclined to entertain challenges to inconclusive inquiry proceedings (unless there exist grave and conclusive evidence to hold such inquiry proceedings to be null and void).

## WRIT REMEDY VERSUS APPEAL REMEDY

It is a settled position of law that where a statute creates a right (and liability) and also prescribes a remedy or procedure of enforcement of that right, then in such case, resort must first be had to the said statutory remedy prior to invoking writ

49 W.P. No. 17798/2022 (09.09.2022, Madras High Court).

jurisdiction of High Courts.[50] Put differently, in the context of the Act, typically, an aggrieved party must first file an appeal before the appellate authority (in case the order is appealable under Section 18 of the Act) and not prefer a writ petition straightway. Writ jurisdiction should ideally not be the preferred course of action when an alternative and efficacious remedy (of appeal) is available. However, this position/proposition is not straitjacket. A litigant may, despite the availability of an appeal, prefer a writ in any of the following situations: (i) Where the remedy of appeal is nothing but an empty formality; (ii) Where there was a complete lack of jurisdiction in the officer or authority to take the action in dispute; (iii) where the order (under challenge) is passed in violation of the principles of natural justice.[51] (iv) abdication of duty or authority by the adjudicating authority; (v) absence of any factual controversy in the matter; (vi) involvement of pure questions of law.

Although the existence of an alternate remedy does not operate as an absolute bar for a High Court from exercising jurisdiction under Article 226 of the Constitution (writ jurisdiction), however, in the absence of any special reasons, the High Court would be loath at such interference.[52]

---

50 *See* Titaghur Paper Mills v. State of Orissa AIR 1983 SC 603; Delhi Cloth & General Mills Co. Ltd. v. CTO Jaipur (1976) 3 SCC 443.

51 A.V. Venkateswaran v. Ramchand Sobhraj Wadhwani AIR 1961 SC 1506. The power of judicial review conferred on courts by Article 226 of the Constitution of India, while examining the matters arising out of disciplinary proceedings, is limited to interfering in set situations: (i) if the disciplinary/inquiry proceedings were conducted in violation of the principles of natural justice; (ii) if the proceedings conducted did not afford adequate opportunity to the accused to defend himself; (iii) the decision of the disciplinary authority being based on no evidence; (iv) the decision of the disciplinary authority suffering from malice or perversity; (v) punishment being totally disproportionate to the prove misconduct of the accused. See generally Shri Milind Mamlekar v. Goa University, W.P. No. 628/2013 (29.01.2021, Bombay High Court, Goa Bench); Indian Oil Corporation v. Ashok Kumar Arora, (1997) 3 SCC 72; Lalit Popli v. Canara Bank, (2003) 3 SCC 583.

52 *See generally* W.P. No. 167/2024 (28.02.2024, High Court of Bombay at Goa).

In Radha Krishan Industries v. State of Himachal Pradesh[53] the Supreme Court summarised the principles governing the exercise of writ jurisdiction when an alternate remedy was available. The Supreme Court held that when a right is created by a statute that prescribes the remedy or procedure for enforcing the right or liability, a resort must be had to that statutory remedy before invoking the discretionary remedy under Article 226 of the Constitution. This rule of exhaustion of statutory remedies is a rule of policy, convenience and discretion.

In Sanjay Sharma v. Union of India[54] the Delhi High Court observed that typically, a writ petition assailing the findings of the ICC will not be entertained in view of the appellate provisions contained in the Act.

In Dr. Satish Kumar S Hosamani v. State of Karnataka[55] a writ petition preferred by government servants assailing the ICC report were rejected by the Karnataka High Court in view of existence of an alternate remedy of appeal before the central administrative tribunal (under the provisions of the State Administrative Tribunals Act 1985). The writ petitions were filed by the petitioners at a stage where, pursuant to an inquiry and the submission of a report by the ICC, a show cause notice was issued to the petitioners seeking their explanation in terms of Rule 14B of the Karnataka Civil Services (Classification, Control and Appeal) Rules, 1957. The High Court dismissed the writ petition on the point of existence of alternate remedy.

In Sharanjeet Kaur v. IDBI Bank Limited[56] a division bench of the Delhi High Court upheld a decision of a single bench which refused to entertain a writ petition on the premise of

53 2021 SCC Online SC 334.

54 W.P. (C) No. 1292/2021 (24.04.2024, Delhi High Court).

55 W.P. No. 11147/2024 (S-RES) and Others (05.02.2025, Karnataka High Court)

56 LPA No. 417/2014 (22.05.2024, Delhi High Court).

availability of an alternative efficacious appellate remedy under the Act.[57]

In Amul v. Union of India[58] the court observed as follows:

> 20. In view of the enunciation of law on this point by the Hon'ble Supreme Court in catena of judgments the general principles on this issue can be broadly summarized as under:
>
> 1. The remedy provided for in Article 226 of the Constitution is a discretionary remedy and the High Court has always the direction to refuse to grant any writ, if it is satisfied that the aggrieved party can have an adequate of suitable relief elsewhere.
> 2. When an alternative and equally efficacious remedy is open to litigant, he should required to pursue that remedy and not invoke the special jurisdiction of the High Court to issue a prerogative writ.
> 3. That the existence of the statutory remedy does not affect the jurisdiction of the High Court to issue a Writ. But the existence of an adequate legal remedy is a need to be taken into consideration in the matter of granting reliefs and where such a remedy exists, it would be sound exercise of discretion refuse to interfere in a writ petition.
> 4. The rule of exhaustion of statutory remedies before a writ is granted is a rule of self imposed limitation, a rule of policy and discretion rather than a rule of law and the Court may, therefore , in exceptional cases issue a writ of certiorari notwithstanding the statutory remedies have not been exhausted.

57 It is important to note that in some cases, the Delhi High Court has indeed entertained repetitions in, interalia, situations where the very constitution of the ICC was challenged (for having been constituted in contravention to the provisions of the Act). One case in point is Ruchika Singh Chhabra v. Air France India (AIR Online 2018 Del 809).

58 OA No. 354/2015 (01.10.2015, Central Administrative Tribunal, Ahmedabad).

5. A writ can be granted when manifest injustice resulting from jurisdictional or grave and material legal infirmity, and the alternative remedy cannot be a bar to remedy such a situation.
6. Whether or not alternative remedy in a given case is equally adequate, efficacious and speedy depends on its peculiar circumstances.
7. Mere existence of an alternative remedy does not itself impose an obligation on the Court to relegate the aggrieved party to such remedy.
8. Where a complaint is made against any act done or purported to be done under any statutory provision, the fact that there exists in the statute itself a possible remedy, is an important fact to be taken into consideration. Whether such provision exists, the Court will be extremely reluctant to interfere by way of high prerogative writs.
9. The existence of an alternative remedy, through an extremely important factor does by no means per se affect, curtail of impinge upon the writ jurisdiction and the same can be invoked by an aggrieved party In a fit case, when the true dictates of justice so demand.

The Supreme Court in Union of India v. P. Gunasekaran[59] has observed thus:

> In disciplinary proceedings the High Court is not and cannot act as a second court of first appeal. The High Court, in exercise of its powers under Article 226/227 of the Constitution of India, shall not venture into re-appreciation of the evidence. The High Court can only see whether:

59 (2015) 2 SCC 610.

a. the inquiry is held by a competent authority;
b. the inquiry is held according to the procedure prescribed in that behalf;
c. there is violation of the principles of natural justice in conducting the proceedings;
d. the authorities have disabled themselves from reaching a fair conclusion by some considerations extraneous to the evidence and merits of the case;
e. the authorities have allowed themselves to be influenced by irrelevant or extraneous considerations;
f. the conclusion, on the very face of it, is so wholly arbitrary and capricious that no reasonable person could ever have arrived at such conclusion;
g. the disciplinary authority had erroneously failed to admit the admissible and material evidence;
h. the disciplinary authority had erroneously admitted inadmissible evidence which influenced the finding;
i. the finding of fact is based on no evidence.

In Pankaj Kumar v. Union of India[60] the Tripura High Court summarised the position as follows:

> Under Article 226/227 of the Constitution of India, the High Court shall not:
> (i) re-appreciate the evidence;
> (ii) interfere with the conclusions in the inquiry, in case the same has been conducted in accordance with law;
> (iii) go into the adequacy of the evidence;
> (iv) go into the reliability of the evidence;
> (v) interfere, if there be some legal evidence on which findings can be based.

60 Pankaj Kumar v Union of India, W P (C) 403/2013 (14.02.2017, Tripura High Court)

(vi) correct the error of fact however grave it may appear to be;

(vii) go into the proportionality of punishment unless it shocks its conscience.

## Judicial Review and Territorial Jurisdiction

In common parlance a High Court within whose territorial limits the opposite party operates, or the cause of action arises, would exercise its powers under judicial review.

The expression "cause of action" refers to the material facts which are imperative for the applicant to plead and obtain relief. In the context of "cause of action", the general rule is that for a High Court to exercise its jurisdiction under judicial review, either the entire or a substantial cause of action should arise within the territorial jurisdiction/limits of that High Court. However, there are some well-known exceptions to this rule. For instance, in case a small part of cause of action arises within the territorial jurisdiction of the High Court, the same, by itself, may not be considered to be a determinative factor to compel that particular High Court to exercise its jurisdiction. Further, in appropriate cases, the High Court may decline to exercise its discretion by invoking the doctrine of forum non conveniens. On the aspect of territorial jurisdiction, the High Court essentially has to arrive at a conclusion on the basis of the averments made in the petition on treating the contents as true and correct. This is a fundamental principle[61]. The doctrine of *forum non conveniens* allows courts to refuse jurisdiction over a case if there is a more appropriate and convenient forum available elsewhere. The principle ensures to reduce hardship and harassment of the parties involved; efficient administration of justice.

61 *See generally* Kusum Ignots & Alloys Limited v. Union of India (2004) 6 SCC 254, Hira Khatoon v. Union of India, W.P. (C) No. 8198/2024 (18.09.2024, Delhi High Court), State of Goa v. Summit Online Trade Solutions Private Limited, (2023) 7 SCC 791.

## PENALTIES

The Act provides for various penalties for non-compliance or violation. The primary purpose behind imposition of penalties is to encourage adherence to law. Penalties under the Act include monetary exactions and moratorium of the violators (employer's) business.

### Penalty for contravention of section 16 of the Act

If any person contravenes the provisions of Section 16 of the Act[62], then the employer shall recover a penalty of Rs. 5,000/- as penalty from such person.[63]

### Penalty for non-compliance with the provisions of the Act

The Act contemplates penalties for the employer in case of non-compliance with the provisions of the Act and for failure to conform to the procedures prescribed therein. These are described below in some detail.

### Fine

A fine (extendable to Rs. 50,000/-) shall be levied on the employer in case it fails to do any of the following:[64]

a. Failure of the employer to constitute an ICC.
b. Failure of the employer to take action, in accordance with the provisions of the Act, on the report of the ICC or the LCC, as the case may be, when such report concludes that sexual harassment has taken place and makes recommendations.[65]

---

62 S. 16 of the Act pertains to confidentiality in the adjudicatory process. For more, *see* Chapter titled 'Confidentiality'.

63 R. 12 of the Rules.

64 S. 26 of the Act.

65 S. 13 (3) of the Act. Note that an employer faces the risk of being exposed to litigation in case it fails to take any disciplinary action for acts of sexual harassment in the workplace. *See generally* Clarinda D' Souza v. McCann Erickson India Limited (2003) 4 Bom CR 292.

c. Failure of the employer to take action, (in accordance with the provisions of the Act) on the report of the ICC or the LCC, as the case may be, when such report concludes that a false or malicious complaint has been knowingly filed by the complainant; or the complainant has submitted forged or misleading documents; or any witness has given false evidence or submitted forged or misleading documents.
d. Failure of the employer to file an annual report in the manner prescribed.[66]
e. Contravention or attempt to contravene or abetment to contravene of any other provision of the Act or the Rules.

## Repeat Offenders

The Act postulates heightened penalty for repeat offenders or recidivists. An employer shall be liable for the following in case of a subsequent conviction:[67]

a. Twice the punishment which might have been imposed on the first conviction. In case a higher punishment is prescribed under any other law (for the time being in force), for the offence for which the accused is being prosecuted under the Act, the concerned authority shall take due cognizance of the same while awarding punishment the Act.
b. Cancellation, withdrawal, non-renewal or non-approval of the employer's business licence or registration by the concerned government or local authority. While such punishment may seem onerous, it appears to have been incorporated by the legislature to provide a strong disincentive for a recalcitrant employer who continues his non-compliance/violations of the provisions of the Act.[68]

66 S. 22 of the Act.

67 S. 26 (2) of the Act.

68 Parliamentary Standing Committee Report (2011), at ¶ 25.3.

## Cognizance of Offence by Courts

No court shall take cognizance of any offence punishable under the Act or the Rules, except on a complaint made by the aggrieved woman or any other authorized person.[69] Further, no court inferior to that of a metropolitan magistrate or a judicial magistrate of the first class shall try any offence punishable under the Act.[70] Every offence under the Act shall be non-cognizable.[71]

## Act Not in Derogation of Any Other Law

As per Section 28 of the Act[72] the remedies prescribed therein are 'in addition to and not in derogation of the provisions of any other law' in force.[73] Clearly the Act is intended to supplement and not supplant. Section 18 provides an additional avenue; another legal option to the aggrieved party. It does not substitute the new for the old.[74]

In S Ravi Selvan v. Central Board of Indirect Taxes[75] one of the questions which arose before the Madras High Court was whether the Act overrides the concerned service rules in matters of inquisitorial procedures. The High Court, by placing reliance on Sections 28 and 11 of the Act, replied in the negative. It was held that the Act does not override the service rules but only supplements the same.

---

69 S. 27 (1) of the Act.

70 S. 27 (2) of the Act.

71 S. 27 (3) of the Act.

72 S. 28 of the Act reads thus: *The provisions of this Act shall be in addition to and not in derogation of the provisions or any other law for the time being in force.*

73 An Ordinance made by a University in terms of the directions of the Vishaka Guidelines cannot be treated as extant law since the Vishaka Guidelines lost its relevance with the enactment of the Act. *See* Amrapali Basumatary v. Union of India W.P. (C) No. 3573/2014 (08.12.2015, Delhi High Court).

74 G.M. Telecom v. M. Krishnan AIR 2003 Ker 152. *See also* J Mani v. Union of India (2021) 170 FLR 23.

75 W.P. No. 17798/2022 (09.09.2022, Madras High Court).

In some matters however, in case of a conflict between the provisions of the Act and the relevant service rules, courts have held that the provisions of the Act should prevail. In Prama Bhattacharjee v. The State of West Bengal[76] a conflict arose between the provisions of the Act (on the one hand) and the UGC Regulations (on the other hand) in connection with the appellate mechanism provided in the service rules/UGC regulations for assailing the findings of an ICC. As per the relevant UGC regulations, the disciplinary authority (which was supposed to proceed on the basis of the findings and recommendations of the ICC) was also designated as the appellate authority over the ICC. This regulation was brought under challenge before the Calcutta High Court by the complainant. The complainant relied upon a decision of the Supreme Court in Nisha Priya Bhatia v. Union of India[77] which observed that the findings or recommendations of an ICC are in the nature of a fact-finding report and forms the basis on which the disciplinary authority would initiate further disciplinary action; and hence the disciplinary authority may not sit as an appellate authority over the recommendations/ findings of an ICC.

The Calcutta High Court upheld the stance of the complainant and observed that such a regulation would render the exercise under Section 13 (3) of the Act as futile. It was ultimately concluded by the Calcutta High Court that, in the said situation, the Act would prevail over the UGC regulations.

In Dr. Tanya Mander v. Rajiv Gandhi National University of Law[78] there existed a conflict between the provisions of the Act (on the one hand) and the UGC regulations (on the other hand) on the issue of constitution (and constituent members) of

76 2024 Lab IC 785.

77 (2020) 13 SCC 56.

78 C.W.P. No. 960/2019 (22.03.2021, Punjab and Haryana High Court).

the complaints committee. For instance, the UGC Regulations provided that the presiding member of the complaints committee must be a person holding the rank of a "professor". Further, the UGC Regulations did not contain any provision for an external number. This was in contrast with the provisions of the Act which mandatorily requires an external member to be a part of the complaints committee. It was argued by the complainant that the complaints committee (which was looking into her complaint of sexual harassment) was constituted in violation of Regulation 4 of the UGC Regulations. The Punjab and Haryana High Court rejected the submission of the complainant and upheld the constitution of the complaints committee on the premise that the complaints committee was constituted in accordance with the provisions of the Act. It was further observed by the court that that "the Act" is a Parliamentary Act where as the UGC Regulations are framed in the exercise of legislative powers conferred upon the executive body and are hence, delegated/subordinate legislation. Therefore, these regulations cannot supersede the Parliamentary Act which is made by the legislature itself. In case of any repugnancy, it is the Parliamentary Act which must prevail. Once a field is occupied by a Parliamentary Act, the regulations, if any, framed by way of subordinate legislation, cannot supersede or over-ride the provisions of the Act.

In sum all extant applicable law in connection with sexual harassment must be harmoniously interpreted with the provisions of the Act.[79] Availability of alternative remedy (for the offence of sexual harassment under any law /apart from the Act) would still not preclude an action under the Act.[80]

---

79 *See generally* Ramesh Pal v. Union of India (2014) 2 MP LJ 500.

80 *See generally* Smt. Kalawati v. United Vaish Co-operative Thrift & Credit Society Ltd. (2002) CPJ 71 (NC).

CHAPTER 8

# Criminal Remedies

Under Indian law, sexual harassment is both a civil and a criminal offence.[1] Accordingly, a victim of sexual harassment at workplace, apart from the right of raising a grievance with the appropriate complaints committee (under the Act), also has a parallel right to initiate criminal action against the perpetrator under the provisions of the Indian Penal Code, 1860 (**IPC**) now the Bhartiya Nyaya Sanhita 2023 (**BNS**). It is pertinent to note that such the civil and criminal actions are not mutually exclusive and may be proceeded with simultaneously.

## CRIMINAL ACTION

Often, under Indian law, civil sanctions (for illegal conduct) are not considered to be sufficient deterrents. This is where criminal remedies gain importance. Generally speaking, there exist numerous reasons for resorting to criminal proceedings (in case an offence under the criminal law regime is made out), some of which are as follows: (i) criminal sanctions include imprisonment which is considered a great deterrent; (ii) adjudication of criminal proceedings is normally speedier than civil proceedings;[2] and

1 Any act done contrary to law or forbidden by law is called an offence. *See* Leena Doley v. State of Assam 2013 (5) GLT 363.

2 Note that the provisions of the Act provide an upper limit of 90 (ninety) days to complete an inquiry. Strict adherence to such provision may make civil remedy speedier.

(iii) the chances of out-of-court settlement(s) in criminal matters are high since criminal conviction tends to negatively affect the wrongdoer's reputation and status thereby pressuring him to try and bring a 'closure' to the matter.[3] Hence, besides its deterrent/ dissuasive value, criminal proceedings appear to offer quick and efficacious results.

However, on the flipside, it may be noted that criminal proceedings do not grant injunctions and financial compensation to the aggrieved.[4] Therefore, ideally, a combination of civil and criminal action is likely to be most efficacious. Accordingly, a victim of sexual harassment may, if deemed necessary, explore the possibility of concurrently availing both criminal and civil remedies to bring about complete vindication of her rights.

Before proceeding further, it is first important to understand the classification of offences under the Indian criminal law regime. In India, the Code of Criminal Procedure 1973 (**CRPC**), now the Bhartiya Nagrik Suraksha Sanhita 2023 (**BNSS**) regulates and governs criminal actions. Criminal offences in India can largely be classified into cognizable and non-cognizable offences; bailable and non-bailable offences.

### Cognizable and Non-Cognizable Offences

The offences in respect of which police authorities can arrest the alleged offender without a warrant are called cognizable

3 In the case of 'sexual harassment at workplace' an aggrieved woman may not be required to invoke criminal remedies if settlement is her desired/potential objective. This is so because the Act already contains provisions relating to 'conciliation' which may be resorted to for exploring elements of settlement. For more on 'conciliation' *see* chapter titled 'Procedure'.

4 Note that S. 357 of the CRPC & S. 395 of the BNSS, clothes the court with the authority to award compensation at the time of passing judgment to a victim who has suffered loss or injury by the offence, when she can recover compensation, in a civil court. In other words, criminal courts are empowered to financially recompense the aggrieved *via* fines imposed on the wrongdoer. However, as on date, no judicial precedent appears to exist on the invocation of this provision to remedy a case of sexual harassment at the workplace.

offences.[5] All serious offences are generally considered cognizable.

On the other hand, offences for which the police authorities have no right to arrest without a warrant are called non-cognizable offences.[6] These offences are normally less serious in nature and are mostly regarded as private criminal wrongs.[7] Note that in case of non-cognizable offences, the onus of collection of evidence and prosecution of the offender is normally left to the initiative and efforts of the aggrieved party. However, a competent magistrate has the power to direct the police to investigate a non-cognizable offence.

**Bailable and Non-Bailable Offences**

As per section 2 (a) of the CRPC & section 2(1)(c) of the BNSS, a 'bailable offence' means an offence which is shown as bailable in the First Schedule to the CRPC & the BNSS (**First Schedule**), or which is made bailable by any other law; and 'non-bailable offence' means any other offence. Note that the CRPC does not prescribe any specific parameter to determine whether any particular offence is bailable or non-bailable. It all depends upon whether the relevant offence has been shown as bailable or non-bailable in the First Schedule. However, by and large, it may be said that serious offences have been declared by law as non-bailable whereas non-serious offences have been declared as bailable.

A pertinent difference between non-bailable and bailable offences is as follows: In case of bailable offence, the grant of bail (to the accused) is a matter of right. It may be either granted by a police officer who has the custody of the accused or by court. On the other hand, in case of a non-bailable offence, the grant of bail is discretionary, which discretion is to be exercised only by court.

5 S. 2 (c) of the CRPC & S. 2(1)(g) of the BNSS.

6 S. 2 (l) of the CRPC & S. 2(1)(o) of the BNSS.

7 All offences under the Act are non-cognizable in nature. *See* S. 27 of the Act.

**Compoundable and Non-Compoundable Offences**

Compoundable offences are those offences with respect to which law permits the parties to enter into a compromise; and by virtue of such compromise, the charges against the offender are dropped.[8] Once the offence is compounded, it has the effect of an acquittal. On the other hand, offences where the law does not permit a compromise are classified as non-compoundable offences. It may be noted that offences which are grave and serious in nature are non-compoundable offences.

## INITIATION OF CRIMINAL ACTION

In case of commission of a cognizable offence, criminal law can be set in motion by providing relevant information about the offence to the officer in charge of the concerned police station and lodging a First Information Report (**FIR**).[9] Note that, in case of a cognizable offence, the police authorities are sufficiently empowered to arrest the accused without a warrant or authority from a competent magistrate and carry out an investigation pursuant to lodging of the FIR.[10] On the other hand, upon receipt of information about commission of a non-cognizable offence, the concerned police officer is required to enter the substance of the information in his station diary and refer the informant to the competent magistrate.[11] The police can investigate the commission of a non-cognizable offence only after receipt of appropriate orders/directions from the magistrate.[12]

It is important to note that criminal action can be initiated by any person. In other words, it is not necessary that only the

8 S. 320 of the CRPC & S. 359 of the BNSS classifies the offences as compoundable and non-compoundable offences.

9 S. 154 of the CRPC & S. 173 of the BNSS.

10 Ss. 156 (1) & 157 of the CRPC & S. 175 & 176 of the BNSS.

11 S. 155 (1) of the CRPC & S. 174 of the BNSS.

12 S. 155 (2) & (3) of the CRPC, now 174 of BNSS.

victim or an eyewitness can initiate criminal proceedings. Any person who has knowledge of commission of the offence can set the criminal machinery in motion.

**First Information Report**

As mentioned above, criminal action against a cognizable offence may be set in motion by filing of an FIR (under Section 154 of the CRPC, now Section 173 of the BNSS). In case the police authorities do not register an FIR then in such case an application (in writing) may be made to the concerned Superintendent of Police for registration of FIR.[13] Even if that does not yield any satisfactory result in the sense that either the FIR is still not registered or that even after registration, no proper investigation is conducted, then the aggrieved may file an application before the concerned Magistrate for a redressal.[14] The Magistrate, if satisfied by such application, can direct the FIR to be registered and a proper investigation to be made. The Magistrate can also monitor the investigation to ensure a proper investigation.[15] Another remedy also exists by making a direct complaint to the Magistrate under the provisions of Section 190 and 200 of the CRPC, now 210 and 223 of BNSS.[16]

**Quashing of FIR**

Criminal proceedings pursuant to an FIR may only be quashed under appropriate proceedings before the relevant High Court (under Section 482 of the CRPC & Section 528 of the BNSS) in

13 S. 154 (3) of the CRPC, now 173 BNSS.

14 S. 156 (3) of the CRPC, now 175 BNSS.

15 *See* Sakiri Vasu v. State of UP 2008 (2) SCC 409; PS v. State of NCT of Delhi W.P. (Crl) 767/2015 (29.02.2016, Delhi High Court).

16 *See generally* Aleque Padamsee v. Union of India 2007 (6) SCC 171.

limited situations[17], including the following: (i) where the FIR *prima facie* does not disclose commission of an offence or make out a case against the accused;[18] or (ii) where the allegations made in the FIR or complaint are so absurd and inherently improbable on the basis of which no prudent person can ever reach a just conclusion that there is sufficient ground for proceeding against the accused; or (iii) where the criminal proceeding is manifestly attended with *mala fide* and/or where the proceeding is maliciously instituted with an ulterior motive for wreaking vengeance on the accused and with a view to spite him due to private and personal grudge[19]; or (iv) where parties to the proceedings settle their disputes.[20]

In Rohit Satindra Sharma v. State of Maharashtra[21] a complaint of sexual harassment was preferred by the complainant against the accused. After an inquiry into the matter, the ICC rejected

---

17 *See generally* Charles Welsh v. State of Maharashtra Cri. W.P. No. 5006/2015 (01.04.2016, Bombay High Court). The inherent powers of the High Court must be exercised sparingly and cautiously to prevent the abuse of process of any court and to secure the ends of justice. N. Soundaram v. P.K Pounraj (2014) 10 SCC 616. The inherent powers should not be exercised to stifle a legitimate protection. Taking the complaint and the allegations as it were, without adding or subtracting anything, if no offence is made out, only then would the court be justified in quashing the proceedings. MCD v. Ram Kishan Rohtagi AIR 1983 SC 67. An investigation should not be shut out at the threshold if the allegations have some substance. Vinod Raghuvanshi v. Ajay Arora 2013 (10) SCC 581.

18 The real test to be applied by court is whether the allegations, if taken at face value and accepted in entirety, *prima facie* establish the offence. *See* Madhavrao Jiwaji Rao Scindia v. S.C. Angre AIR 1988 SC 709.

19 *See generally* Sanjay Babu v. State of Tamil Nadu Criminal Appeal No. 773/2003 (19.02.2009 Supreme Court of India); State of Haryana v. Bhajan Lal 1992 Supp (1) SCC 335.

20 Sanjay Kumar Behera v. State NCT of Delhi Crl. M.C. No. 10/2012 (05.01.2012, Delhi High Court); Sanjay Singh v. State 2008 (1) JCC 650; Mukesh Bansal v. State 2009 (2) JCC 898; Rishiraj v. State, 2009 (1) JCC 265; Shoyab Bijani v. State of Gujarat 2013 (56) PTC 534 (Guj). Note that the High Court in exercise of its inherent power can quash criminal proceedings or F.I.R or complaint and even S.320 of the CRPC, now 359 of BNSS does not limit or affect its powers. B.S. Joshi v. State of Haryana AIR 2003 SC 1386. Note that in case of heinous offences, an FIR may not be quashed even if the parties amicably resolve their dispute.

21 2024 SCC Online Bom 2718.

the complaint for various reasons, including the existence of a consensual relationship between the parties. The complainant did not appeal against the findings of the ICC. In its stead, the complainant lodged an FIR against the accused alleging sexual harassment. At the time of lodging the said FIR, the above mentioned ICC proceedings were suppressed by the complainant. The accused filed a petition before the Bombay High Court for quashing the FIR. The High Court, while allowing the said petition, made the following observations:

a. The complainant completely suppressed the ICC proceedings at the stage of filing a criminal complaint against the accused.
b. The findings of the ICC revealed existence of a consensual relationship between the parties and the complaint of sexual harassment appeared to be lodged only after the spouse of the complainant learnt about this consensual relationship.
c. The accused was not in charge of the complainant's salary and was further not in a position to demand sexual favours from the complainant or to abuse any dominant position over the complainant.
d. The entire case set up by the complainant, on the face of it, appeared to be concocted and fabricated.

### Plea Bargaining

Plea-bargaining, in common parlance, refers to the pre-trial negotiations between the accused and the prosecution during which the accused agrees to plead guilty in exchange for certain concessions by the prosecution.

Prior to introduction of plea-bargaining, the concept of a negotiated settlement in criminal cases was not permissible.[22]

22 *See* State of Uttar Pradesh v. Chandrika AIR 2000 SC 164.

The disposal of cases by means of plea bargaining is considered an efficacious method to deal with the huge arears of criminal cases in India. Plea-bargaining has a two-fold object: (i) to reduce the delay in disposing of criminal trials; and (ii) to alleviate the suffering of under trial prisoners.[23]

The concept of plea bargaining may be invoked in the following situations: (i) where in a police case, the charge sheet/completion report has been filed against the accused that suggests that the offence in question appears to have been committed by such accused; and (ii) where in a complaint case a magistrate has taken cognizance of an offence, and after examining the complainant and the witnesses under section 200 of the CRPC (Section 225 of the BNSS) has issued the process under section 204 of the CRPC (Section 227 of the BNSS).[24]

Plea-bargaining is not available in the following situations[25]: (i) where the punishment for the offence in question is death or imprisonment for life or imprisonment for a term exceeding 7 (seven) years; (ii) where the offence in question affects the social economic condition of the country; (iii) where the offence in question has been committed against a woman, or a child below the age of 14 (fourteen) years; (iv) where the accused is a previous convict of the same offence; and (v) where the accused is a habitual offender.[26]

Plea-bargaining may actually emerge as a potent tool in increasing efficacy of criminal enforcement in India. Approaches like plea bargaining may be helpful in clearing backlogged

---

23 *See* State of Gujarat v. N.H. Thakor 2005 CriLJ 2957.

24 *See* S. 265A of the CRPC. *See also* Ratanlal & Dhirajlal, The Code of Criminal Procedure, 19th Ed., (2011) at 1111 to 1113.

25 *See* Ss. 265A, now 279 of BNSS, 265B & 265L of the CRPC & Sections 289, 290 & 300 of the BNSS.

26 *See* Statement of Objects and Reasons, Criminal Law (Amendment) Act, 2005 (14.08.2003).

dockets, enforcing deadlines for adjudication/resolution of cases, preventing unjustified continuances and encouraging completion of a set number of cases.[27]

## COGNIZANCE OF OFFENCES

No court inferior to that of a metropolitan magistrate or a judicial magistrate of the first class shall try any criminal offence under the Act.[28]

A First Information Report (FIR) lodged by an employer in connection with commission of an offence of sexual harassment is not hit by Section 27 of the Act.[29]

### Jurisdiction

A criminal offence can be inquired into and tried only by a court of competent jurisdiction. The question of jurisdiction is to be determined in accordance with the relevant provisions of the CRPC (now BNSS). Ordinarily, a criminal offence is to be inquired into and tried by a court within whose local jurisdiction the offence was committed.[30] However, where the commission of an offence is spread across various local areas, then the offence may be inquired into or tried by a court having jurisdiction over any of such local areas.[31] To put it succinctly, territorial jurisdiction depends upon the locality of the crime. Jurisdiction to try an offence belongs to the court within whose limits the offence is committed (whether completely or partially).[32]

---

27 *See generally* International Intellectual Property Alliance (IIPA), Special 301 Report on Copyright Protection and Enforcement on India (2011) at 42.

28 S. 27 of the Act.

29 *See generally* Chandan Kumar Soni v. State of Uttarakhand, Criminal Misc Application No. 1028/2015 (24.12.2020, Uttarakhand High Court).

30 S. 177 of the CRPC & S. 197 of the BNSS.

31 S. 178 of the CRPC & S. 198 of the BNSS.

32 Mobarik Ali v. State of Bombay AIR 1957 SC 857.

## LIMITATION

Discussed above is the mode and manner in which criminal law can be set in motion. Criminal machinery should be initiated within a certain prescribed time frame, failing which the courts may not entertain the matter. It is therefore important to be aware of such time frames.[33]

The term 'limitation', in common parlance, refers to the time prescribed by law within which an action may be brought before a competent court or authority. The CRPC (now BNSS) provides that courts shall, after the expiry of the period of limitation, not take cognizance[34] of any offence.[35] The CRPC (now BNSS) prescribes different periods of limitation depending on the gravity of the offence. Such periods of limitation are as follows:[36]

e. 6 (six) months, if the offence is punishable with fine only.
f. 1 (one) year, if the offence is punishable with imprisonment for a term not exceeding 1 (one) year.
g. 3 (three) years if the offence is punishable with imprisonment for a term exceeding 1 (one) year but not exceeding 3 (three) years.
h. There is no limitation period for offences punishable with imprisonment exceeding 3 (three) years.

Generally, limitation period commences from the below mentioned dates, whichever occurs later:[37]

33 Note that the Act prescribes a maximum time limit of 6 (six) months for filing a complaint of sexual harassment with the relevant complaints committee.

34 The term 'cognizance', for the purpose of criminal law, refers to institution of a criminal action against the offender. *See* General Officer Commanding v. CBI 2012 (2) R.A.J 527. Taking 'cognizance' implies application of mind to the materials on record and proceeding to issue process. *See* Ajay Raj Pal v. State Criminal Misc. No. 3100/2005 (19.02.2007, Delhi High Court).

35 S. 468 (1) of the CRPC & S. 514 of BNSS.

36 S. 468 (2) of the CRPC & S. 514 of BNSS.

37 S. 469 of the CRPC & S. 515 of BNSS.

a. The date of the offence;
b. The date on which the aggrieved person or the police becomes aware of the offence; or
c. The date on which the aggrieved person or the police becomes aware of the offender's identity.

In cases where the offence is continuing, a fresh limitation period commences at every moment during which the offences continues.[38] However, a competent court may take cognizance of an offence even after expiry of the above limitation period: (i) if the delay is properly and satisfactorily explained; or (ii) if it is considered necessary to do so in the interests of justice.[39]

## DEPARTMENTAL & CRIMINAL PROCEEDINGS: INTERPLAY

Often, in case of serious misconduct, both departmental and criminal proceedings are initiated simultaneously. It often happens that criminal proceedings are determined earlier with the result being acquittal of the accused. A moot question which arises for consideration is what remains of the disciplinary proceedings in such case. Similarly, the same question arises by examining the situation in reverse i.e. the departmental proceedings concluding earlier with the exoneration of the accused.

The position of law in such cases is follows: The purpose of a departmental inquiry and of a prosecution is different; the criminal prosecution is launched for an offence for a violation of a duty the offender owes to a society, or for breach of which law has provided that the offender shall make satisfaction

38 S. 472 of the CRPC & S. 518 of BNSS.

39 S. 473 of the CRPC & S. 519 of the BNSS; *See also* Ss. 470 & 471 of the CRPC & Ss. 516 & 517 of the BNSS which provide for exclusion of certain time periods in select circumstances while computing the limitation period.

to the public. On the contrary, the purpose of a departmental inquiry is to maintain discipline and efficacy in the service.[40] Departmental proceedings are maintainable even after acquittal in prosecution.[41] At the same time, there have also existed situations where courts have exonerated the accused from criminal proceedings on the basis of a clean chit being given to them in the ICC/departmental enquiries.

This position of law is dealt with in a little more detail in the below mentioned judgements.

In Chairman and M.D. United Commercial Bank v. P.C. Kakkar, the court observed as follows:[42]

> Acquittal in the criminal case is not determinative of the commission of misconduct or otherwise, and it is open to the authorities to proceed with the disciplinary proceeding, not withstanding acquittal in the criminal case. It per se would not entitle the employee to claim immunity from the proceedings. At the most the factum of acquittal may be a circumstance to be considered while awarding punishment. Hence, a criminal trial is conducted for an offence (committed under the applicable criminal law of India) whereas a disciplinary proceedings are conducted for alleged misconduct by the perpetrator. Further, the standard of proof in both the proceedings is different.

In Suresh Pathrela v. Oriental Bank of Commerce[43] it was held as under:

---

40 *See* Noida Entrepreneurs Association v. NOIDA (2007) 10 SCC 385.

41 *See* Shashi Bala v. SBM Sr. Secondary School 218 (2015) DLT 575; Noida Entrepreneurs Association *ibid.*

42 (2003) 4 SCC 364.

43 (2006) 10 SCC 572.

> This Court has taken the view consistently that acquittal in a criminal case would be no bar for drawing up a disciplinary proceeding against the delinquent officer. It is well settled principle of law that the yardstick and standard of proof in a criminal case is different from the disciplinary proceeding. While the standard of proof in a criminal case is a proof beyond all reasonable doubt, the proof in a departmental proceeding is preponderance of probabilities.

In Hindustan Petroleum Corporation v. Sarvesh Berry[44] it was held thus:

> The purposes of departmental inquiry and of prosecution are two different and distinct aspects. Criminal prosecution is launched for an offence for violation of a duty the offender owes to the society, or for breach of which law has provided that the offender shall make a satisfaction to the public. So, crime is an act of commission in violation of law or of omission of public duty. The departmental inquiry is to maintain discipline in the service and efficiency of public service.

In Shri Milind Mamlekar v. Goa University, the court observed thus:[45]

> 27. In case of departmental inquiry which is distinct from a criminal trial, the charges are not to be proved beyond reasonable down doubt but are to be established based on preponderance of probabilities. The disciplinary proceedings are initiated against an erring official by

44 (2005) 10 SCC 471.

45 W.P. No. 628/2013 (29.01.2021, Bombay High Court, Goa Bench).

> the administration according to the prevailing Rules and Regulations governing his service conditions. Some activities which may lead to a departmental action may also coincide with the criminal action initiated against him. But the standard of proof required in both the two proceedings is of different nature. It is well settled that the scope of disciplinary proceedings before authority and the criminal proceedings before the Court of law quite be distinct, exclusive and independent of each other and the standard of proof required in the two are different. It has been held in the catena of the decisions of the Apex Court that interference in the disciplinary proceedings is not permissible unless the orders passed are unreasonable or perverse or manifestly illegal or grossly unjust and it has now being a well settled principle that merely on the basis of acquittal in the criminal case, delinquent official cannot be discharged from the charges in the departmental proceeding and though both the proceedings were based on the same set of facts mere acquittal in the criminal proceedings will not exonerate a delinquent / accused from the departmental proceedings.

In DB Singh v. State of J&K[46] an FIR (lodged by the complainant against the accused with the assistance of the employer for the offence of sexual harassment), was sought to be quashed by the accused on the premise that since the case was one of sexual harassment at the workplace (and covered under the Act), and for which the ICC had already commenced its proceedings; and consequently no criminal proceedings could be instituted in such matter during the pendency of the proceedings of the ICC. The High Court, while rejecting the petition of the accused, made the following observations:

46 CRMC No. 620/2018 (01.0.2019, Jammu and Kashmir High Court).

a. The provisions of the Act are to be construed widely to give effect to its objects and purpose.
b. Reference was made to Section 28 of the Act to hold that the provisions of the Act were in addition to and not in derogation of any other law in force. The court observed that the remedy available under the Act is in the nature of an additional remedy; and there was no conflict between the provisions of the Act and the criminal law provisions.
c. The court permitted simultaneous continuation of ICC proceedings and criminal proceedings.

In K. Unnikrishnan v. Lakshwadeep Administration[47] the court held as follows:

> There is a consensus of judicial opinion that proceedings in a criminal case and disciplinary proceedings can go on simultaneously except where departmental proceedings and criminal case are based on the same set of facts and evidence. But in a departmental proceeding several other factors impinging on the work environment operate in the mind of the disciplinary authority such as enforcement of discipline, respect and good behaviour towards colleagues etc. Maintenance of integrity and the standard of proof required in those proceeding is also different from that required in a criminal case. In a departmental proceeding the standard of proof is one of preponderance of probabilities whereas in a criminal case the charge has to be proved by the prosecution beyond reasonable doubt.
>
> The order of acquittal by a criminal court of charges levelled against the harasser does not preclude a competent court/authority from initiating disciplinary proceedings against him.

47 OA No. 344/2008 (11.08.2015, Central Administrative Tribunal, Ernakulam).

In Union of India v. Naman Singh Shekhawat[48] the court held thus:

> There cannot be any doubt whatsoever, as has been submitted by the learned Additional Solicitor General, that initiation of departmental proceeding is permissible even after the judgment of acquittal is recorded by the criminal court. But the same would not mean that a proceeding would be initiated only because it is lawful to do so. A departmental proceeding could be initiated if the department intended to adduce any evidence which is in its power and possession to prove the charges against the delinquent officer. Such a proceeding must be initiated bona fide. The action of the authority even in this behalf must be reasonable and fair.

In Capt. M. Paul Anthony v. Bharat Gold Mines Ltd.[49] the court held that the departmental proceedings need not be stayed during pendency of the criminal case save and except for cogent reasons.[50] The Court summarized its findings as under:

> (i) Departmental proceedings and proceedings in a criminal case can proceed simultaneously as there is no bar in their being conducted simultaneously, though separately.
>
> (ii) If the departmental proceedings and the criminal case are based on identical and similar set of facts and the charge in the criminal case against the delinquent employee is of a grave nature which involves

48 (2008) 4 SCC 1.

49 JT 1999 (2) SC 456.

50 *See also* Constable Ravinder Rana v. Union of India (2008) ILR 2 Del 915 wherein the law on this aspect is succinctly summarised.

complicated questions of law and fact, it would be desirable to stay the departmental proceedings till the conclusion of the criminal case.

(iii) Whether the nature of a charge in a criminal case is grave and whether complicated questions of fact and law are involved in that case, will depend upon the nature of offence, the nature of the case launched against the employee on the basis of evidence and material collected against him during investigation or as reflected in the charge sheet.

(iv) The factors mentioned at (ii) and (iii) above cannot be considered in isolation to stay the Departmental proceedings but due regard has to be given to the fact that the departmental proceedings cannot be unduly delayed.

(v) If the criminal case does not proceed or its disposal is being unduly delayed, the departmental proceedings, even if they were stayed on account of the pendency of the criminal case, can be resumed and proceeded with so as to conclude them at an early date, so that if the employee is found not guilty his honour may be vindicated and in case he is found guilty, the administration may get rid of him at the earliest.

In Anjan Biswas v. Central Bank of India[51] the position of law was elucidated in the following words:

> It appears that the same test of the nexus of the charge with the line of duty of the concerned employee may be apposite in assessing whether an order of acquittal in the criminal trial should result in the departmental action being quashed. The primary reasons for this is elementary: the standards

51 W.P. No. 86 (W)/2016 (18.01.2016, Calcutta High Court).

> of proof in the two sets of proceedings are completely different. The next reason is that the charge in the criminal proceedings may be wholly unconnected with the functions discharged by the concerned employee in the usual course of his duty and the charge may not have an effect of polluting the work atmosphere. Such a distinction must necessarily be made as personal enmity outside the workplace or reasons completely extraneous to the usual line of duties of the concerned employee may prompt a criminal case being filed against the employee. In such a situation, the acquittal of the employee of the criminal charge should, ordinarily, result in the departmental action following the order of acquittal; though if the charge is of sexual harassment or of moral turpitude, the employer must be left free to assess the facts by a different standard of proof than in criminal proceedings to ensure discipline, integrity and good behaviour at the workplace. But when the similar charges brought against an employee in both criminal and departmental proceedings have some nexus with the workplace or a direct nexus with the usual duties of the concerned employee, the order of acquittal in the criminal proceedings - honourable or otherwise - will only be a relevant consideration in the departmental proceedings. In any event, it cannot be said that as a matter of rule that an order of acquittal in the criminal proceedings - even if honourable - must result in the departmental action being dropped as no contrary view, on a different standard of proof, can be taken at the conclusion of the departmental action.

In select cases and situations, courts have also ordered quashing or discontinuation of criminal proceedings (commenced with respect to an alleged offence of sexual harassment) when the ICC had fully exonerated the accused from the charges. In the case of Usha Padmini v. State of Karnataka[52] the complainant filed a complaint of sexual harassment with the ICC. In addition, the complainant filed a criminal complaint against the accused on the basis of the very same allegations made with the ICC. After inquiry, the ICC exonerated the accused and concluded that a case of sexual harassment was not made out. Thereafter, the accused approached the High Court seeking to quash the criminal proceedings on this basis. The Karnataka High Court after examining the case, observed that the inquiry was conducted by the ICC in respect of the very same allegations which were now the basis of criminal prosecution of the accused for the alleged offence under Section 354 A of the IPC (Section 75 of the BNS). In fact, even the material relied upon by the ICC as well as the investigating agency was one and the same. The High Court ultimately quashed the criminal proceedings.

In Binoy Jacob v. State of Kerala[53] a complaint of sexual harassment was preferred by the complainant against the accused with the ICC. Simultaneously, criminal proceedings were also initiated by the complainant against the accused for the offence of sexual harassment. The ICC, in its final report, exonerated the accused on merits on the ground that allegations of sexual harassment were not proved against him. On the strength and basis of the said final report of the ICC, the accused approached the Kerala High Court and contended that since the ICC had exonerated him, criminal prosecution on the same set of facts and circumstances could not continue. Reliance was also placed by the accused on the case of Usha Padmini v. State of Karnataka *supra* to contend that when the ICC finds no truth or substance to the allegations of sexual harassment, then in such

52 Crl. Petition No. 7492/2015 (28.01.2019, Karnataka High Court).

53 Crl MC No. 847/2022 (01.11.2022, Kerala High Court).

case, prosecution of the accused on the same set of allegations would be unjust.

The Kerala High Court declined to entertain the plea of the accused and did not quash the criminal proceedings for the following principal reasons: (i) complainant had, from the very inception, maintained a consistent stand that she was subjected to sexual harassment at workplace by the accused; (ii) the ICC report did not contain any discussion or reasoning to arrive at a conclusion that a case of sexual harassment was not made out. Further, reliance was also placed by the Kerala High Court on Section 28 of the Act (which stipulates that the provisions of the Act shall be in addition to and not in derogation of the provisions of any other law for the time being in force) to conclude that action under the Act and a criminal complaint registered at the instance of the complainant are independent to each other and permissible under law.

The case of Usha Padmini was distinguished by the Kerala High Court on the following basis: (i) in that matter the complainant had virtually conceded before the ICC that no sexual harassment had taken place; (ii) the complainant had maintained, all through out in her complaint as well as before the ICC that there was no physical contact whatsoever by the accused. It was in such circumstances that the High Court, in that matter, concluded that there was no basis for continuing criminal proceedings against the accused.

In Amjith v. State of Kerala[54] the question which arose before the Kerala High Court was when the ICC report ran contrary to the prosecution case, whether the same alone could be a reason to quash criminal proceedings under Section 528 of the BNSS/ Section 482 of CRPC. After examining various provisions of the Act, the court answered in the negative. The court, while arriving

54 2024:KER:84389

at its conclusion inter alia, observed that, in terms of the Act, even the ICC can recommend measures which include launching of criminal prosecution. Hence, it may not be correct to say that ICC proceedings are subservient to criminal proceedings or *vice versa*. Further, the court held that the report of the ICC is not the final word insofar as the allegations made before the police were concerned (for which the crime was registered).

## DEFAMATION AND SEXUAL HARASSMENT

Generally speaking, laws of defamation are in place to prevent or vindicate a person's damage to reputation or goodwill. Defamation is a potential issue which may arise in the context of sexual harassment complaints because allegations of and an inquiry into a claim of sexual harassment may result in some sort of damage to the harasser's character and reputation. In this regard, it is imperative to note that the law of defamation in the context of sexual harassment may have limited application. A mere complaint of sexual harassment made *bona fide* or in good faith would not, *per se*, qualify to be defamation.

### Defamation as a counter blast to a complaint of Sexual Harassment

In Leena Doley v. State of Assam[55] a question which arose for determination was whether legal proceedings for defamation could be brought against a woman for filing a complaint of sexual harassment. The court observed that permitting a proceeding for defamation on the ground of filing a complaint alleging sexual harassment would amount to discouraging a victim from exercising her right to seek relief against the harassment.

Hence, generally speaking, in the view of the author, courts may not entertain complaints of defamation made by the person against whom allegations of sexual harassment are

55 2013 (5) GLT 363.

brought. Such complaints may perhaps be entertained only when it is established that the claim of sexual harassment by the 'aggrieved' woman was motivated by malice and/or made in bad faith.

**The complainant publicizing the issue of sexual harassment**

As per Leena Doley[56] *supra* prior to the Act, the issue of sexual harassment could be raised in employer-employee meetings (since this was provided for under the Vishaka Guidelines which then occupied the field). Hence, in the view of the author, there appears to be no embargo on the complainant publicising the issue of harassment suffered/experienced by her.

## PENAL PROVISIONS: PRIOR POSITION

Prior to the enactment of the Criminal Law Amendment Act 2013, there existed no specific and/or comprehensive provisions under Indian Criminal law dealing with sexual harassment. Sexual offences were largely covered under sections 509, 354 and 294 of the IPC & Sections 79, 74 and 296 of the BNS. Such provisions were woefully inadequate to effectively and substantially encompass and deal with sexual offences.

### Outraging the Modesty of Women

Sections 509 and 354 of the IPC (Sections 79 and 74 of the BNS) envisage provisions with respect to prevention of outraging the modesty of women. These provisions are discussed below.

Any person who, with the intention to insult the modesty of any woman[57], does any of the below mentioned acts shall be guilty of an offence under section 509 of the IPC (Section 79 of the BNS).

56 *Ibid.*

57 The culpable intention of the accused is the crux of the matter. *See* Sau. Anuradha R. Kshirsagar v. State of Maharashtra (1990) 3 Bom CR 644.

a. Suggests any word or makes any sound or gesture or exhibits any object intending that such word or sound shall be heard or that the gesture or object shall be seen by such woman;
b. Intrudes upon the privacy of such woman.

Meaning of the term 'Modesty'

In Rupan Deol Bajaj v. Kanwar Pal Singh Gill[58]; the term 'modesty' was defined in the following words:

> Modesty is the quality of being modest and in relation to woman means "womanly propriety of behaviour; scrupulous chastity of thought, speech and conduct". The word 'modest' in relation to woman is defined in the above dictionary as "decorous in manner and conduct; not forward or lewd; shame fast". Webster's Third New International Dictionary of the English language defines modesty as "freedom from coarseness, indelicacy or indecency; a regard for propriety in dress, speech or conduct". In the Oxford English Dictionary (1933 Ed) the meaning of the word 'modesty' is given as "womanly propriety of behaviour; scrupulous chastity of thought, speech and conduct (in man or woman); reserve or sense of shame proceeding from instinctive aversion to impure or coarse suggestions.

Simply stated, the concept of 'modesty' concerns with femininity or the like qualities accompanying it. In State of Punjab v. Major Singh[59] the court held that modesty is the quality of being modest which means, as regards women, decent in manner and conduct, scrupulously chaste. Any act done to or in the presence

58 AIR 1996 SC 309.

59 1967 Cri LJ 1. *See also* Aman Kumar v. State of Haryana AIR 2004 SC 1497; Raju Pandurang Mahale v. State of Maharashtra AIR 2004 SC 1677; Turkeshwar Sahu v. State of Bihar (2006) 8 SCC 560).

of a woman which is clearly suggestive of sex according to common notions of mankind must fall within the mischief of section 354 of the IPC (Section 74 of the BNS).[60] Therefore, mere aggressive behaviour devoid of any insult to the women's femininity (or like qualities) may not be sufficient to constitute an offence under this provision.[61]

Prior to the enactment of Sections 354A, 354B, 354C and 354D of the IPC & Sections 76, 77 and 78 of the BNS, sexual harassment complaints were largely registered under Section 509 of the IPC (Section 79 of the BNS).

Punishment under Section 509 of the IPC

An offence under Section 509 of the IPC, now 79 of BNS entails simple imprisonment for a term which may extend to 3 (three) years and fine.

Assault or criminal force to woman with intent to outrage her modesty

Section 354 & Section 74 of the BNS prohibits a person from assaulting or using criminal force to any woman, intending to outrage or knowing that it may likely outrage her modesty.

Punishment under Section 354 of the IPC

An offence under Section 354 of the IPC (Section 74 of the BNS) shall be punishable with imprisonment of either description for

60 The expression 'common notions of mankind' referred to herein should be gauged by contemporary societal standards.

61 *See* Sau. Anuradha R. Kshirsagar v. State of Maharashtra (1990) 3 Bom CR 644. In this case, the accused had used abusive language against women. The utterances included the following: (i) catch the women by the hair; (ii) kick them on the waist; (iii) pull them out etc. The court observed that while such an act constituted an offence under various provisions of the IPC, however, it did not attract S. 509 of the IPC.

a term which shall not be less than 1 (one) year but which may extend to 5 (five) years and with fine.[62]

The provisions of Section 354 of the IPC (Section 74 of the BNS) have been enacted to safeguard public morality and decent behaviour. Prosecution for sexual harassment under Section 354 of the IPC (Section 74 of the BNS) depends on two factors: (i) proof that the accused used criminal force or assaulted the woman; and (ii) such assault was done with an intent and knowledge that it was likely to outrage the modesty of a woman.[63]

The ultimate test for ascertaining whether modesty has been outraged is that whether action of the offender such as could be perceived as one which is capable of shocking the sense of decency of women.[64]

Offence under Section 354 of the IPC (Section 74 of the BNS) is compoundable by the woman assaulted or to whom criminal force was used.[65]

Section 294 of the IPC & Section 296 of the BNS

Section 294 of the IPC (Section 296 of the BNS) prohibits obscene acts or songs causing annoyance to others.

Punishment under Section 294 of IPC & Section 296 of the BNS

Commission of an offence under Section 294 of the IPC & Section 296 of the BNS is punishable with imprisonment of either

---

62 *See* Criminal Law (Amendment) Act 2013. Previously, an offender of S. 354 of the IPC could be punished for a maximum term of 2 (two) years.

63 Proof of intent and knowledge is mandatory to come within the ambit of section 354 of the IPC. Ajahar Ali v. State of West Bengal (2013) 10 SCC 31. *See also* T. Manikadan v. The State, Cr. Rev. Petition No. 404/2016 (10.01.2017, Delhi High Court). The expressions 'Criminal Force' & 'Assault' are defined under Ss. 350 & 351 of the IPC respectively.

64 Rupan Deol Bajaj v. Kanwar Pal Singh Gill AIR 1996 SC 309.

65 As per S. 320 (8) of the CRPC, the composition of an offence under S. 354 will have the effect of acquittal. P. Ramaswamy v. State (2013) 14 SCC 577.

description for a term which may extend to 3 (three) months, or with fine, or with both.

The Criticism to Sections 509 and 294 of the IPC

The Jharkhand High Court, in the case titled 'Court on its own Motion v. State of Jharkhand'[66] criticised Section 294 and 509 in the context of eve teasing, in the following words:

> It is for the prosecution to prove that the accused committed any obscene act or the accused sang, recited or uttered any obscene song; ballad or words and this was done in or near a public place, it was of obscene nature and that it this was done in or near a public place, it was of obscene nature and that it had accused annoyance to others. Normally, it is very difficult to establish those facts and, seldom, complaints are being filed and criminal cases will take years and years and often people get away with no punishment and filing complaint and to undergo a criminal trial itself is an agony for the complainant, over and above the extreme physical or mental agony already suffered.
>
> The burden is on the prosecution to prove that the accused had uttered the words or made the sound or gesture and that such word, sound or gesture was intended by the accused to be heard or seen by some woman. Normally, it is difficult to establish this and, seldom, a woman files a complaints and often the wrongdoers and left unpunished even if the complaint is filed since there is no effective mechanism to monitor and follow up such acts.

## THE CRIMINAL LAW AMENDMENTS OF 2013

Until recently, apart from the above mentioned provisions of the IPC, there existed no other legislation or provision which

66 W.P. (PIL) No. 5497/2011 (06.01.2014, Jharkhand High Court).

addressed the issue of 'sexual harassment' as an offence. The Criminal Law (Amendment) Act 2013 introduced various provisions to tackle the evil of sexual harassment in the workplace as well as on the streets.[67]

The Criminal Law (Amendment) Act, 2013 introduced the following sections to the IPC which envisage the issue of sexual harassment.

**Sexual Harassment**

Section 354A of the IPC (now Section 75 of the BNS) states as follows:

A man committing any of the following acts shall be guilty of the offence of sexual harassment.

i. physical contact and advances involving unwelcome and explicit sexual overtures;
ii. a demand or request for sexual favors; or
iii. showing pornography against the will of a woman; or
iv. making sexually colored remarks.[68]

Punishment under Section 354A & Section 75 of the BNS

Commission of an offence specified under clause (i), (ii) or (iii) above shall be punishable with rigorous imprisonment for a term which may extend to 3 (three) years, or with fine, or with both.

Commission of an offence specified under clause (iv) above shall be punishable with imprisonment (of either description)[69]

67 The Criminal Law (Amendment) Act, 2013 was passed by the Lok Sabha on 19.03.2013 and by the Rajya Sabha on 21.03.2013. It received presidential assent on 02.04.2013 and came into force from 03.04.2013. Prior to the enactment of the Criminal Law (Amendment) Act 2013, there existed no specific comprehensive provision under the IPC which addressed the issue of sexual harassment.

68 An accused may be punished simultaneously under Ss. 354 & 354A of the IPC for the same offence, in case the ingredients are made out. *See* T. Manikadan *supra.*

69 Under Indian law, imprisonment is either simple or rigorous.

for a term which may extend to 1 (one year), or with fine, or with both.

The offence under Section 354A of the IPC (Section 75 of the BNS) is cognizable and bailable.[70]

**Criminal Assault**

Section 354B of the IPC (Section 76 of the BNS) states that any man who assaults or uses criminal force to any woman or abets such act with the intention of disrobing or compelling her to be naked, shall be punishable with imprisonment of either description for a term which shall not be less than 3 (three) years but which may extend to 7 (seven) years, and shall also be liable to fine.

The offence under Section 354B of the IPC & Section 76 of the BNS is cognizable and non-bailable.[71]

**Voyeurism**

Section 354C of the IPC (now Section 77 of the BNS) covers the offence of voyeurism. As per this provision, any man who watches, or captures the image of a woman engaging in a private act[72], or in circumstances where she would usually have the expectation of not being observed either by the perpetrator or by any other person at the behest of the perpetrator or disseminate such image shall be guilty of the offence of voyeurism.

70 *See* First Schedule to the CRPC. Inserted *vide* the Criminal Law (Amendment) Act, 2013.

71 *See* First Schedule to the CRPC. Inserted *vide* the Criminal Law (Amendment) Act, 2013.

72 In law, the term 'private act' includes an act of watching carried out in a place which, in the circumstances, would reasonably be expected to provide privacy and where the victim's genitals, posterior or breasts are exposed or covered only in underwear; or the victim is using a lavatory; the victim is doing a sexual act that is not of a kind ordinarily done in public.

The offence of voyeurism would also cover in its ambit a situation where the victim consents to the capture of the images or any act, but not to the dissemination to third persons and where such image or act is disseminated.

Punishment under Section 354C & Section 77of the BNS

This offence is punishable in the following manner:

a. First Conviction: Imprisonment (of either description) for a term not less than 1 (one) year but which may extend to 3 (three) years and fine.
b. Second or Subsequent Conviction: Imprisonment (of either description) for a term not less than 3 (three) years but which may extend to 7 (seven) years and fine.

The offence under Section 354C of the IPC & Section 77 of the BNS (committed for the first time) is cognizable and bailable.[73] The offence becomes non-bailable for repeat offenders or recidivists.

**Stalking**

Section 354D of the IPC (now Section 78 of the BNS) makes punishable the offence of stalking.

A man who commits the following acts shall be guilty of stalking:

a. following a woman and contacting, or attempting to contact such woman to foster personal interaction repeatedly despite a clear indication of disinterest by such woman; or
b. monitoring the use by a woman of the Internet, email or any other form of electronic communication.

---

73 *See* First Schedule to the CRPC. Inserted *vide* the Criminal Law (Amendment) Act 2013.

Exceptions to the offence of stalking

The above-mentioned acts shall not amount to stalking if the offender proves any of the following:

a. the act was committed for the purpose of preventing or detecting crime and the man accused of stalking had been entrusted with the responsibility of prevention and detection of crime by the state;
b. the act was committed under any law or to comply with any condition or requirement imposed by any person under any law; or
c. in the particular circumstances the act was reasonable and justified.

Punishment under Section 354D & Section 78 of the BNS

a. First Conviction: Imprisonment (of either description) for a term which may extend to 3 (three) years and fine.
b. Second or Subsequent Conviction: Imprisonment (of either description) for a term which may extend to 5 (five) years and fine.

The offence under Section 354D of the IPC & Section 78 of the BNS (committed for the first time) is cognizable and bailable.[74] The offence becomes non-bailable for repeat offenders or recidivists.

**Gender Specific Nature of the Offences**

The offences enumerated under Sections 354, 354A, 354B, 354C and 354D of the IPC (now Sections 74, 75, 76, 77 & 78 of the BNS) are gender specific (*viz.* it only covers women victims).

**EVE TEASING**

Eve Teasing is another form of sexual harassment. It may be described as street sexual harassment which occurs in a public space, such as streets, public transport, public parks, malls etc.

74 *See* First Schedule to the CRPC. Inserted *vide* the Criminal Law (Amendment) Act, 2013.

In Deputy Inspector General of Police v. S. Samuthiram[75] the problem of eve teasing was discussed in a fair bit of detail. Amongst other things, in this judgement, the Supreme Court of India issued the following directions so as to curb the problem of eve teasing:

a. All the State Governments and Union Territories are directed to depute plain clothed female police officers in the precincts of bus- stands and stops, railway stations, metro stations, cinema theatres, shopping malls, parks, beaches, public service vehicles, places of worship, etc. so as to monitor and supervise incidents of eve-teasing.
b. There will be a further direction to the State Government and Union Territories to install CCTV cameras in strategic positions which itself would be a deterrent and if detected, the offender could be caught.
c. Persons in charge of the educations institutions, places of worship, cinema theatres, railway stations, bus-stands have to take steps as they deem fit to prevent eve-teasing, within their precincts and, on a complaint being made, they must pass on the information to the nearest police station or the Women's Help Centre.
d. Where any incident of eve-teasing is committed in a public service vehicle either by the passengers or the persons in charge of the vehicle, the crew of such vehicle shall, on a complaint made by the aggrieved person, take such vehicle to the nearest police station and give information to the police. Failure to do so should lead to cancellation of the permit to ply.
e. The State Governments and Union Territories are directed to establish Women Helpline in various cities and towns, so as to curb eve-teasing within three months.
f. Suitable boards cautioning such act of eve- teasing be exhibited

75 (2013) 1 SCC 598.

in all public places including precincts of educational institutions, bus-stands, railway stations, cinema theatres, parks, benches, public service vehicles, places of worship, etc.

g. Responsibility is also on the passers-by and on noticing such incident, they should also report the same to the nearest police station or to Women Helpline to save the victims from such crimes.

h. The State Governments and Union Territories of India would take adequate and effecting measures by issuing suitable instructions to the authorities concerned including the District Collectors and the District Superintendent of Police so as to take effective and proper measures to curb such incidents of eve-teasing.

The Jharkhand High Court, in the case titled 'Court on its own Motion v. State of Jharkhand'[76] keeping in mind the above observations of the Supreme Court, passed similar directions for curbing eve teasing in the state of Jharkhand.

## MISCELLANEOUS

The Criminal Law (Amendment) Act, 2013 has brought about various other amendments which aid the prosecution process in case of sexual offences. Some notable amendments to the criminal procedure for sexual offences are briefly described below.

**Section 154 of the CRPC & Section 173 of the BNSS:** Section 154 & Section 173 of the BNSS provide for the procedure to be followed in case of receipt of information relating to commission of a cognizable offence. A *proviso* has been added to the said provision which states as follows:

i. If the information is given by the woman against whom an offence under sections 326A, 354, 354A, 354B, 354C, 354D, 376, 376A, 376B,

76 W.P. (PIL) No. 5497/2011 (06.01.2014, Jharkhand High Court).

376C, 376D, 376E or 509 of the IPC (now Sections 124, 74, 75, 76, 77, 78, 64, 66, 67, 68, 70, 71, or 79 of the BNS) is alleged to have been committed or attempted, then such information shall be recorded by a woman police officer. It further provides that in the event that the victim is temporarily or permanently, mentally or physically disabled, then such information shall be recorded by a police officer, at the residence of the person seeking to report such offence or at a convenient place of such person's choice, in the presence of an interpreter or a special educator, as the case may be.

ii. The recording of such information shall be videographed.

iii. The concerned police officer shall get the statement of the person recorded by a judicial magistrate under Section 164 (5A) (a) of the CRPC as soon as possible.

**Section 161 of the CRPC & Section 180 of the BNSS:** Section 161 of the CRPC (now Section 180 of the BNSS) relate to examination of witnesses by police. The Criminal Law (Amendment) Act 2013 had inserted a new *proviso* to Section 161 of the IPC as per which the statement of a victim of a sexual offence shall be recorded by a woman police officer. This seems to have been done to ensure that victims are not subjected to embarrassment/ humiliation in front of male police officers.

**Section 197 of the CRPC & Section 18 of the BNSS:** Section 197 of the CRPC (now Section 18 of the BNSS) provide a safeguard to judges and other public servants against initiation of a prosecution against them in connection with discharge of their official functions. A prior approval/permission of the relevant authorities is normally required to initiate prosecution against judges and public servants in connection with discharge of their official duty. In other words, the appropriate authorities must be satisfied that there is a *prima facie* case for starting a prosecution against the alleged errant public servant or judge. The purpose is to enable them to perform their duties fearlessly.

The Criminal Law (Amendment) Act, 2013 has introduced an *explanation* to Section 197 (1) of the CRPC, now 218 of BNSS which does away with the requirement of obtaining permission for prosecuting a public servant in connection with sexual offences.[77]

**Section 273 of the CRPC & Section 308 of the BNSS:** In section 273 of the CRPC & Section 308 of the BNSS a *proviso* has been introduced whereby the court may take appropriate measures to ensure that a (minor) victim of a sexual offence, at the time of evidence, is not confronted with the accused.[78]

**Section 166A of the IPC & Section 199 of the BNS:** Section 166A has been inserted by the Criminal Law (Amendment) Act, 2013 to the IPC to punish public servants who shirk their responsibility by not acting upon receipt of a complaint of any sexual offences.

---

77 *See* Mahendra Kumar Singh v. Linda Eastwood CRR No. 3451 of 2013 (18.06.2014, Calcutta High Court); Leena Doley v. State of Assam 2013 (5) GLT 363. See generally Suneeti Toteja v. State of U.P 2025 SCC Online 433.

78 Towards this end, various trial courts at Delhi have installed opaque screens behind which the accused sits at the time of evidence.

CHAPTER 9

# Duties of Employers

Typically, in the context of sexual harassment, every individual is personally responsible for: (i) his own acts of sexual harassment; (ii) any retaliatory conduct or victimisation; (iii) any act of causing, inducing, abetting or aiding sexual harassment. However, an employer may also be held vicariously responsible for any act of sexual harassment taking place at its workplace or being carried out by its employees, in case such employer fails to comply with the terms of the Act.[1] Courts, have been willing to intervene on issues and complaints, including inadequate response or action by the employer, resulting in their liability.[2]

Under the Act, the primary liability for an offence of sexual harassment rests on the perpetrator. At the same time, the Act imposes numerous obligations on the employer of the workplace to ensure a harassment free work environment. Under the Act, all employers are under a bounden obligation to prevent creation or proliferation of a sexualised environment; and promptly respond to issues of sexual harassment. This chapter attempts to provide guidance to employers on how to meet their

1 *See* Gayatri Balaswamy v. ISG Novasoft Technologies Ltd. (2014) 6 CTC 602.

2 A.K. Singh v. Union of India W.P. (C) No. 4237/2012 (01.12.2015, Delhi High Court).

legal obligations; and to curb and manage sexual harassment in their workplace.

## COMPLIANCE REQUIREMENTS

There exist legal, social, moral and ethical reasons for an employer to scrupulously comply with the obligations imposed on it under the Act.

Even from an economic standpoint, complying with the Act makes good business sense. Employers who do not take steps to prevent sexual harassment may face losses in the shape of increased absenteeism, decreased productivity, hindered progress, loss of goodwill/image in the market and negative publicity (if cases of sexual harassment within their organisation become public), unnecessary costs of litigation (in case claims of sexual harassment are made) etc.

It is every employer's solemn duty to provide for safe and conducive working conditions for all their employees, regardless of their gender, ethnic background, caste, religion etc. No organisation can afford to put up with conduct which brings down productivity, lowers morale and runs afoul of standards of ethical behaviour expected of all workplace participants. Needless to state, a strict adherence to the terms of the Act would help an employer in effectively dealing with any incidence of sexual harassment at its workplace.

### Statutory Duties of Employer

Generally speaking, Indian law pins primary liability for sexual harassment on the harasser himself and not on the organisation to which the harasser is attached. However, under the Act, every organisation has a statutory, non-delegable duty of care towards its staff and employees. It is incumbent upon an employer to ensure that the workplace is discrimination and harassment free. The employers are required to take all necessary steps to prevent sexual harassment from occurring; and take immediate corrective action in case of its occurrence.

While there exist no homogeneous standards expected of employers in the context of sexual harassment, at the minimum, they are required to comply with the obligations imposed in the Act.[3] As per Section 19 of the Act, an employer has the following duties and responsibilities:

a. provide a safe working environment at the work place, including safety of persons coming into contact with the workplace.
b. display at any conspicuous place in the workplace, the penal consequences of sexual harassment; and the order constituting the ICC.
c. organize workshops and awareness programs at regular intervals for sensitizing the employees with the provisions of the Act; and orientation programs for the members of the ICC.
d. provide necessary facilities to the ICC or the LCC, as the case may be, for dealing with the complaint and conducting an inquiry.
e. assist in securing the attendance of the accused and witnesses before the ICC or the LCC, as the case may be.
f. make available such information to the ICC or the LCC as may be required having regard to the complaint made by the aggrieved woman.[4]
g. provide assistance to the aggrieved woman if she chooses to file a complaint in relation to the offence under the provisions of the Indian Penal Code or any other applicable law.
h. cause to initiate action, under the Indian Penal Code or any other applicable law, against the perpetrator, or if the aggrieved woman so desires, where the perpetrator is not an employee in the workplace at which the incident of sexual harassment took place.

3 S. 19 of the Act & R. 13 of the Rules.

4 Wherever possible, CCTV cameras should be installed at public places/areas.

i. treat sexual harassment as a misconduct under the service rules and initiate action for such misconduct.
j. monitor the timely submission of reports by the ICC.

**ICC Inquiry & Criminal Complaint: Parallel Steps**

In S. Murugan v. The State of Tamil Nadu[5] a question arose as to whether a criminal complaint could be preferred prior to initiation of or during the pendency of an inquiry before the ICC. The Madras High Court, after examining Section 11 and 19 (1) (g) of the Act, observed that an aggrieved woman could straightaway prefer a criminal complaint (instead of waiting for the ICC to investigate the matter) and if such an aggrieved woman chooses to do so, then it is the duty of the employer to provide assistance to the aggrieved woman in this regard. The Madras High Court observed the following:

a. The Act contemplates and permits a two-pronged approach with respect to complaints of sexual harassment. The employer is empowered to constitute an ICC and proceed with the inquiry. Thereafter, based on the inquiry report, the employer may initiate all further actions under the provisions of the Act as well as the service rules in force.
b. That apart, criminal proceedings can also be initiated in the context of sexual harassment. These two separate actions are independent, unconnected and permissible in law.

In addition to the above duties, an employer is required to do the following:[6]

a. Formulate and widely disseminate a sexual harassment policy for prohibition, prevention and redressal of sexual harassment at work

5 2019 (2) MLJ 613.

6 R. 13 of the Rules. The Convention on Elimination of Discrimination Against Women (CEDAW) also imposes similar obligations.

place; and remove underlying factors that contribute towards a hostile work environment against women.

b. Carry out orientation programs and seminars for the members of the ICC.

c. Carry out employee awareness programs and create forums for dialogues which may involve Panchayati Raj Institutions, Gram Sabha women's groups, mother's committees, adolescent groups, urban local bodies etc.

d. Conduct capacity building and skill building programs for the members of the ICC.

e. Declare the names and contact details for all members of the ICC.

f. Use modules developed by the state governments to conduct workshops and awareness programs for sensitizing the employees with the provisions of the Act.

**Penalty for non-compliance with the provisions of the Act**

The Act contemplates penalties for the employer in case of non-compliance with the provisions of the Act and for failure to conform to the prescribed procedures. These are described below in some detail.

<u>Fine</u>

A fine (extendable to Rs. 50,000/-) shall be levied on the employer in case the following:[7]

a. Failure of the employer to constitute an ICC.

b. Failure of the employer to take action, in accordance with the provisions of the Act, on the report of the ICC or the LCC, as the case may be, when such report concludes that sexual harassment has taken place.[8]

---

7 S. 26 of the Act

8 S. 13 (3) of the Act. Note that an employer faces the risk of being exposed to litigation in case it fails to take any disciplinary action for acts of sexual harassment in the workplace. *See generally* Clarinda D' Souza v. McCann Erickson India Limited (2003) 4 Bom CR 292.

c. Failure of the employer to take action (in accordance with the provisions of the Act) on the report of the ICC or the LCC, as the case may be, when such report concludes that a false or malicious complaint has been knowingly filed by the complainant; or the complainant has submitted forged or misleading documents; or any witness has given false evidence or submitted forged or misleading documents.
d. Failure of the employer to file the annual report in the manner prescribed.[9]
e. Contravention or attempt to contravene or abetment to contravene of any other provision of the Act or the Rules.

## Repeat Offenders

The Act postulates heightened penalty for repeat offenders or recidivists. An employer shall be liable for the following in case of a subsequent conviction:[10]

a. Twice the punishment which was imposed on the first conviction.[11]
b. Cancellation, withdrawal, non-renewal or non-approval of the employer's business licence or registration by the concerned government or local authority. (While such punishment may seem onerous, it appears to have been incorporated by the legislature to provide a strong disincentive for a recalcitrant employer who continues his non-compliance/violations of the provisions of the Act).[12]

9 S. 22 of the Act.

10 S. 26 (2) of the Act.

11 Further note that in case a higher punishment is prescribed under any other law for the time being in force, for the offence for which the accused is being prosecuted under the Act, the concerned authority may take due cognizance of the same while awarding the punishment the Act.

12 Parliamentary Standing Committee Report (2011), at 25.3. There exists an apparent lack of clarity on the type of business licences which are sought to be affected.

**Forum for complaint against Employer**

The Act does not appear to explicitly define the forum before whom a complaint can be lost against on errant employer. However, in Tanushree Chopra v. Ministry of Women and Child Development[13] the Delhi High Court took a view that a complaint for violation of Section 19 of the Act may be made to the concerned District Officer under Section 20 of the Act.

Failure of the employer to comply with the provisions of the Act, including: (i) failure to constitute an ICC; (ii) failure to create a conducive work environment; and (iii) failure to prevent creation and continuation of a hostile work environment, can lead to penalties on the employer. In Global Health Private Limited v. Local Complaints Committee[14] the Madhya Pradesh High awarded hefty penalties on the employer in this regard.

## EMPLOYERS ROLE UNDER THE ACT

Employers are mandated to create a climate of security and protection in the workplace, which in turn, requires swift and efficient redressal of grievances of sexual harassment. To achieve this, an employer must be pro-active in confronting the accused; must take appropriate and adequate remedial action; and must ensure that the investigative process is expeditious, efficacious, and in compliance with the principles of natural justice. No complaint of sexual harassment should be trivialized or ignored. Additionally an employer must take all necessary action with regard to the source of the harassment and minimize the chances of its recurrence.[15]

Any laxity or delay on the part of the employer or the ICC in entertaining and inquiring into a complaint of sexual

13 W.P. (C) No. 11759/2015 (17.12.2015, Delhi High Court).

14 W.P. No. 22317/2017 (16.09.2019, Madhya Pradesh High Court, Indore Bench).

15 *See generally* Clarinda D'Souza v. McCann Erickson India Ltd. (2003) 2 Mah LJ 373; Sarita Das v. Union of India 2014 (3) GLD 607 (Gau).

harassment would be antithetical to the purpose of the Act (Sarbajaya Banerjee v. The State of West Bengal).[16]

Prevention is the best tool to eliminate sexual harassment in the workplace. Employers are encouraged to take steps necessary to prevent sexual harassment from occurring. They can do so by providing sexual harassment training to their employees and by establishing an effective complaint or grievance process and taking immediate and appropriate action when an employee makes a complaint of sexual harassment.

Some critical factors which help in deducing an organisation's commitment towards ensuring a sexual harassment free workplace are:

a. The procedures and programmes put in place by the organisation to deal with the issue of sexual harassment.
b. The efficacy with which complaints of sexual harassment are dealt with by the organisation, including the resources made available to the complainant, the response time/turn-around time of the organisation, the seriousness with which the complaint is treated, the appropriate corrective action taken etc.
c. The general and periodical attempts/steps taken by the organisation towards ensuring a harassment free workplace.

Employers send a wrong message to employees if they fail to adequately discipline employees who are found guilty of sexual harassment. At times, the offence is perpetrated by the same people who are expected to set an example for others. Employers have a duty to express strong disapproval of sexual harassment and to develop appropriate sanctions to remedy the same.[17]

16 WPA No. 13588/2024 (13.02.2025, Calcutta High Court)

17 *See generally* Yamaguchi v. Widnall 109 F.3d. 1475 [1997] quoted in A.K. Singh v. Union of India W.P. (C) No. 4237/2012 (01.12.2015, Delhi High Court).

## SECONDARY HARASSMENT BY EMPLOYERS

Inadequate compliance with the Act by the employer or the ICC may result in victimization of the aggrieved.[18] This theory is also called secondary harassment or secondary victimisation. An employer may be held guilty of secondary harassment in case it allows an intimidating, hostile and offensive work environment to exist; or where the management's negligence in controlling working conditions is a cause of the sexual harassment. An employer may be considered negligent with respect to the issue of sexual harassment if it knew or should have known about the conduct and failed to stop/address it.[19] Further, an employer may be responsible for secondary harassment if, after learning of the alleged conduct, it fails to take adequate remedial measures in terms of Act.[20]

In M. Kavya v. Chairman, University Grants Commission[21] the concept of secondary victimisation was discussed by the Madras High Court in the following words:

---

18 *See* M. Kavya v. Chairman, University Grants Commission W.P. No. 11217/2014 (04.12.2014, Madras High Court).

19 *See* Burlington Industries Inc. v. Kimberly B. Ellereth (97-569) 123 F.3d 490 (26.06.1998, Supreme Court of United States). An employer can be held liable if it is negligent in responding to harassment after receiving actual or constructive notice. Abigail Wilson *supra*. 'Actual notice' of harassment is be established by direct proof that the management knew of the harassment, whereas 'constructive notice' will be found where the harassment was so severe and pervasive that the management should have known of it or if it failed to provide reasonable procedures. The following factors are germane to the issue of 'constructive notice': (i) the remoteness of the location of the harassment as compared to the location of the management; (ii) whether the harassment occurs intermittently over a long period of time; (iii) whether the victim was employment on a part time or a full time basis; (iv) whether there were only a few discrete instances of harassment. *See also* Bradley Miller v. Kenworth of Dothan, Inc. 277 F.3d 1269 (11th Circuit, 2002); Allen v. Tyson Foods, Inc. 121 F.3d 642.

20 *See* Puja Dubey v. Union of India W.P (C) 7916/2013 (19.07.2016, Delhi High Court); *See generally* Clarinda D' Souza *supra*.

21 W.P. No. 11217/2014 (04.12.2014, Madras High Court).

47. In 1999, a Hand Book of Justice for Victims was prepared by the United Nations Office for Drug Control and Crime Prevention. It was prepared by a group of experts from more than 40 countries. It was actually in pursuance of the Declaration of Basic Principles of Justice for Victims of Crime and Abuse of Power, which was adopted by the General Assembly of the United Nations 29.11.1985.

48. Chapter I of the Hand Book deals with "Impact of Victimisation". This Chapter covers (1) the physical and financial impact of victimisation; (2) psychological injury and social cost; and (3) secondary victimisation from the Criminal Justice System and Society.

49. Sub-Chapter (c) of Chapter I of the Hand Book points out that secondary victimisation refers to the victimisation that occurs not as a direct result of the criminal act, but through the response of institutions and individuals to the victim. In one of the paragraphs, it is stated as follows:-

"The attitude of individuals is important. Some people with whom the victim has contact (example: family, friends and colleagues) may wish to distance themselves from the distress of the crime by blaming the victim for what has occurred. They may view the victim's behaviour as having contributed to or even cause the victimisation".

By brushing aside the complaints of the petitioners as an outcome of a group clash and rivalry and by branding the petitioners as indulging in political activities, the respondents have belittled the very nature of the complaints. This response on the part of the university and their attempt to blame the victims, is what is pointed out by the U.N. in the aforementioned Hand Book as secondary victimisation.

50. After the case of Nirbhaya, the Government of India constituted a committee headed by former Chief Justice of

> India J.S.Verma. On the invitation of Verma Committee, Professor Sandra Fredman FBA QC (hon), with the assistance of members of Oxford Pro Bono Publico, prepared a report titled "Submissions on the Reform of India's Sexual Violence Laws". One of the recommendations contained therein is to provide "Survivor Support Services", which includes the avoidance of secondary victimisation by the criminal justice system and society.
>
> 51. In the aforesaid report, secondary victimisation is indicated as a victimisation that occurs not as a direct result of a criminal act but through the inadequate response of institutions and individuals to the victims. Such victimisation can range from experiences of isolation and confusion due to lack of support and information, while navigating the criminal justice system, to the shaming and ostracising of survivors and their families.

Simply stated, any employer who creates, condones or fails to check a sexualized environment at the work place, may be liable for secondary harassment.[22] Additionally, failure on the part of the employer to redress a complaint of sexual harassment may also amount to secondary harassment. In Alphi Chugh v. State of Haryana[23] an investigation was directed against the employer by the High Court to determine whether the mechanisms adopted by it to check and control

22 Where there is no policy, or where there is an ineffective or incomplete policy, the employer may be held liable for the perpetrators conduct which is so severe and pervasive so as to confer constructive knowledge, but when an employer promulgates an effective and comprehensive anti harassment policy that is 'aggressively and thoroughly' disseminated to its employees, it may be difficult to cast liability on the employer if the employee fails to utilize the grievance procedures. Further, a policy may be found ineffective when the employer practice indicates a tolerance towards harassment or discrimination. Sandra M. Clark; Rhonda R. Knoop v. United Parcel Service, Inc.; Eli Brock 400 F. 3d 341 (6th Circuit, 2005).

23 Crl. Misc. No. M-29141/2012 (19.09.2012, Punjab & Haryana High Court).

sexual harassment (at its workplace) were adequate or not. The court further observed that it was obligatory for every employer to evolve a specific mechanism to combat sexual harassment in the workplace.

## Establishing Hostile Work Environment

In some cases, it may be possible for the complainant to hold the employer responsible for the discriminatory conduct in the workplace. For holding an employer liable for a hostile work environment, a complainant may have to allege and prove the following elements:[24]

a. The employee belongs to a protected group under the law.
b. The employee was subjected to unwelcome sexual harassment.
c. The harassment complained of was based upon sex; the essence of a disparate treatment claim should be that an employee is intentionally singled out for adverse treatment on the basis of a prohibited criterion.
d. The harassment complained of affected a 'term or condition' of employment. The expression 'term or condition' does not refer to any term or condition in a strict contractual sense but the entire spectrum of employment conditions.
e. The employee must show that the employer knew or should have known of the harassment in question and failed to take prompt remedial action.

## Establishing Quid Pro Quo Harassment

For holding an employer liable for a quid pro quo harassment, a complainant may have to established the following elements:[25]

24 Barbara J. Henson v. City of Dundee 682 F. 2d 897; *See also* Patricia Fuller v. City of Oakland No. 92-16081 (14.02.1995, Court of Appeals, Ninth Circuit).

25 *Ibid.*

a. The employee belongs to a protected group under the law.
b. The employee was subjected to unwelcome sexual harassment.
c. The harassment complained of was based upon sex; the essence of a disparate treatment claim should be that an employee is intentionally singled out for adverse treatment on the basis of a prohibited criterion.
d. The employee's reaction to the harassment affected tangible aspects of the employee's compensation, terms, conditions or privileges of employment. The acceptance or rejection of the harassment by an employee must be an express or implied condition to the receipt of a job benefit or the cause of a tangible job detriment in order to create liability under this theory of sexual harassment.
e. The employee must show that the employer knew or should have known of the harassment in question and failed to take prompt remedial action. In such a situation, an employer may be relieved from liability if prompt remedial action was taken upon notice of the harassment.

Typically, for an employer to be indicted for secondary harassment, it would have to be shown that the employer was negligent in its responsibility of preventing and/or appropriately addressing a case of sexual harassment. To escape any liability for secondary harassment, an employer may be required to establish the following: (i) that it was fully compliant with all its obligations as imposed under the Act; (ii) it exercised reasonable care to prevent and promptly remedy the act of sexual harassment;[26] (iii) the complainant unreasonably failed to take advantage of any preventive or corrective opportunities provided by the employer

26 One way for employers to demonstrate that they exercised reasonable care is to show that they had an anti-harassment policy in place. An employer need not prove success in preventing harassing behaviour in order to demonstrate that it exercised reasonable care in preventing and correcting sexually harassing conduct. Although not necessarily dispositive, the existence of an anti-harassment policy with complaint procedures is an important consideration in this regard. *See* Yasharay Mack v. Otis Elevator Company 326 F.3d 116 (2nd Circuit, 2003).

in this regard.[27] Once the employer has, in good faith, taken all measures which are necessary, feasible and reasonable to combat sexual harassment (as provided in the Act), then in such case such employer may not be charged for secondary harassment.[28]

## EMPLOYER OBLIGATIONS: A GUIDANCE

As discussed above, employers who are aware (or should be aware) that a sexualised environment/atmosphere exists but take no steps to curb it, violate the provisions of the Act and may become accountable for secondary harassment. An employer's negligence and lassitude in relation to the issue of sexual harassment is what may give rise to employer liability. Mere presence of sexual harassment and grievance procedures may not be sufficient. The efforts of the employer will also need to be examined. Such efforts must include immediate and corrective action reasonably calculated for the following: (i) to end the current harassment; and (ii) to deter future harassment from the same offender or others.[29]

In cases where sexual harassment is committed by an employee in the course of his employment, the burden lies on the employer to show that it, in the first instance, took all reasonable steps to prevent the harassment and, in the event of its happening, took all necessary remedial action.[30]

---

27 *See generally* Burlington Industries *supra*; Bradley Miller v. Kenworth of Dothan, Inc. 277 F.3d 1269 (11th Circuit, 2002).

28 *See generally* De Grace v. Rumsfeld 614 F.2d 796 (1980); Robin Anderson v. CRST International Appeal No. 15-55556 (24.03.2017, Court of Appeals, 9th Circuit).

29 *See generally* Yamaguchi v. Widnall 109 F.3d. 1475 [1997]. The concept of secondary harassment is somewhat akin to 'negligence'. *See generally* Laxmi Salt Works v. State of Gujarat 1991 (4) SCC 1; Overseas Tankship (UK) Ltd. v. Morts Docks and Engineering Co. Ltd. (1961) UKPC 1.

30 Once an employer has knowledge of the harassment, the law imposes upon him a duty to take reasonable steps to eliminate it. *See* Torres v. Pisano 116 F.3d 625 (2nd Circuit, 1997).

## Policy, Publicity & Training

Ideally, employers should adopt a zero tolerance policy against sexual harassment. All unscrupulous and delinquent employees must be disciplined. The three essential pillars of a successful anti harassment agenda are: (i) Formulation of effective sexual harassment policies; (ii) Regular and Periodic training(s) for the employees and the complaints committee; and (iii) Wide publicity and dissemination of the Act and the sexual harassment policies at all levels of the organisation. Courts have encouraged conduct of sensitisation and awareness programmes for members of the complaints committee as well as for the members of the workplace.[31]

## The Policy

Every employer must formulate an effective anti-harassment policy, secure measures to effectively implement such policy, and conduct session(s) etc. to ensure that all its employees are fully aware of what constitutes sexual harassment; and the way forward in case one is sexually harassed.

While a majority of employees would be aware that sexual harassment in the workplace is illegal, however, not many would know exactly what constitutes sexual harassment and what should be done to contain this issue at the workplace. In fact, informal empirical study conducted by the author of this work indicates that while many expressly said that they had never experienced or witnessed sexual harassment, however, certain behaviour which they did experience or witness may in fact constitute sexual harassment under the extant law. Clearly, it is the lack of sufficient information and knowledge which results in incidents of sexual harassment going unnoticed.

---

31 *See* Ms. Yangchen Dahdul v. State of Sikkim, W.P. (PIL) No. 5/2015 (25.10.2016, Sikkim High Court).

Employers must develop and adopt anti-sexual harassment policies and ensure that all stakeholders are adequately informed and educated about the nature, effects and consequences of sexual harassment. Employees must be aware of how the organisation intends to discipline violators. Additionally, all penalties/punishments must be made sufficiently public (*albeit* in compliance with the confidentiality related provisions under the Act) to serve as examples for potential violators. A well drafted and charted out policy will help in promoting heightened self-restraint (by the employee) and a prior cognitive analysis of how his conduct may be interpreted by the female workforce before he speaks or acts.

Normally, both men and women may experience sexual harassment; however, the Act only takes within its sweep sexual harassment suffered by women. However, employers are at liberty to make their sexual harassment policies gender neutral.

### Training

All employees of an organisation, including all members of the ICC, are required to be made aware of the seriousness of the offence of sexual harassment. All concerned personnel should be well educated about their specific roles and responsibilities when an issue of sexual harassment arises. Mere presence of a written policy, *per se,* is not sufficient. A policy which is unimplemented or under implemented will be of little assistance in discharging employer liability under the Act. The efficacy of an anti-sexual harassment agenda depends much on the awareness levels in the organization. Therefore, it becomes critical to conduct periodic sexual harassment training at all levels in the organisation.[32] Additionally, training material and

32 In Nunan v. Action Traffic Services Pty Ltd. [2013] QCAT 565, the court observed that the employer had failed to provide adequate training for its employees in relation to workplace policies on sexual harassment.

methodology must be visited (and revisited) if it is found to have no appreciable effect at curbing sexual harassment.

Separately, it is important to train all members of the complaints committees. Unfortunately, today, many members of complaints committees are not sensitised enough and show a general lack of awareness about their duties and roles. This is likely to cause an impediment to the inquiry process and to the successful implementation of the provisions of the Act.

**Publicity**

Rendering large public attention to the issue of sexual harassment is likely to make people more careful and cautious in their official conduct. Methods of publicizing the sexual harassment policy include sending personal copies of the policy to every employee, pasting the policy on the notice board and the website of the organization and discussing the policy during trainings. Serious training and information efforts (on the part of the employer) are likely to have a positive impact in raising workforce sensitivity on the subject of sexual harassment.

**Internal Assessment and Surveys**

It may be prudent for an employer to conduct regular internal audits and assessments to track and monitor the incidence of sexual harassment in its organisation; and the efficacy of its sexual harassment policies. Organising and conducting periodic surveys may be helpful in identifying the problem areas and taking necessary steps to address them. Such surveys would also aid the organisation in gauging its level of success in creating a harassment free work environment.

**Staff Responsibility**

Corresponding to an employer's duty to provide a safe and harassment free working environment for its employees, it is imperative that all employees also do their bit for ensuring that the provisions of the Act are implemented in letter and spirit at their workplace. Even employees have a positive role to play in contributing towards creation of a healthy and conducive environment free from sexual harassment. Employees should be aware that their participation (in any way) in the act(s) of the perpetrator could result in liability for them also.

Mentioned below are some pointers for employees which, in the view of the author, may aid in giving full effect to the ethos of the legislature behind propagating the (Indian) sexual harassment regime.

a. Comply with the organisation's sexual harassment policy.
b. Not spread gossip about the victim or the accused.
c. Not induce, abet or participate in any act causing victimisation to the victim.
d. Offer all possible support to victims of sexual harassment.
e. Maintain confidentiality in case they act as witness or provide any information/documents to the complaints committee during the course of inquiry.
f. Report early concerns about any impermissible behaviour from any quarter so that appropriate steps may be taken by the organisation to curb and contain them before the problem escalates.
g. Ensure that their standard of conduct and behaviour is such that it does not result in any offence under the Act.
h. Discourage colleagues from indulging in any sort of activity prohibited under the Act.

## ROLE OF THE COMPLAINTS COMMITTEE

The complaints committee plays a key role in checking the incidence of sexual harassment within the organisation. The members of the complaints committee must be approachable at all times so as to make it easier for the victim to report any harassing behaviour. Additionally, the members of the committee should possess a genuine concern about the issue and should have the desire to uphold the rule of law and do what is necessary to remedy the situation lest the victims desist from coming forward with their complaints for fear of apathy of the committee or secondary victimisation or retaliatory action.

**Complaints Procedures**

All complaints procedures should be well documented; be based on the principles of procedural fairness and natural justice; and should be periodically audited/updated (when necessary).

**Benefits of a good complaints mechanism**

Having in place an effective complaints mechanism (to counter sexual harassment) has numerous benefits, some of which are listed below.

a. Conveys the message that the organisation takes sexual harassment seriously.
b. Helps to ensure that complaints of sexual harassment are dealt with consistently and in a timely manner.
c. Reduces the risk of the employer being held guilty of vicarious liability.
d. Can help in mitigating the harm suffered by a victim of sexual harassment.

## ROLE OF THE GOVERNMENT

Whilst the employer(s) have various obligations and disclosure requirements under the Act; the government also has several responsibilities. Mentioned below are the statutory obligations of the government under the Act.

**Ensuring appointment of a District Officer in every District**

The government must ensure that every district, at all times, has a district officer to perform the duties under the Act. Any vacancy (created by the retirement of the officer or for any other reason) must be filled up by the government at the earliest. Efforts should be made by the government to ensure that this position is never vacant.[33]

**Monitor Implementation and Maintain Data**

The appropriate government shall monitor the implementation of the Act and maintain data on the number of cases filed and disposed of in respect of all cases of sexual harassment at work place.[34] The purpose of this provision seems to be creation of a centralised database on the number of complaints filed, their disposal, punishments given etc. Such record keeping would aid the government in developing and maintaining an organised database on the subject which would, in turn, improve data accessibility, management and sharing on the issue of sexual harassment.

**Measures to Publicise the Act**

As discussed above, public awareness is a critical tool for effective implementation of this law. Both the employer and the government are obligated to render maximum publicity to the Act. While the employer's duty exits at the organisational level, the government's responsibility extends to the ground level and on a national scale. In Initiatives For Inclusion Foundation v. Union of India[35] the Supreme Court observed that spreading of awareness relating to the Act and the LCCs should be a priority of the highest level for the state.

33 *See* Initiatives For Inclusion Foundation v. Union of India 2023 INSC 927.

34 S. 23 of the Act.

35 2023 INSC 927.

The Act provides that the appropriate government may, subject to availability of financial and other resources[36] do the following:

a. Develop relevant information, education, communication and training materials, and organize awareness programs, to advance the understanding of the public of the provisions of the Act.
b. Formulate orientation and training programs for the members of the LCC.[37]

**Allocation of a Budget**

In Initiatives For Inclusion Foundation v. Union of India[38] the Supreme Court observed that the government would need to setup a designated budget for the purposes of implementation of the Act. It was further observed that in the absence of a delineated budget to pay the concerned officers and conduct events for awareness and training, various LCCS would be rendered infructuous or remain vacant.

**Call for Information and Inspect Records**

The appropriate government, on being satisfied that it is necessary in public interest or in the interest of women employees at the workplace to do so, by order in writing:

a. Call upon any employer or district officer to furnish in writing such information relating to sexual harassment as it may require.
b. Authorize any officer to make inspection of the records and workplace in relation to sexual harassment, who shall submit

36 S. 24 of the Act.

37 It is important that members of the complaints committee receive thorough training so that all inquiries are conducted in a fair manner and in compliance with law.

38 2023 INSC 927.

a report of such inspection to it within such period as may be specified in the order.[39]

The employer or the district officer shall produce on demand before the inspecting officer, all the information, records and other documents in its custody having a bearing on the subject matter of the inspection.[40]

**Court Intervention to ensure compliance**

The government has, over the years, been slow in fully complying with the provisions of the Act. As a result, in the recent past, several petitions have been filed in various high courts seeking directions to government authorities to comply with the provisions of the Act. For instance, in Biyat Pragya Tripathi v. Government of Odhisha[41] directions were sought against the government authorities to put up billboards in public areas displaying the penal consequences of sexual harassment, as well as further directions to the authorities to constitute appropriate ICCs for the respective departments in terms of Section 4 of the Act. In this matter, the Orissa High Court directed all authorities under the central and state government to comply with the provisions of Section 19 (b) of the Act and further directed the authorities to place appropriate billboards showing penal consequences of sexual harassment etc.

In Su Iccha Foundation v. Union of India[42] a petition was filed in the Delhi High Court seeking the following directions: (a) To set up an online portal/mechanism for registration of ICCs for effective implementation of Section 23 of the Act. It was pointed out in the matter that several state governments, including the

39 S. 25 (1) of the Act.

40 S. 25 of the Act.

41 W.P. (C) No. 33000/2022 (15.09.2023, Orissa High Court).

42 W.P. (C) No. 14675/2023 (17.11.2023, Delhi High Court).

governments of Telangana, Karnataka and Maharashtra had already made it mandatory to register ICCs and the detail of its members on their portal/email ids. The Delhi High Court directed the authorities to treat this petition as a representation for consideration of such aspects.

In Initiatives For Inclusion Foundation v. Union of India[43] the Supreme Court passed the following critical directives for the purposes of ensuring compliance with the provisions of the Act:

a. The Women and Child Development Ministry of every State/ Union Territory, through its principal Secretary, should consider identifying a "nodal person" within the department, to oversee and aid in coordination, as contemplated under the Act.
b. The relevant government to ensure appointment of a district officer in each district.
c. The so appointed district officer to take the following further steps: (i) appoint nodal officers in every block, taluka and tehsil in rural or tribal area, ward or municipality in the urban area; (ii) to constitute LCC in the manner prescribed under the Act; (iii) to ensure that the contact details and coordinates of these nodal officers and LCCs are forwarded to the nodal person (as contemplated above).
d. Creation and circulation of a circular/bulletin containing names, details and contact coordinates of all district officers (of every district). Further directions issued by the court to upload such information on the relevant department's website, at a conspicuous place, along with compiled version of the Act, Rules etc.
e. The union government to consider amending the rules, so as to operationalise section 26 of the Act, by recognising are reporting authority and/or a fine collecting authority.
f. The union government to consider amending the Rules, so as to identify one department (preferably the Women and Child department) and creating a post of a "nodal person" who would

43 2023 INSC 927.

be responsible for the coordination required in the implementation of the Act.

g. Imparting training to the District Officers and the LCCs regarding their important responsibilities. The state government to organise periodic and regular training sessions at the district level, which would be attended by all relevant stakeholders.
h. The government to set out financial resources for developing educational, communication and training material for spreading awareness of the provisions of the act of the public.
i. The government to identify non-governmental organisations working with women and their protection within the district, for the purposes of creation of awareness (as discussed above).
j. The government to make efforts to spread awareness amongst the unorganised sector.
k. The government to create a standard operating procedure (SOP) for the purposes of monitoring implementation and maintenance of data.

## SMALL BUSINESSES

The expression 'small business' may be classified as an establishment having less than 10 (ten) workers. There exists no exemption(s) in the Act for small businesses, meaning thereby that all business establishments (whatever the size) are within the ambit of and are required to comply with the Act.

The only limited benefit provided to small businesses under the Act is that they are not mandated to constitute an ICC and consequently are exempt from the complaints committee related obligations under the Act.[44] Therefore, all sexual harassment claims made by or against employees of small businesses would be dealt with by the concerned LCC.[45]

---

44 *viz*. S. 6 (1) of the Act.

45 *See* chapter titled 'Complaints Committee'. Complaints of sexual harassment in such organisations shall be inquired into by the concerned LCC.

CHAPTER 10

# Constitutional Obligations and International Conventions

The protection of women against sexual harassment and her right to work with dignity are universally recognized human rights both by domestic law as well as international conventions and instruments. India's commitment to protection and promotion of women's equality and rights is unequivocal. This chapter briefly analyses India's constitutional obligations in connection with protection of women and some important international instruments executed by India which relate to the issue of women's equality both at the workplace and outside.

## CONSTITUTION OF INDIA

The Constitution of India is the document which lays down the framework of Indian law. Amongst other things, it sets out the structure, powers and duties of the government as also the fundamental rights and directive principles of the citizens. The Constitution came into force on 26.01.1950. As per the Constitution, the State has the primary obligation to secure the fundamental rights of its citizens. The Constitution of India contains various provisions which provide for protection of women. The fundamental rights of women include safety, bodily integrity and right to live with dignity. This also includes provision of secure spaces where they can excise autonomy and free will.[1]Any form of violence or assault, sexual or otherwise, on women, is a violation of their fundamental right.[2] Hence, sexual harassment constitutes a violation of fundamental rights guaranteed under the Constitution.

In this context, it is apt to refer to some constitutional provisions which envisage protection to women, especially in connection with her workplace.

**Article 14 of the Constitution**

The Constitution of India embodies the concept of equality under Article 14. This Article reads thus:

> The State shall not deny to any person equality before the law or the equal protection of the laws within the territory of India.

Article 14 has essentially 2 (two) parts:

i. Equality before law *viz.* equal subjection of all classes to law. Simply put, it means that the same rule must exist for all in similar circumstances.
ii. Equal protection of law *viz.* equals should be treated equally.

Article 14 protects all persons regardless of whether they are citizens of India or not.

**Article 15 of the Constitution**

Article 15 prohibits discrimination on grounds of religion, race, sex, cast or place of birth. Unlike Article 14, Article 15 confers rights only to citizens of India. It reads as follows:

1 *See* Verma Committee Report.

2 *Ibid.*

(1) The State shall not discriminate against any citizen on grounds only of religion, race, caste, sex, place of birth or any of them.
(2) No citizen shall, on grounds only of religion, race, caste, sex, place of birth or any of them, be subject to any disability, liability, restriction or condition with regard to— (a) access to shops, public restaurants, hotels and places of public entertainment; or (b) the use of wells, tanks, bathing ghats, roads and places of public resort maintained wholly or partly out of State funds or dedicated to the use of the general public.
(3) Nothing in this article shall prevent the State from making any special provision for women and children.
(4) Nothing in this article or in clause (2) of Article 29 shall prevent the State from making any special provision for the advancement of any socially and educationally backward classes of citizens or for the Scheduled Castes and the Scheduled Tribes.
(5) Nothing in this article or in sub-clause (g) of clause (1) of article 19 shall prevent the State from making any special provision, by law, for the advancement of any socially and educationally backward classes of citizens or for the Scheduled Castes or the Scheduled Tribes in so far as such special provisions relate to their admission to educational institutions including private educational institutions, whether aided or unaided by the State, other than the minority educational institutions referred to in clause (1) of Article 30.

Article 15, may be broken down into the following parts:

a. Article 15 (1) proscribes discrimination against citizens on any of the following grounds: (i) religion; (ii) race; (iii) caste; (iv) sex; (iv) place of birth.

b. Article 15 (2) prohibits discrimination with regard to: (i) access to shops, public restaurants, hotels and places of public entertainment; (ii) the use of wells, tanks, bathing ghats, roads and places of public resort maintained wholly or partly out of State funds or dedicated to the use of the general public.
c. Article 15 (3) empowers the state to make special provisions for the protection of women and children.
d. Article 15 (4) empowers the State to make special provisions for the advancement of any socially and educationally backward classes of citizens or for the Scheduled Castes and the Scheduled Tribes.
e. Article 15 (5) empowers the State to make special provisions for the advancement of any socially and educationally backward classes of citizens or for Scheduled Castes or Scheduled Tribes for the purpose of admission to educational institutions, including private educational institutions.

**Article 16 of the Constitution**

Article 16 of the Constitution guarantees equality of opportunity to citizens in matters of employment with the State. The relevant excerpt of Article 16 reads as follows:

> (1) There shall be equality of opportunity for all citizens in matters relating to employment or appointment to any office under the State.
> (2) No citizen shall, on grounds only of religion, race, caste, sex, descent, place of birth, residence, or any of them, be ineligible for, or discriminated against in respect of, any employment or office under the State.

This Article, *inter alia,* prohibits any discrimination in respect of employment matters, on the ground of sex.

**Article 19 (1) (g) of the Constitution**

Article 19 (1) (g) of the Constitution reads as follows:

> (1) All citizens shall have the right— (a) to freedom of speech and expression; (b) to assemble peaceably and without arms; (c) to form associations or unions [or co-operative societies]; (d) to move freely throughout the territory of India; (e) to reside and settle in any part of the territory of India; and
>
> (g) to practise any profession, or to carry on any occupation, trade or business.
>
> (6) Nothing in sub-clause (g) of the said clause shall affect the operation of any existing law in so far as it imposes, or prevent the State from making any law imposing, in the interests of the general public, reasonable restrictions on the exercise of the right conferred by the said sub-clause, and, in particular, nothing in the said sub-clause shall affect the operation of any existing law in so far as it relates to, or prevent the State from making any law relating to,— (i) the professional or technical qualifications necessary for practising any profession or carrying on any occupation, trade or business, or (ii) the carrying on by the State, or by a corporation owned or controlled by the State, of any trade, business, industry or service, whether to the exclusion, complete or partial, of citizens or otherwise

This Article guarantees a right to Indian citizens to practice any profession or to carry on any profession, trade or business. This right presupposes the availability of an enabling environment for women, which is safe and secure in every aspect.[3]

---

3 *See* Statement of Objects and Reasons of the Act.

### Article 21 of the Constitution

Article 21 of the Constitution reads as follows:

> 21. No person shall be deprived of his life or personal liberty except according to procedure established by law.

Article 21 lays down that no person shall be deprived of his life or liberty except by procedures established by law. The term 'life' and 'personal liberty' in this article are expression of wide amplitude which include all varieties of life which make up the personal liberties of a man and not merely the right to the continuance of a person's existence.[4] Article 21 includes within its ambit, the right to live with dignity, and in the case of women, it means that they must be treated with due respect, decency and dignity at the workplace.[5]

## DIRECTIVE PRINCIPLES OF STATE POLICY

India is a welfare state *viz.* the welfare of its citizens is the responsibility of the state. The purpose of a welfare state is to, *inter alia,* create economic equality or to assure equitable standards of living for all. The Directive Principles of State Policy (contained in Part IV of the Constitution of India) obligates the State to uphold its conviction of being a welfare state. Unlike Fundamental Rights, the Directive Principles of State Policy are not enforceable in courts, however these provide a discourse to the State on its obligations towards individuals. Some relevant Directive Principles of State Policy are discussed below.

### Article 39 of the Constitution

Article 39 of the Constitution requires the State to, *inter alia,*

4 *See* State of West Bengal v. Committee for Protection of Democratic Rights, West Bengal (2010) 3 SCC 571.

5 *See* Statement of Objects and Reasons of the Act.

direct its policy towards ensuring that: (i) that the citizen, men and women equally, have the right to an adequate means of livelihood; and (ii) that there is equal pay for equal work for both men and women.[6]

Article 39A of the Constitution requires the State to ensure that the operation of the legal system promotes justice, on a basis of equal opportunity, and, in particular, provide free legal aid, by suitable legislation or schemes or in any other way, to ensure that opportunities for securing justice are not denied to any citizen by reason of economic or other disabilities.

### Article 42 of the Constitution

Article 42 of the Constitution requires the State to make provision for securing just and humane conditions of work and for maternity leave.

## INTERNATIONAL CONVENTIONS

India's obligation to ensure gender justice (including protecting women from crime and abuse) arises from many sources of international law and international covenants/instruments, some of which are mentioned below:[7]

### The Universal Declaration of Human Rights, 1948

The Universal Declaration of Human Rights, 1948 (**UDHR**) defines the expressions 'fundamental freedoms' and 'human rights' for the purposes of the Charter of the United Nations (UN Charter).[8] It is generally agreed to be the foundation of

---

6 Articles 39 (a) & (d) of the Constitution of India.

7 *See* Verma Committee Report.

8 A result of the World War II, the Charter of the United Nations is the foundational treaty of the United Nations. It was signed on 26.06.1945 in San Francisco, at the conclusion of the United Nations Conference on International Organization and came into force on 24.10.1945.

international Human Rights Law. India was one of the 48 (forty eight) countries which voted in favour of adoption of the UDHR by the United Nations General Assembly on 10.12.1948. The UDHR was followed up by the International Covenant on Civil and Political Rights, 1966.

**The International Covenant on Civil and Political Rights, 1966**

The International Covenant on Civil and Political Rights, 1966 (**ICCPR**) is a key international human rights treaty, providing a range of protections for civil and political rights. The ICCPR, together with UDHR and the International Covenant on Economic Social and Cultural Rights, are collectively considered the International Bill of Human Rights (which is the pillar for human rights protection within the United Nations). The ICCPR obligates its ratifying countries to protect and preserve basic human rights such as: the right to life and human dignity; equality before the law; freedom of speech, assembly, and association; religious freedom and privacy; freedom from torture, ill-treatment, and arbitrary detention; gender equality; the right to a fair trial, and minority rights. The ICCPR encourages governments to take administrative, judicial and legislative measures in order to protect the rights enshrined therein and to provide effective remedies in connection thereof.[9]

India acceded to the ICCPR on 10.04.1979. However, India has not signed or ratified the optional protocols[10] to the ICCPR (including the Second Optional Protocol which abolishes death penalty).[11]

---

9 *See https://www.aclu.org/faq-covenant-civil-political-rights-iccpr*. *See also* Verma Committee Report.

10 Human Rights Treaties are often followed by 'Optional Protocols' which may either provide for procedures with regard to the treaty or address a substantive area related to the treaty. Optional Protocols are treaties in their own right, and are open to signature, accession or ratification by countries who are party to the main treaty.

11 *See* Verma Committee Report.

## International Covenant on Economic, Social and Cultural Rights, 1966

The Preamble of the International Covenant on Economic, Social and Cultural Rights, 1966 (**ICESCR**) recognises, *inter alia,* that economic, social and cultural rights derive from the 'inherent dignity of the human person' and that 'the ideal of free human beings enjoying freedom of fear and want can only be achieved if conditions are created whereby everyone may enjoy his economic, social and cultural rights, as well as civil and political rights'. The overarching principles of the ICESCR are: (i) Equality and non-discrimination in regard to the enjoyment of all the rights set forth therein; and (ii) Obligations of member states to respect, protect and fulfil economic, social and cultural rights.[12]

## Beijing Principles of the Independence of the Judiciary

The Beijing Principles of the Independence of the Judiciary **(Beijing Principles)** were drawn up and agreed to by the Chief Justices of various countries in the Asia-Pacific region in 1995. As per these principles, the judiciary of participating nations should endeavour to do the following: (i) Ensure that all persons live securely under the rule of law; (ii) Promote, within proper limits of the judicial function, the observance and attainment of human rights; and (iii) Administer the law impartially amongst persons and between persons and the State.[13]

## Convention on the Political Rights of Women, 1954

This Convention, among other things, requires participants to ensure the protection of various political rights of women. India signed this convention on 29.04.1953 and ratified it on 01.11.1961.[14]

---

12 *See* https://www.escr-net.org/docs/i/425251.

13 *See* Verma Committee Report.

14 *Ibid.*

## Declaration on Elimination of Violence against Women 1993

The Declaration on the Elimination of Violence Against Women was adopted by the United Nations General Assembly in its Resolution No. 48/104 of 20.12.1993. A principal aim of the resolution was to overturn the then prevailing governmental stance that violence against women was a private, domestic matter which did not require state intervention. The resolution is often seen as complementary to, and a strengthening of the work of the Convention on the Elimination of All Forms of Discrimination against Women (discussed below). It embodies the same rights and principles as those enshrined in instruments such as the UDHR.[15]

## Convention on Elimination of all forms of Discrimination against Women

The Convention on Elimination of all forms of Discrimination against Women (**CEDAW**) is an international treaty adopted in 1979 by the United Nations General Assembly and is often described as an international bill of rights for women. Consisting of a preamble and 30 (thirty) articles, it defines what constitutes discrimination against women and sets up an agenda for national action to end such discrimination.[16]

Article 11 of the CEDAW requires member states to take all appropriate measures to eliminate discrimination against women in the field of employment. By accepting this convention, states commit to undertake various measures to end discrimination against women in all forms, including the following:[17]

---

15 *See* https://en.wikipedia.org/wiki/Declaration_on_the_Elimination_of Violence_Against_Women.

16 *See* http://www.un.org/womenwatch/daw/cedaw/.

17 *See* http://www.un.org/womenwatch/daw/cedaw/.

a. to incorporate the principle of equality of men and women in their legal system, abolish all discriminatory laws and adopt appropriate ones prohibiting discrimination against women.
b. to establish tribunals and other public institutions to ensure the effective protection of women against discrimination.
c. to ensure elimination of all acts of discrimination against women by persons, organizations or enterprises.
d. to include in their reports information about sexual harassment and on measures to protect women from sexual harassment and others forms of violence in the workplace.

CEDAW, for the first time in the sphere of international law, accorded primacy and supremacy to women's human rights. India is a signatory of CEDAW.[18]

## LAW OF SEXUAL HARASSMENT IN OTHER JURISDICTIONS

It may be relevant to briefly examine the sexual harassment regime existing in some foreign jurisdictions.

### United Kingdom

The United Kingdom enacted the Equality Act, 2010 which consolidated the various statutes and regulations operating in the field of anti-discrimination law, including the Sex Discrimination Act of 1975 and the Employment Equality (Sex Discrimination) Regulations of 2005. The Equality Act provides a legal framework to protect the rights of individuals and to advance equality of opportunity for all.

The Equality Act protects a host of characteristics such as:

i. age;
ii. disability;

18 The CEDAW was ratified by India on 25.06.1993.

iii. gender reassignment;
iv. marriage and civil partnership;
v. pregnancy and maternity;
vi. race;
vii. religion or belief;
viii. sex; and
ix. sexual orientation.

Under the Equality Act, courts and employment tribunals have the jurisdiction to deal with issues arising in context of sexual harassment.[19] This legislation defines 'harassment' and 'victimization' as follows:

> 26. Harassment
> (1) A person (A) harasses another (B) if—
> (a) A engages in unwanted conduct related to a relevant protected characteristic, and
> (b) the conduct has the purpose or effect of—
> (i) violating B's dignity, or
> (ii) creating an intimidating, hostile, degrading, humiliating or offensive environment for B.
>
> (2) A also harasses B if—
> (a) A engages in unwanted conduct of a sexual nature, and
> (b) the conduct has the purpose or effect referred to in subsection (1)(b).
>
> (3) A also harasses B if—
> (a) A or another person engages in unwanted conduct of a sexual nature or that is related to gender reassignment or sex,

19 *See generally* http://www.legislation.gov.uk/ukpga/2010/15/contents.

(b) the conduct has the purpose or effect referred to in subsection (1)(b), and

(c) because of B's rejection of or submission to the conduct, A treats B less favourably than A would treat B if B had not rejected or submitted to the conduct.

(4) In deciding whether conduct has the effect referred to in subsection (1)(b), each of the following must be taken into account—

(a) the perception of B;

(b) the other circumstances of the case;

(c) whether it is reasonable for the conduct to have that effect.

(5) The relevant protected characteristics are—

age;

disability;

gender reassignment;

race;

religion or belief;

sex;

sexual orientation

27. Victimisation

(1) A person (A) victimises another person (B) if A subjects B to a detriment because—

(a) B does a protected act, or

(b) A believes that B has done, or may do, a protected act.

(2) Each of the following is a protected act—

(a) bringing proceedings under this Act;

(b) giving evidence or information in connection with proceedings under this Act;

(c) doing any other thing for the purposes of or in connection with this Act;

(d) making an allegation (whether or not express) that A or another person has contravened this Act.

(3) Giving false evidence or information, or making a false allegation, is not a protected act if the evidence or information is given, or the allegation is made, in bad faith.

(4) This section applies only where the person subjected to a detriment is an individual.

(5) The reference to contravening this Act includes a reference to committing a breach of an equality clause or rule.

As is evident from the above, this law expressly covers both quid pro quo as well as hostile work environment forms of sexual harassment. In fact, even same sex harassment and harassment based on sexual orientation is covered in this legislation.[20] The definition of 'victimisation' is also widely worded and takes within its sweep all detrimental conduct against the complainant, the witnesses or any other person who acts as a whistle blower.

**United States of America**

In the United States, sexual harassment is prohibited by both federal and state statutes. In United States, sexual harassment is a form of sex discrimination that violates Title VII of the Civil Rights Act of 1964. Title VII prohibits employment related discrimination based on sex, race, colour, national origin or religion. Title VII applies to employers with 15 (fifteen) or more

20 The Indian sexual harassment law does not encompass issues such as same-sex harassment and harassment based on sexual orientation.

employees, including state and local governments. In 1980, the Equal Employment Opportunity Commission (EEOC) established under federal law issued guidelines wherein the term sexual harassment was defined in the following words:

> Unwelcome sexual advances, requests for sexual favors, and other verbal or physical conduct of a sexual nature constitute sexual harassment when this conduct explicitly or implicitly affects an individual's employment, unreasonably interferes with an individual's work performance, or creates an intimidating, hostile, or offensive work environment.

Furthermore, the Code of Federal Regulations[21] describes sexual harassment in the following words:

> "29 C.F.R. 1604.11 Sexual Harassment.
> (a) Harassment on the basis of sex is a violation of section 703 of Title VII.
> Unwelcome sexual advances, requests for sexual favors, and other verbal or physical conduct of a sexual nature constitute sexual harassment when (1) submission to such conduct is made either explicitly or implicitly a term or condition of an individual's employment, (2) submission to or rejection of such conduct by an individual is used as the basis for employment decisions affecting such individual, or (3) such conduct has the purpose or effect of unreasonably interfering with an individual's work performance or creating an intimidating, hostile, or offensive working environment."

---

21 The *Code of Federal Regulations* (CFR) is an annual codification of the general and permanent rules published in the Federal Register by the executive departments and agencies of the Federal Government. For more *see* http://www.archives.gov/federal-register/cfr/about.html.

Mentioned below are some principles generally with respect to sexual harassment which are applicable under United States law.[22]

i. United States law on sexual harassment is gender neutral. The victim and harasser may be a woman or a man. The victim does not have to be of the opposite sex.
ii. The harasser can be the victim's supervisor, an agent of the employer, a supervisor in another area, a co-worker, or a non-employee.[23]
iii. The victim does not have to be the person harassed but could be anyone affected by the offensive conduct.[24]
iv. Unlawful sexual harassment may occur without economic injury to the victim.[25]
v. The harasser's conduct must be unwelcome.[26]

22 *See generally http://www.eeoc.gov/eeoc/publications/fs-sex.cfm.* The EEOC is to look into the facts of each case as a whole and in proper context to determine whether the acts complained of amount to sexual harassment. *See also* Punita. K. Sodhi v. Union of India (2010) 172 DLT 409.

23 Superior, subordinate as well as contemporary co-workers/employees are covered. Even third party harassment is covered.

24 An indirect victim of sexual harassment can also make a claim.

25 It is not pertinent that some loss or injury ought to have occasioned to the victim to bring a claim of sexual harassment. Mere occurrence of the offence is sufficient.

26 Reciprocated conduct or behaviour on the part of the victim will not qualify the definition of sexual harassment.

CHAPTER 11

# Service Rules and Other Legislation

Apart from the Act, the subject of sexual harassment is encompassed in many other statutes. This chapter briefly discusses such other legislations under Indian law which govern, regulate and provide a mechanism for adjudication of complaints of sexual harassment in employment/workplace situations. As already discussed previously, post the Vishaka Case, the concept of sexual harassment was introduced to the Indian legal system. Consequently, several statues and service rules were amended to include provisions in this regard. However, prior to promulgation of the Act, there did not exist any 'all pervading' legislation on sexual harassment.

## THE INDUSTRIAL DISPUTES LAW

The Industrial Disputes Act, 1947 (**ID Act**) provides the machinery for the investigation and settlement of industrial disputes.[1] The ID Act is applicable to 'workman'. The Act, *inter alia,* governs 'industrial disputes' arising between workmen and the employers. Indulging in 'unfair labour practices' is one such realm of dispute. It is pertinent to briefly examine some important terms under the ID Act.

1 The ID Act is a benign measure which seeks to pre-empt industrial tensions, provide the mechanics of dispute-resolutions and set-up the necessary infrastructure for achieving industrial justice.

### Workman

'Workman' means any person (including an apprentice) employed in any industry to do any manual, unskilled, skilled, technical, operational, clerical or supervisory work for hire or reward, whether the terms of employment be express or implied, and for the purposes of any proceeding under this Act in relation to an industrial dispute, includes any such person who has been dismissed, discharged or retrenched in connection with, or as a consequence of, that dispute, or whose dismissal, discharge or retrenchment has led to that dispute, but does not include any such person[2]:

i. who is subject to the Air Force Act, 1950 or the Army Act, 1950 or the Navy Act, 1957; or
ii. who is employed in the police service or as an officer or other employee of a prison; or
iii. who is employed mainly in a managerial or administrative capacity; or
iv. who, being employed in a supervisory capacity, draws wages exceeding Rs. 10,000/- or exercises, either by the nature of the duties attached to the office or by reason of the powers vested in him, functions mainly of a managerial nature.

### Industry

'Industry' means any business, trade, undertaking, manufacture or calling of employers and includes any calling, service, employment, handicraft, or industrial occupation or avocation of workmen.[3]

### Industrial Dispute

'Industrial Dispute' means any dispute or difference between employers and employers or between employers and workmen,

2 S. 2(s) of the ID Act.

3 S. 2 (j) of the ID Act.

or between workmen and workmen, which is connected with the employment or non-employment or the terms of employment or with the conditions of labour, of any person.[4]

**Unfair Labour Practice**

In common parlance, unfair labour practice refers to any unfair act or omission that arises between an employer and employee. Under the ID Act, it is impermissible for an employer or workman or a trade union to indulge in unfair labour practice.[5]

**Constituents of Unfair Labour Practice**

Under the ID Act, *inter alia,* the following activities (enlisted in Schedule V therein) qualify to be 'unfair trade practice':[6]

1. To dismiss or discharge a workman:
    a. by way of victimisation.
    b. not in good faith, but in the colourable exercise of the employer's rights.
    c. by falsely implicating a workman in a criminal case on false evidence or on concocted evidence.
    d. for patently false reasons.
    e. on untrue or trumped up allegations of absence without leave.
    f. in utter disregard of the principles of natural justice in the conduct of domestic inquiry or with undue haste.
    g. for misconduct of a minor or technical character, without having any regard to the nature of the particular misconduct or the past record or service of the workman, thereby leading to a disproportionate punishment.

4 S. 2 (k) of the ID Act.

5 S. 25T of the ID Act.

6 S. 2 (ra) of the ID Act.

2. To transfer a workman *mala fide* from one place to another, under the guise of following management policy.
3. To show favouritism or partiality to one set of workers regardless of merit.
4. To discharge or discriminate against any workman for filing charges or testifying against an employer in any inquiry or proceeding relating to any industrial dispute.
5. To indulge in acts of force or violence.

Under the ID Act, all of the above discriminatory practices are punishable. It is noteworthy that an act of sexual harassment has not been specifically defined or described as an 'unfair trade practice'. However, any unfair trade practice in an industrial workplace which is a consequence of or an adjunct of unwelcome sexual behaviour may be actionable under the Standing Orders Act (described below in more detail).

**Penalty for Unfair Labour Practice**

Any person who commits any unfair labour practice shall be punishable with imprisonment for a term which may extend to 6 (six) months or with fine which may extend to Rs. 1,000/- or with both.[7]

## INDUSTRIAL STANDING ORDERS ACT

The Industrial Disputes (Standing Orders Act), 1946 ("**Standing Orders Act**"), makes it obligatory for employers of an industrial establishment where 100 (hundred) or more workers are employed, to clearly define the conditions of employment, by way of standing orders/services rules and to make them known to all workmen.[8] These standing orders deal with a wide range

7 S. 25U of the ID Act.

8 In several states like Karnataka, Gujarat, the N.C.T. of Delhi, the Standing Orders Act applies to industrial establishments where 50 (fifty) or more workmen are employed or were employed in the preceding 12 (twelve) months.

of issues, including the day to day affairs of the establishment, leaves, procedures for misconduct, termination etc. Standing Orders once certified by the relevant authority acquire the force of law.

### Sexual Harassment under the Model Orders

The Industrial Standing Order Central Rules 1946 (**Standing Order Rules**) provide for model standing orders which may be adopted by industrial establishments. Sexual harassment is both defined as well as classified as a misconduct in the Model Standing Order Rules.[9] The model standing orders further prescribe a procedure for holding an inquiry for complaints of sexual harassment.

### Penalty

The Act provides for punishments in the form of fines in case of failure to establish appropriate standing orders or for contravention of the standing orders.

## ARTICLE 311 OF THE CONSTITUTION

Before proceeding further, it would be relevant to take note of Article 311 of the Constitution of India, which applies to civil servants in service related issues.

Article 311 of the Constitution of India provides certain safeguards to civil servants in matters of dismissal, removal, or reduction in rank. It is part of the constitutional framework aimed at ensuring the security of tenure and fair treatment of government employees employed by the union or state governments. Article 311 strikes a balance between the rights of civil servants and the necessity of ensuring accountability and discipline in public administration.

9 Order 14 of Schedule I to the Standing Order Rules.

Article 311 (1) provides that no civil servant holding a civil post under the union or a state shall be dismissed or removed by an authority subordinate to the one that appointed them. This clause ensures that the concerned person cannot be dismissed or removed by someone who is at a lower rank than the officer who appointed them. This safeguard prevents arbitrary or vengeful actions against the concerned person by ensuring a certain level of authority in such decisions.

Article 311 (2) provides that no civil servant shall be dismissed, removed, or reduced in rank except after an inquiry in which they have been informed of the charges against them and given a reasonable opportunity to defend themselves. This provision upholds principles of natural justice, namely, right of the delinquent to be informed of the charges against him and an adequate opportunity of defence (includes procedural safeguards such as cross-examination and access to relevant documents etc.)

Article 311 also contains certain exceptions where the safeguards of Article 311 (2) (discussed above) may not apply. These are as follows:

a. Where an inquiry is impracticable or not required, i.e. if the authority empowered to dismiss, remove, or reduce the rank of the person is satisfied that conducting an inquiry is not practicable, provided the reasons are reasonable and based on some evidence.
b. Where the inquiry would be against the interests of national security (security of the state). In other words, in cases like national security, the executive's discretion is given importance, provided that the reasons are genuine and not arbitrary.
c. Where the person is convicted of a criminal charge by a court and the conviction itself justifies dismissal, removal, or reduction in rank.

In sum, the provisions of Article 311 (2) can be dispensed with in the following situations: (i) The process of holding an inquiry is impractical due to the circumstances, to the subjective satisfaction of the inquiring authority. (ii) National security considerations warrant that no inquiry be conducted (the understand is that national security considerations take precedence over procedural fairness). (iii) A court conviction negates the need for a separate departmental inquiry[10].

## THE CENTRAL CIVIL SERVICE RULES

The service conditions of government employees are regulated and governed by the Central Civil Services (Classification, Control and Appeal) Rules, 1965 [**CCA (CCS) Rules**] and Central Civil Services (Conduct) Rules, 1964 [**CCS Rules**].

### Applicability

The CCA (CCS) Rules apply to the below mentioned personnel:

- Every government servant including every civilian government servant in the Defence Services, except the following: (i) any railway servant, as defined in Rule 102 of Volume I of the Indian Railways Establishment Code; (ii) any member of the All India Services; (iii) any person in casual employment; (iv) any person subject to discharge from service on less than one month's notice.

### Sexual Harassment under the Rules

The term 'sexual harassment' is defined in the CCS Rules. The modalities for inquiring into a complaint of sexual harassment are described in the CCA (CCS) Rules. The definition of the

10 See generally Bhim Singh Bairwa v. Delhi Police, 2024 SCC Online CAT 537

expression 'sexual harassment' under these rules is similar to that under the Act and the relevant excerpt is as follows:[11]

> 3C. Prohibition of sexual harassment of working women (1) No Government servant shall indulge in any act of sexual harassment of any woman at any work place. (2) Every Government servant who is in charge of a work place shall take appropriate steps to prevent sexual harassment to any woman at the work place.
>
> Explanation - (I) For the purpose of this rule, - (a) "sexual harassment" includes any one or more of the following acts or behaviour (whether directly or by implication) namely: - (i) physical contact and advances; or (ii) a demand or request for sexual favours; or (iii) making sexually coloured remarks; or (iv) showing pornography; or (i) any other unwelcome physical, verbal, non-verbal conduct of a sexual nature.
>
> (b) the following circumstances, among other circumstances, if it occurs or is present in relation to or connected with any act or behaviour of sexual harassment may amount to sexual harassment: - (i) implied or explicit promise of preferential treatment in employment; or (ii) implied or explicit threat of detrimental treatment in employment; or (iii) implied or explicit threat about her present or future employment status; or (iv) interference with her work or creating an intimidating or offensive or hostile work environment for her; or (v) humiliating treatment likely to affect her health or safety.
>
> (c) "workplace" includes- (i) any department, organisation, undertaking, establishment, enterprise, institution, office, branch or unit which is established, owned, controlled or wholly or substantially financed by funds provided directly

11 R. 3 C of the CCS Rules.

> or indirectly by the Central Government; (ii) hospitals or nursing homes; (iii) any sports institute, stadium, sports complex or competition or games venue, whether residential or not used for training, sports or other activities relating thereto; (iv) any place visited by the employee arising out of or during the course of employment including transportation provided by the employer for undertaking such journey; (v) a dwelling place or a house.

The CCA (CCS) Rules provide the constitution of a disciplinary authority to initiate and adjudicate disciplinary proceedings against the delinquent government servant.[12]

Rule 14 of the CCA (CCS) Rules describes the procedure for inquiry[13] in cases where the charges are so serious as to call for major punishments, such as, dismissal, removal, reduction in rank etc. (A summary procedure is prescribed therein for less serious charges).

This Rule 14 of the CCA (CCS) Rules prescribes the procedure required to be followed for conducting an inquiry by a public authority, which entails issuance of a charge sheet, furnishing details of the articles of charge, enclosing statements of imputations in respect of each article of charge, forwarding of a list of witnesses and the documents sought to be relied upon by the management/employer.

In Sandeep Khurana v. Delhi Transco Limited[14] in the context of the Central Civil Services (CCA) Rules, 1964, the Delhi High Court has observed that the procedure for conducting an

---

12 R. 11 of the CCA (CCS) Rules make a distinction between major and minor penalties.

13 The provisions of Rule 14 have been designed to, *inter alia*, ensure compliance with a salutary principle of justice and public policy which has also been incorporated in Article 311 of the Constitution of India *viz.* no man should be condemned or punished without a reasonable opportunity to defend himself.

14 135 (2006) DLT 346.

inquiry under Rule 14 of the said rules, "as far as practicable" must be adhered to.

In Aureliano Fernandes v. State of Goa[15] the Supreme Court, in the context of Rule 14 of the CCA CCS Rules, observed that proceedings stood vitiated in as much as that the "as far as practicable" norm was violated by the disciplinary authority (conducting the disciplinary proceedings in the context of a complaint of sexual harassment) for, *inter alia,* the following reasons: (i) the "tearing hurry" in which the proceedings were conducted and concluded (within less than one month); (ii) the unilateral advancing of dates of hearings by the disciplinary authority; (iii) the "almost back-to-back" hearings which were conducted by the disciplinary authority without cause or reason (which limited the time for the participants to properly prepare and participate in the matter).

In P. Murugesan v. Tamil Nadu State Transport Corporation[16], the Madras High Court, after examining various judicial precedent, indicated the procedure to be followed for dealing with a complaint of sexual harassment with respect to government employees who are governed by the CCA CCS Rules. In this regard, the following broad principles would emerge:

a. Every complaint of sexual harassment must be referred to the ICC.
b. The provisions of the CCA CCS Rules should be complied with as far as practicable. Minor deviation with respect to procedure may not result in violation of principles of natural justice.
c. Failure to frame specific charges at the time of commencement of inquiry but not vitiate the process in the event the complaint

---

15 Civil Appeal No. 2482/2014 (12.05.2023, Supreme Court of India).

16 2024 SCC Online Mad 2233

of sexual harassment (which clearly discloses the allegations against the accused) are duly supplied to the accused.

d. The accused should be granted adequate opportunity of representation in the inquiry process. This includes an opportunity to file its reply/version and an opportunity to cross examine the complainant and the witnesses.
e. Considering the sensitivity and balance of power equations, there can be elasticity in the manner of cross examination.
f. Once the inquiry report is submitted, it would be open for the disciplinary authority to issue a second show cause notice and after considering the further explanation of the accused, punishment can be imposed.
g. The timelines for the inquiry and taking further action are all meant to expedite prompt action. By the timelines should be observed, any deviation in this regard may not vitiate the inquiry process.

## THE ALL INDIA SERVICES (DISCIPLINE & APPEAL) RULES

The All India Services (Discipline and Appeal) Rules, 1969 provide the manner in which disciplinary proceedings are to be undertaken against members of the All India Services.

### All India Services (Prevention of Sexual Harassment) Regulations, 1998

These regulations prohibit all members of the service from indulging in any act of sexual harassment of any woman at the working place. Further, every member of the service who is in-charge of a work place is required to take appropriate steps to prevent sexual harassment to any woman at such working place. An inquiry for a complaint of sexual harassment made against any member of the service is required to be made in accordance with the procedure specified in the CCA (CCS) Rules.

## THE INDECENT REPRESENTATION OF WOMEN (PROHIBITION) ACT, 1986

The Indecent Representation of Women (Prohibition) Act, 1986 has been enacted to prohibit indecent representation of women through advertisements or in publications, writings, paintings, figures or in any other manner.

### Indecent Representation of Women-Meaning

The expression 'indecent representation of women' is defined as follows:

> 'indecent representation of women' means the depiction in any manner of the figure of a woman; her form or body or any part thereof in such way as to have the effect of being indecent, or derogatory to, or denigrating women, or is likely to deprave, corrupt or injure the public morality or morals.

### Prohibition

The Indecent Representation Act proscribes the following acts[17]:

a. Publishing or causing to be published, or arranging or taking part in the publication or exhibition of, any advertisement which contains indecent representation of women in any form.
b. Producing or cause to be produced, selling, letting on hire, distributing, circulating or sending by post any book, pamphlet, paper, slide, film, writing, drawing, painting, photograph, representation or figure which contains indecent representation of women in any form.

---

17 Ss. 3 and 4 of the Indecent Representation Act.

**Punishment for Violation**

Any person who contravenes the provisions of the Indecent Representation Act shall be punished in the following manner:

First Conviction: Imprisonment of either description for a term which may extend to 2 (two) years, and with fine which may extend to Rs. 2,000/-.

Second/Subsequent Conviction: Imprisonment for a term of not less than 6 (six) months but which may extend to 5 (five) years and also with a fine not less than Rs. 10,000/- but which may extend to Rs.1,00,000/-.[18]

An offence committed under this legislation is cognizable and bailable.[19]

18 S. 6 of the Indecent Representation Act.

19 S. 8 of the Indecent Representation Act.

CHAPTER 12

# Epilogue

Through this work, the author has attempted to deeply analyse the extant law on sexual harassment in India. The author has earnestly attempted to provide necessary insight on the issue of sexual harassment under Indian law along with necessary guidance to employers and other stakeholders on how to meet their legal obligations; and to curb and eradicate sexual harassment from the workplace.

## AN END ANALYSIS

As discussed in the previous chapters, the object of the Act is to ensure that employees behave in a manner that female co-employees do not feel threatened or harassed. The purpose of the Act (and of the sexual harassment prohibition policies) is to stop unwanted attention towards female employees. The law attempts to strike at the root of the power imbalance between males and females at the workplace. The larger social goal is to achieve an equal and safe workplace where the worth of the individual matters, not her or his gender or looks.[1] However the moot question remains: What is the 'on the ground' reality and what practices must be developed/evolved to actually achieve the desired purpose of the Act.

1 *See* Arvind v. Union of India W.P. (C) No. 5863/2014 (21.09.2015, Delhi High Court).

## Problems relating to Enforcement of the Act

Recently, the Supreme Court, in Aureliano Fernandes v. State of Goa[2] highlighted serious lapses on the part of the stakeholder in the enforcement of the Act even after such a long passage of time. The observation of the Supreme Court in this regard is best described in its own words which are reproduced thus:

> 75. It is disquieting to note that there are serious lapses in the enforcement of the Act even after such a long passage of time. This glaring lacuna has been recently brought to the fore by a National daily newspaper that has conducted and published a survey of 30 national sports federations in the country and reported that 16 out of them have not constituted an ICC till date. Where the ICC have been found to be in place, they do not have the stipulated number of members or lack the mandatory external member. This is indeed a sorry state of affairs and reflects poorly on all the State functionaries, public authorities, private undertakings, organizations and institutions that are duty bound to implement the PoSH Act in letter and spirit. Being a victim of such a deplorable act not only dents the selfesteem of a woman, it also takes a toll on her emotional, mental and physical health. It is often seen that when women face sexual harassment at the workplace, they are reluctant to report such misconduct. Many of them even drop out from their job. One of the reasons for this reluctance to report is that there is an uncertainty about who to approach under the Act for redressal of their grievance. Another is the lack of confidence in the process and its outcome. This social malady needs urgent amelioration through robust and efficient implementation of the Act. To achieve this, it is imperative to educate the complainant victim about the import and working of the Act. They must be made aware of

2 Civil Appeal No. 2482/2014 (12.05.2023, Supreme Court of India).

> how a complaint can be registered, the procedure that would be adopted to process the complaint, the objective manner in which the ICC/LC/IC is expected to function under the Statute, the nature of consequences that the delinquent employee can be visited with if the complaint is found to be true, the result of lodging a false or a malicious complaint and the remedies that may be available to a complainant if dissatisfied with the Report of the ICC/LC/IC etc.

Consequently, the Supreme Court was compelled to pass the following directions for bettering the enforcement and implementation of the Act:

> 77. To fulfil the promise that the PoSH Act holds out to working women all over the country, it is deemed appropriate to issue the following directions:
>
> i. The Union of India, all State Governments and Union Territories are directed to undertake a timebound exercise to verify as to whether all the concerned Ministries, Departments, Government organizations, authorities, Public Sector Undertakings, institutions, bodies, etc. have constituted ICCs/LCs/ICs, as the casemay be and that the composition of the said Committees are strictly in terms of the provisions of the PoSH Act.
>
> ii. It shall be ensured that necessary information regarding the constitution and composition of the ICCs/LCs/ICs, details of the e-mail IDs and contact numbers of the designated person(s), the procedure prescribed for submitting an online complaint, as also the relevant rules, regulations and internal policies are made readily available on the website of the concerned Authority/Functionary/ Organisation/ Institution/Body, as the case may be. The information furnished shall also be updated from time to time.

iii. A similar exercise shall be undertaken by all the Statutory bodies of professionals at the Apex level and the State level (including those regulating doctors, lawyers, architects, chartered accountants, cost accountants, engineers, bankers and other professionals), by Universities, colleges, Training Centres and educational institutions and by government and private hospitals/nursing homes.

iv. Immediate and effective steps shall be taken by the authorities/ managements/employers to familiarize members of the ICCs/LCs/ICs with their duties and the manner in which an inquiry ought to be conducted on receiving a complaint of sexual harassment at the workplace, from the point when the complaint is received, till the inquiry is finally concluded and the Report submitted.

v. The authorities/management/employers shall regularly conduct orientation programmes, workshops, seminars and awareness programmes to upskill members of the ICCs/ LCs/ICs and to educate women employees and women's groups about the provisions of the Act, the Rules and relevant regulations.

vi. The National Legal Services Authority(NALSA) and the State Legal Services Authorities(SLSAs) shall develop modules to conduct workshops and organize awareness programmes to sensitize authorities/managements/employers, employees and adolescent groups with the provisions of the Act, which shall be included in their annual calendar.

vii. The National Judicial Academy and the State Judicial Academies shall include in their annual calendars, orientation programmes, seminars and workshops for capacity building of members of the ICCs/LCs/ICs established in the High Courts and District Courts and for drafting Standard Operating Procedures (SOPs) to conduct an inquiry under the Act and Rules.

viii. A copy of this judgment shall be transmitted to the Secretaries of all the Ministries, Government of India who shall ensure implementation of the directions by all the concerned Departments, Statutory Authorities, Institutions, Organisations etc. under the control of the respective Ministries. A copy of the judgment shall also be transmitted to the Chief Secretaries of all the States and Union Territories who shall ensure strict compliance of these directions by all the concerned Departments. It shall be the responsibility of the Secretaries of the Ministries, Government of India and the Chief Secretaries of every State/Union Territory to ensure implementation of the directions issued.

ix. The Registry of the Supreme Court of India shall transmit a copy of this judgment to the Director, National Judicial Academy, Member Secretary, NALSA, Chairperson, Bar Council of India and the Registrar Generals of all the High Courts. The Registry shall also transmit a copy of this judgment to the Medical Council of India, Council of Architecture, Institute of Chartered Accountants, Institute of Company Secretaries and the Engineering Council of India for implementing the directions issued.

x. Member-Secretary, NALSA is requested to transmit a copy of this judgment to the Member Secretaries of all the State Legal Services Authorities. Similarly, the Registrar Generals of the State High Courts shall transmit a copy of this judgment to the Directors of the State Judicial Academies and the Principal District Judges/District Judges of their respective States.

xi. The Chairperson, Bar Council of India and the Apex Bodies mentioned in sub-para (ix) above, shall in turn, transmit a copy of this judgment to all the State Bar Councils and the State Level Councils, as the case may be.

In Initiatives for Inclusion Foundation v. Union of India[3] the Supreme Court ruled the failure of or inadequacies in the implementation of the provisions of the Act. The following excerpts are relevant in this regard:

> 12. We have perused the replies/affidavits filed by numerous states pursuant to receiving notice; seen together, they are marked by a lack of uniformity in terms of implementation of the Act. Numerous states have tried to force-fit the institutional requirements of the Act, within their existing bureaucratic frameworks (for instance, some states have assigned its implementation to departments other than their Women and Child Development Ministry, like the departments dealing with Social Welfare, Social Security, Legislative Affairs, etc.). The affidavit filed by the petitioner in response to the replies by the States, highlights the many lacunae and lack of uniformity in the implementation of the POSH Act, by various state governments. District Officers were in most states notified after notice of this writ petition was served on them, and even among those states that have taken action – they have simply notified a specific post as District Officer, without providing any specific details of the officers, their contact information, etc. Most states have failed to provide documentation on constitution of LCs, and even those who have, many have not constituted one in each district. Only a handful of states have provided any details of 'nodal officers'– but even among these, the nodal officers are specific posts notified, and not individuals at every taluka, ward, municipality, etc. as contemplated under Section 6(2). The information on annual reports is perhaps most alarming– only three have provided a consolidated report (relying on differing sources, or just the LCs). Each State, has notified a

3 2023 INSC 927

> different Ministry as the 'nodal' ministry for implementation of the Act – some have notified the Social Welfare Ministry or its allied departments, while others rely on the Women and Child Development department. 13. The general thrust of the affidavits, especially that of the Union of India has been to highlight the generation of awareness through a massive publicity campaign and issuance of advisories, publication of handbooks, etc. However, it is quite plainly clear that though the generation of awareness is necessary, if a woman suffers sexual harassment at the workplace – the framework for redressal has to in fact exist. The failure to notify district officers specifically, has a snowballing effect on appointment of the LCs and nodal officers, in addition to other aspects. The complaint mechanism, and larger framework - no matter how effective, remain inadequate if the authorities set out in the Act, are not duly appointed/notified. Therefore, the State/ UT government must ensure that every district, at all times has a notified District Officer; in case of vacancy caused by retirement, or any other reason, it must be duly remedied, to enable smooth transition between officers, and ensure that there is always someone incharge of this position. Furthermore, effort has to be undertaken to orient, train and sensitise these district officers, with regards to the provisions of the Act and Rules, with an emphasis on their roles and obligations. Similar range of activities must be conducted for the nodal officers appointed and LCs constituted by each district officer.

Thereafter, the Supreme Court passed the following directions for the purpose of operationalizing the Act, spreading awareness regarding the LCC, setting up budgets and disbursal of funds to the District Officer and usage of anonymised data.

## Spreading awareness regarding the LCC

On this aspect, the Supreme Court observed as follows:

> Consider next, the composition and role of the LC - which is the foundational body in the district, especially so for the unorganized sector. This committee is headed by a nominated chairperson who is an eminent woman in the field of social work and committed to the cause of women; one member is nominated from the women working in a block/taluka/tehsil (rural) or ward/municipality (urban); two more, of which at least one has to be a woman to be nominated amongst NGOs or associations committed to cause of women or a person familiar with the issues relating to sexual harassment. Further one must be with legal background/ knowledge of the law, and one must belong to a Scheduled Caste, Scheduled Tribe, or Other Backward Class. An LC is as per Section 6 and 7 of the Act. The District Officer is empowered with powers equivalent to a civil court to conduct inquiry, issue summons, enforce attendance, etc., which is reflective of its importance in the framework. The inclusion of nominees from such NGOs is also helpful, because in a context where LCs may convey a sense of formality, women find it easier to approach local NGOs; this is one of the finding in a 2015 International Labour Organization (ILO) report. However as pointed out, there is no avenue in the law for these NGOs to register or pursue the matter on behalf of such consenting women. Thus, the spreading of awareness relating to LCs and dispelling the air of formality, should form a priority of the highest level State, that seeks to implement the Act.

## Setting up of budgets and disbursal of funds to the District Officer

> Lastly, it is relevant to note a major limitation of the Act, which depends on the Union Government to disburse funds to the States, which using an agency, can transfer the same to the district officer.

In the absence of a delineated budget to pay the concerned officers and conduct events for awareness and training, various LCs are rendered infructuous or remain vacant. Therefore, the requirement of setting the budget for the implementation of this Act, at each district level, and thereafter state-level, to ascertain disbursal of grants from the Union Government.

Usage of anonymised data

While the Act does not contemplate such publication in the public domain, there is certainly merit in using this anonymised data on cases lodged and disposed, to consolidate statistics, that will reflect efficacy of the implementation of the Act. Therefore, while there is no need for such an express direction by this court, the Central Government, and State Government, as the case may be, in the interest of transparency and good governance may consider to make these statistics public- the access to which, would certainly have a positive impact on various stakeholders. This in turn will also strengthen the monitoring of the implementation of this Act.

Finally, the following set of directions were passed by the Supreme Court in the matter:

A. Coordination between Union Government and State/UT Governments

(i) The Women and Child Development Ministry of every State/ UT, through its Principal Secretary, should consider identifying a "nodal person" within the Department, to oversee and aid in coordination as contemplated under the PoSH Act. This person would also be able to coordinate with the Union Government on matters relating to this Act and its implementation.

(ii) Each State/UT Government is to submit a consolidated report of its compliance with the below directions to the Union Government within 8 weeks. The latter is hereby directed to consolidate the various reports, identify any lapses in the compliance by the State and try to remedy it, before filing a consolidated affidavit of compliance – detailing the States' compliance, and the Union Government's action taken in regard to the direction within 12 weeks from the date of this judgment.

## B. Appointment of public authorities

(iii) The Principal Secretary concerned of the State/UT Ministry of Women and Child [or any other Department, subject to amendment of the Rules as per Direction (vii) below], will personally ensure appointment of a District Officer in each district within their territorial jurisdiction, as contemplated under Section 5 within four weeks from the date of this judgment.

(iv) Thereafter, each appointed District Officer
(a) must in compliance of Section 6(2) appoint nodal officers in every block, taluka and tehsil in rural or tribal area and ward or municipality in the urban area;
(b) must constitute a LC, as contemplated under Sections 6 and 7 of the Act; and
(c) ensure the contact details of these nodal officers, and LCs, shall be forwarded to the nodal person within the State Government, Ministry of Women and Child Development within 6 weeks from the date of this judgment.

(v) Thereafter, a circular/bulletin containing names of all District Officers, and their contact details (phone, address, and email), along with a district wise chart of the various nodal officers and their contact details, must be uploaded on the department's website (or in the absence of one, on the main State Government website) in a conspicuous location, along with a compiled version of the Act, Rules, and simple charts/explainers on the basics of the Act, within 6 weeks from the date of this judgment.

## C. Amendments and gaps in Rules that State must fill

(vi) The Union Government ought to consider amending the Rules, so as to operationalise Section 26 of the Act, by recognising a reporting authority, and/or a fine collecting authority. This direction must be read in light of the discussion in para 9 (role of District Officer with regards to annual compliance reports) and para 24 (on the penalty regime contemplated in the Act and resulting lacunae in the Rules) above.

(vii) The Union Government may also consider amending the Rules so as to identify one Department (preferably the Women and Child Department), and creating a "nodal person" post within the said Department to be responsible for the coordination required in the implementation of the Act [see Direction (i)]. This will ensure greater uniformity in the implementation of the Act across the country.

## D. Training and capacity building

(viii) The District Officers and LCs should be mandatorily trained regarding their important responsibilities. Given their position in the redressal framework contemplated in the Act, they must first be sensitised to the nature of sexual harassment, the gendered interactions that occur in the workspace, etc. The State Governments, must organise periodic, and regular training sessions at the district level which are to be attended by the District Officer, members of the LC, and nodal officers [ref : Section 24(b)].

## E. Larger efforts towards awareness

(ix) In furtherance of Section 24, the State/UT Governments, and Union Government are hereby directed to set out the financial resources allocated and/or needed, to developing educational, communication and training material for spreading awareness of the provisions of this Act to the public, and formulate orientation and training programmes as elaborated in Direction (viii) above. This plan of action, must form part of the compliance affidavit filed by each State. The discussion in para 19 is to be read along with this Direction.

(x) The District Officers, once nominated by the State are hereby directed to identify the non-governmental organisations working with women and their protection within the district, and take action pursuant to their duty under Section 20(b) for creation of awareness.

(xi) The appropriate Government or District Officers in question, must also undertake effort to spread awareness on the existence of LCs, and make them approachable for the unorganised sector – thus operationalising the horizontal import of this Act.

(xii) Directions 87.4 and 87.5 passed in Aureliano Fernandes v. State of Goa [Aureliano Fernandes v. State of Goa, (2024) 1 SCC 632] cover specifically the direction to authorities, management and employers to familiarise the members of the ICCs and LCs of their duties and detailed step-wise manner in which an inquiry ought to be conducted on receiving a complaint of sexual harassment; conduct orientation programmes, workshops, seminars, awareness programmes, etc. and to educate women employees and women groups about the Act, Rules, and Regulations are reiterated. The modules prepared by Nalsa [as per Direction 87.6

in Aureliano Fernandes [Aureliano Fernandes v. State of Goa, (2024) 1 SCC 632] to conduct workshops and organise awareness programmes to sensitise authorities, managements, employers could be used in this regard.

(xiii) It is relevant to add here that the Ministry of Women and Child Development, Government of India, has prepared a Handbook for implementation of the PoSH Act [ Government of India, Handbook on Sexual Harassment of Women at Workplace (2015) <https://wcd.nic.in/sites/default/files/Handbook%20on%20Sexual%20Harassment%20of%20Women%20at %20Workplace.pdf> (accessed on 26-9-2023).] , which serves as a useful guide for not just employees seeking information, but also more pertinently those who are nominated or appointed as members of the ICs (by the employer) or LCs (by the District Officer). It is hereby directed that a targeted effort be made to share this information with each District Officer, who may in turn disseminate it to their respective LCs, the nodal officers appointed under Section 6(2), and employers who constitute their own ICCs.

## F. Annual compliance reports

(xiv) Due compliance with Sections 21(1) and (2), and Section 22, must be undertaken by each District Officer, of the State – including collecting the reports from the IC/employers (or information where no report is available), and from the LC, and preparation of a brief report to be shared with the State Government. The State/UT Governments is hereby directed to create a standard operating procedure ("SOP") including the procedure, and timelines for this process, so as to enable it to, in turn, comply with Section 23 of the Act i.e. monitoring implementation and maintaining data. This Direction may be read in light of the discussion contained in para 21 above.

## G. Monitoring of ICs and compliance by employers

(xv) The directions passed in Aureliano Fernandes v. State of Goa [Aureliano Fernandes v. State of Goa, (2024) 1 SCC 632] address most specifically, the constitution of ICs – in public establishments [falling broadly within Section 2(o)(i)] and some private establishments – such as bodies governing professional associations, etc.; those directions are hereby reiterated, to avoid multiplicity or overlap of efforts. It is however further, directed that efforts made must be in line with the scheme of the Act, and through the authorities so designated for the various roles.

(xvi) Similarly, directions are hereby made to hospitals, nursing homes, sports institutes, stadiums, sports complex, or competition or games venues [as defined in Sections 2(o)(iii) and (iv)] to establish ICs, and report compliance as per the duties under this Act.

(xvii) The District Officer must be supplied a list of establishments (compiled by the relevant departments of the State/UT Government) that fall within the scope of Section 2(o), so that they may write to them and ensure that they are well versed with the provisions relating to employers, and their duties (including constitution of ICC under Section 4, duties under Section 19, etc.) and are implementing them in letter and spirit. This will also enable collection of annual reports, as contemplated under Section 21. The consequent direction to all private sector workplaces under Section 2(o)(ii) can be passed once the District Officer is able to discern an exhaustive list of entities.

### Eradication of Sexual Harassment

Sexual harassment is an endemic problem which is entrenched in the Indian workplace ecosystem and requires systematic elimination. Sexual harassment in the workplace is not a complaint that is easily made because of various issues associated with it (such as stigma, ridicule, reprisal etc.); it often tends to put the complainant's position in jeopardy. Further, unfortunately, there also appears to exist a significant lack of understanding as to what sexual harassment is and what are the methods to contain this problem. Efforts towards creation of a culture that does not tolerate sexual harassment; and taking swift and effective action to curb sexual harassment can have a positive overall impact on the work environment.

Clearly, promulgation of the law itself cannot eradicate the problem. Having a law in place is only a means to an end. Proper and effective implementation of the Act and its periodical monitoring is the key. The extant directions of the Supreme Court for ensuring effective implementation of Act have just been discussed in the preceding heading. In the view of the author, the following further steps may also be explored:

1. Creating an enhanced prosecution model for sexual harassment and related offences both in work places as well as outside. Victims of sexual harassment must experience better outcomes in the adjudicatory processes.

- Creation of cells/departments to provide free and independent legal advice to victims of sexual harassment.
- Increased training for employees of all organisations and members of the complaints committee.
- Making provisions for rehabilitation and protection of victims of sexual harassment, including victim counselling.
- Creating a general change in attitudes and behaviours. This would include the following: (i) training to the police on the subject so that they understand the concept of sexual harassment and respond to victims/complainants in an appropriate manner; (ii) creation and implementation of educational programs on the issue in schools

and other educational institutions, so that the awareness levels on the subject can be raised early on; and (iii) raising general public awareness on sexual harassment.

**Concluding Remarks**

Sexual harassment is a sad reality of today's time. It represents a moral degradation of the society. While the law has attempted to put in place robust provisions to tackle this menace, however, it may not be able to change the moral fabric of the society. It is in such situations that, apart from the steps mentioned above, the need for cultural education and inculcating a sense of true respect for women is necessary. In other words, the patriarchal attitudes and behaviour needs to change.

All employers must take charge of the situation at their workplace and strive to achieve the objects of the Act. By taking a strong stance on sexual harassment, employers can send a clear message to employees that there is no place for sexual harassment at their workplace. Additionally, even members of the complaints committees, employees at the workplace and governmental authorities have a role to play.

It took upwards of 15 (fifteen) years to convert the Vishaka Guidelines into a full-fledged legislation. The era of the Vishaka Guidelines was marked by various ups and downs. Now the success of the Sexual Harassment Act is in our hands. With concerted effort from all, we can succeed in establishing a sexual harassment free work culture in Indian workspaces.

Labour should be a joy; it is an extension of the self. It gives the worker the chance to freely develop his or her own intrinsic talents and skills[4]; and contribute to the nation. This should not be taken away or diluted by the evil of sexual harassment.

4 Mary Nell Dinkins v. Charoen Pokphand USA, Inc. 133 F. Supp. 2d 1254 (M.D. Ala. 2001).

ANNEXURE I

# The Sexual Harassment Policy

Sexual harassment was traditionally understood to be an act of private transgression and consequently was often ignored or trivialized. Now, we are aware that it is actually a manifestation of gender-based discrimination; a violation of fundamental rights; and an infraction of the right of a safe work environment.

In order to give a true and full effect to the provisions of the Act, it is imperative to draw up and implement an appropriate mechanism that is accessible to all stakeholders and will ensure confidentiality, apart from ensuring fair and accountable procedures for redressal and resolution.[1]

The policy of prohibiting sexual harassment in the workplace is to recognize that the dignity of an employee is paramount. It is a policy of respect for the many human qualities of an employee which are relevant to employment or advancement; it is a proscription of coercive sexual encounters or a sexually demeaning work environment.[2] Law requires every organization to have in place a clear and comprehensive

1 *See generally* Dr. B.N. Ray v. Ramjas College W.P. (C) No. 4427/2008 (21.05.2012, Delhi High Court).

2 Cuff v. Gypsy Restaurant (1987) BOI 87-004 (06.02.1987, Human Rights Tribunal of Ontario/Board of Inquiry).

policy dealing with the issue of sexual harassment. This policy must clearly set out the manner in which the issue of sexual harassment will be dealt with along with the rights, roles and responsibilities of each party.[3] A well drafted and implemented policy serves as an indicator to employees that their employer cares about how they treat one another. An effective and comprehensive policy also aids an employer in establishing its affirmative defence in case it is sued for secondary victimisation.[4]

Additionally, law postulates widest possible dissemination of the policies and rules relating to sexual harassment so that all members of the workplace are aware of it and know what is expected of them. Some steps which may be adopted by organizations for ensuring wide accessibility and dissemination of the policy are:

a. Making the policy of part of the employment contract.
b. spreading awareness about the policy by including it in the orientation programs of all new inductees of the organization.
c. Translating (or transliterating) the policy into relevant community languages, where required, for greater accessibility to employees from linguistically diverse backgrounds.
d. Educating and training all persons (at all levels), including persons in positions of responsibility about the policy on a periodical basis.

---

3 The objective is to develop an internal self regulatory and sustainable mechanism for addressing the issue of sexual harassment.

4 In case an employer's anti-harassment policy is questioned, then an inquiry may be undertaken that looks behind the face of a policy to determine whether it was effective in practice and in reasonably preventing and correcting any harassing behaviour. *See* Sandra M. Clark; Rhonda R. Knoop v. United Parcel Service, Inc.; Eli Brock 400 F. 3d 341 (6th Circuit, 2005). The effectiveness of an employer's sexual harassment policy depends on the effectiveness of those who are designated to implement it.

## FEATURES AND CONTENTS OF A SEXUAL HARASSMENT POLICY

Some salient features (and contents) of an effective anti-harassment policy are as follows:

a. A clear explanation of the term 'sexual harassment'.
b. Assurance to employees who bring about or participate in a claim of sexual harassment that they will be protected.
c. Provisions to protect the confidentiality of the complaint, the complainant, the witnesses and the investigation process.
d. A clearly described procedure for adjudicating claims of sexual harassment.
e. Contact coordinates of all members of the ICC.
f. Appropriate mechanisms for correction or reversal of the after-effects of sexual harassment.
g. Provisions for protecting complainants and witnesses, both during the pendency of a complaint and thereafter.[5]
h. Making the policy gender neutral so that the focus remains on checking in appropriate behaviour and making the work environment dignified for both men and women.
i. If deemed necessary, provisions for covering aspects of same sex harassment as well as harassment based on sexual orientation.[6]

Additionally, the policy must contain specific details on the following:

a. The policy's outreach, scope and extent.
b. The availability of the alternative dispute resolution (conciliation) to resolve the complaint.

5 *See generally* M. Kavya v. Chairman, University Grants Commission W.P. No. 11217 of 2014 (04.12.2014, Madras High Court).

6 Note that Indian law does not mandate a complaints and adjudicatory mechanism for same sex harassment, male harassment and sexual harassment based on sexual orientation.

c. the manner in which the complaint will be investigated.
d. the time frame within which the investigation process will be completed.
e. availability of interim relief to the complainant (and the witnesses).
f. manner of dealing with complaints when the harasser is unknown or an outsider.
g. remedies available if the claim of sexual harassment is proved.

**Updating the Policy**

Every employer must periodically undertake a self-diagnosis on the issue of sexual harassment within its organisation, identify the trouble spots, if any, and thereafter customize (and re-customize) the policy as well as the training programs for greater impact. An updation exercise may also be carried out periodically after taking into account latest developments on the subject.

**TEMPLATE SEXUAL HARASSMENT POLICY**

The author has created a draft sexual harassment policy which may be referred to and utilised by employers while drafting or updating their internal policies.

**POLICY ON PREVENTION OF SEXUAL HARASSMENT**

**Introduction**

[_] ("Company") is an equal opportunity employer and is committed to creating an atmosphere of mutual trust and building healthy working environment that enables its Employees (as defined below) to work without fear of discrimination. The Company also believes in providing to all Employees a disciplined and harassment free environment. The Company has a zero-tolerance approach to sexual harassment and aims to protect all its Employees, irrespective of their gender, against sexual harassment at its workplace. Sexual harassment at the workplace or otherwise of employees of the Company, is a grave offence and is punishable under law. The Company has adopted this policy ("Policy") which lays down guidelines for preventing, prohibiting and redressing issues in connection with sexual harassment and provides a forum for redressal of grievances related to sexual harassment. Not only is this Policy compliant with the Sexual Harassment of Women at Workplace (Prevention, Prohibition and Redressal) Act, 2013 ("Act"), but it is a step forward in recognizing and addressing vulnerabilities of all genders, to this grave offence, and to that extent the Policy is gender neutral.

1. **Scope**

   1.1 This Policy is a guide to prevent, prohibit and deter the commission of acts of sexual harassment, and also, to guide, assist and provide the procedure for redressal of complaints pertaining to sexual harassment.

   1.2 This Policy is applicable to all complaints of sexual harassment at a workplace, made by and/or against employees of the Company, as well as other independent consultants, temporary and contractual staff.

   1.3 This Policy is applicable to all Employees of the Company, as well as any employees of its agents/contractors as referred below, and to the extent that any breach of this policy is committed by an Employee or upon the premises of the Company, to all such instances of breach of the terms hereof.

   1.4 This Policy covers not only harassment at the office premises of the Company, but also at other premises, where employees of the Company carry out official duties in connection with their employment, such as business trips, off site training programs, social events, etc.

## 2. Definitions

2.1 For the purposes of this Policy, the following words and expressions shall have the meanings ascribed hereunder:

i. "Act" shall mean and include the Sexual Harassment of Women at Workplace (Prevention, Prohibition and Redressal) Act, 2013, the Sexual Harassment of Women at Workplace (Prevention, Prohibition and Redressal) Rules, 2013, and any other rules framed thereunder, regulations, circulars, notifications, clarifications, orders or guidelines issued pursuant to the Act, as amended from time to time, and also includes any statutory replacement or re-enactment thereof, if the context so requires.

ii. "Complainant" in relation to a workplace means a person of any age, whether employed of not, who alleges to have been subjected to any act of Sexual Harassment by a Respondent.

iii. "Employee" shall mean all individuals engaged by the Company for any work on regular, temporary, or contractual basis, employee on ad-hoc or daily wage basis, employees who are serving the Company on deputation from other organization(s), either directly or through an agent, including a contractor, with or without the knowledge of the Company, whether for remuneration or not, or working on a voluntary basis or otherwise, and whether the terms of employment are express or implied. This also includes co-workers, probationers, trainees, fellows, apprentices or other people engaged by the Company, by whatever name called.

iv. "Employer" means—

- in relation to any department, organisation, undertaking, establishment, enterprise, institution, office, branch, the head of that department, organisation, undertaking, establishment, enterprise, institution, office, branch or unit or such other officer as the appropriate Government or the local authority, as the case may be, may by an order specify in this behalf;

- in any workplace not covered under sub-clause (a), any person responsible for the management, supervision and control of the workplace.

Explanation - For the purposes of this sub-clause "management" includes the person or board, or committee responsible for formulation and administration of policies for such organization.

v. "ICC" shall mean the Internal Complaints Committee constituted by the Company to address complaints of Sexual Harassment. The membership of the ICC is as specified under clause 3 of this Policy.
vi. "LCC" shall mean the Local Complaints Committee of the relevant local district, constituted in accordance with the provisions of the Act.
vii. "Policy" shall mean this Policy for Prevention of Sexual Harassment.
viii. "Respondent" shall mean the person against whom a complaint has been made.
ix. "Sexual Harassment" shall mean and include any one or more of the following unwelcome acts or behaviour (whether directly or by implication):
    - Physical contact and advances; or
    - A demand or request for sexual favours; or
    - Making sexually colored remarks; or
    - Showing pornography; or

- Any other unwelcome physical, verbal, or non-verbal conduct of sexual nature.

2.2 Words and expressions used and not defined in this Policy but defined in the Act shall have the meaning respectively assigned to them in the Act.

3. **Internal Complaints Committee**

3.1 The Internal Complaints Committee ("ICC") shall comprise of a minimum of 4 members appointed by the Board of Directors of the Company, in the manner prescribed under the Indian sexual harassment law regime.

3.2 A quorum of three (3) members is required to be present for conducting any inquiry/ proceedings by the ICC. The quorum shall include the Presiding Officer and at least one other woman member.

3.3 In the event of inability to hold a meeting of the ICC physically, owing to administrative and/or other difficulties/issues, the members may convene a meeting using electronic means over any one of the following virtual communications platforms/software:

- Zoom Meetings; or
- Microsoft Teams Meetings; or
- Any other suitable platform.

3.4 The constitution of the ICC may be changed if found necessary including, but not limited to: transfer(s), resignation(s), determination/termination of employment, conflict of interest situations, role change(s), and location change(s) of any of the ICC members.

**NOTE – Counsellor:**

*While this is not a requirement under the Act, the employer may explore the possibility of having in place a counsellor (a third party) whom victims may approach for confidential advice in case they face sexual harassment. Such persons can serve as the first point of contact for a complainant of sexual harassment and assist in educating the victim on the subject of sexual harassment.*

*The role of such counsellor may be limited to hearing out the complainant, providing information on sexual harassment, the legal avenues available etc. However, it must be ensured that such person possesses all necessary skills, experience and training for providing the right guidance to the victim and effectively tacking all issues which may arise.*

## 4. Redressal Process

### 4.1 Complaint/Inquiry:

A complaint by or against any Employee of the Company may be filed by following the procedure set out below:

a. Any complainant who has been subjected to Sexual Harassment, directly or indirectly, may file a formal written complaint of the alleged incident (along with all the reasonable supporting documents and evidence), by addressing an email to [ ], or to any member/s of the ICC at their respective e-mail ID/s. In the alternative, the complaint (along with all the reasonable supporting documents and evidence) may be filed by physically submitting the same to any of the members of the ICC.

b. In cases where the Complainant is not able to file the Complaint personally, the same may be filed on behalf of such Complainant, as per the provisions of the Act. In such a situation, guidance may be obtained from the Human Resource team of the Company on the mode and manner of making of such a complaint.

c. The complaint should be filed within a period of 3 months from the date of the incident or within a period of 3 months from the date of the last incident (if the incidents are recurring).

Any delay beyond this period of 3 months must be adequately explained in the complaint. The ICC will be competent to determine as to whether any delay in filing of a complaint of sexual harassment is sufficiently explained and is required to be condoned.

d. The complaint must contain the information/details, and must be filed only in the standard Complaint Form of the Company. The said Complaint Form is available with the Human Resources contact of the Company for use and/or reference by any Employee(s) of the Company.

e. The ICC will maintain a record of every complaint received and keep the contents thereof confidential, except that the same may be used for the purpose, as contemplated under the Act.

4.2 If a complaint is to be filed against any person falling within the definition of "Employer", the Complaint shall be filed with the LCC. In such a case, the members of the ICC must assist the Complainant with filing of such complaint.

**4.3 Conciliation**

i. In the event the Complainant requests for a settlement, the ICC shall circulate the terms of the same to the Respondent within two (2) working days. Before accepting any proposed settlement, the ICC shall ensure that monetary compensation alone does not form the entire basis for the said settlement.

ii. If the terms of the settlement are accepted by the Respondent, the ICC shall communicate such acceptance within two (2) working days to the Complainant. In case the settlement is accepted partially, the ICC shall mediate between the parties to enable them to arrive at a final settlement.

iii. In the event the conciliation process is successful, both parties must agree and accept the settlement in writing ("Settlement Agreement"). Where a settlement has been arrived at, the

ICC shall submit the Settlement Agreement to the Board of Directors of the Company, so that action can be taken in the manner specified in the Settlement Agreement. A copy of the Settlement Agreement shall also be handed over to the Complainant and the Respondent.

iv. The Board of Directors acting through an authorized director, shall ensure compliance with the terms of the Settlement Agreement within thirty (30) working days of its execution, and such director shall furnish a compliance report to the ICC, along with a copy to the Complainant and the Respondent.

**4.4 Inquiry Process**

i. As soon as a complaint is received by the ICC, and where there is no request for settlement from the Complainant, the Presiding Officer of the ICC shall (within two (2) working days) convene a meeting of the ICC at which each member must submit a "Conflict-of-Interest Disclosure Form" in the format available with the Human Resources contact of the Company, to the Presiding Officer.

ii. In case any member of the ICC has a conflict of interest, in respect of any specific complaint he/she shall be replaced by any other person (who shall be an ad-hoc/temporary member of the ICC) for all proceedings and matters concerning such complaint in accordance with the provisions of clause 3.4 of this Policy.

iii. In case the Presiding Officer of the ICC has a conflict of interest in respect of any specific complaint, she shall be replaced as a member of the ICC as stated in clause 4.4. (ii) above, for all proceedings and matters concerning such complaint and the senior most female member of the ICC shall take charge as the Presiding Officer.

iv. Within seven (7) working days from the date when the ICC receives the complaint, the ICC shall forward one (1) copy of the complaint to the Respondent. The Respondent shall file his/her response (along with supporting documents, if any) within ten (10) working days from the date of receipt of the complaint by the Respondent.

v. In case the Respondent does not file a response to the complaint, the ICC may take further action, as deemed necessary, or proceed ex-parte against the Respondent.

vi. The Complainant and the Respondent shall not be allowed to be represented by a legal practitioner at any stage of the proceedings before the ICC. However, the Complainant may be accompanied by a colleague, friend, or such other support person for psychological or emotional support. Such colleague, friend, or other support person will not be permitted to speak at, or otherwise interfere with the proceedings of the ICC, and shall only be an observer.

vii. All persons who are part of the ICC proceedings will need to sign a confidentiality agreement.

viii. The ICC must notify the Complainant and the Respondent of the Company of the time and dates of its meetings in writing, not less than five (5) working days in advance of any such meeting. Minutes of meeting/s will be taken down to record the proceedings by a designated ICC member.

ix. If the Complainant or Respondent desires any witness/es to be called, they shall communicate to the ICC the names of witness/es whom they propose to call in writing. The ICC shall call upon all the witnesses (i.e. witnesses sought to be relied upon by both the parties) after providing not less than three (3) working days in advance of any such meeting.

x. In the event the Complainant wishes to withdraw the complaint after initiation of the formal proceeding, the ICC shall permit the same only upon satisfaction that the Complainant has not been threatened, forced, or otherwise improperly induced to do so. The same shall be recorded in writing by both parties.

xi. If the ICC forms a reasoned opinion that the complaint was withdrawn owing to the complaint having been malicious or mischievous in nature, then the ICC may initiate a detailed inquiry or decide upon the penalty, which may be levied against the Complainant, in such cases.

xii. The ICC shall have the right to terminate the inquiry proceedings or to make an ex-parte decision on the complaint if the Complainant or the Respondent fails, without sufficient cause, to present herself/himself for three (3) consecutive hearings of the ICC. However, such termination or ex-parte decision may not be passed without giving a prior written notice of fifteen (15) working days to the party concerned.

xiii. In the event that the ICC arrives at the conclusion that the allegation against the Respondent has been proved, possible disciplinary action will be in direct proportion to the seriousness of the offence and may include, but is not limited to a written apology, warning, reprimand, withholding of promotion, withholding of salary, withholding of salary increments or termination of employment of the Respondent.

xiv. The ICC shall issue its report along with its recommendations to the Board of Directors of the Company within ten (10) working days from the date of completion of the inquiry. The report of the ICC is an Inquiry Report within the meaning ascribed thereto under the Act.

xv. The Board of Directors acting through an authorized director will ensure corrective action in accordance with the recommendation proposed by the ICC within sixty (60) working days from the date of receipt of the inquiry report and such director shall furnish a compliance report to the ICC as well as the Complainant. Corrective action may include, but is not limited to any of the following:

- Formal apology;
- Counselling;

- Reprimand;
- Written warning to the perpetrator and copy thereof maintained in the service record/file of the perpetrator;
- Withholding a promotion;
- Withholding a salary;
- Withholding of salary increments;
- Change of work assignment/transfer of either the Respondent or the Complainant;
- Suspension or termination of services of the Respondent.

## 5. Confidentiality

5.1 The ICC and the Board of Directors shall ensure that the contents of the complaint, the identity and addresses of the Complainant(s), Respondent(s), and witnesses, any information relating to conciliation and inquiry proceedings, recommendations of the ICC, and the action taken by the Board of Directors shall not be published, communicated, or made known to the public, press and media in any manner.

5.2 Any person responsible for breach of confidentiality of the proceedings conducted in terms of this Policy shall be liable to pay a sum of Rs. 5,000/-(Rupees Five Thousands only), as penalty and be subject to further penalty or disciplinary action, as directed by the ICC or the Company.

## 6. Appeal

6.1 Any person aggrieved by the decision of the ICC in connection with a complaint filed by or on behalf of a Complainant who is a female, or the implementation of such decision, may prefer an appeal, before the appellate authority as notified under Clause 2 (a) of the Industrial Employment (Standing Orders) Act, 1946 (20 of 1946).

6.2 Any person aggrieved by the decision of the ICC arising from a complaint filed by or on behalf of a Complainant who is a male, or implementation of such decision, does not have a right to appeal under the Act and may prefer an appeal under applicable law, if any.

7. **Third Party Harassment**

The Company also stands committed towards adopting appropriate preventive and remedial action to prevent sexual harassment of its Employees by non-employees. Where Sexual Harassment occurs from any act by any third party or outsider, the Employer shall take all steps necessary and reasonable to assist the victim in terms of support and preventive action.

8. **Miscellaneous Provisions**

8.1 The ICC will be entitled to seek legal advice to determine whether the alleged acts of the Respondent as mentioned in a complaint constitute a criminal offence. If such acts constitute a criminal offence and/or where the Complainant desires that appropriate criminal proceedings be initiated against the Respondent, then this fact shall be mentioned by the ICC in its Inquiry Report. In such a case, appropriate action (i.e. criminal proceedings) may be initiated by the complainant with the assistance of the Employer and in accordance with the Act.

8.2 Upon completion of the inquiry and implementation of the recommendations/directions set out in the Inquiry Report, in the interest of the organization and safety of other Employees, the ICC shall follow up with the Complainant every three (3) months for a span of a year or till he/she is employed with the organization, to ensure that there have been no further similar incidents perpetrated against the said Complainant, unless the Complainant requests the ICC in writing to cease such follow-ups.

## 9. Non-Retaliation

The Company will not accept, support, or tolerate retaliation in any form against any Employee/ Complainant who, acting in good faith, reports suspected misconduct, asks questions, or raises concerns. Any person who engages in such retaliation, directly or indirectly, or encourages others to do so, may be subject to appropriate disciplinary action.

i. Retaliation will be treated as a major misconduct per the Employee Handbook of the Company.
ii. Retaliation against those reporting Sexual Harassment is prohibited by this Policy.
iii. Retaliation means and includes any action to the detriment of an individual(s), be it with respect to the professional or other comforts enjoyed by the said individual, prior to raising such Complaint.
iv. Anyone suspecting or experiencing retaliation should report the same to the ICC.
v. Retaliation cases are treated as seriously as an alleged case of Sexual Harassment, even if the original Complaint has/had not been proven.

## 10. Review Of Policy

The Policy will be reviewed annually, and in case any amendments are required, whether under the Act or that may be recommended by the ICC, such amendments shall be incorporated, as necessary.

ANNEXURE II

# Conciliation

As discussed earlier in this handbook[1] conciliation is an informal dispute resolution mechanism offered under the Act. The objective of conciliation is to put an end to the offending behaviour rather than judge the offender and adjudicate the alleged offence. Also, in the conciliation process, the focus is more often on future relationships between the concerned parties rather than what transpired in the past.

## WHY CHOOSE CONCILIATION

Conciliation may be a procedure of choice in the following situations:

a. Where the complainant simply wishes that the offending behaviour should stop and is not particularly interested in seeking punishment for the offender.
b. Where the unwanted behaviour emanates from a past personal relationship between the parties.
c. Where the complainant feels that the conduct of the offender may not have been deliberate; or an outcome of his inability to understand that his conduct is being perceived negatively by the complainant.

1 *See* chapter titled 'Procedure'.

A classical distinction between conciliation and the regular adjudicatory process (envisaged under the Act) is as follows: The conciliation normally ends when pursuant to an attempt by the parties to settle, the complainant is satisfied with the outcome and decides to bring a quietus to the matter. On the contrary, the formal adjudicatory procedure ends when the complaints committee concludes its investigation, decides on the guilt or innocence of the alleged harasser and sends its recommendation(s) on the matter to the employer who then takes appropriate steps in accordance with the recommendations.

Mentioned below is a brief procedure which may be resorted to by the complaints committee (following a request by the complainant) for the purposes of determining a complaint of sexual harassment through conciliation. This procedure may be adopted as a part of the sexual harassment policy by all organisations.

## THE CONCILIATION PROCESS

### Initiation of Conciliation

In case the complainant wishes to resort to conciliation, then she shall send to the complaints committee a written request to conciliate the matter (Conciliation Request).

### Preliminary Examination

The Conciliators shall, upon receipt of the Conciliation Request, examine the same in light of the facts of the case.

In case the Conciliators form an opinion that the matter is fit for conciliation, then they shall initiate the conciliation process in accordance with this policy.

In case the Conciliators form an opinion that the Conciliation Request may not be appropriate in view of the facts of the case, then they shall hold a preliminary hearing with the complainant to satisfy themselves that the Conciliation Request has been preferred by her out of her own free will and desire, without any compulsion, coercion, fraud, misrepresentation, undue influence or allurement of any kind whatsoever from anyone (Other Reasons).

If after the preliminary hearing, the Conciliators are satisfied that there exist no other reasons for making the Conciliation Request, then they shall initiate the conciliation process.

**The Conciliators**

The Presiding Member and the External Member of the complaints committee shall act as conciliators in the matter.[2] Both conciliators shall act jointly. The conciliator shall act in an impartial manner.

**Procedure**

The Conciliators, upon their appointment, shall request the complainant to submit a brief statement describing the general nature of her grievance.

The Conciliators may request each party to submit a written statement of their position and the facts and grounds in support thereof, supplemented by any documents and other evidence that such party deems appropriate. Each party shall send a copy of such statement, documents and other evidence to the other party.

At any stage of the conciliation proceedings, the Conciliators may request a party to submit such additional information as deemed appropriate.

The Conciliators shall assist the parties in an independent and impartial manner in their attempt to reach an amicable settlement of their dispute. The Conciliators shall be guided by principles of objectivity, fairness and justice, giving consideration

---

2 *See* chapter titled 'Complaints Committee'.

to, among other things, the rights and obligations of the parties and the circumstances surrounding the dispute.

**Administrative Assistance**

In order to facilitate the conduct of the conciliation proceedings, the Conciliators, with the consent of the parties, may arrange for administrative assistance by a suitable institution or person.

**Time and Place of Sittings**

The Presiding Officer shall fix the time and place for the meetings.

**Communication between Conciliator and Parties**

The Conciliators may invite the parties to meet him or may communicate with them orally or in writing. They may meet or communicate with the parties together or with each of them separately.

The conciliation proceedings shall be held at such place as determined by the conciliators.

**Disclosure of information**

When the Conciliators receive factual information concerning the dispute from a party, they may disclose the substance of that information to the other party in order that the other party may have the opportunity to present any explanation to the same. All information and explanations shared with the Conciliators shall be kept confidential.

**Cooperation of parties with conciliator**

The parties are expected to cooperate with the conciliators and, in particular, endeavour to comply with the requests by the conciliators to submit written materials, provide evidence and attend meetings.

**Settlement**

When it appears to the Conciliators that there exist elements of a settlement which may be acceptable to the parties, they shall formulate the terms of a possible settlement and submit them to the parties for their observations. After receiving the observations of the parties, the conciliators may reformulate the terms of a possible settlement in the light of such observations.

If the parties reach a consensus on a settlement of the dispute, they shall draw up and sign a written settlement agreement. If requested by the parties, the conciliators may draw up, or assist the parties in drawing up, the settlement agreement.

The Conciliators shall jointly authenticate the settlement agreement and furnish a copy thereof to each of the parties.

**Confidentiality**

The Conciliators and the parties shall keep confidential all matters relating to the conciliation proceedings. Confidentiality shall extend also to the settlement agreement, except where its disclosure is necessary for purposes of implementation and enforcement.

**Resort to other proceedings**

The parties may not initiate, during the conciliation proceedings, any legal proceedings in respect of a dispute that is the subject matter of the Conciliation proceedings

**Admissibility of Evidence in other proceedings**

The parties shall not rely on or introduce as evidence in any quasi judicial or judicial proceedings, whether or not such proceedings relate to the dispute that is the subject of the Conciliation proceedings,-

a. the contents of the Conciliation Request and the documents filed by the parties before the Conciliators.
b. any proposal(s) made by the conciliator(s) during the course of the proceedings.
c. views expressed or suggestions made by any other party in respect of a possible settlement of the dispute.
d. admissions made by the other party in the courseof the Conciliation proceedings.
e. the fact that the other party had indicated his willingness to accept a proposal for settlement made by the Conciliators.
f. The proceeding sheets of the Conciliation.

**Timelines**

The Conciliators shall conclude the Conciliation process within a period of 30 (thirty) days from the date of receipt of the Conciliation Request.

ANNEXURE III

# Confidentiality Undertaking

Every party/ participant in inquiry proceedings may execute a confidentiality under takings in the below mentioned format.

**TO WHOMSOEVER IT MAY CONCERN**

**Subject Matter:** Complaint of Sexual Harassment preferred by [_] against [_] with the ICC of [_].

I understand, acknowledge and agree that any and all information or documents supplied/made available/informed (by or) to me by any person in connection with the complaint of sexual harassment (specified above) whether in written form, electronically or orally, shall be held by me in strictest confidence **("Confidential Information")**. I shall ensure that all Confidential Information is kept safe and secured at all times and is properly protected against theft, damage, loss or unauthorized access, hacking, etc.

I shall, at all times, remain in compliance with the provisions of the Sexual Harassment of Women at Workplace (Prevention, Prohibition, and Redressal) Act, 2013 (as amended from time to time) **("POSH Act")**. I understand that a violation of the present Confidentiality Undertaking shall constitute a violation of and be actionable under the provisions of the POSH Act as well as the Sexual Harassment Policy of [_].

All Confidential Information available with me in connection with the complaint of the sexual harassment and the proceedings before the ICC shall be promptly returned by me within ten (10) days a written notice from the PO of the ICC requesting a return of the Confidential Information.

This Confidentiality Undertaking shall be valid in perpetuity.

**Name:**
**Date:**
**Designation in [_], if applicable:**
**Capacity:** Complainant / Accused / Witness / ICC Member / Other [Please specify]

ANNEXURE IV

# Conflict of Interest Declaration Form

Every member of the ICC may execute a conflict of interest declaration in the below mentioned format.

I, [Name], being a member of the Internal Complaints Committee of [_] (**"ICC"**) do hereby state that I have read and understood the complaint dated [Date] submitted by [Name of Complainant] / [Name of Next Friend] on behalf of [Name of Complainant] against [Name of Accused].

I hereby declare to the best of my knowledge:

1. That I do not have any interest, personal or professional, in the decision to be made by the Internal Complaints Committee.
2. I am not personally related or professionally answerable to either the complainant, aggrieved individual or respondent.

I hereby likewise declare that in case I receive any information during the course of the conciliation or inquiry proceedings that, in my view and in the view of the ICC, may cause me to be in a position of a conflict of interest with regard to my duties and responsibilities as a member of the ICC, then I shall immediately inform the Presiding Officer of the ICC and recuse myself from the proceedings

______________________________

*[Designation of ICC Member]*

Date:

ANNEXURE V

# Complaint Form

## (Aggrieved Individual)

A complainant may make a complaint of sexual harassment in the below mentioned format.

### I. Details of Individual Aggrieved by Sexual Harassment

| Name | Division & Department | Designation/ Title | Contact Details: Email address & Mobile phone (if known) |
|---|---|---|---|
| | | | |

### II. Details of the Accused/ Respondent(s)

| Name | Division & Department (if known) | Designation/ Title (if known) | Contact Details: Email address & Mobile phone (if known) |
|---|---|---|---|
| | | | |
| | | | |
| | | | |

### III. Details of the incident(s)

| Sr. No. | Nature/ Description of incident | Date of incident | Time of incident (approximate) | Place of incident | Name and contact details of witnesses (if any) |
|---|---|---|---|---|---|
| | | | | | |
| | | | | | |
| | | | | | |
| | | | | | |
| | | | | | |

IV. **Whether the Accused/ Respondent/Complainant is a member of the Internal Complaints Committee**

Yes ( ) No ( )

V. **Has a report regarding these incidents been filed with any other agency/ governmental organization?**

Yes ( ) No ( )

If yes, with which agency/ governmental organization?

VI. **Additional information and comments if any:**

____________________________ ________________

Signature of Aggrieved Individual Date

ANNEXURE VI

# Complaint Form

## (Complainant on behalf of the Aggrieved Individual)

I. **Whether the Aggrieved Individual is unable to file the Complaint personally?**

Yes ( ) No ( )

If yes, then what are the reasons for such inability?

______________________________________________

______________________________________________

______________________________________________

II. **Details of Complainant:**

| Name | Relationship with Aggrieved Individual | Contact Details: Email address & Mobile phone |
|---|---|---|
| | | |

III. **Details of Individual Aggrieved by Sexual Harassment:**

| Name | Division & Department | Designation | Contact Details: Email address & Mobile phone |
|---|---|---|---|
| | | | |

IV. **Details of the Accused/ Respondent(s):**

| Name | Division & Department | Designation | Contact Details: Email address & Mobile phone |
|---|---|---|---|
| | | | |
| | | | |
| | | | |
| | | | |

V. **Details of the incident(s):**

| Sr. No. | Nature/ Description of incident | Date of incident | Time of incident (approx.) | Place of incident | Name and contact details of witnesses (if any) |
|---|---|---|---|---|---|
| | | | | | |
| | | | | | |
| | | | | | |
| | | | | | |
| | | | | | |

VI. **Whether the Accused/ Respondent/Complainant(s) is a member of the Internal Complaints Committee:**

Yes ( ) No ( )

VII. **Has a report regarding these incidents been filed with any other agency/ governmental organization?**

Yes ( ) No ( )

If yes, with which agency/ governmental organization?

VIII. **Additional information and comments if any:**

____________________ ____________

Signature of Complainant Date

ANNEXURE VII

# Annual Return

Organisations may use the below mentioned format for annual filings under the Act.

**COVERING LETTER**

Date: [_]

To,
District Officer

Dear Sir/Madam,

**Subject:** Annual return under Section 21 of the Sexual Harassment of Women at Workplace (Prevention, Prohibition and Redressal) Act, 2013 for the calendar year ended on [Date].

Please find enclosed herewith the Annual Return (along with Annexures) required to be filed by [_], under Section 21 of the Sexual Harassment of Women at Workplace (Prevention, Prohibition and Redressal) Act, 2013 for its workplace situated at [Address] with regards to complaints received and their redressal for the year ended on [Date] for your information and record.

For [_]

______________________

[Name of Presiding Officer]
**Presiding Officer**

[Name of Director]
Encl:

1. Annual Return for the calendar year [Date]
2. Certified Copy of Policy against Sexual Harassment.
3. Certified Copy of Notice for display of Internal Complaints Committee.
4. Certified Copy of pictures taken during training session on Sexual Harassment of Women at Workplace (Prevention, Prohibition and Redressal) Act, 2013.
5. Certified Copy of the attendance record of training session on Sexual Harassment of Women at Workplace (Prevention, Prohibition and Redressal) Act, 2013.

## ANNUAL RETURN

Date: [_]
To,
District Officer

**Subject:** Annual return under the Sexual Harassment of Women at Workplace (PreventionProhibition and Redressal) Act, 2013 for the calendar year ended on [Date].

Dear Madam /Sir,

We, [_], a Company registered under the Companies Act, 2013, bearing CIN/registration no. [Number] (hereinafter referred to as the "**Company**"), having our workplace situated at [*Address*] have enclosed herewith the Annual Return under Sexual Harassment of Women at Workplace (Prevention, Prohibition and Redressal) Act, 2013, with regards to complaints received and their redressal for the calendar year ended on [Date], thereby certifying as follows:-

1. That the Company has formulated, circulated and implemented an updated internal Sexual Harassment of Women at Workplace (Prevention, Prohibition and Redressal) Act, 2013 Policy ("Policy") in the year [Date] to all its employees. A certified copy of the Policy is attached herewith and marked as Annexure A for your kind perusal.
2. That the number of Employees of the Company as on date of filing this Return is [Number].
3. That the Company has duly appointed an Internal Complaints Committee ("ICC") for its offices located at the aforementioned addresses as per the Sexual Harassment of Women at Workplace (Prevention, Prohibition and redressal) Act, 2013. The names of the ICC members are as follows:

| S. No. | Name of the members | Office Designation | Contract Number | Email Id |
|---|---|---|---|---|
| 1. | [] | [] | [] | [] |
| 2. | [] | [] | [] | [] |
| 3. | [] | [] | [] | [] |
| 4. | [] | [] | [] | [] |
| 5. | [] | [] | [] | [] |

4. That the Company has duly displayed the notice of appointment of the ICC at the office of the Company. The true copies of the notice specifying the names, designation, email ids and contact details of all the ICC members are attached herewith and marked as Annexure B for your kind perusal.

5. That the Company has duly informed its employees about the Company's policy on Sexual Harassment as well the consequences of violation thereof and has also displayed the aforementioned notices at the office of the Company. A true copy of the photograph of the notice board displaying this Notice at the office of the Company, is attached herewith and marked as Annexure C for your kind perusal.

6. That the Company has duly conducted a workshop attendance whereof was mandatory for all Employees of the Company on [Date] for the calendar year ended on [Date], thereby informing all the employees about the offence(s) connected with or involving sexual harassment, its consequences, the investigation and inquiry process and the terms and conditions of Company's Sexual Harassment Policy. The photographs of the workshop attended by the employees along with a copy of the attendance record, are attached herewith and marked as Annexures D and E respectively, for kind perusal.

7. That the Company has made all due efforts to inform the employees about their rights provided under the Sexual Harassment of Women at Workplace (Prevention, Prohibition and Redressal) Act, 2013 in the aforementioned workshop.

8. That as per the Policy, the Company has duly devised a formal process to provide assistance to any Employee who may have been sexually harassed, in approaching its Internal Complaints Committee and in dealing with the psychological and other repercussions of the same including provision of assistance in lodging a complaint with the police. The Employees of the Company have also been made aware of the said Policy and have been duly sensitized towards all issues concerned therewith.

9. That the Company has duly conducted an orientation program/ capacity and skill building workshop for the ICC Members on [Date] for calendar year ended on [Date].

10. That the Company has provided necessary facilities to the ICC for dealing with Sexual Harassment proceedings and has duly followed the recommendations of the ICC regarding the interim measures.

11. That the report of Internal Complaints Committee in respect of Complaints received during the calendar year ended on [Date] under the Sexual Harassment of Women at Workplace (Prevention, Prohibition and Redressal) Act, 2013 and the rules framed there under as per Section 21 of the Act is as follows:-

    a) No. of Complaints of sexual harassment received during the year: [_]

    b) No. of Complaints disposed off during the year: [_]

    c) No. of Cases pending for more than 90 days: [_]

    d) Nature of action taken by the employer: [_]

    e) No. of Workshops or Awareness Program(s) against Sexual Harassment carried out: [_]

    f) Does a separate anti sexual harassment policy exist? Yes ( ) No ( )

    g) The Policy is in compliance with the Sexual Harassment of Women at Workplace (Prevention, Prohibition and Redressal) Act, 2013? Yes ( ) No ( )

h) The policy is relevant to the functioning of the organization.

i) The disciplinary action to be taken against, as well as the procedure to be adopted with respect to complaints concerning sexual harassment is dealt with in Sexual Harassment Policy of the Company inter alia at Clause 5 therein.

12. That the Company duly includes information concerning the pending and/or resolved complaints/conciliation proceedings with respect to Sexual Harassment cases concerning its Employees in its annual report each year.

Yours Sincerely,

**For the Company:**

_______________

[Name of Presiding Officer]

**Presiding Officer**

_______________

[Name of Director]

# THE SEXUAL HARASSMENT OF WOMEN AT WORKPLACE (PREVENTION, PROHIBITION AND REDRESSAL) ACT, 2013

ACT NO. 14 OF 2013

[*22nd April,* 2013]

An Act to provide protection against sexual harassment of women at workplace and for the prevention and redressal of complaints of sexual harassment and for matters connected therewith or incidental thereto.

WHEREAS sexual harassment results in violation of the fundamental rights of a woman to equality under articles 14 and 15 of the Constitution of India and her right to life and to live with dignity under article 21 of the Constitution and right to practice any profession or to carry on any occupation, trade or business which includes a right to a safe environment free from sexual harassment;

AND WHEREAS the protection against sexual harassment and the right to work with dignity are universally recognised human rights by international conventions and instruments such as Convention on the Elimination of all Forms of Discrimination against Women, which has been ratified on the 25th June, 1993 by the Government of India;

AND WHEREAS it is expedient to make provisions for giving effect to the said Convention for protection of women against sexual harassment at workplace.

BE it enacted by Parliament in the Sixty-fourth Year of the Republic of India as follows: —

## CHAPTER I

### PRELIMINARY

**1. Short title, extent and commencement.**—(*1*) This Act may be called the Sexual Harassment of Women at Workplace (Prevention, Prohibition and Redressal) Act, 2013.

(*2*) It extends to the whole of India.

(*3*) It shall come into force on such date[1] as the Central Government may, by notification in the Official Gazette, appoint.

**2. Definitions.**—In this Act, unless the context otherwise requires, —

(*a*) "aggrieved woman" means—

(*i*) in relation to a workplace, a woman, of any age whether employed or not, who alleges to have been subjected to any act of sexual harassment by the respondent;

(*ii*) in relation to dwelling place or house, a woman of any age who is employed in such a dwelling place or house;

(*b*) "appropriate Government" means—

(*i*) in relation to a workplace which is established, owned, controlled or wholly or substantially financed by funds provided directly or indirectly—

(*A*) by the Central Government or the Union territory administration, the Central Government;

(*B*) by the State Government, the State Government;

1. 9th December, 2013, *vide* notification No. S.O. 3606(E), dated 9th December, 2013, *see* Gazette of India, Extraordinary, Part II, sec. 3(*ii*).

(*ii*) in relation to any workplace not covered under sub-clause (*i*) and falling within its territory, the State Government;

(*c*) "Chairperson" means the Chairperson of the Local Complaints Committee nominated under sub-section (*1*) of section *7*;

(*d*) "District Officer" means on officer notified under section 5;

(*e*) "domestic worker" means a woman who is employed to do the household work in any household for remuneration whether in cash or kind, either directly or through any agency on a temporary, permanent, part time or full time basis, but does not include any member of the family of the employer;

(*f*) "employee" means a person employed at a workplace for any work on regular, temporary, *ad hoc* or daily wage basis, either directly or through an agent, including a contractor, with or, without the knowledge of the principal employer, whether for remuneration or not, or working on a voluntary basis or otherwise, whether the terms of employment are express or implied and includes a co-worker, a contract worker, probationer, trainee, apprentice or called by any other such name;

(*g*) "employer" means—

(*i*) in relation to any department, organisation, undertaking, establishment, enterprise, institution, office, branch or unit of the appropriate Government or a local authority, the head of that department, organisation, undertaking, establishment, enterprise, institution, office, branch or unit or such other officer as the appropriate Government or thc local authority, as the case may be, may by an order specify in this behalf;

(*ii*) in any workplace not covered under sub-clause (*i*), any person responsible for the management, supervision and control of the workplace.

*Explanation.* —For the purposes of this sub-clause "management" includes the person or board or committee responsible for formulation and administration of polices for such organisation;

(*iii*) in relation to workplace covered under sub-clauses (*i*) and (*ii*), the person discharging contractual obligations with respect to his or her employees;

(*iv*) in relation to a dwelling place or house, a person or a household who employs or benefits from the employment of domestic worker, irrespective of the number, time period or type of such worker employed, or the nature of the employment or activities performed by the domestic worker;

(*h*) "Internal Committee" means an Internal Complaints Committee constituted under section 4;

(*i*) "Local Committee" means the Local Complaints Committee constituted under section 6;

(*j*) "Member" means a Member of the Internal Committee or the Local Committee, as the case may be;

(*k*) "prescribed" means prescribed by rules made under this Act;

(*l*) "Presiding Officer" means the Presiding Officer of the Internal Complaints Committee nominated under sub-section (*2*) of section 4;

(*m*) "respondent' means a person against whom the aggrieved woman has made a complaint under section 9;

(*n*) "sexual harassment" includes any one or more of the following unwelcome acts or behavior (whether directly or by implication) namely:—

(*i*) physical contact and advances; or

(*ii*) a demand or request for sexual favours; or

(*iii*) making sexually coloured remarks; or

(*iv*) showing pornography; or

(*v*) any other unwelcome physical, verbal or non-verbal conduct of sexual nature;

(*o*) "workplace" includes—

(*i*) any department, organisation, undertaking, establishment, enterprise, institution, office, branch or unit which is established, owned, controlled or wholly or substantially financed by funds provided directly or indirectly by the appropriate Government or the local authority or a Government company or a corporation or a co-operative society;

(*ii*) any private sector organisation or a private venture, undertaking, enterprise, institution, establishment, society, trust, non-governmental organisation, unit or service provider carrying on commercial, professional, vocational, educational, entertainmental, industrial, health services or financial activities including production, supply, sale, distribution or service;

(*iii*) hospitals or nursing homes;

(*iv*) any sports institute, stadium, sports complex or competition or games venue, whether residential or not used for training, sports or other activities relating thereto;

(*v*) any place visited by the employee arising out of or during the course of employment including transportation by the employer for undertaking such journey;

(*vi*) a dwelling place or a house;

(*p*) "unorganised sector" in relation to a workplace means an enterprise owned by individuals or self-employed workers and engaged in the production or sale of goods or providing service of any kind whatsoever, and where the enterprise employs workers, the number of such workers is less than ten.

**3. Prevention of sexual harassment.**—(*1*) No woman shall be subjected to sexual harassment at any workplace.

(*2*) The following circumstances, among other circumstances, if it occurs, or is present in relation to or connected with any act or behavior of sexual harassment may amount to sexual harassment:—

(*i*) implied or explicit promise of preferential treatment in her employment; or

(*ii*) implied or explicit threat of detrimental treatment in her employment ; or

(*iii*) implied or explicit threat about her present or future employment status; or

(*iv*) interference with her work or creating an intimidating or offensive or hostile work environment for her; or

(*v*) humiliating treatment likely to affect her health or safety.

## CHAPTER II

### CONSTITUTION OF INTERNAL COMPLAINTS COMMITTEE

**4. Constitution of Internal Complaints Committee.**— (*1*) Every employer of a workplace shall, by an order in writing, constitute a Committee to be known as the "Internal Complaints Committee":

Provided that where the offices or administrative units of the workplace are located at different places or divisional or sub-divisional level, the Internal Committee shall be constituted at all administrative units or offices.

(*2*) The Internal Committees shall consist of the following members to be nominated by the employer, namely: —

(*a*) a Presiding Officer who shall be a woman employed at a senior level at workplace from amongst the employees:

Provided that in case a senior level woman employee is not available, the Presiding Officer shall be nominated from other offices or administrative units of the workplace referred to in sub-section*(1)*:

Provided further that in case the other offices or administrative units of the workplace do not have a senior level woman employee, the Presiding Officer shall be nominated from any other workplace of the same employer or other department or organisation;

(*b*) not less than two Members from amongst employees preferably committed to the cause of women or who have had experience in social work or have legal knowledge;

(*c*) one member from amongst non-governmental organisations or associations committed to the cause of women or a person familiar with the issues relating to sexual harassment:

Provided that at least one-half of the total Members so nominated shall be women.

(*3*) The Presiding Officer and every Member of the Internal Committee shall hold office for such period, not exceeding three years, from the date of their nomination as may be specified by the employer.

(*4*) The Member appointed from amongst the non-governmental organisations or associations shall be paid such fees or allowances for holding the proceedings of the Internal Committee, by the employer, as may be prescribed.

(*5*) Where the Presiding Officer or any Member of the Internal Committee, —

(*a*) contravenes the provisions of section 16; or

(*b*) has been convicted for an offence or an inquiry into an offence under any law for the time being in force is pending against him; or

(*c*) he has been found guilty in any disciplinary proceedings or a disciplinary proceeding is pending against him; or

(*d*) has so abused his position as to render his continuance in office prejudicial to the public interest,

such Presiding Officer or Member, as the case may be, shall be removed from the Committee and the vacancy so created or any casual vacancy shall be filled by fresh nomination in accordance with the provisions of this section.

## CHAPTER III

### CONSTITUTION OF LOCAL COMPLAINTS COMMITTEE

**5. Notification of District Officer.**—The appropriate Government may notify a District Magistrate or Additional District Magistrate or the Collector or Deputy Collector as a District Officer for every District to exercise powers or discharge functions under this Act.

**6. Constitution and jurisdiction of** [1][Local Committee].—(*1*) Every District Officer shall constitute in the district concerned, a committee to be known as the "[1][Local Committee]" to receive complaints of

1. Subs. by Act 23 of 2016, s. 3 and the Second Schedule, for "Local Complaints Committee" (w.e.f. 6-5-2016).

sexual harassment from establishments where the [1][Internal Committee] has not been constituted due to having less than ten workers or if the complaint is against the employer himself.

(*2*) The District Officer shall designate one nodal officer in every block, taluka and tehsil in rural or tribal area and ward or municipality in the urban area, to receive complaints and forward the same to the concerned [2][Local Committee] within a period of seven days.

(*3*) The jurisdiction of the [2][Local Committee] shall extend to the areas of the district where it is constituted.

**7. Composition, tenure and other terms and conditions of [2][Local Committee].**—(*1*) The [2][Local Committee] shall consist of the following members to be nominated by the District Officer, namely: —

(*a*) a Chairperson to be nominated from amongst the eminent women in the field of social work and committed to the cause of women;

(*b*) one Member to be nominated from amongst the women working in block, taluka or tehsil or ward or municipality in the district;

(*c*) two Members, of whom at least one shall be a woman, to be nominated from amongst such non-governmental organisations or associations committed to the cause of women or a person familiar with the issues relating to sexual harassment, which may be prescribed:

Provided that at least one of the nominees should, preferably, have a background in law or legal knowledge:

Provided further that at least one of the nominees shall be a woman belonging to the Scheduled Castes or the Scheduled Tribes or the Other Backward Classes or minority community notified by the Central Government, from time to time;

(*d*) the concerned officer dealing with the social welfare or women and child development in the district, shall be a member *ex officio*.

(*2*) The Chairperson and every Member of the Local Committee shall hold office for such period, not exceeding three years, form the date of their appointment as may be specified by the District Officer.

(*3*) Where the Chairperson or any Member of the [2][Local Committee]—

(*a*) contravenes the provisions of section 16; or

(*b*) has been convicted for an offence or an inquiry into an offence under any law for the time being in force is pending against him; or

(*c*) has been found guilty in any disciplinary proceedings or a disciplinary proceeding is pending against him; or

(*d*) has so abused his position as to render his continuance in office prejudicial to the public interest,

such Chairperson or Member, as the case may be, shall be removed from the Committee and the vacancy so created or any casual vacancy shall be filled by fresh nomination in accordance with the provisions of this section.

(*4*) The Chairperson or Members of the Local Committee other than the Members nominated under clauses (*b*) and (*d*) of sub-section (*1*) shall be entitled to such fees or allowances for holding the proceedings of the Local Committee as may be prescribed.

**8. Grants and audit.**—(*1*) The Central Government may, after due appropriation made by Parliament by law in this behalf, make to the State Government grants of such sums of money as the Central

1. Subs. by Act 23 of 2016, s. 3 and the Second Schedule, for "Internal Complaints Committee" (w.e.f. 6-5-2016).
2. Subs. by s. 3 and the Second Schedule, *ibid.*, for "Local Complaints Committee" (w.e.f. 6-5-2016).

Government my think fit, for being utilised for the payment of fees or allowances referred to in sub-section (*4*) of section 7.

(*2*) The State Government may set up an agency and transfer the grants made under sub-section (*1*) to that agency.

(*3*) The agency shall pay to the District Officer, such sums as may be required for the payment of fees or allowances referred to in sub-section (*4*) of section 7.

(*4*) The accounts of the agency referred to in sub-section (*2*) shall be maintained and audited in such manner as may, in consultation with the Accountant General of the State, be prescribed and the person holding the custody of the accounts of the agency shall furnish, to the State Government, before such date, as may be prescribed, its audited copy of accounts together with auditors' report thereon.

## CHAPTER IV

## COMPLAINT

**9. Complaint of sexual harassment.**—(*1*) Any aggrieved woman may make, in writing, a complaint of sexual harassment at workplace to the Internal Committee if so constituted, or the Local Committee, in case it is not so constituted, within a period of three months from the date of incident and in case of a series of incidents, within a period of three months from the date of last incident:

Provided that where such complaint cannot be made in writing, the Presiding Officer or any Member of the Internal Committee or the Chairperson or any Member of the Local Committee, as the case may be, shall render all reasonable assistance to the woman for making the complaint in writing:

Provided further that the Internal Committee or, as the case may be, the Local Committee may, for the reasons to be recorded in writing, extend the time limit not exceeding three months , if it is satisfied that the circumstances were such which prevented the woman from filing a complaint within the said period.

(*2*) Where the aggrieved woman is unable to make a complaint on account of her physical or mental incapacity or death or otherwise, her legal heir or such other person as may be prescribed may make a complaint under this section.

**10. Conciliation.**—(*1*) The Internal Committee or, as the case may be, the Local Committee, may, before initiating an inquiry under section 11 and at the request of the aggrieved woman take steps to settle the matter between her and the respondent through conciliation:

Provided that no monetary settlement shall be made as a basis of conciliation.

(*2*) Where settlement has been arrived at under sub-section (*1*), the Internal Committee or the Local Committee, as the case may be, shall record the settlement so arrived and forward the same to the employer or the District Officer to take action as specified in the recommendation.

(*3*) The Internal Committee or the Local Committee, as the case may be, shall provide the copies of the settlement as recorded under sub-section (*2*) to the aggrieved woman and the respondent.

(*4*) Where a settlement is arrived at under sub-section (*1*), no further inquiry shall be conducted by the Internal Committee or the Local Committee, as the case may be.

**11. Inquiry into complaint.**— (*1*) Subject to the provisions of section 10, the Internal Committee or the Local Committee, as the case may be, shall, where the respondent is an employee, proceed to make inquiry into the complaint in accordance with the provisions of the service rules applicable to the respondent and where no such rules exist, in such manner as may be prescribed or in case of a domestic worker, the Local Committee shall, if *prima facie* case exist, forward the complaint to the police, within a period of seven days for registering the case under section 509 of the Indian Penal Code (45 of 1860), and any other relevant provisions of the said Code where applicable:

Provided that where the aggrieved woman informs the Internal Committee or the Local Committee, as the case may be, that any term or condition of the settlement arrived at under sub-section *(2)* of section 10 has not been complied with by the respondent, the Internal Committee or the Local Committee shall proceed to make an inquiry into the complaint or, as the case may be, forward the complaint to the police:

Provided further that where both the parties are employees, the parties shall, during the course of inquiry, be given an opportunity of being heard and a copy of the findings shall be made available to both the parties enabling them to make representation against the findings before the Committee.

(*2*) Notwithstanding anything contained in section 509 of the Indian Penal Code (45 of 1860), the court may, when the respondent is convicted of the offence, order payment of such sums as it may consider appropriate, to the aggrieved woman by the respondent, having regard to the provisions of section 15.

(*3*) For the purpose of making an inquiry under sub-section (*1*), the Internal Committee or the Local Committee, as the case may be, shall have the same powers as are vested in a civil court the Code of Civil Procedure, 1908 (5 of 1908) when trying a suit in respect of the following matters, namely:—

(*a*) summoning and enforcing the attendance of any person and examining him on oath;

(*b*) requiring the discovery and production of documents; and

(*c*) any other matter which may be prescribed.

(*4*) The inquiry under sub-section (*1*) shall be completed within a period of ninety days.

## CHAPTER V

### INQUIRY INTO COMPLAINT

**12. Action during pendency of inquiry.**—(*1*) During the pendency of an inquiry on a written request made by the aggrieved woman, the Internal Committee or the local Committee, as the case may be, may recommend to the employer to—

(*a*) transfer the aggrieved woman or the respondent to any other workplace; or

(*b*) grant leave to the aggrieved woman up to a period of three months; or

(*c*) grant such other relief to the aggrieved woman a may be prescribed.

(*2*) The leave granted to the aggrieved woman under this section shall be in addition to the leave she would be otherwise entitled.

(*3*) On the recommendation of the Internal Committee or the Local Committee, as the case may be, under sub-section (*1*), the employer shall implement the recommendations made under sub-section (*1*) and send the report of such implementation to the Internal Committee or the Local Committee, as the case may be.

**13. Inquiry report.**—(*1*) On the completion of an inquiry under this Act, the Internal Committee or the Local Committee, as the case may be, shall provide a report of its findings to the employer, or as the case may be, the District Officer within a period of ten days from the date of completion of the inquiry and such report be made available to the concerned parties.

(*2*) Where the Internal Committee or the Local Committee, as the case may be, arrives at the conclusion that the allegation against the respondent has not been proved, it shall recommend to the employer and the District Officer that no action is required to be taken in the matter.

(*3*) Where the Internal Committee or the Local Committee, as the case may be, arrives at the conclusion that the allegation against the respondent has been proved, it shall recommend to the employer or the District Officer, as the case may be—

(*i*) to take action for sexual harassment as a misconduct in accordance with the provisions of the service rules applicable to the respondent or where no such service rules have been made, in such manner as may be prescribed;

(*ii*) to deduct, notwithstanding anything in the service rules applicable to the respondent, from the salary or wages of the respondent such sum as it may consider appropriate to be paid to the aggrieved woman or to her legal heirs, as it may determine, in accordance with the provisions of section 15:

Provide that in case the employer is unable to make such deduction from the salary of the respondent due to his being absent from duty or cessation of employment it may direct to the respondent to pay such sum to the aggrieved woman:

Provided further that in case the respondent fails to pay the sum referred to in clause (*ii*), the Internal Committee or as, the case may be, the Local Committee may forward the order for recovery of the sum as an arrear of land revenue to the concerned District Officer.

(*4*) The employer or the District Officer shall act upon the recommendation within sixty days of its receipt by him.

**14. Punishment for false or malicious complaint and false evidence.**—(*1*) Where the Internal Committee or the Local Committee, as the case may be, arrives at a conclusion that the allegation against the respondent is malicious or the aggrieved woman or any other person making the complaint has made the complaint knowing it to be false or the aggrieved woman or any other person making the complaint has produced any forged or misleading document, it may recommend to the employer or the District Officer, as the case may be, to take action against the woman or the person who has made the complaint under sub-section (*1*) or sub-section (*2*) of section 9, as the case may be, in accordance with the provisions of the service rules applicable to her or him or where no such service rules exist, in such manner as may be prescribed:

Provided that a mere inability to substantiate a complaint or provide adequate proof need not attract action against the complainant under this section:

Provided further that the malicious intent on part of the complainant shall be established after an inquiry in accordance with the procedure prescribed, before any action is recommended.

(*2*) Where the Internal Committee or the Local Committee, as the case may be, arrives at a conclusion that during the inquiry any witness has given false evidence or produced any forged or misleading document, it may recommend to the employer of the witness or the District Officer, as the case may be, to take action in accordance with the provisions of the service rules applicable to the said witness or where no such service rules exist, in such manner as may be prescribed.

**15. Determination of compensation.**—For the purpose of determining the sums to be paid to the aggrieved woman under clause (*ii*) of sub-section (*3*) of section 13, the Internal Committee or the Local Committee, as the case may be, shall have regard to—

(*a*) the mental trauma, pain, suffering and emotional distress caused to the aggrieved woman;

(*b*) the loss in the career opportunity due to the incident of sexual harassment;

(*c*) medical expenses incurred by the victim for physical or psychiatric treatment;

(*d*) the income and financial status of the respondent;

(*e*) feasibility of such payment in lump sum or in instalments.

**16. Prohibition of publication or making known contents of complaint and inquiry proceedings.**—Notwithstanding anything contained in the Right to Information Act, 2005 (22 of 2005), the contents of the complaint made under section 9, the identity and addresses of the aggrieved woman, respondent and witnesses, any information relating to conciliation and inquiry proceedings, recommendations of the Internal Committee or the Local Committee, as the case may be, and the action taken by the employer or the District Officer under the provisions of this Act shall not be published, communicated or made known to the public, press and media in any manner:

Provided that information may be disseminated regarding the justice secured to any vicitim of sexual harassment under this Act without disclosing the name, address, identity or any other particulars calculated to lead to the identification of the aggrieved woman and witnesses.

**17. Penalty for publication or making known contents of complaint and inquiry proceedings.**—Where any person entrusted with the duty to handle or deal with the complaint, inquiry or any recommendations or action to be taken under the provisions of this Act, contravenes the provisions of section 16, he shall be liable for penalty in accordance with the provisions of the service rules applicable to the said person or where no such service rules exist, in such manner as may be prescribed.

**18. Appeal.**—(*1*) Any person aggrieved from the recommendations made under sub-section (*2*) of section 13 or under clause (*i*) or clause (*ii*) of sub-section (*3*) of section 13 or sub-section (*1*) or sub-section (*2*) of section 14 or section 17 or non-implementation of such recommendations may prefer an appeal to the court or tribunal in accordance with the provisions of the service rules applicable to the said person or where no such service rules exist then, without prejudice to provisions contained in any other law for the time being in force, the person aggrieved may prefer an appeal in such manner as may be prescribed.

(*2*) The appeal under sub-section (*1*) shall be preferred within a period of ninety days of the recommendations.

## CHAPTER VI

### DUTIES OF EMPLOYER

**19. Duties of employer.**— Every employer shall—

(*a*) provide a safe working environment at the workplace with shall include safety from the persons coming into contact at the workplace;

(*b*) display at any conspicuous place in the workplace, the penal consequences of sexual harassments; and the order constituting, the Internal Committee under sub-section (*1*) of section 4;

(*c*) organise workshops and awareness programmes at regular intervals for sensitising the employees with the provisions of the Act and orientation programmes for the members of the Internal Committee in the manner as may be prescribed;

(*d*) provide necessary facilities to the Internal Committee or the Local Committee, as the case may be, for dealing with the complaint and conducting an inquiry;

(*e*) assist in securing the attendance of respondent and witnesses before the Internal Committee or the Local Committee, as the case may be;

(*f*) make available such information to the Internal Committee or the Local Committee, as the case be, as it may require having regard to the complaint made under sub-section (*1*) of section 9;

(*g*) provide assistance to the woman if she so chooses to file a complaint in relation to the offence under the Indian Penal Code (45 of 1860) or any other law for the time being in force;

(*h*) cause to initiate action, under the Indian Penal Code (45 of 1860) or any other law for the time being in force, against the perpetrator, or if the aggrieved woman so desires, where the perpetrator is not an employee, in the workplace at which the incident of sexual harassment took place;

(*i*) treat sexual harassment as a misconduct under the service rules and initiate action for such misconduct;

(*j*) monitor the timely submission of reports by the Internal Committee.

## CHAPTER VII

### DUTIES AND POWERS OF DISTRICT OFFICER

**20. Duties and powers of District Officer.**—The District Officer shall, —

(*a*) monitor the timely submission of report furnished by the Local Committee;

(*b*) take such measures as may be necessary for engaging non-governmental organisations for creation of awareness on sexual harassment and the rights of the women.

## CHAPTER VIII

### MISCELLANEOUS

**21. Committee to submit annual report.**— (*1*) The Internal Committee or the Local Committee, as the case may be, shall in each calendar year prepare, in such form and at such time as may be prescribed, an annual report and submit the same to the employer and the District Officer.

(*2*) The District Officer shall forward a brief report on the annual reports received under sub-section (*1*) to the State Government.

**22. Employer to include information in annual report.**—The employer shall include in its report the number of cases filed, if any, and their disposal under this Act in the annual report of his organisation or where no such report is required to be prepared, intimate such number of cases, if any, to the District Officer.

**23. Appropriate Government to monitor implementation and maintain data.**—The appropriate Government shall monitor the implementation of this Act and maintain date on the number of cases filed and disposed of in respect of all cases of sexual harassment at workplace.

**24. Appropriate Government to take measures to publicise the Act.**—The appropriate Government may, subject to the availability of financial and other resources, —

(*a*) develop relevant information, education, communication and training materials, and organise awareness programmes, to advance the understanding of the public of the provisions of this Act providing for protection against sexual harassment of woman at workplace;

(*b*) formulate orientation and training programmes for the members of the [1][Local Committee].

**25. Power to call for information and inspection of records.**—(*1*) The appropriate Government, on being satisfied that it is necessary in the public interest or in the interest of women employees at a workplace to do so, by order in writing,—

(*a*) call upon any employer or District Officer to furnish in writing such information relating to sexual harassment as it may require;

(*b*) authorise any officer to make inspection of the records and workplace in relation to sexual harassment, who shall submit a report of such inspection to it within such period as may be specified in the order.

(*2*) Every employer and District Officer shall produce on demand before the officer making the inspection all information, records and other documents in his custody having a bearing on the subject matter of such inspection.

**26. Penalty for non-compliance with provisions of Act.**—(*1*) Where the employer fails to—

(*a*) constitute an Internal Committee under sub-section (*1*) of section 4;

1. Subs. by Act 23 of 2016, s. 3 and the Second Schedule, for "Local Complaints Committee" (w.e.f. 6-5-2016).

(*b*) take action under sections 13, 14 and 22; and

(*c*) contravenes or attempts to contravene or abets contravention of other provisions of this Act or any rules made thereunder,

he shall be punishable with fine which may extend to fifty thousand rupees.

(*2*) If any employer, after having been previously convicted of an offence punishable under this Act subsequently commits and is convicted of the same offence, he shall be liable to—

(*i*) twice the punishment, which might have been imposed on a first conviction, subject to the punishment being maximum provided for the same offence:

Provided that in case a higher punishment is prescribed under any other law for the time being in force, for the offence for which the accused is being prosecuted, the court shall take due cognizance of the same while awarding the punishment;

(*ii*) cancellation, of his licence or withdrawal, or non-renewal, or approval, or cancellation of the registration, as the case may be, by the Government or local authority required for carrying on his business or activity.

**27. Cognizance of offence by courts.**—(*1*) No court shall take cognizance of any offence punishable under this Act or any rules made thereunder, save on a complaint made by the aggrieved woman or any person authorised by the Internal Committee or Local Committee in this behalf.

(*2*) No court inferior to that of a Metropolitan Magistrate or a Judicial Magistrate of the first class shall try any offence punishable under this Act.

(*3*) Every offence under this Act shall be non-cognizable.

**28. Act not in derogation of any other law.**—The provisions of this Act shall be in addition to and not in derogation of the provisions of any other law for the time being in force.

**29. Power of appropriate Government to make rules.**—(*1*) The Central Government may, by notification in the Official Gazette, make rules for carrying out the provisions of this Act.

(*2*) In particular and without prejudice to the generality of the foregoing power, such rules may provide for all or any of the following matters, namely:—

(*a*) the fees or allowances to be paid to the Members under sub-section (*4*) of section 4;

(*b*) nomination of members under clause (*c*) of sub-section (*1*) of section 7;

(*c*) the fees or allowances to be paid to the Chairperson, and Members under sub-section (*4*) of section 7;

(*d*) the person who may make complaint under sub-section (*2*) of section 9;

(*e*) the manner of inquiry under sub-section (*1*) of section 11;

(*f*) the powers for making an inquiry under clause (*c*) of sub-section (*2*) of section 11;

(*g*) the relief to be recommended under clause (*c*) of sub-section (*1*) of section 12;

(*h*) the manner of action to be taken under clause (*i*) of sub-section (*3*) of section 13;

(*i*) the manner of action to be taken under sub-sections (*1*) and (*2*) of section 14;

(*j*) the manner of action to be taken under section 17;

(*k*) the manner of appeal under sub-section (*1*) of section 18;

(*l*) the manner of organising workshops, awareness programmes for sensitising the employees and orientation programmes for the members of the Internal Committee under clause (*c*) of section 19; and

(*m*) the form and time for preparation of annual report by Internal Committee and the Local Committee under sub-section (*1*) of section 21.

(*3*) Every rule made by the Central Government under this Act shall be laid as soon as may be after it is made, before each House of Parliament, while it is in session, for a total period of thirty days which may be comprised in one session or in two or more successive sessions, and if, before the expiry of the session immediately following the session or the successive sessions aforesaid, both Houses agree in making any modification in the rule or both Houses agree that the rule should not be made, the rule shall thereafter have effect only in such modified form or be of no effect, as the case may be; so, however, that any such modification or annulment shall be without prejudice to the validity of anything previously done under that rule.

(*4*) Any rule made under sub-section (*4*) of section 8 by the State Government shall be laid, as soon as may be after it is made, before each House of the State Legislature where it consists of two Houses, or where such Legislature consists of one House, before that House.

**30. Power to remove difficulties.**— (*1*) If any difficulty arises in giving effect to the provisions of this Act, the Central Government may, by order published in the Official Gazette, make such provisions, not inconsistent with the provisions of this Act, as may appear to it to be necessary for removing the difficulty:

Provided that no such order shall be made under this section after the expiry of a period of two years from the commencement of this Act.

(*2*) Every order made under this section shall be laid, as soon as may be after it is made, before each House of Parliament.

(घ) लैंगिक उत्पीड़न के विरुद्ध क्रियान्वित कार्यशालाओं या जागरुकता कार्यक्रमों की संख्या;

(ङ) नियोक्ता या जिला अधिकारी द्वारा की गई कार्रवाई का स्वरूप।

[फा. सं. 19–5/2013–डब्ल्यूडब्ल्यू]

डॉ. श्रीरंजन, संयुक्त सचिव

## MINISTRY OF WOMEN AND CHILD DEVELOPMENT

## NOTIFICATION

New Delhi, the 9th December, 2013

**G.S.R. 769(E).**—In exercise of the powers conferred by section 29 of the Sexual Harassment of Women at Workplace (Prevention, Prohibition and Redressal) Act, 2013 (14 of 2013), the Central Government hereby makes the following rules, namely:—

1. **Short title and commencement.** – (1) These rules may be called the Sexual Harassment of Women at Workplace (Prevention, Prohibition and Redressal) Rules, 2013.

(2) They shall come into force on the date of their publication in the Official Gazette.

2. **Definitions.** – In these rules, unless the context otherwise requires,-

(a) "Act" means the Sexual Harassment of Women at Workplace (Prevention, Prohibition and Redressal) Act, 2013 (14 of 2013);
(b) "complaint" means the complaint made under section 9;
(c) "Complaints Committee" means the Internal Committee or the Local Committee, as the case may be;
(d) "incident" means an incident of sexual harassment as defined in clause (n) of section 2;
(e) "section" means a section of the Act;
(f) "special educator" means a person trained in communication with people with special needs in a way that addresses their individual differences and needs;
(g) words and expressions used herein and not defined but defined in the Act shall have the meanings respectively assigned to them in the Act.

3. **Fees or allowances for Member of Internal Committee.-** (1) The Member appointed from amongst non-government organisations shall be entitled to an allowance of two hundred rupees per day for holding the proceedings of the Internal Committee and also the reimbursement of travel cost incurred in travelling by train in three tier air condition or air conditioned bus and auto rickshaw or taxi, or the actual amount spent by him on travel, whichever is less.

The employer shall be responsible for the payment of allowances referred to in sub-rule (1).

4. **Person familiar with issues relating to sexual harassment.-** Person familiar with the issues relating to sexual harassment for the purpose of clause (c) of sub-section (1) of section 7 shall be a person who has expertise on issues relating to sexual harassment and may include any of the following:-

(a) a social worker with at least five years' experience in the field of social work which leads to creation of societal conditions favourable towards empowerment of women and in particular in addressing workplace sexual harassment;
(b) a person who is familiar with labour, service, civil or criminal law.

1. **Fees or allowances for Chairperson and Members of Local Committee.-** (1) The Chairperson of the Local Committee shall be entitled to an allowance of two hundred and fifty rupees per day for holding the proceedings of the said Committee.

(2) The Members of the Local Committee other than the Members nominated under clauses (b) and (d) of sub-section (1) of section 7 shall be entitled to an allowance of two hundred rupees per day for holding the proceedings of the said Committee and also the reimbursement of travel cost incurred in travelling by train in three tier air condition or air conditioned bus and auto rickshaw or taxi, or the actual amount spent by him on travel, whichever is less.

The District Officer shall be responsible for the payment of allowances referred to in sub-rules (1) and (2).

6. **Complaint of sexual harassment.** – For the purpose of sub-section (2) of Section 9,-

(i) where the aggrieved woman is unable to make a complaint on account of her physical incapacity, a complaint may be filed by –

(a) her relative or friend; or
(b) her co-worker; or
(c) an officer of the National Commission for Women or State Women's Commission; or
(d) any person who has knowledge of the incident, with the written consent of the aggrieved woman;

(ii) where the aggrieved woman is unable to make a complaint on account of her mental incapacity, a complaint may be filed by-
(a) her relative of friend; or
(b) a special educator; or
(c) a qualified psychiatrist or psychologist; or
(d) the guardian or authority under whose care she is receiving treatment or care; or
(e) any person who has knowledge of the incident jointly with her relative or friend or a special educator or qualified psychiatrist or psychologist, or guardian or authority under whose care she is receiving treatment or care;

(iii) where the aggrieved woman for any other reason is unable to make a complaint, a complaint may be filed by any person who has knowledge of the incident, with her written consent;

(iv) where the aggrieved woman is dead, a complaint may be filed by any person who has knowledge of the incident, with the written consent of her legal heir.

**7. Manner of inquiry into complaint.-** (1) Subject to the provisions of section 11, at the time of filing the complaint, the complainant shall submit to the Complaints Committee, six copies of the complaint along with supporting documents and the names and addresses of the witnesses.

(2) On receipt of the complaint, the Complaints Committee shall send one of the copies received from the aggrieved woman under sub-rule (1) to the respondent within a period of seven working days.

(3) The respondent shall file his reply to the complaint along with his list of documents, and names and addresses of witnesses, within a period not exceeding ten working days from the date of receipt of the documents specified under sub-rule (1).

(4) The Complaints Committee shall make inquiry into the complaint in accordance with the principles of natural justice.

(5) The Complaints Committee shall have the right to terminate the inquiry proceedings or to give an *ex-parte* decision on the complaint, if the complainant or respondent fails, without sufficient cause, to present herself or himself for three consecutive hearings convened by the Chairperson or Presiding Officer, as the case may be:

Provided that such termination or ex-parte order may not be passed without giving a notice in writing, fifteen days in advance, to the party concerned.

(6) The parties shall not be allowed to bring in any legal practitioner to represent them in their case at any stage of the proceedings before the Complaints Committee.

(7) In conducting the inquiry, a minimum of three Members of the Complaints Committee including the Presiding Officer or the Chairperson, as the case may be, shall be present.

**8. Other relief to complainant during pendency of inquiry.-**The Complaints Committee at the written request of the aggrieved woman may recommend to the employer to-
(a) restrain the respondent from reporting on the work performance of the aggrieved woman or writing her confidential report, and assign the same to another officer;
(b) restrain the respondent in case of an educational institution from supervising any academic activity of the aggrieved woman.

**9. Manner of taking action for sexual harassment.-** Except in cases where service rules exist, where the Complaints Committee arrives at the conclusion that the allegation against the respondent has been proved, it shall recommend to the employer or the District Officer, as the case may be, to take any action including a written apology, warning, reprimand or censure, withholding of promotion, withholding of pay rise or increments, terminating the respondent from service or undergoing a counselling session or carrying out community service.

**10. Action for false or malicious complaint or false evidence.-** Except in cases where service rules exist, where the Complaints Committee arrives at the conclusion that the allegation against the respondent is malicious or the aggrieved woman or any other person making the complaint has made the complaint knowing it to be false or the aggrieved woman or any other person making the complaint has produced any forged or misleading document, it may recommend to the employer or District Officer, as the case may be, to take action in accordance with the provisions of rule 9.

**11. Appeal.-** Subject to the provisions of section 18, any person aggrieved from the recommendations made under sub-section (2) of section 13 or under clauses (i) or clause (ii) of sub-section (3) of section 13 or sub-section (1) or sub-section (2) of section 14 or section 17 or non-implementation of such recommendations may prefer an appeal to the appellate authority notified under clause (a) of section 2 of the Industrial Employment (Standing Orders) Act, 1946 (20 of 1946).

**12. Penalty for contravention of provisions of section 16.-** Subject to the provisions of section 17, if any person contravenes the provisions of section 16, the employer shall recover a sum of five thousand rupees as penalty from such person.

**13. Manner to organise workshops, etc.–** Subject to the provisions of section 19, every employer shall-

(a) formulate and widely disseminate an internal policy or charter or resolution or declaration for prohibition, prevention and redressal of sexual harassment at the workplace intended to promote gender sensitive safe spaces and remove underlying factors that contribute towards a hostile work environment against women;

(b) carry out orientation programmes and seminars for the Members of the Internal Committee ;

(c) carry out employees awareness programmes and create forum for dialogues which may involve Panchayati Raj Institutions, Gram Sabha, women's groups, mothers' committee, adolescent groups, urban local bodies and any other body as may be considered necessary;

(d) conduct capacity building and skill building programmes for the Members of the Internal Committee;

(e) declare the names and contact details of all the Members of the Internal Committee;

(f) use modules developed by the State Governments to conduct workshops and awareness programmes for sensitising the employees with the provisions of the Act.

**14. Preparation of annual report.-** The annual report which the Complaints Committee shall prepare under Section 21, shall have the following details:-

(a) number of complaints of sexual harassment received in the year;

(b) number of complaints disposed off during the year;

(c ) number of cases pending for more than ninety days;

(d) number of workshops or awareness programme against sexual harassment carried out;

(e) nature of action taken by the employer or District Officer.

[F. No. 19-5/2013-WW]

Dr. SHREERANJAN, Jt. Secy.

Printed by the Manager, Government of India Press, Ring Road, Mayapuri, New Delhi-110064
and Published by the Controller of Publications, Delhi-110054.

# BILL NO. I OF 2024

*A Bill further to amend the Sexual Harassment of Women at Workplace (Prevention, Prohibition and Redressal) Act, 2013.*

BE it enacted by Parliament in the Seventy- fifth Year of the Republic of India as follows:—

**1.** (*1*) This Act may be called the Sexual Harassment of Women at Workplace (Prevention, Prohibition and Redressal) Amendment Act, 2024. Short title and commencement.

(*2*) It shall come into force on such date as the Central Government may, by notification in the Official Gazette, appoint.

Amendment of section 9

**2.** In the Sexual Harassment of Women at Workplace (Prevention, Prohibition and Redressal) Act, 2013 (hereinafter referred to as the principal Act), in section 9:— 14 of 2013

(*a*) in sub-section (*1*), for the words "within a period of three months from the date of incident" and "within a period of three months from the date of last incident", the words "within a period of one year from the date of incident" and "within a period of one year from the date of last incident" respectively, shall be substituted; and

(*b*) in the second proviso to sub-section (*1*), the words "not exceeding three months" shall be omitted.

Omission of section 10.

**3.** In the principal Act, section 10 shall be omitted.

## STATEMENT OF OBJECTS AND REASONS

The Sexual Harassment of Women at Workplace (Prevention, Prohibition and Redressal) Act, 2013 represents a significant step towards protection of women against sexual harassment at the workplace. However, considering the lived experiences of the women workforce and the realities of the modern workplace, the Act needs to address two important issues.

Pensions Section 9 stipulates a limitation period of three months for filing complaints, further extendable by three months, provided that the Internal Committee or Local Committee (as the case may be) is satisfied that the circumstances were such which prevented the woman from filing a complaint within the said period. This limitation period is inapposite since in cases involving sexual harassment, women may be so traumatised as to render filing of the complaint impossible until such time they have recouped their strength. Placing a maximum limit of six months on such complaints does great injustice to the aggrieved woman.

Section 10 provides the aggrieved woman with the option of settling the complaint through conciliation. This provision is highly problematic since it fails to take into account the possibility of influencing, coercing, pressuring or intimidating the complainant to arrive at a settlement. While there are certain areas (such as contractual matters) where conciliation may be fruitful, an attempt to reach a compromise in matters of sexual harassment of women greatly undermines the dignity of women.

This Bill intends to remedy these problems by amending the Sexual Harassment of Women at Workplace (Prevention, Prohibition and Redressal) Act, 2013. It provides that the basic limitation period for filing complaints shall be fixed at one year, which shall be further extendable, without any upper limit, by the Internal Committee or Local Committee (as the case may be), upon satisfaction that the circumstances prevented the woman from filing the complaint within the limitation period. Additionally, it proposes the deletion of the provision for conciliation in its entirety.

This Bill seeks to achieve the above objectives.

SASMIT PATRA.

REPORT OF THE COMMITTEE ON

# AMENDMENTS TO CRIMINAL LAW


JUSTICE J.S. VERMA (RETD)
CHAIRMAN

JUSTICE LEILA SETH (RETD)
MEMBER

GOPAL SUBRAMANIUM
MEMBER


JANUARY 23, 2013

जस्टिस वर्मा
आपराधिक कानूनों के
संशोधन संबंधी समिति
विज्ञान भवन एनैक्सी
नई दिल्ली - 110003

सत्यमेव जयते

**Justice Verma**
**Committee on Amendmen**
**to Criminal Law,**
**E-mail : justice.verma@nic.**
**Vigyan Bhawan Annexe,**
**New Delhi-110003**

**Justice (Smt.) Leila Seth**
**Member**

**Justice J. S. Verma**
**Chairman**

**Gopal Subramaniam**
**Member**

January 23, 2013

Dear Prime Minister,

This Committee was constituted by GOI Notification No. SO (3003)E, dated December 23, 2012 to look into possible amendments of the Criminal Law to provide for quicker trial and enhanced punishment for criminals committing sexual assault of extreme nature against women. In view of the significance and urgency of the task, the Committee undertook to perform it within 30 days, which task has been completed.

Accordingly, the Committee has prepared its Report, which is enclosed herewith.

It is the Committee's hope that the promptitude with which this Committee was constituted within a few days of the brutal gang rape in Delhi on December 16, 2012, will continue to accomplish the task by speedy implementation of its Recommendations to retain public confidence in good governance.

With Regards,

Yours Sincerely

J. S. Verma

( J. S. Verma )

Hon'ble Dr. Manmohan Singh
Prime Minister of India
7, Race Course Road,
New Delhi

# CHAPTER FOUR

# SEXUAL HARASSMENT AT THE WORKPLACE

1. While much has been said and done in the past several years about sexual harassment at the workplace, it is evident that this evil is still rampant in Indian society. Parliament is therefore considering the Sexual Harassment of Women at Workplace (Prevention, Prohibition and Redressal) Bill, 2012. We however notice that there was no debate in the Lok Sabha on 3rd September 2012 when this Bill was introduced, and it is now pending approval in the Rajya Sabha.

2. We are also aware that in compliance with the judgment in *Vishakha v. State of Rajasthan*[97], universities such as the Jawaharlal Nehru University and the University of Delhi have formulated policies and constituted mechanisms to prevent and redress complaints of sexual harassment. We have taken note of the suggestion that those universities whose anti-sexual harassment policy rules and committee mechanism meet the standards of *Vishakha* are proposed to be exempted from the purview of the Sexual Harassment Bill, 2012, as these committees are more democratic and are better related to ensure prevention and prohibition of sexual harassment in educational institutions. We do notice that there is an anomaly in the Bill that it does not include within its ambit the students of universities, colleges or schools. We will deal with

[97] AIR 1997 Supreme Court 3011

other shortcomings of the proposed Bill subsequently.

3. We must, however, first revisit the Supreme Court's judgment in *Vishakha*. Here, the petitioner in question sought to enforce the fundamental rights of working women. The said petition wanted an enforcement of Article 14, 19 and 21 '*in view of the prevailing climate in which the violation of these rights is not uncommon*'. Regrettably, notwithstanding the directions of the Supreme Court in *Vishakha*, there is no empirical evidence to suggest that conditions of working women have distinctly improved in the recent past. We also notice that the petition was presented as a class action by certain social activists and NGOs with the aim of focusing attention towards the 'societal aberration' and also to a system finding suitable methods for realisation of the true concept of gender equality. There was also a prayer that sexual harassment of women in all workplaces must be injuncted through judicial orders until the vacuum in the existing legislation was replaced.

4. The Court, in *Vishakha,* took notice of Articles 15 and Article 42 of the Constitution. We would like to emphasise Article 42:-

> *"The State shall make provision for securing just and humane conditions of work and for maternity relief."*

5. Article 42, naturally, needs to be read along with the other provisions which are contained in the fundamental rights and the Preamble and it emphasises, in the light of the preamble of values, that the State is meant to be caring and

compassionate about those who are underprivileged or those who are disadvantaged and those who may not even need special provisions but may insist upon the simple compliance with constitutional guarantees.

6. We do take note of a shift in the manner in which the women's organisations have presented themselves as a 'rising community', a more conscious and aware community, and not wanting the 'succour' of any special provisions. Women want constitutional guarantees to be simply and plainly enforced and we think that it is the duty of the State to make special provisions to ensure that they are granted. We would like to reiterate that the Indian society is a sovereign, socialist, secular and a republic. The words 'socialist', 'secular' and 'republic' bear great meaning. We are therefore of the opinion that the Indian State appears to have been out of tune with its own Constitution. It does not view that the State is meant to be a just and a humane State where it cares for the rights of citizens. We also would like to say that in the discourse of rights, we are aware that there must be economic policies which actually take forward growth but not at the expense of the obligations of the State towards the poor.

7. Article 51 of the Constitution provides that the State shall endeavour to foster respect for international law and treaty obligations in the dealings of organised people with one another.

8. Article 253 of the Constitution which provides that Parliament can legislate for the whole or any part of the territory of India for implementing any treaty, agreement or convention with any other

country or countries or any decision made at any international conference association or other body.

9. We also would like to point out that Entry 14 of List 1 provides that Parliament can enter into treaties and agreements with foreign countries and implement treaties, agreements and conventions with foreign countries. We are also of the opinion that such international conventions which are consistent with fundamental rights and in harmony with its spirit, must actually be read into the provisions of the fundamental rights because they actually impart clarity and perhaps more vigour to the content of the Article. We also notice that under Article 51(c) of the Constitution and under Article 253 read with Entry 54, the power of Parliament to enact laws to implement international conventions exists.

10. We also notice therefore that we have a large number of provisions in the Constitution that mandate the State and its various organs to guarantee gender equality. If laws have to give effect to the same, it is necessary that laws which involve crime against women must also be sufficiently structured to give effect to these guarantees.

11. In *Vishakha*, it was observed that:-

> *"Gender equality includes protection from sexual harassment and right to work with dignity, which is a universally recognised basic human right. The common minimum requirement of this right has received global acceptance. The international conventions and norms are, therefore, are of great significance in the formulation of the guidelines to achieve this purpose."*

12. In a certain sense, the judiciary is also the enforcing authority for fundamental rights. In *Vishakha,* the principles of independence of the judiciary were also referred to and in particular the objective and function of the judiciary was stated as follows:-

   a) To ensure that all persons are able to live securely under the rule of law;
   b) To promote within the proper limits of the judicial function, the observance and attainment of human rights;
   c) To administer the law impartially among persons and between persons and the State.

13. In this context, we must add a note about the lower judiciary in the words of the Commissioner appointed by the Supreme Court in *Sheela Barse* (infra):

*"Usually the most important encounter which the citizen has with the law is at the primary level. This level, in fact, frightens many citizens, and has\ given a feeling of helplessness that the administration of law does not necessarily lead to justice in the predominance of Truth. Even the secondary and the Tertiary level courts i.e. the High Court and the Supreme Court to function, they too depend upon the impressions of the primary level courts. Thus, if an error creeps in there, it becomes an error which may not perceptible of correction by the secondary and the tertiary levels."*

14. The *Vishakha* judgment made it clear that gender equality and the right to a secure workspace was part of the fundamental rights guaranteed under the Constitution, and that it was the duty of the judiciary to ensure (as a part of the Constitutional machinery) that the State enforced these rights, especially in view of the nation's obligation to

comply with covenants of international treaties and conventions.

15. It is necessary that the judicial system must also cooperate in enhancing the credibility and faith of people in the rule of law. We are of the utmost confidence that judiciary will lead by example and will ensure that speedy justice to rape victims is given. We must point out that apart from the various recommendations which we have made for the protection of the juveniles including the females and children who are rescued from trafficking, we are of the opinion that the inadequacy of judicial personnel, which is cited as a reason for non-expeditious disposal of cases can be immediately and effectively addressed in the following manner:

(a) Retired Judges of the Supreme Court, High Court and the District Courts could be appointed as ad-hoc judges to expeditiously dispose pending cases;

(b) Parliament should consider equalisation of age of retirement of the subordinate judiciary, the High Court and the Supreme Court so that manpower will be immediately available;

(c) Infrastructure for ad hoc judges can be easily identified in respect of unutilised government buildings and be made available.

(d) Adjournment should not be allowed as a matter of course in respect of cases specially fixed for hearing before the ad-hoc courts, or even before regular courts.

(e) Public prosecutors should be appointed on the basis of merit in accordance with the recommendations made by the Chief Justice of the High Court and not on the basis of any political considerations.

(f) Cases of rape and sexual assault should be tried by women prosecutors, and, to the extent possible, by women judges. In any event, all judges of the subordinate and higher judiciary should receive training in gender sensitivity.

16. We would also like to refer to the decision in *Nilabati Behera v, State of Orissa & Others*[98]. This was an important pronouncement to ensure that an enforceable right of compensation was also a part of the enforcement of guaranteed rights. Thus, what can happen in respect of an offence like rape is that there could be not only an offence as defined in the IPC but simultaneously there would be a constitutional violation of Articles 14, 14, 19 and 21 and which would also enable the victim to claim right to compensation. We are of the view that a right to claim compensation will lie against the State in the event the State is unable to secure safe conditions / safe spaces for women. It is under these circumstances that the norms and guidelines were actually prescribed in *Vishakha* by the Supreme Court.

17. In 2000, in *Municipal Corporation of Delhi v. Female Workers' Muster Roll*[99], we notice the constitutional

---

[98] (1993) 2 SCC 746

[99] AIR 2000 SC 1274

position vis-à-vis the Indian reality noted by the Supreme Court:

*"Not long ago, the place of a woman in rural areas has been traditionally her home; but the poor illiterate women forced by sheer poverty now come out to seek various jobs so as to overcome the economic hardship. They also lake up jobs which involve hard physical labour. The female workers who are engaged by the Corporation on muster roll have to work at the site of construction and repairing of roads. Their services have also been utilised for digging of trenches. Since they are engaged on daily wages, they, in order to earn their daily bread, work even in advance stage of pregnancy and also soon after delivery, unmindful of -detriment to their health or to the health of the new-born. It is in this background that we have to look to our Constitution which, in its Preamble, promises social and economic justice. We may first look at the Fundamental Rights contained in Chapter III of the Constitution. Article 14 provides that the State shall not deny to any person equality before law or the equal protection of the laws within the territory of India. Dealing with this Article vis-a-vis the Labour Laws, this Court in Hindustan Antibiotics Ltd. v. Workmen , has held that labour to whichever sector it may belong in a particular region and in a particular industry will be treated on equal basis. Article 15 provides that the State shall not discriminate against any citizen on grounds only of religion, race, caste, sex, place of birth or any of them. Clause (3) of this Article provides as under:*

*(3) Nothing in this article shall prevent the State from making any special provision for women and children.*

18. The Court also noticed Article 39(e) of the Constitution:

*8. From Part III, we may shift to Part IV of the Constitution containing Directive Principles of State Policy. Article 38 provides that the State shall strive to promote the welfare of the people by securing and protecting, as effectively as it may, a social order in which justice, social, economic and political shall inform all the institutions of the national life. Sub-clause (2) of this Article mandates that the State shall strive to minimise the inequalities in income and endeavour to eliminate inequalities in status, facilities and opportunities.*

19. In our considered view, the time has come when women must be able to feel liberated and emancipated from what could be fundamentally oppressive conditions against which an autonomous choice of freedom can be exercised and made available by women. Thus, we notice the guaranteeing of the private space to the women, which is to choose her religious and private beliefs and also her capacity to assert equality which is in the public space is vitally important. Very often, a woman may have to assert equality vis-à-vis her own family and that is why it is necessary to understand the subtle dimension of a woman being able to exercise autonomy and free will at all points of time in the same way a man can. This, we will later see, is sexual autonomy in the fullest degree.

20. We now examine the proposed Bill in greater detail.

21. We note that Section 10(1) of the Sexual Harassment Bill, 2012 stipulates that on receipt of complaint of sexual harassment, conciliation must be attempted between the complainant and respondent. This is in violation of the mandate prescribed by the Supreme Court in *Vishakha,* which was a direction to the State '*to ensure a safe workplace / educational institution for women*'. In this context, we think that the attempts to get justice cannot be muscled by attempts at conciliation.

There are certain areas, such as contractual matters where there could be conciliation, but in matters of harassment and humiliation of women an attempt to compromise the same is indeed yet another way in which the dignity of women is undermined. We are in agreement with the objections raised by many women's organisations that the said provision actually shows very little regard for the dignity of women. We think that Section 10(1) of the Bill, in so far as it proposes conciliation as a first step, must be deleted.

22. We now wish to look at Section 14 of the Sexual Harassment Bill, 2012. We notice from the provisions of the Bill that Section 14 appears to penalise a woman for filing a false complaint. We think that such a provision is a completely abusive provision and is intended to nullify the objective of the law. We think that these 'red-rag' provisions ought not to be permitted to be introduced and they show very little thought.

23. As far as Section 11(ii) is concerned, which has enabled the internal complaints committee to be given powers of a civil court for summoning discovery and production of documents is concerned, this amounts to colourable legislation because powers of courts cannot be simply conferred upon domestic committees, particularly when the composition of the internal committee does not have any legal background. We are also of the opinion that the Bill does not specify any training to the committee for fulfilling these duties. This is in distinction to the composition of the local complaints committee in which at least one member has to preferably have a background in law or legal knowledge.

24. As far as clause 6 of the Bill is concerned, which contains ambiguous guidelines for constitution of the local complaints committee, we notice that the Bill provides that every district officer shall constitute a local complaints committee in the district. It also prescribes that an additional local complaints committee shall be constituted at the block level to address complaints in certain cases. However, the jurisdiction and functions of these commissions is unclear. This needs to be clarified.

25. We are further of the opinion that suitable provisions should be added to the Bill to make payment of compensation for a woman who has suffered sexual harassment which should be paid by the company which compensation will be determined by a Tribunal.

26. Pursuant to a review of the Sexual Harassment Bill as passed by the Lok Sabha, applicable case laws, a review of available literature and various conversations with Indian and international experts, we have arrived at the conclusion that, read as a whole, the Sexual Harassment Bill is unsatisfactory. While the Sexual Harassment Bill purports to be in effectuation of the Hon'ble Supreme Court's dictum in *Vishakha v. State of Rajasthan*[100], it is clear from a reading of the said Bill that the spirit of the judgment in *Vishakha* is not adequately reflected. It is our aim that the applicable law relating to sexual harassment at the workplace ought to ensure that not even an imperceptible influence of any gender bias is felt against the female workforce either in the performance of their duties or in their career progression. Our analysis of the Sexual

---

[100] (1997) 6 SCC 241

Harassment Bill and suggestions for a more effective legislation are as follows:

(a) **Definition of Sexual Harassment:** We are of the view that the present definition of "sexual harassment" contained in Section 2(n) and the consequential provision relating to the prevention of sexual harassment contained in Section 3 of the Sexual Harassment Bill is satisfactory and should be retained in any future bill.

However, it is important to note that the definition requires some clarification inasmuch as any interpretation of the word "unwelcome" as contained in the said definition must give due weight to both objective as well as subjective criteria in order to ensure that women of differing perceptions and comfort levels are given appropriate protection. Therefore, we suggest that after the definition of "sexual harassment", the following explanation may be inserted:

> *"Explanation: In determining whether the behaviour or act complained of is unwelcome, one of the factors to be given due weight shall be the subjective perception of the complainant."*

(b) **Employment Tribunal:** We are of the view that the present structure mandating the setting up of an Internal Complaints Committee to which any complaint must be filed is counter-productive to the ends sought to be met. While each employer may opt for an internal mechanism for redressal of complaints of sexual harassment, it would better serve the ends sought to be achieved to set up a separate Tribunal to be termed as the Employment Tribunal to receive and adjudicate all complaints.

It is our apprehension that the in-house dealing of all grievances would dissuade women from filing complaints and may promote a culture of suppression of legitimate complaints in order to avoid the concerned establishment falling into disrepute. Consequently the setting up of a Tribunal as proposed herein would obviate the need for both the Internal Complaints Committee as well as the Local Complaints Committee as envisaged under the present Sexual Harassment Bill.

(c) **Constitution and jurisdiction of an Employment Tribunal**: We propose that an Employment Tribunal be set up which should comprise of two retired judges (of which one must be a woman), two eminent sociologists and one social activist, who has sufficient experience in the field of gender-based discrimination. The members of the Tribunal should be appointed by a collegium consisting of the Chief Justice of the High Court (or his nominee judge) of the concerned state or a District Judge, if the appointment is to be made in a *Taluka*, as the case may be, along with no less than one eminent female sociologist and one female advocate of the local High Court or District Court, as the case may be.

We further propose that the proposed Employment Tribunal's operation should not be trammelled by the application of complex procedures found in civil suits under the CPC or allied legislation. We therefore suggest that the Tribunal ought to follow a summary procedure for the disposal of complaints so as to expedite the resolution of disputes. It is apprehended that if the complaint of sexual harassment is tried as a full blown civil trial then the parties concerned will be adversely affected in the workplace for a prolonged period of time which can cause a prejudicial effect to both or either party. It is expected that typical complaints of sexual harassment will not be evidence-intensive and hence should not require either a plethora of documents or witnesses. It is therefore proposed that, under the principle of *kompetenz kompetenz,* the Tribunal ought to be free to choose its own procedure for each complaint. Specifically, it is suggested that parties shall not as a matter of right be free to call upon witnesses, unless permitted by the Tribunal in the facts of the case.

(d) **Establishments to which the proposed Act shall apply**: Since each and every act of sexual harassment at the workplace is a form of sex discrimination which in effect denies a woman her fundamental rights guaranteed under the Constitution, it is proposed that any legislation dealing with the said issue should have the widest possible application so as to take within its scope every female member of the national workforce. Therefore, any legislation must apply to all government institutions, all public bodies, all *panchayats,* all establishments covered under the Factories Act and the Industrial Disputes Act and all employers in the private sector who are not otherwise covered by the categories listed above. The present definition of "workplace" contained in Section 2(o) is of wide amplitude and in that sense is acceptable. However, it bears mentioning that a clarification may be inserted in the said definition that the "unorganized sector" is not exempt from the ambit of the proposed legislation. To this end, we suggest that the proposed legislation should also cover women in the armed forces and police, agricultural workers and women students and staff of all schools and educational institutions. The present definition appears to exclude government and other educational institutions.

It is also proposed that domestic workers should also fall within the ambit of the proposed legislation. This would facilitate protection from situations where their wages are withheld arbitrarily as also to provide a basis for monetary compensation in the event of sexual harassment/assault besides steps taken under the general criminal law. Since education and behaviour at home is the most valuable form of learning, we feel that providing dignity to domestic workers is one of the most effective ways to humanize the treatment meted out to those of lower castes or economic class. We note that the present Sexual Harassment Bill does in fact cover domestic workers. We only reiterate the need for such protection to highlight the importance of covering every single female member of the national workforce.

(e) **Mode of Enforcement**: The intendment of the proposed legislation ought to be the widest possible dissemination of the rules relating to sexual harassment so that all persons at the workplace are aware of what is expected. We therefore suggest that the sexual harassment policy of each establishment ought to be prominently displayed within the premises with complete details on the procedure for making a complaint. Further, it is suggested that the policy should form part and parcel of the letter of appointment to ensure every person joining the establishment is made aware of their rights against sexual harassment. Any dereliction in the duty of the employer to prominently disseminate the sexual harassment policy in the work place and the mode for making a complaint ought to be met with a fine in the first instance, and imprisonment of the concerned officer for a repeat offence.

(f) **Requirement of Complaint to be made only in writing**: This Committee is of the view that ground realities and the fact that the proposed legislation shall be applicable to the widest possible amplitude of workplaces, it would be too onerous a burden to expect a complaint to be made only in writing. Often the more underprivileged members of the female workforce are not in a position to make a complaint in writing for various reasons, such as, illiteracy, lack of education to permit them to put down on paper that which they have experienced and which may otherwise be clear in their minds. We propose that complainants may be free to approach the Tribunal directly to state a complaint orally, which may then be transcribed into the written form in the manner prescribed by the Tribunal.

(g) **Limitation:** We are of the view that period of limitation of 3 months for the making of a complaint contained in Section 9(1) of the Sexual Harassment Bill may be misused to defeat the ends sought to be achieved. It may often transpire that a woman may fail to make a complaint on the occurrence of the first instance of sexual harassment and may only do so upon a repetition of such instances. It would in those circumstances be unfair for only the last of such incidents (or those that fall within the three month limitation) to form the basis of her complaint when evidence of prior instances may reveal a systemic flaw at the workplace which is promotive of gender-based discrimination. It is therefore suggested that no fixed time period of limitation be prescribed and that the only expectation be that a complaint shall be made within a reasonable period of time with regard to the facts and circumstances surrounding the making of such a complaint and the personal circumstances of the complainant. A determination of what amounts to a reasonable period of time shall be made by the Tribunal which may then be refined through the development of case law on the point.

(h) **Conciliation:** The Committee is of the view that conciliation in cases of sexual harassment is antithetical to the intended result, inasmuch as the concept of conciliation pre-supposes the existence of a valid complaint. If in fact a false complaint is made or one which is incapable of proof, there will be no need for a conciliation. Alternatively, since conciliation arises at a time prior to action being taken on a complaint it may be used as an effective tool to muzzle the Tribunal's primary duty of investigating and prosecuting cases of sexual harassment so as to lend sufficient teeth to the legislation. If a valid complaint is made, then the consequences that ensue must only be those mandated by the proposed legislation. We are further of the view that the complainant shall not be permitted to withdraw a complaint once made so as to ensure that all cases of sexual harassment are properly dealt with under the law of the land. We apprehend that permitting either mandatory conciliation, even if at the instance of the complainant, or permitting the complainant to withdraw her complaint will negatively impact the ability of women to bring valid complaints before the Tribunal. It cannot be gainsaid that the myriad pressurizing influences that are brought to bear upon women in our society may act to disable her from pursuing a valid complaint.

(i) **Role of the Employer**: While we have proposed the elimination of a mandatory Internal Complaints Committee, we are of the view that the best source for prevention of incidents of sexual harassment is an enlightened employer. Our suggestions should not be read to mean that we wish to restrict the various optional measures that an employer may take to prevent sexual harassment. They should be free to set up an internal committee, if they so desire, however, a complainant cannot be compelled to approach such an internal committee prior to approaching the proposed Employment Tribunal. They are also free to take other measures such as education programmes within their premises to further strengthen anti-sexual harassment measures within their establishments. Employers must take all steps necessary to prevent sexual harassment from occurring, such as affirmatively raising the subject, expressing strong disapproval, developing appropriate sanctions internally when an instance of sexual harassment is brought to their notice, informing employees of their right to raise, and how to raise, the issue of harassment, and developing methods to sensitize all concerned. Particularly, all employers must have a nodal officer to whom all complaints of sexual harassment may be made, whether in writing or otherwise. Such a person should always be a female member of the workforce and should be granted sufficient training to deal with such situations. It shall be such nodal officer's duty to assist an aggrieved party to make a complaint to the Tribunal, if necessary. We would like to clarify that it shall not be mandatory for a complainant to approach such nodal officer prior to the filing of a complaint with the Tribunal.

(j) **Liability of the Employer**: We are of the view that it would be inequitable to visit the employer with liability in all cases of sexual harassment though the primary responsibility for avoiding situations of sexual harassment lies with the employer. We therefore propose that the liability of the employer will be limited to case where the employer has (a) by an act or omission facilitated the specific act of sexual harassment complained of; (b) permitted the creation of an environment at the workplace where acts of sexual harassment have become widespread and systemic; or (c) been found in breach of any other obligation under the Act, including but not limited to, the proper disclosure of the sexual harassment policy and the mode of filing of a complaint or the forwarding of any complaint received by either the employer, or by any person appointed by the employer on its behalf, to the Tribunal at the instance of the complainant.

(k) **Action during Pendency of the Enquiry/Case**: The proposed Section 12 of the Sexual Harassment Bill empowers the Internal Complaints Committee or the Local Complaints Committee to direct the employer to either transfer the aggrieved woman or the respondent or to grant leave to the aggrieved woman if it deems fit. Once an

Employment Tribunal, as envisaged by these recommendations, is put into place, it follows that this power will be exercisable by the Tribunal. However, we are of the view that the Tribunal should not have the power to compulsorily transfer or grant leave to the aggrieved woman. It is our view that either of these powers should only be exercised with the consent of the aggrieved woman. In the event that the aggrieved woman is not amenable to either transfer or grant of leave then no such action ought to be taken against her will so as to ensure that she does not foster either a sense of bias or alienation merely on account of the fact that she exercised her rights under the proposed legislation to file a complaint of sexual harassment. However, to facilitate a feasible working environment, both the aggrieved woman and the respondent should not be compelled to work together on any project. They should be separated at the workplace such that they do not need to come into contact with one another pending the adjudication of the complaint. Additionally, it is suggested that leave may be granted to the respondent pending adjudication in the event that the aggrieved woman is neither amenable to transfer or leave or that given the structure of the workplace or the nature of the work it is infeasible or impossible for the aggrieved woman and the respondent to be separated in the discharge of their duties. The present act seems to regard the granting of leave as a beneficial provision for the aggrieved woman without taking into account her wishes. This, to our mind, is contrary to the ends sought to be achieved by the proposed legislation inasmuch as there should not be any provision that enhances a sense of victimhood in the aggrieved woman.

(l) **Action in relation to False or Malicious Complaints or Giving of False Evidence**:
The present Section 14 of the Sexual Harassment Bill appears to be a provision which is liable to misuse. Where an aggrieved woman makes a complaint it is possible that she will be faced with opposition from the employer as well. In such cases it is often possible that evidence may be manipulated by the employer or those acting in concert with the employer so as to ostensibly falsify the allegations of the aggrieved woman. Therefore the fear is that such a provision may be used to counter the complaint of the aggrieved woman and would promote a culture among employers with means to render false the genuine complaint of an aggrieved woman.

Accordingly, it is our recommendation that the said provision be deleted so as to foster an environment conducive to the making of complaints under the proposed legislation. The Tribunal shall always have the option of reprimanding the aggrieved woman or the witness, as the case may be, in its order in relation to any falsification. It is our belief that such an order of reprimand will have far reaching consequences for the future employment prospects of the aggrieved woman which may be punishment enough.

(m) **Review of Premises by the Tribunal**: The Tribunal ought to also be mandated to conduct periodic inspection of various establishments within their jurisdiction to obtain information on the state of the enforcement of the proposed legislation and to assess various steps taken by employers to ensure proper compliance with the terms of the proposed legislation. The purpose of these inspections should not be limited to the enforcement of the proposed legislation but should also extend to activities relating to gender sensitization based on the experiences collated by them. This may be through various education programmes or assessments received by those that have interacted with a specific employer as either workers or as clients or in any other capacity.

(n) **Special Provisions as to Universities**: While in the preceding Recommendation No. 2 we have recommended that students and staff of all educational institutions may also be included within the definition of "workplace" under the proposed legislation, we are in receipt of certain submissions made the Jawahar Lal Nehru University which, in part, deal with the issue of sexual harassment. Those universities, in which Internal Complaint Committees have functioned successfully to deal with sexual harassment, should share their internal guidelines on combating sexual harassment in their University with other Universities across India. As an example, the internal complaint committee of JNU is known as Gender Sensitisation Committee against Sexual Harassment, which is stated to have been extremely effective in its working partly due to the diverse nature of its constituent members. This model may be examined.

Further with regards to the constitution of ICC's within Universities in the *Dr. B. N Ray v. Ramjas*

*College & Ors*[101] judgment on 21st May 2012, the Delhi High Court ruled that:

*"It was very much in the domain and competence of the University to provide, by way of Ordinance, that the members of the Committee would include representatives from all the sections of the college community".*

The High Court then went on to say that in fact such a constitution would be welcome on the basis that it

*"...meets the objective of ensuring that all sections of the college community have full faith in the functioning of the Committee on account of presence of their representatives on it. The findings of such a broad based Committee are likely to be better received and accepted by all the sections of the college community".*

The court held that the mere fact that the chairperson of the committee was ranked junior to the accused was not violative of his rights under Article 14 of the Constitution.

We note that the court in *Dr. B. N Ray v. Ramjas College & Ors* stated that whilst the principles of natural justice should be followed in the procedures of the University's ICC, it is not imperative that the complainant(s) in a case of sexual harassment need be cross examined in the presence of the accused.

---

[101] Judgment dated May 21, 2012 in Writ Petition (C) No. 4427 of 2008.

# Index

## Words/Expressions

## Section Wise

### Sexual Harassment at Workplace (Prevention, Prohibition and Redressal) Act, 2013

**The Sexual Harassment of Women at Workplace Rules, 2013**

Acknowledgements

*(First Edition)*

This book has taken a long time to complete. The law of sexual harassment at workplace is at nascent stage. One had to bid his time and wait for sufficient judicial precedents to evolve on the subject before a useful authorship could be crafted. I hope that this time was well spent.

I am extremely grateful to Hon'ble Justice Jayant Nath, Hon'ble Justice V. Kameshwar Rao and Hon'ble Justice Manju Goel for their gracious notes and endorsements.

A special thanks to my colleague Ayush Beotra, Advocate for assisting me in all facets of this work, including research, case law analysis, editing etc. He put in long hours for this book despite a gruelling work regime.

I would also like to thank Mrs. Sanjivini Kaul Raina, Assistant Professor, Faculty of Law, Delhi University for her valuable inputs. Ms. Pooja Tiwari, a budding law graduate, also deserves a special mention for her efforts towards case research and preparation of notes.

I would like to thank my friends, colleagues and staff at work who all have, in some way or the other, made a contribution to this authorship.

I have also to acknowledge the efforts put in by the entire team at Niyogi Books.

New Delhi
12 July 2017

**Amish Tandon**
Advocate

# Acknowledgements

*(Revised Edition)*

I am happy to present a thoroughly revised and edited version of my book, *The Law of Sexual Harassment at Workplace: Practice and Procedure*.

I have endeavoured to trace and cover every judicial precedent on the subject between the period 2017 and the present. Additionally, I have tried to make this edition more user-friendly by introducing a word based and a legal provision-based index.

Further, on the aspect of templates, I have updated the template sexual harassment policy. I have also added various other templates (from a compliance point of view), which include template complaint forms, confidentiality undertaking, and conflict of interest declarations. All the above-mentioned templates can be readily used by organisations at the time of implementing the provisions of this law in their workplace.

I am extremely grateful to Hon'ble Justice Amit Bansal and Hon'ble Justice Mini Pushkarna for their gracious endorsements.

I am deeply thankful to Mr Harsh Prabhakar, Advocate, for reviewing the draft and providing valuable feedback, which was extremely helpful in shaping this edition. I thank him for accommodating me and taking out substantial time from his busy schedule for this exercise.

Mr Aditya Sharan, a law student at Symbiosis Law School, Noida, deserves a special mention. He worked extensively with me during the finalisation of the current edition. He collated and examined recent judicial precedents on the subject. He also ably assisted me in proofreading and finalising multiple chapters of this book. His suggestions and inputs have been valuable.

Mr. Rohit Pitti, a budding lawyer and a final-year law student at Amity Law School, Noida, must also be appreciated for his valuable efforts at during the final stages of this book. He diligently assisted me in all the meticulous aspects of the finalisation process, including research contribution, proofreading, etc. His commitment and attention to detail have been invaluable. I sincerely thank him for his hard work and conscientious approach in ensuring the successful completion of this academic endeavour.

I thank Niyogi Books for bringing out this edition.

New Delhi
3 August 2025

**Amish Tandon**
Advocate

# About the Author

**Mr. Amish Tandon** is an Advocate practicing in New Delhi for more than 16 years, with extensive experience in litigation, arbitration and corporate advisory.

He has also been actively associated with not-for-profit organisations providing legal aid to the needy on a *pro bono* basis.

He is the author of the treatise titled Indian Citizenship and Immigration Laws published in 2022.

Mr. Tandon regularly conducts seminars, talks and trainings on the subject of 'sexual harassment at workplace'.

He can be reached at amishtandon@gmail.com